**Microsoft**

Exam Ref 70-410: Installing and Configuring Windows Server 2012 R2

Craig Zacker

PUBLISHED BY
Microsoft Press
A Division of Microsoft Corporation
One Microsoft Way
Redmond, Washington 98052-6399

Library of Congress Control Number: 2014931253
ISBN: 978-0-7356-8424-9

Printed and bound in the United States of America.

Third Printing: August 2014

Microsoft Press books are available through booksellers and distributors worldwide. If you need support related to this book, email Microsoft Press Book Support at mspinput@microsoft.com. Please tell us what you think of this book at http://www.microsoft.com/learning/booksurvey.

Acquisitions Editor: Anne Hamilton
Developmental Editor: Karen Szall
Editorial Production: Box Twelve Communications
Technical Reviewer: Brian Svidergol
Cover: Twist Creative • Seattle

Contents at a glance

Contents

What do you think of this book? We want to hear from you!

Microsoft is interested in hearing your feedback so we can continually improve our
books and learning resources for you. To participate in a brief online survey, please visit:

www.microsoft.com/learning/booksurvey/

Chapter 5   Installing and administering Active Directory   257

What do you think of this book? We want to hear from you!

Microsoft is interested in hearing your feedback so we can continually improve our
books and learning resources for you. To participate in a brief online survey, please visit:

www.microsoft.com/learning/booksurvey/

Introduction

Most books take a very low-level approach, teaching you how to use basic concepts to accomplish fine-grained tasks. Like the Microsoft 70-410 certification exam, this book takes a high-level approach, building on your existing knowledge of lower-level Microsoft Windows system administration and extending it into higher-level server concepts needed for Windows Server 2012 R2.

Candidates for this exam are Information Technology (IT) Professionals who have Windows Server 2012 R2 operating system knowledge and experience and want to validate the skills and knowledge necessary to implement the Windows Server 2012 R2 core infrastructure services.

The 70-410 exam is the first in a series of three exams that validate the skills and knowledge necessary to implement a core Windows Server 2012 R2 Infrastructure into an existing enterprise environment. This book covers the initial implementation and configuration of the Windows Server 2012 R2 core services, such as Active Directory and the networking services. This book, along with the Exam Reference books covering the 70-411 and 70-412 exams, will collectively illustrate the skills and knowledge necessary for implementing, managing, maintaining and provisioning services and infrastructure in a Windows Server 2012 R2 environment.

This book covers every exam objective, but it does not cover every exam question. Only the Microsoft exam team has access to the exam questions themselves and Microsoft regularly adds new questions to the exam, making it impossible to cover specific questions. You should consider this book a supplement to your relevant real-world experience and other study materials. If you encounter a topic in this book that you do not feel completely comfortable with, use the links you'll find in text to find more information and take the time to research and study the topic. Great information is available on MSDN, TechNet, and in blogs and forums.

Microsoft certifications

Microsoft certifications distinguish you by proving your command of a broad set of skills and experience with current Microsoft products and technologies. The exams and corresponding certifications are developed to validate your mastery of critical competencies as you design and develop, or implement and support, solutions with Microsoft products and technologies both on-premises and in the cloud. Certification brings a variety of benefits to the individual and to employers and organizations.

Errata & book support

We've made every effort to ensure the accuracy of this book and its companion content. Any errors that have been reported since this book was published are listed at:

http://aka.ms/ER410R2/errata

If you find an error that is not already listed, you can report it to us through the same page.

If you need additional support, email Microsoft Press Book Support at mspinput@microsoft.com.

Please note that product support for Microsoft software is not offered through the addresses above.

We want to hear from you

At Microsoft Press, your satisfaction is our top priority, and your feedback our most valuable asset. Please tell us what you think of this book at:

http://aka.ms/tellpress

The survey is short, and we read every one of your comments and ideas. Thanks in advance for your input!

Stay in touch

Let's keep the conversation going! We're on Twitter: *http://twitter.com/MicrosoftPress*.

Preparing for the exam

Microsoft certification exams are a great way to build your resume and let the world know about your level of expertise. Certification exams validate your on-the-job experience and product knowledge. While there is no substitution for on-the-job experience, preparation through study and hands-on practice can help you prepare for the exam. We recommend that you round out your exam preparation plan by using a combination of available study materials and courses. For example, you might use the Training Guide and another study guide for your "at home" preparation and take a Microsoft Official Curriculum course for the classroom experience. Choose the combination that you think works best for you.

CHAPTER 1

Installing and configuring servers

Installing new Windows servers on your network is not something to be done casually—you must plan the installation well in advance. Among other things, you must decide what edition of the operating system to install, whether you are installing the full graphical user interface (GUI) or the Server Core option, what your virtualization strategy will be, if any, and what roles you intend to implement on the server. If you are installing Windows Server 2012 R2 for the first time, you might also have to decide whether to add the server to your production network or install it on a test network.

This chapter discusses the process of installing Windows Server 2012 R2 using either a clean install or a server upgrade and the server configuration tasks you must perform immediately following the installation. Finally, it considers the configuration of various types of hard disk technologies used for local storage and the deployment of roles to servers all over the network.

> **IMPORTANT**
> ### Have you read page xiii?
> It contains valuable information regarding the skills you need to pass the exam.

Objectives in this chapter:

- Objective 1.1: Install servers
- Objective 1.2: Configure servers
- Objective 1.3: Configure local storage

EXAM TIP

Some exam questions are in a multiple-choice format, where answers are either right or wrong. If, while taking the exam, it seems as though two answers could be right but you can choose only one answer, you've likely missed a clue in the question text that would enable you to discard one of these answers. When exams are authored, the question writer has to provide logical reasons as to why one answer is correct as well as valid reasons as to why the other answers are incorrect. Although there is a small chance that you've come across a poorly worded question, it's not likely. It's more likely, however, that under the duress of a stressful exam situation, you've overlooked a vital bit of evidence that discounts an answer that you suspect is correct.

Objective 1.1: Install servers

Installation is a key topic and has been extensively tested in previous Windows Server exams. The 70-410 exam is no different. This objective discusses planning a Windows Server 2012 R2 installation. It looks at the preinstallation requirements and how you can prepare your installation hardware. It also considers the server roles you can implement during installation.

To review the topics in this objective, this section takes you through a clean installation of Windows Server 2012 R2 using the Server Core option and describes how the Features on Demand function enables you to optimize resources by removing all the files associated with a deleted server role or feature. The objective also looks at the options for upgrading a server running Windows Server 2008 or Windows Server 2008 R2 to Windows Server 2012 R2 and migrating roles from an existing server to a new one.

> **This objective covers how to:**
> - Plan for a server installation
> - Plan for server roles
> - Plan for a server upgrade
> - Install a server using Server Core
> - Optimize resource utilization using Features on Demand
> - Migrate roles from previous versions of Windows Server

Planning for a server installation

In versions of Windows Server prior to Windows Server 2008 R2, installation planning could be a complex task. You had to decide from the outset what edition of the operating system to install, whether to install the 32-bit or 64-bit version, and whether you should perform a Server Core installation or whether you should use the full GUI. All of these decisions affected the server hardware requirements and all of these decisions were irrevocable. To change the edition, the platform, or the interface, you had to reinstall the server from the beginning.

With Windows Server 2012, you have far fewer options to choose from and far fewer installation decisions to make. Since Windows Server 2008 R2, there has been no 32-bit version; only a 64-bit operating system is available, reflecting the fact that most major applications are now 64-bit and that modern server configurations are typically supported on hardware that requires 64 bits. There are only four Windows Server 2012 R2 editions from which to choose, two fewer than the six editions in Windows Server 2008 R2. The Server Core installation option and the full GUI installation option remain, along with a third option called the *Minimal Server Interface*. However, it is now possible to switch between these options without reinstalling the operating system each time.

Selecting a Windows Server 2012 R2 edition

Microsoft releases all of its operating systems in multiple editions, which provides consumers with varying price points and feature sets. When planning a server deployment, the operating system edition you choose should be based on multiple factors, including the following:

- The roles you intend the servers to perform
- The virtualization strategy you intend to implement
- The licensing strategy you plan to use

Compared to Windows Server 2008, Microsoft has simplified the process of selecting a server edition by reducing the available products. As with Windows Server 2008 R2, Windows Server 2012 R2 requires a 64-bit processor architecture. All of the 32-bit versions have been eliminated, and there is no build that supports Itanium processors. This leaves Windows Server 2012 R2 with the following core

editions:

- **Windows Server 2012 R2 Datacenter**   The Datacenter edition is designed for large and powerful servers with up to 64 processors and include fault-tolerance features such as hot-add processor support. As a result, this edition is available only through the Microsoft volume-licensing program and is bundled with a server from original equipment manufacturers (OEMs).

- **Windows Server 2012 R2 Standard**   The Standard edition includes the full set of Windows Server 2012 R2 features and differs from the Datacenter edition only in the number of virtual machine (VM) instances permitted by the license.

- **Windows Server 2012 R2 Essentials**   The Essentials edition includes nearly all the features in the Standard and Datacenter editions; it does not include Server Core, Hyper-V, and Active Directory Federation Services. The Essentials edition is limited to one physical or virtual server instance and a maximum of 25 users.

- **Windows Server 2012 R2 Foundation**   The Foundation edition is a scaled-down version of the operating system; it is designed for small businesses that require only basic server features, such as file and print services and application support. The Foundation edition comes pre-installed with server hardware, includes no virtualization rights, and is limited to 15 users.

The price of each edition is commensurate with its respective capabilities. Obviously, the goal of administrators planning server deployments is to purchase the most cost-effective edition that meets their needs. The following sections examine the primary differences among the Windows Server 2012 R2 editions.

Supporting server roles

Windows Server 2012 R2 includes predefined combinations of services, called *roles*, which implement common server functions. Computers running the Windows Server 2012 R2 operating system can perform a wide variety of tasks, using both the software included with the product and third-party applications. After you install the Windows Server 2012 R2 operating system, you can use Server Manager or Windows PowerShell to install one or more roles on that computer.

Some of the Windows Server 2012 R2 editions include all of the available roles, whereas others include only some of them. Selecting the appropriate edition of Windows Server has always been a matter of anticipating the roles that the computer must perform. At one time, this was a relatively simple process. You planned your server deployments by deciding which ones would be domain controllers, which ones would be certificate servers, which ones would use failover clustering, and so forth. Once you made these decisions, you were done because server roles were largely static.

With the increased focus on virtualization in Windows Server 2012 R2, however, more administrators are forced to consider not only what roles a server must perform at the time of the deployment but what roles a server might perform in the future.

By using virtualized servers, you can modify your network's server strategy at will to accommodate changing workloads and business requirements or to adapt to unforeseen circumstances. Therefore, the process of anticipating the roles a server will perform must account for the potential expansion of your business and possible emergency needs.

Supporting server virtualization

The Windows Server 2012 R2 Datacenter edition and the Standard edition each includes support for Hyper-V, but each edition varies in the number of VMs permitted by its license. Each running instance of the Windows Server 2012 R2 operating system is classified as being in a *physical operating system environment (POSE)* or in a *virtual operating system environment (VOSE)*. When you purchase a Windows Server 2012 R2 license, you can perform a POSE installation of the operating system, as always. After installing the Hyper-V role, you can then create VMs and perform VOSE installations on them. The number of VOSE installations permitted by your license depends on the edition you purchased, as shown in Table 1-1.

TABLE 1-1 Physical and virtual instances supported by Windows Server 2012 R2 editions

Edition	POSE Instances	VOSE Instances
Datacenter	1	Unlimited
Standard	1	2
Essentials	1 (POSE or VOSE)	1 (POSE or VOSE)
Foundation	1	0

EXAM TIP

The 70-410 exam can contain questions about licensing in which you must figure out how many copies of Windows are needed for a particular number of virtual machines on a Hyper-V server and which version of Windows would best meet the requirements while minimizing the cost.

Server licensing

Microsoft provides several different sales channels for Windows Server 2012 R2 licenses, and not all of the editions are available through all of the channels. Licensing Windows Server 2012 R2 includes purchasing licenses for both servers and clients, and there are many options for each one.

If you are already involved in a licensing agreement with Microsoft, you should already be aware of the server editions that are available to you through that agreement. If you are not aware, however, you should investigate the licensing options available to you before you select a server edition.

Table 1-2 lists the sales channels through which you can purchase each of the Windows Server 2012 R2 editions.

TABLE 1-2 Windows Server sales channel availability by edition

	Retail	Volume Licensing	Original Equipment Manufacturer
Datacenter	No	Yes	Yes
Standard	Yes	Yes	Yes
Essentials	Yes	Yes	Yes
Foundation	No	No	Yes

Installation requirements

If your computer does not meet the following hardware specifications, Windows Server 2012 R2 will not install correctly (or possibly at all):

- 1.4-GHz 64-bit processor

- 512 MB RAM
- 32 GB available disk space
- Super VGA (1024 x 768) or higher resolution monitor
- Keyboard and mouse (or other compatible pointing device)
- Internet access

32 GB of available disk space should be considered an absolute minimum. The system partition will need extra space if you install the system over a network or if your computer has more than 16 GB of RAM installed. The additional disk space is required for paging, hibernation, and dump files. In practice, you are unlikely to come across a computer with 32 GB of RAM and only 32 GB of disk space. If you do, free more disk space or invest in additional storage hardware.

As part of Microsoft's increased emphasis on virtualization and cloud computing in its server products, it has significantly increased the maximum hardware configurations for Windows Server 2012 R2. These maximums are listed in Table 1-3.

TABLE 1-3 Maximum hardware configurations in Windows Server versions

	Windows Server 2012 R2	Windows Server 2008 R2
Processors	640	256
RAM	4 TB	2 TB
Failover cluster nodes	64	16

Choosing installation options

Many enterprise networks today use servers that are dedicated to a particular role. When a server is performing a single role, it does not make sense to have so many other processes running on the server that contribute little or nothing to that role. Windows Server 2012 R2 provides installation options that enable administrators to keep the unnecessary resources installed on a server to a minimum.

Using Server Core

Windows Server 2012 R2 includes an installation option that minimizes the user interface on a server. When you select the Windows *Server Core* installation option, you will install a stripped-down version of the operating system. There is no Start menu, no desktop Explorer shell, no Microsoft Management Console (MMC), and virtually no graphical applications. All you see when you start the computer is a single window with a command prompt, as shown in Figure 1-1.

FIGURE 1-1 The default Server Core interface

There are several advantages to running servers using Server Core:

- **Hardware resource conservation**   Server Core eliminates some of the most memory-intensive and processor-intensive elements of the Windows Server 2012 R2 operating system, thus devoting more of the system hardware to running essential services.

- **Reduced disk space**   Server Core requires less disk space for the installed operating system elements and less swap space, which maximizes the utilization of the server's storage resources.

- **Reduced patch frequency**   The graphical elements of Windows Server 2012 R2 are among the most frequently updated, so running Server Core reduces the number of updates that administrators must apply. Fewer updates also mean fewer server restarts and less downtime.

- **Reduced attack surface**   The less software there is running on the computer, the fewer entrance points for attackers to exploit. Server Core reduces the potential openings presented by the operating system, increasing its overall security.

When Microsoft first introduced the Server Core installation option in Windows Server 2008, it was an intriguing idea, but few administrators took advantage of it. The main reason for this was that most server administrators were not sufficiently conversant with the command-line interface that is used to manage a Windows server without a GUI.

In Windows Server 2008 and Windows Server 2008 R2, the decision to install the operating system using the Server Core option was irrevocable. Once you installed the operating system using Server Core, there was no way to get the GUI back except to perform a complete reinstallation. That has all changed in Windows Server 2012 and Windows Server 2012 R2. You can now switch a server from the Server Core option to the Server with a GUI option and back again, at will, by using Windows PowerShell commands.

> **MORE INFO** **THERE AND BACK AGAIN**
>
> For more information on converting from the Server Core option to the Server with a GUI option and back again, see "Objective 1.2: Configure servers," later in this chapter.

This ability means that administrators can install Windows Server 2012 R2 using the Server with a GUI option, configure the server using the familiar graphical tools, and then switch the server to Server Core to take advantage of the benefits listed earlier.

SERVER CORE DEFAULTS

In Windows Server 2012 R2, Server Core is the default installation option for reasons other than simply providing administrators with the ability to switch options after installing. In Windows Server 2012 R2, Microsoft is attempting to fundamentally modify the way that administrators work with their servers. Server Core is now the default installation option because in the new way of managing servers, administrators should rarely, if ever, have to work at the server console, either physically or remotely.

Windows Server has long been capable of remote administration, but this capability has been piecemeal. Some Microsoft Management Console (MMC) snap-ins enabled administrators to connect to remote servers, and Windows PowerShell 2.0 provided some remote capabilities from the command line, but Windows Server 2012 R2, for the first time, includes comprehensive remote administration tools that nearly eliminate the need to work at the server console.

The new Server Manager application in Windows Server 2012 R2 enables administrators to add servers from all over the enterprise and create server groups to facilitate the simultaneous configuration of multiple systems. The new Windows PowerShell 4.0 environment increases the number of available cmdlets from 230 to well over 2,000.

With tools like these, you can install your servers using the Server Core option, execute a few commands to join each server to an Active Directory Domain Services domain, and then never touch the server console again. You can perform all subsequent administration tasks, including the deployment of roles and features, by using Server Manager and Windows PowerShell from a remote workstation.

SERVER CORE CAPABILITIES

In addition to omitting most of the graphical interface, a Server Core installation omits some of the server roles found in a Server with a GUI installation. However, the Server Core option in Windows Server 2012 R2 includes 12 of the 19 roles, plus support for SQL Server 2012, as opposed to only 10 roles in Windows Server 2008 R2 and nine in Windows Server 2008.

Table 1-4 lists the roles and features that are available and not available in a Windows Server 2012 R2 Server Core installation.

TABLE 1-4 Windows Server 2012 R2 Server Core roles

Roles Available in Server Core Installation	Roles Not Available in Server Core Installation
Active Directory Certificate Services	Active Directory Federation Services
Active Directory Domain Services	Application Server (deprecated)
Active Directory Lightweight Directory Services	Fax Server
Active Directory Rights Management Services	Network Policy and Access Services
DHCP Server	Remote Desktop Gateway Remote Desktop Session Host Remote Desktop Web Access
DNS Server	Volume Activation Services
File and Storage Services	Windows Deployment Services
Hyper-V	
Print and Document Services	
Remote Access	
Web Server (IIS)	
Windows Server Update Services	

Using the Minimal Server Interface

If the advantages of Server Core sound tempting, but there are traditional server administration tools you don't want to give up, Windows Server 2012 R2 provides a compromise called the Minimal Server Interface.

The *Minimal Server Interface* is a setting that removes some of the most hardware-intensive elements from the graphical interface. These elements include Internet Explorer and the components of the Windows shell, including the desktop, File Explorer, and the Windows 8 desktop apps. Also omitted are the Control Panel items implemented as shell extensions, including the following:

- Programs and Features
- Network and Sharing Center

- Devices and Printers Center
- Display
- Firewall
- Windows Update
- Fonts
- Storage Spaces

What's left in the Minimal Server Interface are the Server Manager application, the MMC application, Device Manager, and the entire Windows PowerShell interface. This provides administrators with most of the tools they need to manage local and remote servers.

To configure a Windows Server 2012 R2 Server with a GUI installation to use the Minimal Server Interface, you must remove the Server Graphical Shell feature by using Windows PowerShell or the Remove Roles And Features Wizard, as shown in Figure 1-2.

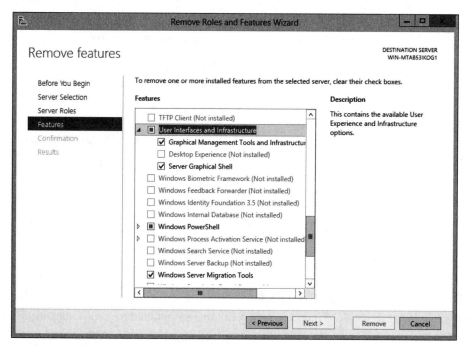

FIGURE 1-2 Using the User Interfaces And Infrastructure feature in the Remove Roles And Features Wizard

Using Features on Demand

During a Windows Server 2012 R2 installation, the Setup program copies the files for all the operating system components from the installation medium to a directory called *WinSxS*, the side-by-side component store. This enables you to activate any of the features included with Windows Server 2012 R2 without having to supply an installation medium.

The only drawback of this arrangement is that the WinSxS directory permanently occupies approximately 5 GB of disk space, much of which is, in many cases, devoted to data that will never be used after the initial server deployment.

With the increasing use of VMs to distribute server roles, enterprise networks often have more copies of the server operating system than ever before, and therefore they have more wasted disk space. In addition, the advanced storage technologies often used by today's server infrastructures, such as storage area networks (SANs) and solid state drives (SSDs), are making that disk space more expensive.

Features on Demand, introduced in Windows Server 2012, is a third state for operating system features that enables administrators to conserve disk space by removing specific features, not only from operation but also from the WinSxS directory.

Features on Demand provides a third installation state for each of the features in Windows Server 2012 R2. In versions of the operating system prior to Windows Server 2012, features could only be Enabled or Disabled. Features on Demand provides the following three states:

- Enabled
- Disabled
- Disabled with payload removed

To implement this third state, you must use the Windows PowerShell Uninstall-Windows-Feature cmdlet, which now supports a new –Remove flag. Thus, the Windows PowerShell command to disable the Server Graphical Shell and remove its source files from the WinSxS directory would be as follows:

```
Uninstall-WindowsFeature Server-Gui-Shell -Remove
```

Once you delete the source files for a feature from the WinSxS folder, they are not irretrievable. If you attempt to enable that feature again, the system will download it from Windows Update or, alternatively, retrieve it from an image file you specify by using the –Source flag with the Install-WindowsFeature cmdlet. This enables you to retrieve the required files from a removable disk or from an image file on the local network. You can also use Group Policy to specify a list of installation sources.

> **NOTE FEATURES ON DEMAND**
> This ability to retrieve source files for a feature from another location is the actual functionality to which the name Features on Demand refers. Microsoft often uses this capability to reduce the size of updates downloaded from the Internet. When the user installs the update, the program downloads the additional files required and completes the installation.

Upgrading servers

An in-place upgrade is the most complicated form of Windows Server 2012 R2 installation. It is also the lengthiest and the most likely to cause problems during its execution. Whenever possible, Microsoft recommends that administrators perform a clean installation or migrate required roles, applications, and settings instead.

Although in-place upgrades often proceed smoothly, the complexity of the upgrade process and the large number of variables involved means that there are many things that can go wrong. To minimize the risks involved, it is important for you to take the upgrade process seriously, prepare the system beforehand, and have the ability to troubleshoot any problems that might arise. The following sections discuss these subjects in greater detail.

Upgrade paths

Upgrade paths for Windows Server 2012 R2 are limited. In fact, it's easier to specify when you can perform an upgrade than when you can't. If you have a 64-bit computer running Windows Server 2008 or Windows Server 2008 R2, you can upgrade it to Windows Server 2012 R2 as long as you use an appropriate operating system edition.

Windows Server 2012 R2 does not support the following:

- Upgrades from Windows Server versions prior to Windows Server 2008
- Upgrades from pre-RTM editions of Windows Server 2012 R2
- Upgrades from Windows workstation operating systems
- Cross-platform upgrades, such as 32-bit Windows Server 2008 to 64-bit Windows Server 2012 R2
- Upgrades from any Itanium edition
- Cross-language upgrades, such as from Windows Server 2008, U.S. English to Windows Server 2012 R2, French

In any of these cases, the Windows Setup program will not permit the upgrade to proceed.

Preparing to upgrade

Before you begin an in-place upgrade to Windows Server 2012 R2, you should perform a number of preliminary procedures to ensure that the process goes smoothly and that the server data is protected.

Consider the following before you perform any upgrade to Windows Server 2012 R2:

- **Check hardware compatibility**   Make sure that the server meets the minimum hardware requirements for Windows Server 2012 R2.
- **Check disk space**   Make sure that there is sufficient free disk space on the partition where the old operating system is installed. During the upgrade procedure, sufficient disk space is needed to simultaneously hold both operating systems. After the upgrade is complete, you can remove the old files, freeing up some additional space.

- **Confirm that software is signed**   All kernel-mode software on the server, including device drivers, must be digitally signed or the software will not load. This can result in an aborted upgrade process, hardware failures after the upgrade is completed, or failure of the system to start after the upgrade. If you cannot locate a software update for the application or driver that is signed, then you should uninstall the application or driver before you proceed with the installation.

> **IMPORTANT   DISABLING THE DRIVER SIGNATURE**
>
> If an unsigned driver prevents the computer from starting, you can disable the driver signature requirement by pressing F8 during the startup, selecting Advanced Boot Options, and then selecting Disable Driver Signature Enforcement.

- **Save mass storage drivers on removable media**   If a manufacturer has supplied a separate driver for a device in your server, save the driver to a CD, a DVD, or a USB flash drive in either the media root directory or the /amd64 folder. To provide the driver during Setup, click Load Driver or press F6 on the disk selection page. You can browse to locate the driver or you can have Setup search the media.

- **Check application compatibility**   The Setup program displays a Compatibility Report page that can notify you of possible application compatibility problems. You can sometimes solve these problems by updating or upgrading the applications. Create an inventory of the software products installed on the server and check the manufacturers' websites for updates, availability of upgrades, and announcements regarding support for Windows Server 2012 R2. In an enterprise environment, you should test all applications for Windows Server 2012 R2 compatibility, no matter what the manufacturer says, before you perform any operating system upgrades.

- **Ensure computer functionality**   Make sure that Windows Server 2008 or Windows Server 2008 R2 is running properly on the computer before you begin the upgrade process. You must start an in-place upgrade from within the existing operating system, so you cannot count on Windows Server 2012 R2 to correct any problems that prevent the computer from starting or running the Setup program.

- **Perform a full backup**   Before you perform any upgrade procedure, you should back up the entire system or, at the very least, the essential data files. Your backup should include all data and configuration information that is necessary for your target computer to function. When you perform the backup, be sure to include the boot and system partitions and the system state data. Removable hard drives make this a simple process, even if there is not a suitable backup device in the computer.

- **Disable virus protection software**   Virus protection software can make installations much slower by scanning every file that is copied locally to your computer. If installed, you should disable this software before performing the upgrade.

- **Disconnect the UPS device**   If you have an uninterruptible power supply (UPS) connected to your target computer, disconnect the data cable before performing the upgrade. Setup automatically attempts to detect connected devices; UPS equipment can cause issues with this process.

- **Purchase the correct Windows Server 2012 R2 edition** Be sure to purchase the appropriate Windows Server 2012 R2 edition for the upgrade and have the installation disk and product key handy.

During the upgrade process, when the system restarts, the boot menu provides an option to roll back to the previous operating system version. However, once the upgrade is complete, this option is no longer available and it is not possible to uninstall Windows Server 2012 R2 and revert to the old operating system version.

Migrating roles

Migration is the preferred method of replacing an existing server with one running Windows Server 2012 R2. Unlike an in-place upgrade, a migration copies vital information from an existing server to a clean Windows Server 2012 R2 installation.

When migrating, nearly all the restrictions listed earlier in regard to upgrades do not apply. By using the Windows Server Migration Tools and migration guides supplied with Windows Server 2012 R2, you can migrate data between servers under any of the following conditions:

- **Between versions** You can migrate data from any Windows Server version from Windows Server 2003 SP2 to Windows Server 2012 R2. This includes migrations from one server running Windows Server 2012 R2 to another.

- **Between platforms** You can migrate data from a 32-bit or 64-bit server to a 64-bit server running Windows Server 2012 R2.

- **Between editions** You can migrate data between servers running different Windows Server editions.

- **Between physical and virtual instances** You can migrate data from a physical server to a virtual one, or the reverse.

- **Between installation options** You can migrate data from one server to another, even when one server is using the Server Core installation option and the other is using the Server with a GUI option.

Migration at the server level is different from any migrations you might have performed on workstation operating systems. Instead of performing a single migration procedure that copies all the user data from the source to the destination computer at once, in a server migration you migrate roles or role services individually.

Windows Server 2012 R2 includes a collection of migration guides that provide individualized instructions for each of the roles supported by Windows Server 2012 R2. Some of the roles require the use of Windows Server Migration Tools; others do not.

Installing Windows Server Migration Tools

Windows Server Migration Tools is a Windows Server 2012 R2 feature that consists of Windows PowerShell cmdlets and help files that enable administrators to migrate certain roles between servers.

Before you can use the migration tools, however, you must install the Windows Server Migration Tools feature on the destination server running Windows Server 2012 R2 and then copy the appropriate version of the tools to the source server.

Windows Server Migration Tools is a standard feature that you install on Windows Server 2012 R2 by using the Add Roles And Features Wizard in Server Manager, as shown in Figure 1-3, or the Install-WindowsFeature Windows PowerShell cmdlet.

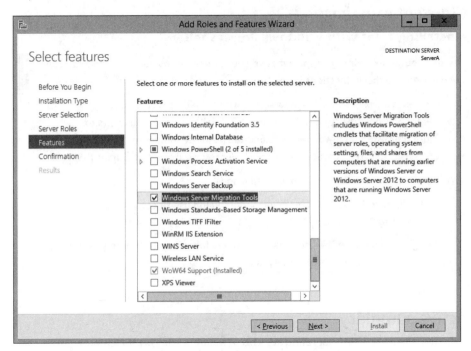

FIGURE 1-3 The Select Features page of the Add Roles And Features Wizard

Using migration guides

Once you have installed the Windows Server Migration Tools on both the source server and the destination server, you can proceed to migrate data between the two.

By using the migration tools, administrators can migrate certain roles, features, shares, operating system settings, and other data from the source server to the destination server running Windows Server 2012 R2. Some roles require the use of the migration tools, whereas others that have their own internal communication capabilities do not.

There is no single procedure for migrating all the Windows Server roles, whether they have their own migration tools or not. Instead, Microsoft provides detailed migration guides for individual roles; in some instances, Microsoft provides detailed migration guides for individual role services within a role.

> **MORE INFO MIGRATION GUIDES**
>
> Up-to-date migration guides are available at the Windows Server Migration Portal at the Windows Server 2012 R2 TechCenter (*http://technet.microsoft.com/en-us/library/jj134039*).

Thought experiment
Installing roles with Windows PowerShell

In this thought experiment, apply what you've learned about this objective. You can find answers to these questions in the "Answers" section at the end of this chapter.

Ralph recently took delivery of a new server with Windows Server 2012 R2 Datacenter edition already installed with the full GUI option. Ralph wants to configure the system as a web server, using the absolute minimum of hardware resources. His first step is to use Server Manager to install the Web Server (IIS) role.

With this in mind, answer the following questions.

1. What Windows PowerShell command should Ralph use to convert the full GUI installation to Server Core?

2. What Windows PowerShell command should Ralph use to completely remove the GUI installation files from the system?

Objective summary

- Microsoft releases all its operating systems in multiple editions, which provides consumers with varying price points and feature sets.

- When you select the Windows Server Core installation option, you get a stripped-down version of the operating system.

- The Minimal Server Interface is a setting that removes some of the most hardware-intensive elements from the graphical interface.

- An in-place upgrade is the most complicated form of a Windows Server 2012 R2 installation. It is also the lengthiest and the most likely to cause problems during its execution. Whenever possible, Microsoft recommends that administrators perform a clean installation or migrate required applications and settings instead.

■ Migration is the preferred method of replacing an existing server with one running Windows Server 2012 R2. Unlike an in-place upgrade, a migration copies vital information from an existing server to a clean Windows Server 2012 R2 installation.

Objective review

Answer the following questions to test your knowledge of the information in this objective. You can find the answers to these questions and explanations of why each answer choice is correct or incorrect in the "Answers" section at the end of this chapter.

1. Which of the following processor architectures can be used for a clean Windows Server 2012 R2 installation? (Choose all that apply.)

   A. 32-bit processor only

   B. 64-bit processor only

   C. 32-bit or 64-bit processor

   D. 64-bit or Itanium processor

2. Which of the following paths is a valid upgrade path to Windows Server 2012 R2?

   A. Windows Server 2003 Standard to Windows Server 2012 R2 Standard

   B. Windows Server 2008 Standard to Windows Server 2012 R2 Standard

   C. Windows Server 2008 32-bit to Windows Server 2012 R2 64-bit

   D. Windows 7 Ultimate to Windows Server 2012 R2 Essentials

3. Which of the following features must be added to a Windows Server 2012 R2 Server Core installation to convert it to the Minimal Server Interface?

   A. Graphical Management Tools and Infrastructure

   B. Server Graphical Shell

   C. Windows PowerShell

   D. Microsoft Management Console

4. Which of the following terms is the name of the directory where Windows stores all the operating system modules it might need to install at a later time?

   A. Windows

   B. System32

   C. bin

   D. WinSxS

5. Which of the following statements are valid reasons as to why administrators might want to install their Windows Server 2012 R2 servers by using the Server Core option? (Choose all that apply.)

   A. A Server Core installation can be converted to the full GUI without reinstalling the operating system.

   B. The Windows PowerShell 4.0 interface in Windows Server 2012 R2 includes more than 10 times as many cmdlets as Windows PowerShell 2.0.

   C. The new Server Manager in Windows Server 2012 R2 makes it much easier to administer servers remotely.

   D. A Windows Server 2012 R2 Server Core license costs significantly less than a full GUI license.

Objective 1.2: Configure servers

A server is rarely ready to perform all the tasks you have planned for it immediately after installation. Typically some postinstallation configuration is required and further configuration changes might become necessary after the server is in service.

> **This objective covers how to:**
> - Configure Server Core
> - Delegate administration
> - Add and remove features in offline images
> - Deploy roles on remote servers
> - Convert Server Core to and from full GUI
> - Configure services
> - Configure NIC teaming
> - Install and configure Windows PowerShell Desired State Configuration (DSC)

Completing postinstallation tasks

As part of the new emphasis on cloud-based services in Windows networking, Windows Server 2012 R2 contains a variety of tools that have been overhauled to facilitate remote server management capabilities.

The new Server Manager, for example, is designed to enable administrators to manage Windows servers without having to interact directly with the server console, either physically or remotely. However, there are some tasks that administrators might have to perform immediately after the operating system installation that require direct access to the server console:

- Configuring the network connection
- Setting the time zone
- Enabling Remote Desktop
- Renaming the computer
- Joining a domain

Using GUI tools

In Windows Server 2012 R2, the Properties tile in Server Manager, as shown in Figure 1-4, provides the same functionality as the Initial Configuration Tasks window in previous Windows Server versions. To complete any or all of the postinstallation configuration tasks on a GUI Windows Server 2012 R2 installation, you can use the tools in the Properties tile, either by working directly at the server console or by using Remote Desktop to access the server from another computer.

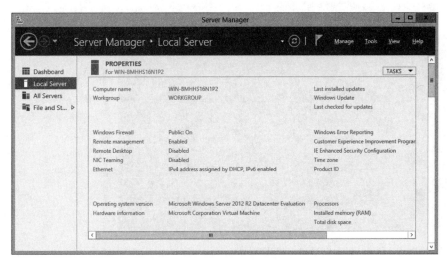

FIGURE 1-4 The Properties tile of the local server in Server Manager

The Ethernet entry in the Properties tile specifies the current status of the computer's network interface. If there is an active Dynamic Host Configuration Protocol (DHCP) server on the network, the server will have already retrieved an IP address and other settings and used them to configure the interface. If there is no DHCP server on the network, or if you must configure the computer with a static IP address, click the Ethernet hyperlink to display the Network Connections window from the Control Panel. You can use this to open the Ethernet Properties sheet and the Internet Protocol Version 4 (TCP/IPv4) Properties sheet, where you can configure the TCP/IP client.

Accurate computer clock time is essential for Active Directory Domain Services communication. If the server is located in a time zone other than the default Pacific zone, click the Time Zone hyperlink to open the Date and Time dialog box, where you can correct the setting.

By default, Windows Server 2012 R2 does not allow Remote Desktop connections. To enable them, click the Remote Desktop hyperlink to open the Remote tab of the System Properties sheet.

In a manual operating system installation, the Windows Setup program assigns a unique name beginning with WIN to the computer. To change the name of the computer and join it to a domain, click the Computer Name hyperlink to open the System Properties sheet and click Change to open the Computer Name/Domain Changes dialog box.

Using command-line tools

If you selected the Server Core option when installing Windows Server 2012 R2, you can perform the same postinstallation tasks from the command line. At the very minimum, you will have to rename the computer and join it to a domain. To do this, you can use the Sconfig. exe or Netdom.exe program.

To rename a computer, run Netdom.exe with the following syntax, as shown in Figure 1-5:

```
netdom renamecomputer %ComputerName% /NewName: <NewComputerName>
```

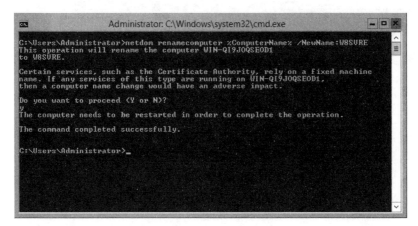

FIGURE 1-5 Renaming a computer from the command line

To restart the computer as directed, use the following command:

```
shutdown /r
```

Then, to join the computer to a domain, use the following syntax:

```
netdom join %ComputerName% /domain: <DomainName> /userd: <UserName> /passwordd:*
```

In this command, the asterisk (*) in the /passwordd parameter causes the program to prompt you for the password to the user account you specified.

These commands assume that a DHCP server has already configured the computer's TCP/IP client. If this is not the case, you must manually configure it before you can join a domain. To assign a static IP address to a computer using Server Core, you can use the Netsh.exe program or the New-NetIPAddress cmdlet in Windows PowerShell.

Converting between GUI and Server Core

In Windows Server 2012 R2, you can convert a computer installed with the full GUI option to Server Core and add the full GUI to a Server Core computer. This is a major improvement in the usefulness of Server Core over the version in Windows Server 2008 R2, in which you can only change the interface by reinstalling the entire operating system.

With this capability, administrators can install servers with the full GUI, use the graphical tools to perform the initial setup, and then convert them to Server Core to conserve system resources. If it later becomes necessary, it is possible to reinstall the GUI components.

To convert a full GUI installation of Windows Server 2012 R2 to Server Core by using Server Manager, you must run the Remove Roles And Features Wizard and uninstall the following features, as shown in Figure 1-6:

- Graphical Management Tools And Infrastructure
- Server Graphical Shell

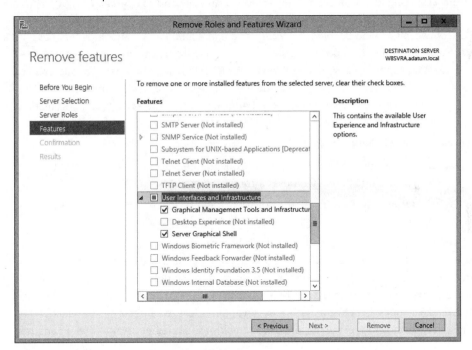

FIGURE 1-6 Uninstalling features using the Remove Features page in Server Manager

To add the full GUI to a Server Core computer, you must use Windows PowerShell to install the same features you removed in the previous procedure. To convert a Windows Server 2012 R2 Server Core installation to the full GUI option, use the following Windows PowerShell command:

```
Install-WindowsFeature Server-Gui-Mgmt-Infra,Server-Gui-Shell –Restart
```

To convert a full GUI server installation to Server Core, use the following command:

```
Uninstall-WindowsFeature Server-Gui-Mgmt-Infra,Server-Gui-Shell -Restart
```

Configuring NIC teaming

NIC teaming is a feature in Windows Server 2012 R2 that enables administrators to combine the bandwidth of multiple network interface adapters, providing increased performance and fault tolerance. Virtualization enables administrators to separate vital network functions on different systems without having to purchase a separate physical computer for each one. However, one of the drawbacks of this practice is that a single server hosting multiple VMs is still a single point of failure for all of them. A single malfunctioning network adapter, a faulty switch, or even an unplugged cable can bring down a host server and all its VMs.

EXAM TIP

The objectives for the 70-410 exam specifically mention the use of the NIC teaming feature. Exam candidates should be familiar with this feature and its operation.

NIC teaming, also called *bonding, balancing,* and *aggregation,* is a technology that has been available for some time, but it was always tied to specific hardware implementations. The NIC teaming capability in Windows Server 2012 R2 is hardware independent and enables you to combine multiple physical network adapters into a single interface. The results can include increased performance by combining the throughput of the adapters and protection from adapter failures by dynamically moving all traffic to the functioning NICs.

NIC teaming in Windows Server 2012 R2 supports two modes:

- **Switch Independent Mode** All the network adapters are connected to different switches, providing alternative routes through the network.
- **Switch Dependent Mode** All the network adapters are connected to the same switch, providing a single interface with their combined bandwidth.

In Switch Independent Mode, you can choose between two configurations. The active/active configuration leaves all the network adapters functional, providing increased throughput. If one adapter fails, all the traffic is shunted to the remaining adapters. In the active/standby configuration, one adapter is left offline to function as a failover in the event the active adapter fails. In active/active mode, an adapter failure causes a performance reduction; in active/standby mode, the performance remains the same before and after an adapter failure.

In Switch Dependent Mode, you can choose static teaming, a generic mode that balances the traffic between the adapters in the team, or you can opt to use the Link Aggregation Control Protocol defined in IEEE 802.3ax, assuming that your equipment supports it.

In Windows Server 2012, there is one significant limitation to NIC teaming. If your traffic consists of large TCP sequences, such as a Hyper-V live migration, the system will avoid using multiple adapters for those sequences to minimize the number of lost and out-of-order TCP segments. You will therefore not realize any performance increase for large file transfers using

TCP. In Windows Server 2012 R2, a new Dynamic Mode splits these large TCP sequences into smaller units and distributes them among the NICs on a team. This is now the default load-balancing mode in Windows Server 2012 R2.

You can create and manage NIC teams by using Server Manager or Windows PowerShell. To create a NIC team by using Server Manager, follow these steps.

1. In Server Manager, in the Properties tile, click NIC Teaming. The NIC Teaming window opens, as shown in Figure 1-7.

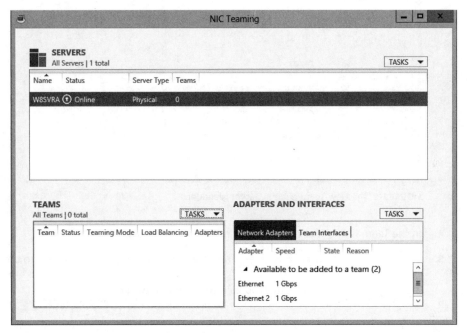

FIGURE 1-7 The NIC Teaming window in Server Manager

2. In the Teams tile, click Tasks and select New Team to open the New Team page.

3. Click the Additional Properties arrow to expand the window, as shown in Figure 1-8.

FIGURE 1-8 The New Team page in Server Manager

4. In the Team Name text box, type the name you want to assign to the team.

5. In the Member Adapters box, select the network adapters you want to add to the team.

6. In the Teaming Mode drop-down list, select one of the following options:

   - Static Teaming
   - Switch Independent
   - LACP

7. In the Load Balancing Mode drop-down list, select one of the following options:

   - Address Hash
   - Hyper-V Port
   - Dynamic

8. If you selected Switch Independent for the Teaming Mode value, use the Standby Adapter drop-down list to select one of the adapters to function as the offline standby.

9. Click OK. The new team is listed in the Teams tile, as shown in Figure 1-9.

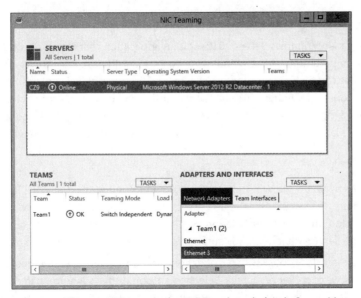

FIGURE 1-9 The new NIC team in the NIC Teaming window in Server Manager

Once you have created a NIC team, the NIC Teaming window enables you to monitor the status of the team and the team interface you have created. The team itself and the individual adapters all have status indicators that inform you if an adapter goes offline.

If this occurs, the indicator for the faulty adapter immediately switches to disconnected, as shown in Figure 1-10, and depending on which teaming mode you chose, the status of the other adapter might also change.

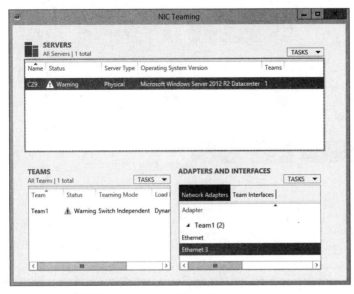

FIGURE 1-10 A NIC team showing a failed adapter

Using Server Manager

The Server Manager tool in Windows Server 2012 R2 is an application that is the most obvious evidence of a major paradigm shift in Windows Server administration. Prior to Windows Server 2012, an administrator who wanted to install a role by using graphical controls had to work at the server console by either physically sitting at the keyboard or by connecting to it by using Remote Desktop Services (formerly Terminal Services). In contrast, the Windows Server 2012 R2 Server Manager can install roles and features to any server on the network.

Adding servers

The primary difference between the Windows Server 2012 and Windows Server 2012 R2 Server Managers and previous versions is the ability to add and manage multiple servers at once. When you log on to a GUI installation of Windows Server 2012 R2 with an administrative account, Server Manager loads automatically, displaying the Welcome tile.

The Server Manager interface consists of a navigation pane on the left containing icons representing various views of server resources. Selecting an icon displays a home page in the right pane, which consists of a number of tiles containing information about the resource. The Dashboard page, which opens by default, contains, in addition to the Welcome tile, thumbnails that summarize the other views available in Server Manager, as shown in Figure 1-11. These other views include a page for the Local Server, one for All Servers, and others for server groups and role groups.

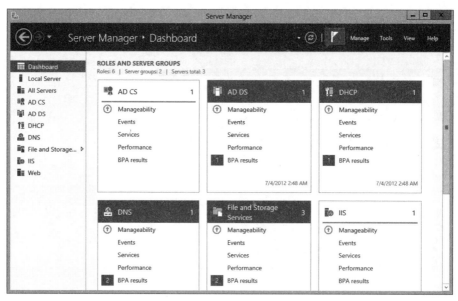

FIGURE 1-11 Dashboard thumbnails

Although only the local server appears in Server Manager when you first run it, you can add other servers, enabling you to manage them together. The servers you add can be physical or virtual and can be running any version of Windows Server since Windows Server 2003. After you add servers to the interface, you can create groups containing collections of servers, such as the servers at a particular office location or those performing a particular function. These groups appear in the navigation pane, enabling you to administer them as a single entity.

To add servers in Server Manager, use the following procedure.

1. Open Server Manager and, in the navigation pane, click All Servers. The All Servers home page opens, as shown in Figure 1-12.

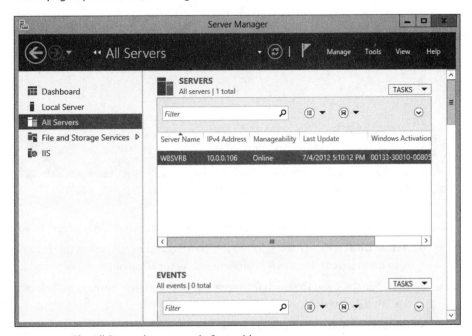

FIGURE 1-12 The All Servers home page in Server Manager

2. From the Manage menu, select Add Servers. The Add Servers dialog box opens, as shown in Figure 1-13.

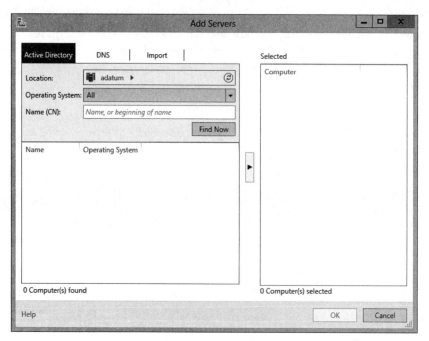

FIGURE 1-13   The Add Servers dialog box in Server Manager

3. Select one of the following tabs to specify how you want to locate servers to add:

   - **Active Directory**   Enables you to search for computers running specific operating systems in specific locations in an Active Directory Domain Services domain

   - **DNS**   Enables you to search for servers in your currently configured Domain Name System (DNS) server

   - **Import**   Enables you to supply a text file containing the names of the servers you want to add

4. Initiate a search or upload a text file to display a list of available servers, as shown in Figure 1-14.

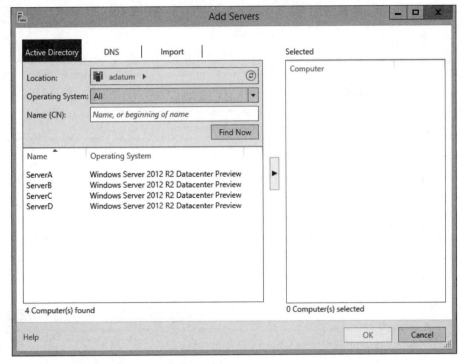

FIGURE 1-14 Searching for servers in Server Manager

5. Select the servers you want to add and click the right arrow button to add them to the Selected list.

6. Click OK. The servers you selected are added to the All Servers home page.

For administrators of enterprise networks, it might be necessary to add a large number of servers to Server Manager. To avoid having to work with a long scrolling list of servers, you can create server groups based on server locations, functions, or any other organizational paradigm.

Adding roles and features

The Server Manager program in Windows Server 2012 R2 combines what used to be separate wizards for adding roles and features into one, the Add Roles And Features Wizard. Once you add multiple servers to the Server Manager interface, they are integrated into the Add Roles And Features Wizard, so you can deploy roles and features to any of your servers.

To install roles and features by using Server Manager, use the following procedure.

1. In Server Manager, from the Manage menu, select Add Roles And Features. The Add Roles And Features Wizard starts, displaying the Before You Begin page.

2. Click Next to open the Select Installation Type page, as shown in Figure 1-15.

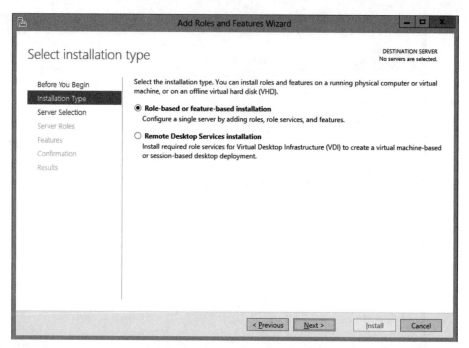

FIGURE 1-15 Configuring the Select Installation Type page in the Add Roles And Features Wizard

3. Leave the Role-Based Or Feature-Based Installation option selected and click Next. The Select Destination Server page opens, as shown in Figure 1-16.

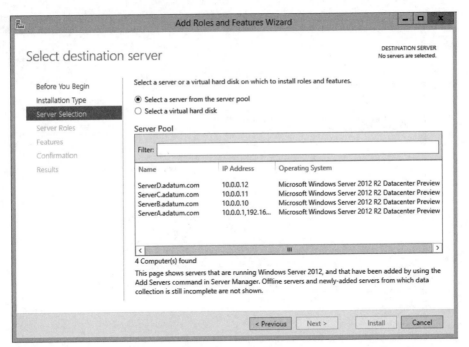

FIGURE 1-16 Configuring the Select Destination Server page in the Add Roles And Features Wizard

4. Select the server on which you want to install the roles or features. If the server pool contains a large number of servers, you can use the Filter text box to display a subset of the pool based on a text string. When you have selected the server, click Next. The Select Server Roles page opens, as shown in Figure 1-17.

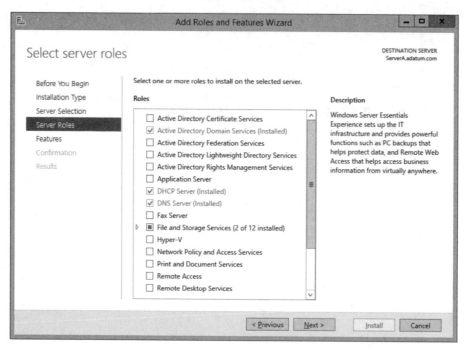

FIGURE 1-17 The Select Server Roles page in the Add Roles And Features Wizard

---

NOTE **INSTALLING COMPONENTS TO MULTIPLE SERVERS**

Although you can use the Add Roles And Features Wizard to install components to any server you have added to Server Manager, you cannot use it to install components to multiple servers at once. You can, however, do this by using Windows PowerShell.

---

5. Select the role or roles you want to install on the selected server. If the roles you select have other roles or features as dependencies, an Add Features That Are Required dialog box opens.

NOTE **SELECTING ALL ROLES AND FEATURES**

Unlike earlier versions of Server Manager, the Windows Server 2012 R2 version enables you to select all the roles and features for a particular server configuration at once, rather than making you run the wizard multiple times.

---

6. Click Add Features to accept the dependencies and then click Next to open the Select Features page, as shown in Figure 1-18.

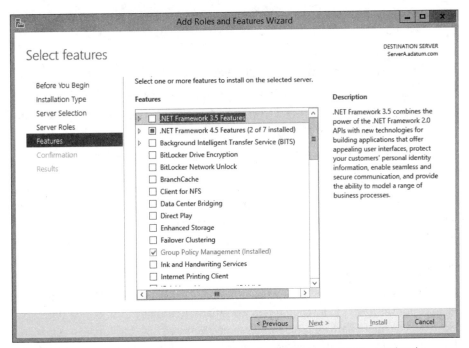

FIGURE 1-18 Configuring the Select Features page in the Add Roles And Features Wizard

7. Select any features you want to install in the selected server and click Next. Dependencies might appear for your feature selections.

8. The wizard then displays pages specific to the roles or features you have chosen. Most roles have a Select Role Services page, on which you can select which elements of the role you want to install. Complete each of the role-specific or feature-specific pages and click Next. A Confirm Installation Selections page opens.

9. You can select from the following optional functions:

   ■ **Restart The Destination Server Automatically If Desired** Causes the server to restart automatically when the installation is completed, if the selected roles and features require it

   ■ **Export Configuration Settings** Creates an XML script documenting the procedures performed by the wizard, which you can use to install the same configuration on another server by using Windows PowerShell

   ■ **Specify An Alternate Source Path** Specifies the location of an image file containing the software needed to install the selected roles and features. Use this option when you have previously deleted the source files from the system using Features on Demand.

10. Click Install to open the Installation Progress page. Depending on the roles and features installed, the wizard might display hyperlinks to the tools needed to perform required

postinstallation tasks. When the installation is complete, click Close to complete the wizard.

> **NOTE USING AN EXPORTED CONFIGURATION FILE**
>
> To use an exported configuration file to install roles and features on another computer running Windows Server 2012 R2, use the following command in a Windows PowerShell session with elevated privileges:
>
> ```
> Install-WindowsFeature –ConfigurationFilePath <ExportedConfig.xml>
> ```

Once you install roles on your servers, the roles appear as icons in Server Manager's navigation pane. These icons actually represent role groups. Each role group contains all the instances of that role found on any of your added servers. You can therefore administer the role across all of the servers on which you have installed it.

Deploying roles to VHDs

In addition to installing roles and features to servers on the network, Server Manager also enables administrators to install them to VMs that are currently in an offline state. For example, you might have an offline web server VM stored on a backup host server, in case the computer hosting your main web server VMs should fail. Server Manager enables you to select a virtual hard disk (VHD) file and install or remove roles and features without having to deploy the VM.

To install roles or features to an offline VHD file, use the following procedure.

1. In Server Manager, from the Manage menu, select Add Roles and Features. The Add Roles And Features Wizard starts, displaying the Before You Begin page.

2. Click Next to open the Select Installation Type page.

3. Leave the Role-Based Or Feature-Based Installation option selected and click Next. The Select Destination Server page opens.

4. Select the Select A Virtual Hard Disk option. A Virtual Hard Disk text box appears at the bottom of the page.

5. In the Virtual Hard Disk text box, type or browse to the location of the VHD file you want to modify.

6. In the Server Pool box, select the server that the wizard should use to mount the VHD file, as shown in Figure 1-19, and click Next. The Select Server Roles page opens.

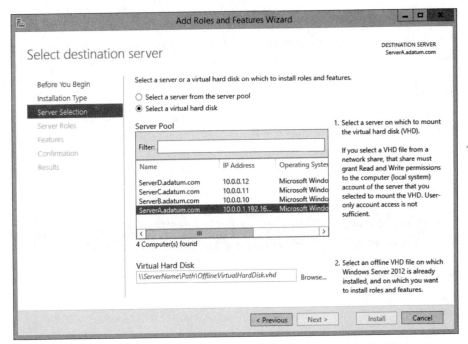

FIGURE 1-19 Configuring the Select Destination Server page in the Add Roles And Features Wizard

> **NOTE WHAT IT MEANS TO MOUNT THE VHD FILE**
>
> The wizard must mount the VHD file on the server you select to look inside and determine which roles and features are already installed and which are available for installation. Mounting a VHD file only makes it available through the computer's file system; it is not the same as starting the VM by using the VHD.

7. Select the role or roles you want to install on the selected server, adding the required dependencies if necessary, and click Next. The Select Features page opens.

8. Select any features you want to install on the selected server and click Next. Dependencies might appear for your feature selections.

9. The wizard then displays pages specific to the roles or features you have chosen, enabling you to select role services and configure other settings. Complete each of the role-specific or feature-specific pages and click Next. A Confirmation page opens.

10. Click Install. The Installation Progress page opens. When the installation is complete, click Close to dismount the VHD and complete the wizard.

Configuring services

Most Windows Server roles and many of the features include services, which are programs that run continuously in the background, typically waiting for a client process to send a request to them. Server Manager provides access to services running on servers all over the network.

When you first look at the Local Server home page in Server Manager, one of the tiles you find there is the Services tile, shown in Figure 1-20. This tile lists all the services installed on the server and specifies their operational status and their Start Type. When you right-click a service, the shortcut menu provides controls that enable you to start, stop, restart, pause, and resume the service.

FIGURE 1-20 The Services tile in Server Manager

The Services tile in the Server Manager display is similar to the traditional Services snap-in for MMC found in previous versions of Windows Server. However, although you can start and stop a service in Server Manager, you cannot modify its Start Type, which specifies whether the service should start automatically with the operating system. To do that you must use the Services MMC snap-in or the Set-Service cmdlet in Windows PowerShell.

Another difference of the Services tile in Windows Server 2012 R2 Server Manager is that this tile appears in many locations throughout Server Manager and in each place it displays a list of services for a different context. This is a good example of the organizational principle of the new Server Manager. The same tools, repeated in many places, provide a consistent management interface to different sets of components.

For example, when you select the All Servers icon in the navigation pane, you first see the Servers tile, as usual, containing all the servers you have added to the Server Manager console. When you select some or all of the servers and scroll down to the Services tile, you see the same display as before, but now it contains all the services for all the computers you selected. This enables you to monitor the services on all the servers at once.

In the same way, when you select one of the role group icons, you can select from the servers running that role and the Services tile will contain only the services associated with that role for the servers you selected.

To manipulate other server configuration settings, you must use the Services snap-in for MMC as mentioned earlier. However, you can launch that, and many other snap-ins, by using Server Manager.

After selecting a server from the Servers pane in any group home page, click the Tools menu to display a list of the utilities and MMC snap-ins, including the Services snap-in. To manage a remote server with an MMC snap-in, you must manually connect it.

Delegating server administration

As networks grow, so does the number of administrative tasks there are to perform on a regular basis, and so does the IT staff that is needed to perform them. Delegating administrative tasks to specific individuals is a natural part of enterprise server management, as is assigning those individuals the permissions they need—and only the permissions they need—to perform those tasks.

> **NOTE DELEGATING PRIVILEGES**
>
> For information on delegating printer privileges, see Objective 2.2, "Configure print and document services." For information on delegating administrative control via Active Directory, see Objective 5.3, "Create and manage Active Directory groups and organizational units."

On smaller networks with small IT staffs, it is not uncommon for task delegation to be informal and for everyone in the IT department to have full access to the entire network. However, on larger networks with larger IT staffs, this becomes increasingly impractical. For example, you might want the newly hired junior IT staffers to be able to create new user accounts but not be able to redesign your Active Directory tree or change the CEO's password.

Delegation is the practice by which administrators grant other users a subset of the privileges that they possess. As such, delegation is as much a matter of restricting permissions as it is of granting them. You want to provide individuals with the privileges they need while protecting sensitive information and delicate infrastructure.

Using Windows PowerShell Desired State Configuration (DSC)

Desired State Configuration (DSC) is the next phase in the development of Windows PowerShell, a process that began over a decade ago and first appeared as a Windows component in Windows PowerShell 1.0 (released in 2006). Windows Server 2012 expanded the functionality of Windows PowerShell by using the command line infrastructure as an underlayment for all of the new graphical capabilities in the operating system. Windows PowerShell 3.0 added thousands of new cmdlets, making it possible to use the command line to accomplish any task you might otherwise perform in Server Manager.

In Windows PowerShell 4.0, DSC provides a new scripting model that enables administrators to create modules called *configurations*, which consist of *nodes* representing computers and *resources* that define elements that administrators want to define as part of the configuration for a particular node.

For example, a relatively simple script to deploy a Web server might appear as follows:

```
Configuration CompanyWeb
{
    Node "ServerB"
    {
        WindowsFeature InstallIIS
        {
            Ensure = "Present"
            Name = "Web-Server"
        }
        File CopyWebSite
        {
            Ensure = "Present"
            Type = "Directory"
            Recurse = $true
            SourcePath = $WebsitePath
            DestinationPath = "C:\inetpub\wwwroot"
            Requires = "[WindowsFeature]InstallIIS"
        }
    }
}
```

In this script, the Node block identifies the computer to be configured and the WindowsFeature and File blocks are both built-in resources that you can use to define the configuration you want to deploy. The WindowsFeature block specifies that the configuration must install the Web-Server role, and the File block copies the content files for a website to the node from a location defined by the $WebsitePath variable. DSC includes many other built-in resources that you can use to define more complex configuration elements, such as system services, registry settings, environment variables, and user and group accounts. It is also possible for administrators to create their own custom resources.

Once you have created a configuration script, you can deploy it by executing the defined configuration name—in this case CompanyWeb—from a Windows PowerShell prompt.

In large enterprise deployments, administrators can create a centralized DSC server by installing the *PowerShell Desired State Configuration Service*, a Windows PowerShell feature that uses the Internet Information Services Web server to deploy configuration logic and data to nodes all over the network. After storing DSC configuration scripts on the server, administrators can configure nodes to check periodically for changes in their configurations or configure the server to push new configurations to nodes as needed.

Thought experiment
Configuring Server Core using Windows PowerShell

In this thought experiment, apply what you've learned about this objective. You can find answers to these questions in the "Answers" section at the end of this chapter.

Deepak is an IT technician who has been assigned the task of configuring a new server running Windows Server 2012 R2 Server Core, called ServerA, which is to be shipped out to the company's branch office. The server must be configured to function as a file server with support for the Distributed File System (DFS), a print server with support for Internet printing, and a secured intranet web/FTP server for domain users.

With this in mind, answer the following questions.

1. What Windows PowerShell command should Deepak use to install the required roles on the servers?

2. What Windows PowerShell command can Deepak use to obtain the short names for the roles used by Windows PowerShell?

3. List the commands that Deepak must run on the new server to install the required modules.

Objective summary

- Server Manager is designed to enable administrators to fully manage Windows servers without ever having to interact directly with the server console, either physically or remotely.

- There are some tasks that administrators might have to perform immediately after the operating system installation that require direct access to the server console.

- If you selected the Server Core option when installing Windows Server 2012 R2, you can perform postinstallation tasks from the command line.

- In Windows Server 2012 R2, the Properties tile in Server Manager provides the same functionality as the Initial Configuration Tasks window in previous versions.

- In Windows Server 2012 R2, you can convert a computer installed with the full GUI option to Server Core and add the full GUI to a Server Core computer.

- NIC teaming is a new feature in Windows Server 2012 R2 that enables administrators to combine the bandwidth of multiple network interface adapters, providing increased performance and fault tolerance.

- For administrators of enterprise networks, it might be necessary to add a large number of servers to Server Manager. To avoid having to work with a long scrolling list of servers, you can create server groups based on server locations, functions, or any other organizational paradigm.

- In addition to installing roles and features to servers on the network, Server Manager enables administrators to install them to VMs that are currently in an offline state.

Objective review

Answer the following questions to test your knowledge of the information in this objective. You can find the answers to these questions and explanations of why each answer choice is correct or incorrect in the "Answers" section at the end of this chapter.

1. Which features must be removed from a full GUI installation of Windows Server 2012 R2 in order to convert it to a Server Core installation? (Choose all that apply.)

   A. Windows Management Instrumentation (WMI)

   B. Graphical Management Tools and Infrastructure

   C. Desktop Experience

   D. Server Graphical Shell

2. Which of the following NIC teaming modes provides fault tolerance and bandwidth aggregation?

   A. Hyper-V live migration

   B. Switch Independent Mode

   C. Switch Dependent Mode

   D. Link Aggregation Control Protocol

3. Which of the following command-line tools are used to join a computer to a domain?

   A. Net.exe

   B. Netsh.exe

   C. Netdom.exe

   D. Ipconfig.exe

4. Which of the following statements about Server Manager is *not* true?

   A. Server Manager can deploy roles to multiple servers at the same time.

   B. Server Manager can deploy roles to VHDs while they are offline.

   C. Server Manager can install roles and features at the same time.

   D. Server Manager can install roles and features to any Windows Server 2012 R2 server on the network.

5. Which of the following operations can you *not* perform on a service by using Server Manager? (Choose all that apply.)

   A. Stop a running service

   B. Start a stopped service

   C. Disable a service

   D. Configure a service to start when the computer starts

Objective 1.3: Configure local storage

Although Windows Server 2012 R2 is designed to take advantage of remote storage and cloud computing, the configuration of local storage remains an important consideration.

> **This objective covers how to:**
> - Design storage spaces
> - Configure basic and dynamic disks
> - Configure MBR and GPT disks
> - Manage volumes
> - Create and mount virtual hard disks (VHDs)
> - Configure storage pools and disk pools
> - Create storage pools by using disk enclosures

Planning server storage

A Windows server can conceivably perform its tasks using the same type of storage as a workstation; that is, one or more standard hard disks connected to a standard drive interface such as Serial ATA (SATA). However, the I/O burdens of a server are different from those of a workstation; a standard storage subsystem can easily be overwhelmed by file requests from dozens or hundreds of users. In addition, standard hard disks offer no fault tolerance and are limited in their scalability.

A variety of storage technologies are better suited for server use. The process of designing a storage solution for a server depends on several factors, including the following:

- The amount of storage the server needs
- The number of users who will be accessing the server at the same time
- The sensitivity of the data to be stored on the server
- The importance of the data to the organization

The following sections examine these factors and the technologies you can choose when creating a plan for your network storage solutions.

How many servers do I need?

When is one big file server preferable to several smaller ones? This is one of the most frequently asked questions when planning a server deployment. In the past, you might have considered the advantages and disadvantages of using one server to perform several roles versus distributing the roles among several smaller servers. Today, however, the emphasis is on virtualization, which means that although you might have many VMs running different roles, they could all be running on a single large physical server.

If you are considering large physical servers or if your organization's storage requirements are extremely large, you must also consider the inherent storage limitations of Windows Server 2012 R2.

The number of sites your enterprise network encompasses and the technologies you use to provide network communication among those sites can also affect your plans. If, for example, your organization has branch offices scattered around the world and uses relatively expensive wide area network (WAN) links to connect them, it would probably be more economical to install a server at each location than to have all your users access a single server by using the WAN links.

Within each site, the number of servers you need can depend on how often your users work with the same resources and how much fault tolerance and high availability you want to build into the system. For example, if each department in your organization typically works with its own applications and documents and rarely needs access to those of other departments, deploying individual servers to each department might be preferable. If everyone in your organization works with the same set of resources, centralized servers might be a better choice.

Estimating storage requirements

The amount of storage space you need in a server depends on a variety of factors, not just the initial requirements of your applications and users. In the case of an application server, start by allocating the amount of space needed for the application files themselves plus any other space the application needs, as recommended by the developer. If users will be storing documents on the server, then allocate a specific amount of space for each user the server will support. Then factor in the potential growth of your organization and your network, both in terms of additional users and additional space required by each user and of data files and updates to the application itself.

Using Storage Spaces

Windows Server 2012 R2 includes a disk virtualization technology called *Storage Spaces*, which enables a server to concatenate storage space from individual physical disks and allocate that space to create virtual disks of any size supported by the hardware.

This type of virtualization is a feature often found in SAN and network attached storage (NAS) technologies, which require a substantial investment in specialized hardware and administrative skill. Storage Spaces provides similar capabilities by using standard direct-attached disk drives or simple external "Just a Bunch of Disks" (JBOD) arrays.

Storage Spaces uses unallocated disk space on server drives to create storage pools. A *storage pool* can span multiple drives invisibly, providing an accumulated storage resource that administrators can expand or reduce as needed by adding disks to or removing them from the pool. By using the space in the pool, administrators can create *virtual disks* of any size.

Once created, a virtual disk behaves just like a physical disk, except that the actual bits might be stored on any number of physical drives in the system. Virtual disks can also provide fault tolerance by using the physical disks in the storage pool to hold mirrored or parity data.

After creating a virtual disk, you can create volumes on it just as you would on a physical disk. Server Manager provides the tools you need to create and manage storage pools and virtual disks and provides you with the ability to create volumes and file system shares, with some limitations.

Understanding Windows disk settings

When you install Windows Server 2012 R2 on a computer, the setup program automatically performs all the preparation tasks for the primary hard disk in the system. However, when you install additional hard disk drives on a server, or when you want to use settings that differ from the system defaults, you must perform the following tasks manually:

- **Select a partitioning style**   Windows Server 2012 R2 supports two hard disk partition styles: the master boot record (MBR) partition style and the GUID (globally unique identifier) partition table (GPT) partition style. You must choose one of these partition styles for a drive; you cannot use both.

- **Select a disk type**   Windows Server 2012 R2 supports two disk types: the basic disk type and the dynamic disk type. You cannot use both types on the same disk drive, but you can mix disk types in the same computer.

- **Divide the disk into partitions or volumes**   Although many professionals use the terms partition and volume interchangeably, it is correct to refer to partitions on basic disks and volumes on dynamic disks.

- **Format the partitions or volumes with a file system**   Windows Server 2012 R2 supports the NTFS file system, the FAT file system (including the FAT16, FAT32, and exFAT variants), and the new ReFS file system (covered later in this chapter, in the "Understanding file systems" section.)

The following sections examine the options for each of these tasks.

Selecting a partition style

The term *partition style* refers to the method that Windows operating systems use to organize partitions on the disk. Servers running Windows Server 2012 R2 computers can use either of the following two hard disk partition styles:

- **MBR**   The MBR partition style has been around since before Windows and is still a common partition style for x86-based and x64-based computers.

- **GPT** GPT has existed since the late 1990s, but no x86 version of Windows prior to Windows Server 2008 and Windows Vista supports it. Today, most operating systems support GPT, including Windows Server 2012 R2.

Before Windows Server 2008 and Windows Vista, all x86-based Windows computers used only the MBR partition style. Computers based on the x64 platform could use either the MBR or GPT partition style, as long as the GPT disk was not the boot disk.

Unless the computer's architecture provides support for an Extensible Firmware Interface (EFI)–based boot partition, it is not possible to boot from a GPT disk. If this is the case, the system drive must be an MBR disk and you can use GPT only on separate nonbootable disks for data storage.

When you use Server Manager to initialize a disk in Windows Server 2012 R2, it uses the GPT partition style, whether it is a physical or a virtual disk. There are no controls in Server Manager supporting MBR, although it displays the partition style in the Disks tile.

Understanding disk types

Most personal computers use basic disks because they are the easiest to manage. Advanced volume types require the use of dynamic disks. A *basic disk* using the MBR partition style organizes data by using primary partitions, extended partitions, and logical drives. A primary partition appears to the operating system as though it is a physically separate disk and can host an operating system, in which case it is known as the active partition.

When you work with basic MBR disks in Windows Server 2012 R2 using the Disk Management snap-in, you can create three volumes that take the form of primary partitions. When you create the fourth volume, the system creates an extended partition, with a logical drive on it, of the size you specified. If there is free space left on the disk, the system allocates it to the extended partition, as shown in Figure 1-21, where you can use it to create additional logical drives.

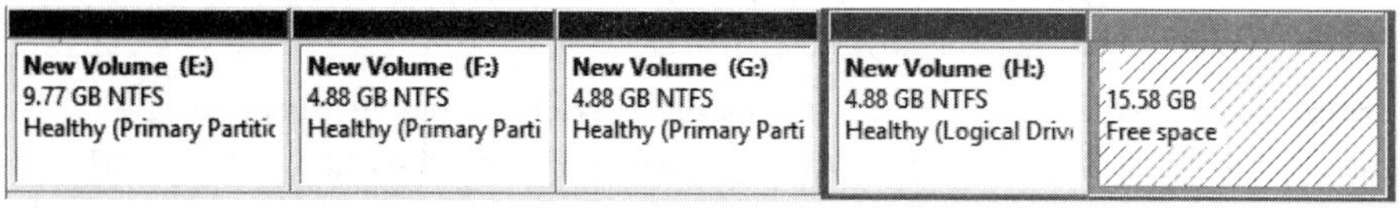

FIGURE 1-21 Primary and extended partitions on a basic disk using MBR

When you select the GPT partition style, the disk still appears as a basic disk, but you can create up to 128 volumes, each of which appears as a primary partition, as shown in Figure 1-22. There are no extended partitions or logical drives on GPT disks.

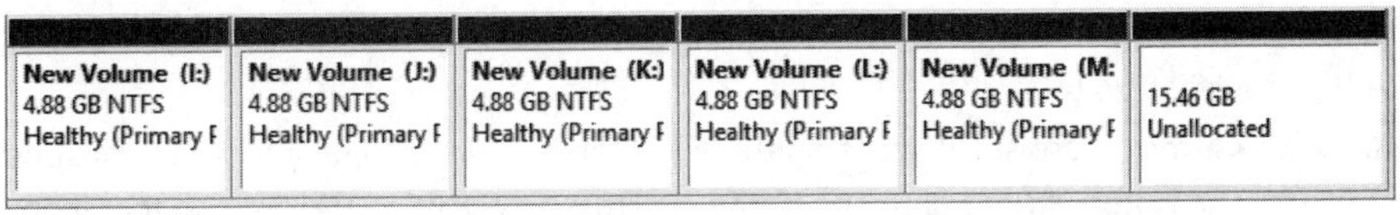

FIGURE 1-22 Primary partitions on a basic disk using GPT

The alternative to using a basic disk is to convert it to a *dynamic disk*. The process of converting a basic disk to a dynamic disk creates a single partition that occupies the entire disk. You can then create an unlimited number of volumes out of the space in that partition. Dynamic disks support several different types of volumes, as described in the next section.

Understanding volume types

A dynamic disk can contain an unlimited number of volumes that function much like primary partitions on a basic disk, but you cannot mark an existing dynamic disk as active. When you create a volume on a dynamic disk by using the Disk Management snap-in in Windows Server 2012 R2, you choose from the following five volume types:

- **Simple volume** Consists of space from a single disk. After you have created a simple volume, you can extend it to multiple disks to create a spanned or striped volume, as long as it is not a system volume or boot volume. You can also extend a simple volume into any adjacent unallocated space on the same disk or, with some limitations, shrink the volume by deallocating any unused space in the volume.

- **Spanned volume** Consists of space from 2 to 32 physical disks, all of which must be dynamic disks. A spanned volume is essentially a method for combining the space from multiple dynamic disks into a single large volume. Windows Server 2012 R2 writes to the spanned volume by filling all the space on the first disk and then filling each of the additional disks in turn. You can extend a spanned volume at any time by adding disk space. Creating a spanned volume does not increase the disk's read/write performance or provide fault tolerance. In fact, if a single physical disk in the spanned volume fails, all the data in the entire volume is lost.

- **Striped volume** Consists of space from 2 to 32 physical disks, all of which must be dynamic disks. The difference between a striped volume and a spanned volume is that in a striped volume, the system writes data one stripe at a time to each successive disk in the volume. Striping provides improved performance because each disk drive in the array has time to seek the location of its next stripe while the other drives are writing. Striped volumes do not provide fault tolerance, however, and you cannot extend them after creation. If a single physical disk in the striped volume fails, all the data in the entire volume is lost.

- **Mirrored volume** Consists of an identical amount of space on two physical disks, both of which must be dynamic disks. The system performs all read and write operations on both disks simultaneously so they contain duplicate copies of all data stored on the volume. If one disk fails, the other continues to provide access to the volume until the failed disk is repaired or replaced.

- **RAID-5 volume**   Consists of space on three or more physical disks, all of which must be dynamic. The system stripes data and parity information across all the disks so that if one physical disk fails, the missing data can be re-created by using the parity information on the other disks. RAID-5 volumes provide improved read performance because of the disk striping, but write performance suffers due to the need for parity calculations.

Understanding file systems

To organize and store data or programs on a hard drive, you must install a file system. A file system is the underlying disk drive structure that enables you to store information on your computer. You install file systems by formatting a partition or volume on the hard disk.

In Windows Server 2012 R2, five file system options are available:

- NTFS
- FAT32
- exFAT
- FAT (also known as FAT16)
- ReFS

NTFS is the preferred file system for a server; the main benefits are improved support for larger hard drives than FAT and better security in the form of encryption and permissions that restrict access by unauthorized users.

Because the FAT file systems lack the security that NTFS provides, any user who gains access to your computer can read any file without restriction. Additionally, FAT file systems have disk size limitations: FAT32 cannot handle a partition greater than 32 GB or a file greater than 4 GB. FAT cannot handle a hard disk greater than 4 GB or a file greater than 2 GB. Because of these limitations, the only viable reason for using FAT16 or FAT32 is the need to dual boot the computer with a non-Windows operating system or a previous version of Windows that does not support NTFS, which is not a likely configuration for a server.

ReFS is a new file system first appearing in Windows Server 2012 R2 that offers practically unlimited file and directory sizes and increased resiliency that eliminates the need for error-checking tools, such as Chkdsk.exe. However, ReFS does not include support for NTFS features such as file compression, Encrypted File System (EFS), and disk quotas. ReFS disks also cannot be read by any operating systems older than Windows Server 2012 and Windows 8.

Working with disks

Windows Server 2012 R2 includes tools that enable you to manage disks graphically or from the command prompt. All Windows Server 2012 R2 installations include the File and Storage Services role, which causes Server Manager to display a menu when you click the icon in the navigation pane, as shown in Figure 1-23. This menu provides access to home pages that enable administrators to manage volumes, disks, storage pools, shares, and iSCSI devices.

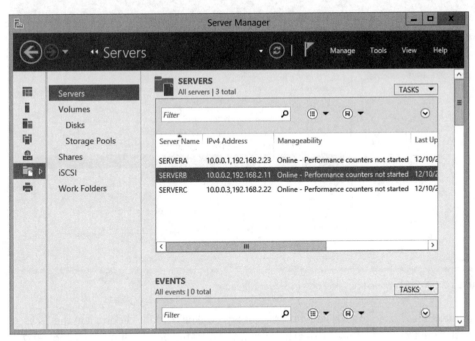

FIGURE 1-23 Using the File and Storage Services menu in Server Manager

Server Manager is the only graphical tool that can manage storage pools and create virtual disks. It can also perform some—but not all—of the standard disk and volume management operations on physical disks. Like the other Server Manager home pages, the File page and the Storage Services page enables you to perform tasks on any servers you have added to the interface.

Disk Management is an MMC snap-in that is the traditional tool for performing disk-related tasks. To access the Disk Management snap-in, open the Computer Management console and select Disk Management.

You can also manage disks and volumes from the command line by using the DiskPart.exe utility.

Adding a new physical disk

When you add a new hard disk to a Windows Server 2012 R2 computer, you must initialize the disk before you can access its storage. To add a new secondary disk, shut down the computer and install or attach the new physical disk per the manufacturer's instructions. A newly added physical disk is listed in Server Manager in the Disks tile, as shown in Figure 1-24, with a status of Offline and an unknown partition style.

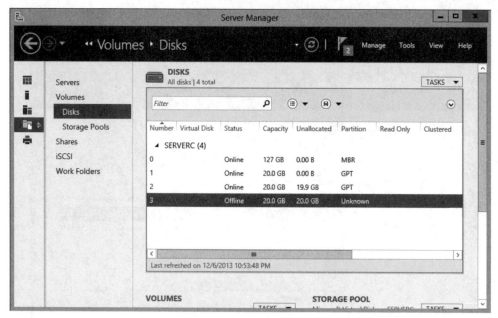

FIGURE 1-24 A newly added physical disk in Server Manager

To make the disk accessible, you must first bring it online by right-clicking it in the Disks tile and, from the shortcut menu, selecting Bring Online. After you confirm your action and the disk status changes to Online, right-click it and select Initialize.

Unlike the Disk Management snap-in, Server Manager does not allow you to choose the partition style for the disk. A Task Progress window opens; when the process is completed, click Close. The disk then appears in the list with a partition style of GPT.

You can convert a disk from one partition style to another at any time using Disk Management by right-clicking the disk you need to convert and then, from the shortcut menu, selecting Convert To GPT Disk or Convert To MBR Disk. However, be aware that converting the disk partition style is a destructive process. You can perform the conversion only on an unallocated disk, so if the disk you want to convert contains data, you must back up the disk and then delete all existing partitions or volumes before you begin the conversion.

Creating and mounting virtual hard disks (VHDs)

Hyper-V relies on the virtual hard disk (VHD or VHDX) format to store virtual disk data in files that can easily be transferred from one computer to another. The Disk Management snap-in in Windows Server 2012 R2 enables you to create VHD and VHDX files and mount them on the computer. Once they are mounted, you can treat them just like physical disks and use them to store data. When dismounting a VHD or VHDX, the stored data is packaged in the file so you can copy or move it as needed.

To create a VHD in Disk Management, use the following procedure.

1. In Server Manager, click Tools, Computer Management. The Computer Management console opens.

2. Click Disk Management to open the Disk Management snap-in.

3. From the Action menu, select Create VHD. The Create And Attach Virtual Hard Disk dialog box opens, as shown in Figure 1-25.

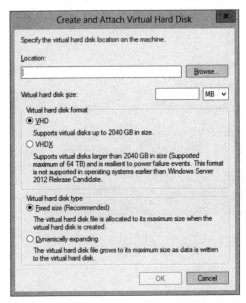

FIGURE 1-25 Configuring the Create And Attach Virtual Hard Disk settings

4. In the Location text box, type the path and file name for the file you want to create.

5. In the Virtual Hard Disk Size box, type the maximum size of the disk you want to create.

6. Select one of the following Virtual Hard Disk Format options:

   - **VHD**   The original and more compatible format, which supports files of up to 2,040 GB

   - **VHDX**   A new version of the format that supports files of up to 64 TB but can be read only by computers running Windows Server 2012 and Windows Server 2012 R2

7. Select one of the following Virtual Hard Disk Type options:

   - **Fixed Size (Recommended)**   Allocates all the disk space for the VHD/VHDX file at once

   - **Dynamically Expanding**   Allocates disk space to the VHD/VHDX file as you add data to the virtual hard disk

8. Click OK. The system creates the VHD or VHDX file and attaches it so that it appears as a disk in the snap-in.

Once you have created and attached the VHD or VHDX file, it appears as an uninitialized disk in the Disk Management snap-in and in Server Manager. By using either tool, you can initialize the disk and create volumes on it, just as you would a physical disk. After storing data on the volumes, you can detach the VHD or VHDX file and move it to another location or mount it on a Hyper-V VM.

Creating a storage pool

Once you have installed your physical disks, you can concatenate their space into a storage pool, from which you can create virtual disks of any size.

To create a storage pool by using Server Manager, follow this procedure.

1. In Server Manager, click the File and Storage Services icon and, in the menu that opens, click Storage Pools. The Storage Pools tile then opens, as shown in Figure 1-26.

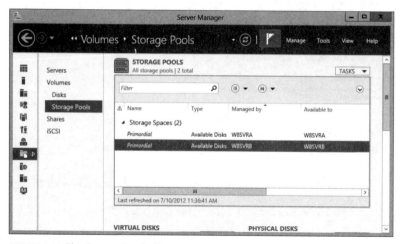

FIGURE 1-26 The Storage Pools tile

2. In the Storage Pools tile, select the primordial space on the server where you want to create the pool and, from the Tasks menu, select New Storage Pool. The New Storage Pool Wizard starts, displaying the Before You Begin page.

3. Click Next. The Specify A Storage Pool Name and Subsystem page opens, as shown in Figure 1-27.

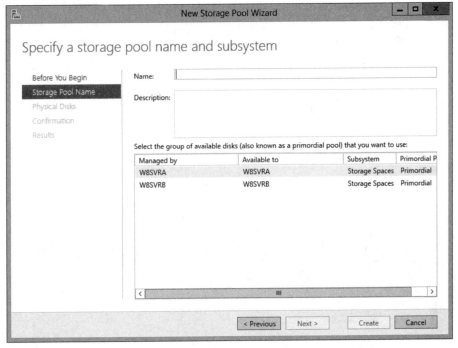

FIGURE 1-27 The Specify A Storage Pool Name and Subsystem page

4. In the Name text box, type the name you want to assign to the storage pool. Then select the server on which you want to create the pool and click Next. The Select Physical
Disks For the Storage Pool page opens, as shown in Figure 1-28.

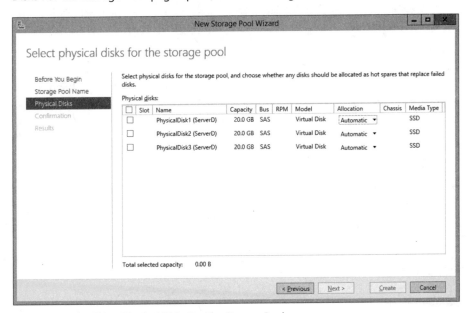

FIGURE 1-28 The Select Physical Disks For The Storage Pool page

5. Select the check boxes for the disks you want to add to the pool and click Next to open the Confirm Selections page.

6. Click Create. The wizard creates the new storage pool and the View Results page opens.

7. Click Close. The wizard closes and the new pool appears on the Storage Pools tile, as shown in Figure 1-29.

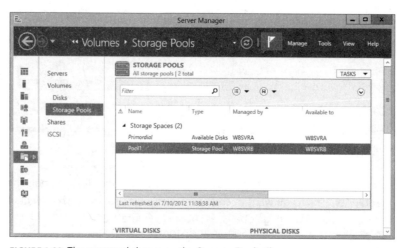

FIGURE 1-29 The new pool shown on the Storage Pools tile

8. Close the Server Manager window.

After you have created a storage pool, you can modify its capacity by adding or removing physical disks. The Tasks menu in the Physical Disks tile on the Storage Pools home page contains the following options:

- **Add Physical Disk** Enables you to add a physical disk to the pool as long as it is initialized and does not contain any volumes

- **Remove Disk** Removes the space provided by a physical disk from the storage pool. This option is available only if all data has already been evicted from the disk.

To create a new storage pool by using Windows PowerShell, you use the New-StoragePool cmdlet with the following basic syntax:

```
New-StoragePool -FriendlyName <pool name> -StorageSubSystemFriendlyName <subsystem name>
-PhysicalDisks <CIM instances>
```

To obtain the correct designations for the storage subsystem and the physical disks, use the Get-StorageSubsystem and Get-PhysicalDisk cmdlets.

In addition to the required parameters, the New-StoragePool cmdlet also accepts the following options, which are not available in the wizard.

- **-EnclosureAwareDefault**   Specifies whether the storage pool is being created from disks housed in a disk enclosure that supports SCSI Enclosure Services. This enables the pool to use additional information provided by the enclosure, such as slot locations, to balance data storage among the hardware devices.
- **-ProvisioningTypeDefault**   Specifies the type of provisioning (Unknown, Fixed, or Thin) to be used for the creation of virtual disks from this pool
- **-ResiliencySettingsNameDefault**   Specifies the resiliency setting (Simple, Mirror, or Parity) that the system should use by default when creating virtual disks from the pool

Creating virtual disks

After you have created a storage pool, you can use the space to create as many virtual disks as you need.

To create a virtual disk by using Server Manager, use the following procedure.

1. In Server Manager, click the File And Storage Services icon and, in the menu that opens, click Storage Pools. The Storage Pools home page opens.

2. Scroll down (if necessary) to expose the Virtual Disks tile and, from the Tasks menu, select New Virtual Disk. The New Virtual Disk menu opens, displaying the Before You Begin page.

3. Click Next to open the Select The Server And Storage Pool page.

4. Select the pool in which you want to create a virtual disk and click Next. The Specify The Virtual Disk Name page opens.

5. In the Name text box, type a name for the virtual disk and click Next. The Select The Storage Layout page opens, as shown in Figure 1-30.

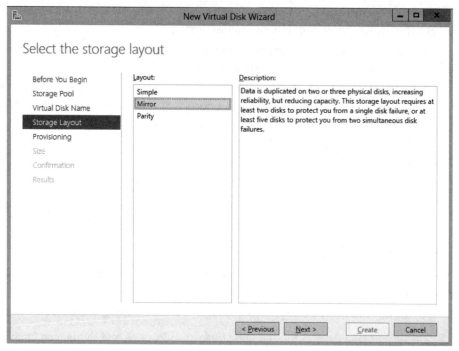

FIGURE 1-30 The Select The Storage Layout page

6. Select one of the following layout options and click Next.

- **Simple** Requires the pool to contain at least one physical disk and provides no fault tolerance. When more than one physical disk is available, the system stripes data across the disks.

- **Mirror** Requires the pool to contain at least two physical disks and provides fault tolerance by storing identical copies of every file. Two physical disks provide protection against a single disk failure; five physical disks provide protection against two disk failures.

- **Parity** Requires the pool to contain at least three physical disks and provides fault tolerance by striping parity information along with data.

IMPORTANT DISK-LEVEL FAULT TOLERANCE

The fault tolerance built into Storage Spaces is provided at the disk level, not the volume level, as in the Disk Management snap-in. Theoretically, you can use Disk Management to create mirrored or RAID-5 volumes out of virtual disks, but this would defeat the purpose of creating them in the first place because the virtual disks might be located on the same physical disk.

---

7. The Specify The Provisioning Type page opens, as shown in Figure 1-31.

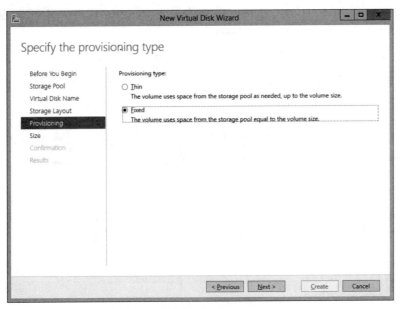

FIGURE 1-31 The Specify The Provisioning Type page

8. Select one of the following Provisioning Type options and click Next.

- **Thin** The system allocates space from the storage pool to the disk as needed, up to the maximum specified size.

- **Fixed** The system allocates the maximum specified amount of space to the disk immediately on creating it.

The Specify The Size Of The Virtual Disk page opens, as shown in Figure 1-32.

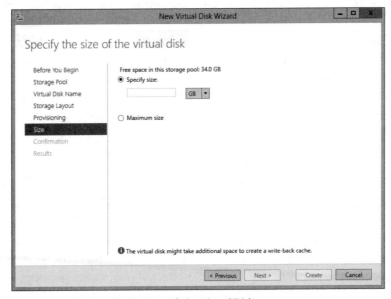

FIGURE 1-32 The Specify The Size Of The Virtual Disk page

9. In the Specify Size text box, specify the size of the disk you want to create and click Next. The Confirm Selections page opens.

10. Click Create. The View Results page opens as the wizard creates the disk.

11. Click Close. The wizard closes and the new disk opens in the Virtual Disks tile, as shown in Figure 1-33.

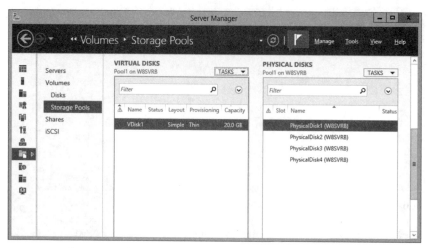

FIGURE 1-33 The new disk is shown in the Virtual Disks tile in Server Manager

12. Close the Server Manager window.

By default, the New Volume Wizard launches when you create a new virtual disk. At this point, the disk is a virtual equivalent of a newly installed physical disk. It contains nothing but unallocated space, and you must create at least one volume before you can store data on it.

Creating a simple volume

Technically speaking, you create partitions on basic disks and volumes on dynamic disks. This is not just an arbitrary difference in nomenclature. Converting a basic disk to a dynamic disk actually creates one big partition, occupying all the space on the disk. The volumes you create on the dynamic disk are logical divisions within that single partition.

Windows versions prior to 2008 use the correct terminology in the Disk Management snap-in. The menus enable you to create partitions on basic disks and volumes on dynamic disks. Windows Server 2012 R2 uses the term volume for both disk types and enables you to create any of the available volume types, whether the disk is basic or dynamic. If the volume type you select is not supported on a basic disk, the wizard converts it to a dynamic disk as part of the volume creation process.

Despite the menus that refer to basic partitions as volumes, the traditional rules for basic disks remain in effect. The New Simple Volume menu option on a basic disk creates up to three primary partitions. When you create a fourth volume, the wizard actually creates an extended partition and a logical drive of the size you specify. If there is any remaining space on the disk, you can create additional logical drives in the extended partition.

> **IMPORTANT BE CAREFUL IF USING THE DISKPART.EXE UTILITY**
>
> When you use DiskPart.exe (a command-line utility included with Windows Server 2012 R2) to manage basic disks, you can create four primary partitions or three primary partitions and one extended partition. The DiskPart.exe utility contains a superset of the commands supported by the Disk Management snap-in. In other words, DiskPart can do everything Disk Management can do and more. However, whereas the Disk Management snap-in prevents you from unintentionally performing actions that might result in data loss, DiskPart has no safeties and thus does not prohibit you from performing such actions. For this reason, Microsoft recommends that only advanced users use DiskPart and that they use it with due caution.

To create a new simple volume on a basic or dynamic disk by using the Disk Management snap-in, use the following procedure.

1. In Server Manager, click Tools and click Computer Management. The Computer Management console opens.

2. Click Disk Management to launch the Disk Management snap-in.

3. In the Graphical View, right-click an unallocated area in the disk on which you want to create a volume and, from the shortcut menu, select New Simple Volume. The New Simple Volume Wizard starts.

4. Click Next to bypass the Welcome page. The Specify Volume Size page opens, as shown in Figure 1-34.

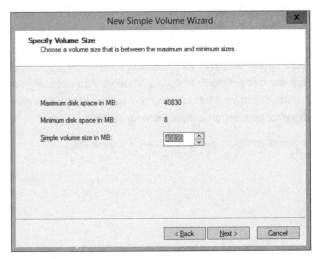

FIGURE 1-34 Configuring the Specify Volume Size page

5. Select the size for the new partition or volume, within the maximum and minimum limits stated on the page, by using the Simple Volume Size In MB spin box, and then click Next. The Assign Drive Letter Or Path page opens, as shown in Figure 1-35.

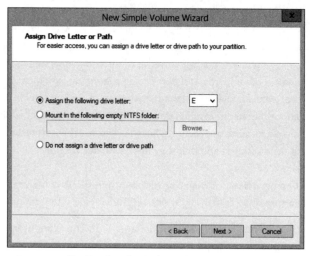

FIGURE 1-35 Configuring the Assign Drive Letter Or Path page

6. Configure one of the following three options:

- **Assign The Following Drive Letter**   If you select this option, click the associated drop-down list for a list of available drive letters and select the letter you want to assign to the drive.

- **Mount In The Following Empty NTFS Folder**   If you select this option, either type the path to an existing NTFS folder or click Browse to search for or create a new folder. The entire contents of the new drive will appear in the folder you specify.

- **Do Not Assign A Drive Letter Or Drive Path**   Select this option if you want to create the partition but are not yet ready to use it. When you do not assign a volume a drive letter or path, the drive is left unmounted and inaccessible. When you want to mount the drive for use, assign a drive letter or path to it.

7. Click Next to open the Format Partition page, as shown in Figure 1-36.

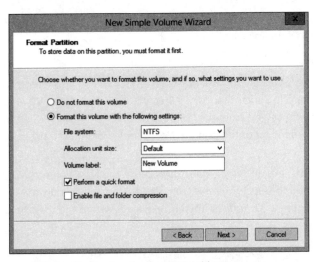

FIGURE 1-36 Configuring the Format Partition page

8. Specify whether the wizard should format the volume and if so, how. If you do not want to format the volume at this time, select the Do Not Format This Volume option. If you want to format the volume, select the Format This Volume With The Following Settings option, and then configure the associated options as follows.

- **File System** Select the desired file system. The options available depend on the size of the volume and can include ReFS, NTFS, exFAT, FAT32, and FAT.

- **Allocation Unit Size** Specify the file system's cluster size. The cluster size signifies the basic unit of bytes in which the system allocates disk space. The system calculates the default allocation unit size based on the size of the volume. You can override this value by clicking the associated drop-down list and then selecting one of the values. For example, if your client uses consistently small files, you might want to set the allocation unit size to a smaller cluster size.

- **Volume Label** Specify a name for the partition or volume. The default name is New Volume, but you can change the name to anything you want.

- **Perform A Quick Format** When this check box is selected, Windows formats the disk without checking for errors. This is a faster method to format the drive, but Microsoft does not recommend it. When you check for errors, the system looks for and marks bad sectors on the disk so that your clients will not use those portions of the disk.

- **Enable File And Folder Compression** Selecting this check box turns on folder compression for the disk. This option is available only for volumes being formatted with the NTFS file system.

9. Click Next. The Completing The New Simple Volume Wizard page opens.

10. Review the settings to confirm your options and then click Finish. The wizard creates the volume according to your specifications.

11. Close the console containing the Disk Management snap-in.

This procedure can create volumes on physical or virtual disks. You can also create simple volumes by using a similar wizard in Server Manager. When you launch the New Volume Wizard in Server Manager, which you can do from the Volumes or Disks home page, the options the wizard presents are nearly identical to those in the New Simple Volume Wizard in Disk Management.

The primary difference is that, like all Server Manager wizards, the New Volume Wizard includes a page that enables you to select the server and the disk on which you want to create the volume, as shown in Figure 1-37. You can therefore use this wizard to create volumes on any disk on any of your servers.

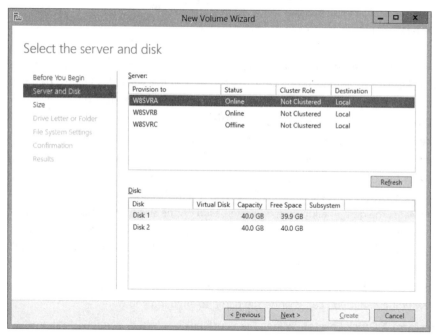

FIGURE 1-37 The Select The Server And Disk page in the New Volume Wizard in Server Manager

Creating a striped, spanned, mirrored, or RAID-5 volume

The procedure for creating a striped, spanned, mirrored, or RAID-5 volume is almost the same as that for creating a simple volume, except that the Specify Volume Size page is replaced by the Select Disks page.

To create a striped, spanned, mirrored, or RAID-5 volume, use the following procedure.

1. In Server Manager, click Tools and click Computer Management. The Computer Management console opens.

2. Click Disk Management to open the Disk Management snap-in.

3. Right-click an unallocated area on a disk and then, from the shortcut menu, select the command for the type of volume you want to create. A New Volume Wizard starts, named for your selected volume type.

4. Click Next to bypass the Welcome page. The Select Disks page opens, as shown in Figure 1-38.

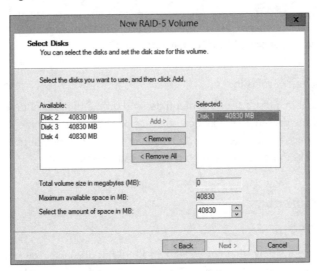

FIGURE 1-38 Configuring the Select Disks page

5. On the Select Disks page, select the disks you want to use for the new volume from the Available list box and then click Add. The disks you chose are moved to the Selected list box, joining the original disk you selected when launching the wizard. For a striped, spanned, or mirrored volume, you must have at least two disks in the Selected list; for a RAID-5 volume, you must have at least three.

6. Specify the amount of space you want to use on each disk by using the Select the Amount of Space in MB spin box. Then click Next. The Assign Drive Letter or Path page opens.

   If you are creating a spanned volume, you must click each disk in the Selected list and specify the amount of space to use on that disk. The default value for each disk is the size of the unallocated space on that disk.

   If you are creating a striped, mirrored, or RAID-5 volume, you specify only one value because these volumes require the same amount of space on each disk. The default value is the size of the unallocated space on the disk with the least free space.

7. Specify whether you want to assign a drive letter or path and then click Next. The Format Partition page opens.

8. Specify if or how you want to format the volume and then click Next. The Completing The New Simple Volume Wizard page opens.

9. Review the settings to confirm your options and then click Finish. If any of the disks you selected to create the volume are basic disks, a Disk Management message box opens, warning you that the volume creation process will convert the basic disks to dynamic disks.

10. Click Yes. The wizard creates the volume according to your specifications.

> **MORE INFO** **ADDITIONAL OPTIONS**
>
> See "Creating a simple volume" earlier in this chapter for more information about the options on the Assign Drive Letter or Path and Format Partition pages.

11. Close the Disk Management snap-in.

The commands that appear in a disk's shortcut menu depend on the number of disks installed in the computer and the presence of unallocated space on them. For example, at least two disks with unallocated space must be available to create a striped, spanned, or mirrored volume, and at least three disks must be available to create a RAID-5 volume.

Thought experiment
Using storage pools

In this thought experiment, apply what you've learned about this objective. You can find answers to these questions in the "Answers" section at the end of this chapter.

On a new server running Windows Server 2012 R2, Morris created a storage pool that consists of two physical drives holding 1 TB each. Then he created three simple virtual disks out of the space in the storage pool. Using the Disk Management snap-in, Morris then created a RAID-5 volume out of the three virtual disks.

With this in mind, answer the following questions.

1. In what way is Morris's storage plan ineffectual at providing fault tolerance?

2. Why will adding a third disk to the storage pool fail to improve the fault tolerance of the storage plan?

3. How can Morris modify the storage plan to make it fault tolerant?

Objective summary

- Windows Server 2012 R2 supports two hard disk partition types: MBR and GPT; two disk types: basic and dynamic; five volume types: simple, striped, spanned, mirrored, and RAID-5; and three file systems: ReFS, NTFS, and FAT.

- The Disk Management snap-in can initialize, partition, and format disks on the local machine. Server Manager can perform many of the same tasks for servers all over the network.

- Windows Server 2012 R2 includes a new disk virtualization technology called Storage Spaces, which enables a server to concatenate storage space from individual physical disks and allocate that space to create virtual disks of any size supported by the hardware.

- All Windows Server 2012 R2 installations include the File and Storage Services role, which causes Server Manager to display a menu when you click the icon in the navigation pane. This menu provides access to home pages that enable administrators to manage volumes, disks, storage pools, shares, and iSCSI devices.

- The Disk Management snap-in in Windows Server 2012 R2 enables you to create VHD files and mount them on the computer.

- Once you have installed your physical disks, you can concatenate their space into a storage pool, from which you can create virtual disks of any size. Once you have created a storage pool, you can use the space to create as many virtual disks as you need.

Objective review

Answer the following questions to test your knowledge of the information in this objective. You can find the answers to these questions and explanations of why each answer choice is correct or incorrect in the "Answers" section at the end of this chapter.

1. Which of the following statements are true of striped volumes? (Choose all that apply.)

   A. Striped volumes provide enhanced performance over simple volumes.

   B. Striped volumes provide greater fault tolerance than simple volumes.

   C. You can extend striped volumes after creation.

   D. If a single physical disk in the striped volume fails, all the data in the entire volume is lost.

2. Which of the following statements best describes the requirements for extending a volume on a dynamic disk? (Choose all that apply.)

   A. If you want to extend a simple volume, you can use only the available space on the same disk if the volume is to remain simple.

   B. The volume must have a file system (a raw volume) before you can extend a simple or spanned volume.

   C. You can extend a simple or spanned volume if you formatted it by using the FAT or FAT32 file systems.

   D. You can extend a simple volume across additional disks if it is not a system volume or a boot volume.

3. Which of the following volume types supported by Windows Server 2012 R2 provide fault tolerance? (Choose all that apply.)

   A. Striped

   B. Spanned

   C. Mirrored

   D. RAID-5

4. A JBOD drive array is an alternative to which of the following storage technologies?

   A. SAN

   B. SCSI

   C. RAID

   D. iSCSI

Answers

This section contains the solutions to the thought experiments and answers to the objective review questions in this chapter.

Objective 1.1: Thought experiment

```
Uninstall-WindowsFeature Server-Gui-Mgmt-Infra,Server-Gui-Shell -Restart
Uninstall-WindowsFeature Server-Gui-Mgmt-Infra,Server-Gui-Shell -Remove
```

Objective 1.1: Review

1. **Correct answer:** B

    A. **Incorrect:** Windows Server 2012 R2 cannot run on a 32-bit processor.

    B. **Correct:** Windows Server 2012 R2 can run only on a 64-bit processor.

    C. **Incorrect:** Windows Server 2012 R2 cannot run on a 32-bit processor.

    D. **Incorrect:** Windows Server 2012 R2 cannot run on an Itanium processor.

2. **Correct answer:** B

    A. **Incorrect:** You cannot upgrade any version of Windows Server 2003 Standard to Windows Server 2012 R2 Standard.

    B. **Correct:** You can upgrade Windows Server 2008 Standard to Windows Server 2012 R2 Standard.

    C. **Incorrect:** You cannot upgrade Windows Server 2008 R2 32-bit, or any 32-bit version, to Windows Server 2012 R2 64-bit.

    D. **Incorrect:** You cannot upgrade Windows 7 Ultimate, or any workstation operating system, to Windows Server 2012 R2 Essentials.

3. **Correct answer:** A

    A. **Correct:** Installing the Graphical Management Tools and Infrastructure module—and only that module—on a Server Core installation results in the Minimal Server Interface.

    B. **Incorrect:** Installing the Server Graphical Shell with the Graphical Management Tools and Infrastructure converts a Server Core installation to the full GUI.

    C. **Incorrect:** Windows PowerShell is a command-line interface that has no effect on the Minimal Server Installation.

    D. **Incorrect:** MMC is one of the graphical applications available in the Minimal Server Installation, but you do not install it individually.

4. **Correct answer:** D

   A. **Incorrect:** The Windows directory contains live operating system files, not the installation files.

   B. **Incorrect:** The System32 directory contains live operating system files, not the installation files.

   C. **Incorrect:** There is no bin directory associated with the Windows operating system.

   D. **Correct:** Windows stores all the operating system installation modules in the WinSxS directory.

5. **Correct answers:** A, C

   A. **Correct:** It is possible to convert a computer running Windows Server 2012 R2 between the Server Core and the Full GUI interface as needed.

   B. **Incorrect:** The inclusion of additional cmdlets in Windows PowerShell 3.0 is not a benefit exclusive to Server Core.

   C. **Correct:** Server Manager incorporates a server selection interface into many of its wizards.

   D. **Incorrect:** There are no different licenses for Server Core and Full GUI versions of Windows Server 2012 R2.

Objective 1.2: Thought experiment

1. Install-WindowsFeature

2. Get-WindowsFeature

3. Install-WindowsFeature FS-FileServer
   Install-WindowsFeature FS-DFS-Namespace
   Install-WindowsFeature FS-DFS-Replication
   Install-WindowsFeature FS-NFS-Service
   Install-WindowsFeature Print-InternetServices –allsubfeatures
   Install-WindowsFeature Web-Server
   Install-WindowsFeature Web-Windows-Auth
   Install-WindowsFeature Web-Ftp-Service

The Install-WindowsFeature FS-Fileserver command is not necessary, as it installs as dependency for DFS. The Install-WindowsFeature Web-Server and Install-WindowsFeature Web-Windows-Auth commands are not necessary, as they install as dependencies for Print-Internet.

Objective 1.2: Review

1. **Correct answers:** B, D

   A. Incorrect: Windows Management Instrumentation (WMI) is a set of driver extensions often used with Windows PowerShell. You do not have to remove it to convert to a Server Core installation.

   B. Correct: Removing the Graphical Management Tools and Infrastructure feature is required to convert to a Server Core installation.

   C. Incorrect: Desktop Experience is not installed by default on a full GUI or a Server Core installation.

   D. Correct: Server Graphical Shell provides support for the Windows graphical interface, including the desktop and File Explorer. You must remove it to convert to a Server Core installation.

2. **Correct answer:** B

   A. Incorrect: Hyper-V live migration is not a NIC teaming mode.

   B. Correct: In Switch Independent Mode, the NICs in the team are connected to different switches, providing alternate paths through the network.

   C. Incorrect: In Switch Dependent Mode, the NICs in the team are connected to the same switches, providing link aggregation but no fault tolerance.

   D. Incorrect: Link Aggregation Control Protocol is not a NIC teaming mode.

3. **Correct answer:** C

   A. Incorrect: Net.exe is a Windows command-line tool that provides many different functions, but it cannot join a computer to a domain.

   B. Incorrect: Netsh.exe is a network shell program that you can use to configure the network interface, but it cannot join a computer to a domain.

   C. Correct: Netdom.exe is the Windows command-line domain manager application.

   D. Incorrect: Ipconfig.exe can display network configuration settings and reset DHCP settings, but it cannot join a computer to a domain.

4. **Correct answer:** A

   A. Correct: Server Manager cannot deploy roles to multiple servers at the same time.

   B. Incorrect: Server Manager can mount offline VHD files and install roles and features to them.

   C. Incorrect: Server Manager combines the role and feature installation processes into a single wizard.

   D. Incorrect: Server Manager can install roles and features to any Windows Server 2012 R2 server on the network.

5. **Correct answers:** C, D

   A. **Incorrect:** You can stop a running service by using Server Manager.

   B. **Incorrect:** You can start a stopped service by using Server Manager.

   C. **Correct:** You cannot disable a service by using Server Manager.

   D. **Correct:** You cannot configure a service to start when the computer starts by using Server Manager.

Objective 1.3: Thought experiment

1. Morris has created a RAID-5 volume out of virtual disks created out of a storage pool that has only two physical disks in it. A RAID-5 volume can only provide fault tolerance by storing data on three physical disks.

2. Adding a third disk will not guarantee fault tolerance because there is no assurance that each of the three virtual disks exists on a separate individual disk.

3. To make the plan fault-tolerant, Morris should delete the three simple virtual disks and create one new virtual disk by using either the mirror or parity layout option.

Objective 1.3: Review

1. **Correct answers:** A, D

   A. **Correct:** Striping provides improved performance because each disk drive in the array has time to seek the location of its next stripe while the other drives are writing.

   B. **Incorrect:** Striped volumes do not contain redundant data and therefore do not provide fault tolerance.

   C. **Incorrect:** Striped volumes cannot be extended after creation without destroying the data stored on them in the process.

   D. **Correct:** If a single physical disk in the striped volume fails, all the data in the entire volume is lost.

2. **Correct answers:** A, D

   A. **Correct:** When extending a simple volume, you can use only the available space on the same disk. If you extend the volume to another disk, it is no longer simple.

   B. **Incorrect:** You can extend a simple or spanned volume, even if it does not have a file system (a raw volume).

   C. **Incorrect:** You can extend a volume if you formatted it by using the NTFS file system. You cannot extend volumes by using the FAT or FAT32 file systems.

   D. **Correct:** You can extend a simple volume across additional disks if it is not a system volume or a boot volume.

3. **Correct answers:** C, D

   A. Incorrect: A striped volume spreads data among multiple disks, but it writes the data only once. Therefore, it does not provide fault tolerance.

   B. Incorrect: A spanned volume uses space on multiple drives, but it writes the data only once. Therefore, it does not provide fault tolerance.

   C. Correct: A mirrored volume writes duplicate copies of all data to two disks, thereby providing fault tolerance.

   D. Correct: A RAID-5 volume writes data and parity information on multiple disks, thereby providing fault tolerance.

4. **Correct answer:** C

   A. Incorrect: A SAN is a separate network dedicated to storage and a JBOD is a drive array that can be installed on a SAN or on a standard network.

   B. Incorrect: SCSI is disk interface, not a type of drive array.

   C. Correct: A JBOD array is an alternative to a RAID array that treats each disk as an independent volume.

   D. Incorrect: A JBOD array is not an alternative to iSCSI, which is a protocol used for SAN communications.

CHAPTER 2

Configuring server roles and features

This chapter covers some of the fundamental services that most Windows servers perform. In the business world, file and printer sharing were the reasons computers were networked in the first place, and with Windows Server 2012 R2, remote management has become a critical element of server administration.

Objectives in this chapter:

- Objective 2.1: Configure file and share access
- Objective 2.2: Configure print and document services
- Objective 2.3: Configure servers for remote management

Objective 2.1: Configure file and share access

One of the critical daily functions of server administrators is deciding where users should store their files and who should be permitted to access them.

> **This objective covers how to:**
> - Create and configure shares
> - Configure share permissions
> - Configure offline files
> - Configure NTFS permissions
> - Configure access-based enumeration (ABE)
> - Configure Volume Shadow Copy Service (VSS)
> - Configure NTFS quotas
> - Create and configure Work Folders

Creating folder shares

Sharing folders makes them accessible to network users. After you have configured the disks on a file server, you must create shares to enable network users to access those disks. As noted in the planning discussions in Chapter 1, "Installing and configuring servers," you should have a sharing strategy in place by the time you are ready to create your shares. This strategy should consist of the following information:

- What folders you will share
- What names you will assign to the shares
- What permissions you will grant users to the shares
- What Offline Files settings you will use for the shares

If you have the necessary permissions for a folder, you can share it on a Windows Server 2012 R2 computer by right-clicking the folder in any File Explorer window, selecting Share With, Specific People from the shortcut menu, and following the instructions in the File Sharing dialog box, as shown in Figure 2-1.

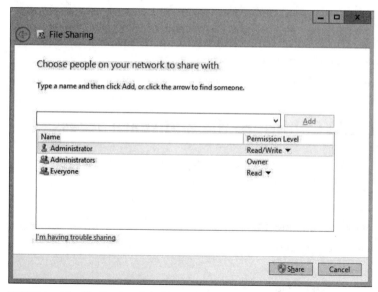

FIGURE 2-1 The File Sharing dialog box

This method of creating shares provides a simplified interface that contains only limited control over elements such as share permissions. You can specify only that the share users receive Read permissions or Read/Write permissions to the share. If you are not the Creator Owner of the folder, you can access the Sharing tab of the folder's Properties sheet instead. Clicking the Share button launches the same File Sharing dialog box. Clicking the Advanced Sharing button displays the Advanced Sharing dialog box, shown in Figure 2-2, which provides greater control over share permissions.

FIGURE 2-2 The Advanced Sharing dialog box

NOTE **NETWORK DISCOVERY**

For the users on the network to be able to browse the shares you create on the file server in File Explorer, you must make sure the Network Discovery settings and the File Sharing settings are turned on in the Network and Sharing Center control panel.

To take control of the shares on all your disks on all your servers and exercise granular control over their properties, you can use the File and Storage Services home page in Server Manager.

Windows Server 2012 R2 supports two types of folder shares:

- **Server Message Blocks (SMB)**   *SMB* is the standard file sharing protocol used by all versions of Windows.
- **Network File System (NFS)**   *NFS* is the standard file sharing protocol used by most UNIX and Linux distributions.

When you install Windows Server 2012 R2, the setup program installs the Storage Services role service in the File and Storage Services role by default. However, before you can create and manage SMB shares by using Server Manager, you must install the File Server role service; to create NFS shares, you must install the Server for NFS role service.

To create a folder share by using Server Manager, use the following procedure.

1. In Server Manager, click the File and Storage Services icon and, in the submenu that appears, click Shares. The Shares home page appears.

2. From the Tasks menu, select New Share. The New Share Wizard starts, displaying the Select The Profile For This Share page, as shown in Figure 2-3.

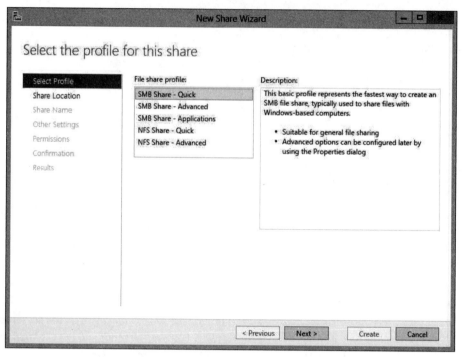

FIGURE 2-3 Configuring the Select The Profile For This Share page in the New Share Wizard

3. From the File Share Profile list, select one of the following options:

- **SMB Share–Quick**   Provides basic SMB sharing with full share and NTFS permissions

- **SMB Share–Advanced**   Provides SMB sharing with full share and NTFS permissions and access to services provided by File Server Resource Manager

- **SMB Share–Applications**   Provides SMB sharing with settings suitable for Hyper-V and other applications

- **NFS Share–Quick**   Provides basic NFS sharing with authentication and permissions

- **NFS Share–Advanced**   Provides NFS sharing with authentication and permissions and access to services provided by File Server Resource Manager

4. Click Next. The Select The Server And Path For This Share page appears.

5. Select the server on which you want to create the share and either select a volume on the server or specify a path to the folder you want to share. Click Next. The Specify Share Name page appears.

MORE INFO   NFS SHARING

Selecting one of the NFS share profiles adds two pages to the wizard: The Specify Authentication Methods page and the Specify The Share Permissions page. Each page provides access to functions implemented by the Server for NFS role service, as covered in Objective 2.1, "Configure Advanced File Services," in Exam 70-412, "Configuring Advanced Windows Server 2012 R2 Services."

6. In the Share Name text box, specify the name you want to assign to the share and click Next. The Configure Share Settings page appears, as shown in Figure 2-4.

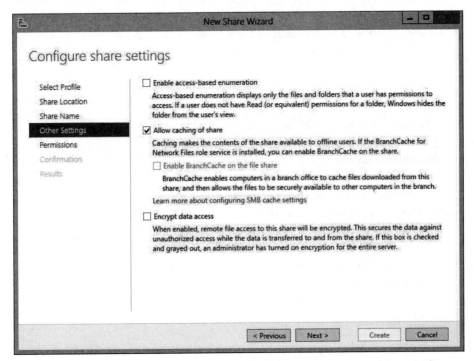

FIGURE 2-4 Configuring Other Settings on the Configure Share Settings page of the New Share Wizard

7. Select any or all of the following options:

- **Enable Access-Based Enumeration**   Prevents users from seeing files and folders they do not have permission to access

- **Allow Caching Of Share**   Enables offline users to access the contents of this share

- **Enable BranchCache On The File Share**   Enables BranchCache servers to cache files accessed from this share

- **Encrypt Data Access**   Causes the server to encrypt remote file access to this share

---

NOTE ACCESS-BASED ENUMERATION

Access-based enumeration (ABE), a feature first introduced in Windows Server 2003 R2, applies filters to shared folders based on the individual user's permissions to the files and subfolders in the share. Simply put, users who cannot access a particular shared resource are unable to see that resource on the network. This feature prevents users from seeing files and folders they cannot access. You can enable or disable ABE for a share at any time by opening the share's Properties sheet in the Sharing and Storage Management console and clicking Advanced, which displays the same Advanced dialog box displayed by the Provision a Shared Folder Wizard.

NOTE OFFLINE FILES

Offline Files, also known as *client-side caching*, is a Windows feature that enables client systems to maintain local copies of files they access from server shares. When a client selects the Always Available Offline option for a server-based file, folder, or share, the client system copies the selected data to the local drive and updates it regularly so the client user can always access it, even if the server is offline. To enable clients to use the Offline Files feature, the share must have the Allow Caching Of Share check box selected. Windows Server 2012 R2 and Windows 8.1 also have an Always Offline mode for the Offline Files feature that causes clients to always use the cached copy of server files, providing better performance. To implement this mode, you must set the Configure slow-link mode Group Policy setting on the client to a value of 1 millisecond.

---

8. Click Next to move to the Specify Permissions To Control Access page.

9. Modify the default share and NTFS permissions as needed and click Next. The Confirm Selections page appears.

NOTE ADVANCED SHARE PROFILES

Selecting one of the Advanced share profiles on the Select The Profile For This Share page adds two more pages to the wizard: The Specify Folder Management Properties page and the Apply A Quota To A Folder Or Volume page. Each page provides access to functions of the File Server Resource Manager application, as covered in Objective 2.2, "Configure File Server Resource Manager (FSRM)," in Exam 70-411, "Administering Windows Server 2012 R2."

---

10. Click Create. The View Results page appears as the wizard creates the share.

11. Close the New Share Wizard.

After you create a share by using the wizard, the new share appears in the Shares tile on the Shares home page in Server Manager. You can now use the tile to manage a share by right-clicking it and opening its Properties sheet or by clicking Stop Sharing.

Assigning permissions

Using Windows Server 2012 R2, you can control access to a file server to provide network users the access they need while protecting other files against possible intrusion and damage, whether deliberate or not. To implement this access control, Windows Server 2012 R2 uses permissions.

Permissions are privileges granted to specific system entities, such as users, groups, or computers, enabling them to perform a task or access a resource. For example, you can grant a specific user permission to read a file while denying that same user the permissions needed to modify or delete the file.

Windows Server 2012 R2 has several sets of permissions, which operate independently of each other. For the purpose of file sharing, you should be familiar with the operation of the following permission systems:

- **Share permissions**   Control access to folders over a network. To access a file over a network, a user must have appropriate share permissions (and appropriate NTFS permissions if the shared folder is on an NTFS volume).
- **NTFS permissions**   Control access to the files and folders stored on disk volumes formatted with the NTFS file system. To access a file, either on the local system or over a network, a user must have the appropriate NTFS permissions.

All these permission systems operate independently of each other and sometimes combine to provide increased protection to a specific resource. For network users to be able to access a shared folder on an NTFS drive, you must grant them both share permissions and NTFS permissions. As you saw earlier, you can grant these permissions as part of the share creation process, but you can also modify the permissions at any time afterward.

Understanding the Windows permission architecture

To store permissions, Windows elements have an *access control list (ACL)*. An ACL is a collection of individual permissions in the form of *access control entries (ACEs)*. Each ACE consists of a security principal (that is, the name of the user, group, or computer granted the permissions) and the specific permissions assigned to that security principal. When you manage permissions in any of the Windows Server 2012 R2 permission systems, you are actually creating and modifying the ACEs in an ACL.

To manage permissions in Windows Server 2012 R2, you can use a tab in the protected element's Properties sheet, like the one shown in Figure 2-5, with the security principals listed at the top and the permissions associated with them at the bottom. Share permissions are typically found on a Share Permissions tab and NTFS permissions are located on a Security tab. All the Windows permission systems use the same basic interface, although the permissions themselves differ. Server Manager also provides access to NTFS and share permissions by using a slightly different interface.

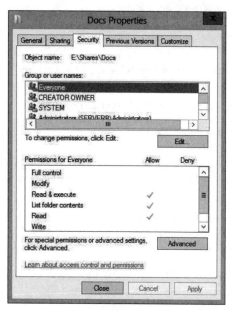

FIGURE 2-5 Configuring the Security tab of a Properties dialog box

Understanding basic and advanced permissions

The permissions protecting a particular system element are not like the keys to a lock, which provide either full access or no access at all. Permissions are designed to be granular, enabling you to grant specific degrees of access to security principals.

To provide this granularity, each Windows permission system has an assortment of permissions you can assign to a security principal in any combination. Depending on the permission system with which you are working, you might have dozens of different permissions available for a single system element.

Windows provides preconfigured permission combinations suitable for most common access control tasks. When you open the Properties sheet for a system element and look at its Security tab, the NTFS permissions you see are called *basic permissions*. Basic permissions are actually combinations of advanced permissions, which provide the most granular control over the element.

EXAM TIP

Prior to Windows Server 2012, basic permissions were known as standard permissions and advanced permissions were known as special permissions. Candidates for certification exams should be aware of these alternative terms.

For example, the NTFS permission system has 14 advanced permissions you can assign to a folder or file. However, there are also six basic permissions, which are various combinations of the 14 advanced permissions. You can also assign both types of permissions in a single ACE, combining a basic permission with one or more advanced permissions, to create a customized combination. In most cases, however, administrators work only with basic permissions. Many administrators rarely, if ever, have reason to work directly with advanced permissions.

If you find it necessary to work directly with advanced permissions, Windows makes it possible. When you click the Advanced button on the Security tab of any Properties sheet, an Advanced Security Settings dialog box appears, as shown in Figure 2-6, which enables you to access directly the ACEs for the selected system element. System Manager provides access to the same dialog box through a share's Properties sheet.

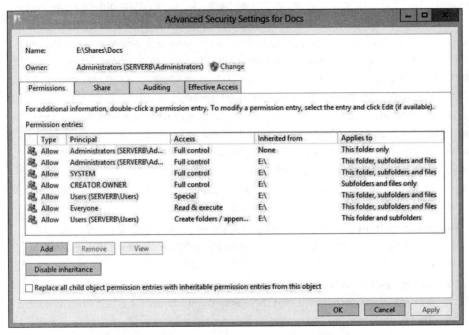

FIGURE 2-6 The default settings of the Advanced Security Settings dialog box.

Allowing and denying permissions

When you assign permissions to a system element, you are, in effect, creating a new ACE in the element's ACL. There are two basic types of ACE: Allow and Deny. This makes it possible to approach permission management tasks from two directions:

- **Additive** Start with no permissions and then grant Allow permissions to individual security principals to give them the access they need.

- **Subtractive** Start by granting all possible Allow permissions to individual security principals, giving them full control over the system element, and then grant them Deny permissions for the access you don't want them to have.

Most administrators prefer the additive approach, because Windows, by default, attempts to limit access to important system elements. In a properly designed permission hierarchy, the use of Deny permissions is often unnecessary. Many administrators frown on their use, because combining Allow and Deny permissions in a hierarchy can make it difficult to determine the effective permissions for a specific system element.

Inheriting permissions

The most important principle in permission management is that permissions tend to run downward through a hierarchy. This is called *permission inheritance*. Permission inheritance means that parent elements pass their permissions down to their subordinate elements. For example, when you grant Alice Allow permissions to access the root of the D drive, all the folders and subfolders on the D drive inherit those permissions, which means Alice can access them.

The principle of inheritance greatly simplifies the permission assignment process. Without it, you would have to grant individual Allow permissions to security principals for every file, folder, share, object, and key they need to access. With inheritance, you can grant access to an entire file system by creating one set of Allow permissions.

In most cases, whether consciously or not, system administrators take inheritance into account when they design their file systems and their Active Directory Domain Services OU structures. The location of a system element in a hierarchy is often based on how the administrators plan to assign and delegate permissions.

In some situations, an administrator might want to prevent subordinate elements from inheriting permissions from their parents. There are two ways to do this:

- **Turn off inheritance**   When you assign advanced permissions, you can configure an ACE not to pass its permissions down to its subordinate elements. This effectively blocks the inheritance process.

- **Deny permissions**   When you assign a Deny permission to a system element, it overrides any Allow permissions that the element might have inherited from its parent objects.

Understanding effective access

A security principal can receive permissions in many ways, and it is important for an administrator to understand how these permissions combine. The combination of Allow permissions and Deny permissions a security principal receives for a given system element—whether explicitly assigned, inherited, or received through a group membership—is called the *effective access* for that element. Because a security principal can receive permissions from so many sources, it is not unusual for those permissions to overlap. The following rules define how the permissions combine to form the effective access.

- **Allow permissions are cumulative.**   When a security principal receives Allow permissions from more than one source, the permissions are combined to form the effective access permissions.

- **Deny permissions override Allow permissions.** When a security principal receives Allow permissions—whether explicitly, by inheritance, or from a group—you can override those permissions by granting the principal Deny permissions of the same type.

- **Explicit permissions take precedence over inherited permissions.** When a security principal receives permissions by inheriting them from a parent or from group memberships, you can override those permissions by explicitly assigning contradicting permissions to the security principal itself.

Of course, instead of examining and evaluating all the possible permission sources, you can just open the Advanced Security Settings dialog box and click the Effective Access tab. On this tab, you can select a user, group, or device and view its effective access, without accounting for group membership or while accounting for group membership.

Setting share permissions

In Windows Server 2012 R2, shared folders have their own permission system, which is independent from the other Windows permission systems. For network users to access shares on a file server, you must grant them the appropriate share permissions. By default, the Everyone special identity receives the Allow Read Full Control share permission to any new shares you create using File Explorer. In shares you create using Server Manager, the Everyone special identity receives the Allow Full Control share permission.

To modify the share permissions for an existing share by using File Explorer, you open the Properties sheet for the shared folder, select the Sharing tab, click Advanced Sharing, and then click Permissions to open the Share Permissions tab, as shown in Figure 2-7.

FIGURE 2-7 The Share Permissions tab for a shared folder

By using this interface, you can add security principals and allow or deny them the three share permissions. To set share permissions by using Server Manager, either while creating a share or modifying an existing one, use the following procedure.

1. In Server Manager, click the File and Storage Services icon and, in the submenu that appears, click Shares to open the Shares home page.

2. In the Shares tile, right-click a share and, from the shortcut menu, select Properties. The Properties sheet for the share opens.

3. Click Permissions. The Permissions page opens.

4. Click Customize Permissions. The Advanced Security Settings dialog box for the share opens.

5. Click the Share tab to display the interface shown in Figure 2-8.

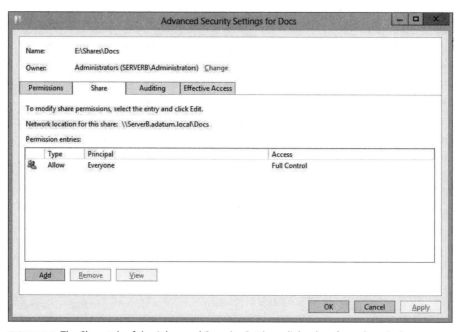

FIGURE 2-8 The Share tab of the Advanced Security Settings dialog box for a share in Server Manager

6. Click Add to open a Permission Entry dialog box for the share.

7. Click the Select A Principal link to display the Select User, Computer, Service Account, Or Group dialog box.

8. Type the name of or search for the security principal to whom you want to assign share permissions and click OK. The security principal you specified appears in the Permission Entry dialog box.

9. Select the type of permissions you want to assign (Allow or Deny).

10. Select the check boxes for the permissions you want to assign and click OK.

11. The new ACE you just created appears in the Advanced Security Settings dialog box.

> *NOTE* **BYPASSING SHARE PERMISSIONS**
>
> **Many file server administrators simply leave the Allow Full Control share permission to the Everyone special identity in place, essentially bypassing the share permission system, and rely solely on NTFS permissions for granular file system protection. NTFS permissions control access by both local and remote users, rendering share permissions redundant.**

12. Click OK to close the Advanced Security Settings dialog box.

13. Click OK to close the share's Properties sheet.

14. Close the Server Manager window.

Understanding NTFS authorization

The majority of Windows installations today use the NTFS file systems as opposed to FAT32. One of the main advantages of NTFS is that they support permissions, which FAT32 does not. As described earlier in this chapter, every file and folder on an NTFS drive has an ACL that consists of ACEs, each of which contains a security principal and the permissions assigned to that principal.

In the NTFS permission system, the security principals involved are users and groups, which Windows refers to by using security identifiers (SIDs). When a user attempts to access an NTFS file or folder, the system reads the user's security access token, which contains the SIDs for the user's account and all the groups to which the user belongs. The system then compares these SIDs to those stored in the file or folder's ACEs to determine what access the user should have. This process is called *authorization*.

Assigning basic NTFS permissions

Most file server administrators work almost exclusively with basic NTFS permissions because there is no need to work directly with advanced permissions for most common access control tasks.

To assign basic NTFS permissions to a shared folder, the options are essentially the same as with share permissions. You can open the folder's Properties sheet in File Explorer and select the Security tab or you can open a share's Properties sheet in Server Manager, as described in the following procedure.

1. In Server Manager, open the Shares home page.

2. Open the Properties sheet for a share and click Permissions to open the Permissions
    page.

3. Click Customize Permissions to open the Advanced Security Settings dialog box for the
    share, displaying the Permissions tab, as shown in Figure 2-9. This dialog box is as close
    as the Windows graphical interface can come to displaying the contents of an ACL.

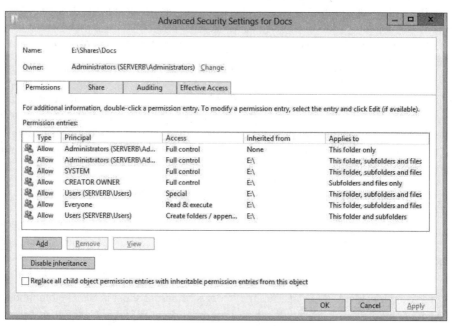

FIGURE 2-9 The Advanced Security Settings dialog box for a share in Server Manager

4. Click Add. This opens the Permission Entry dialog box for the share.

5. Click the Select A Principal link to display the Select User, Computer, Service Account, or Group dialog box.

6. Type the name of or search for the security principal to whom you want to assign NTFS permissions and click OK. The security principal you specified appears in the Permission Entry dialog box.

7. In the Type drop-down list, select the type of permissions you want to assign (Allow or Deny).

8. In the Applies To drop-down list, specify which subfolders and files should inherit the permissions you are assigning.

9. Select the check boxes for the basic permissions you want to assign and click OK. The new ACE you just created appears in the Advanced Security Settings dialog box.

10. Click OK twice to close the Advanced Security Settings dialog box and the Properties sheet.

11. Close the Server Manager window.

Assigning advanced NTFS permissions

In Windows Server 2012 R2, the ability to manage advanced permissions is integrated into the interface you use to manage basic permissions.

In the Permission Entry dialog box, clicking the Show Advanced Permissions link changes the list of basic permissions to a list of advanced permissions. You can then assign advanced permissions in any combination, just as you would basic permissions.

Combining share permissions with NTFS permissions

It is important for file server administrators to understand that the NTFS permission system is completely separate from the share permission system and that for network users to access files on a shared NTFS drive, the users must have the correct NTFS share permissions and the correct share permissions.

The share and NTFS permissions assigned to a file or folder can conflict. For example, if a user has the NTFS Write and Modify permissions for a folder but lacks the Change share permission, that user will not be able to modify a file in that folder.

The share permission system is the simplest of the Windows permission systems and it provides only basic protection for shared network resources. Share permissions provide only three levels of access, in contrast to the far more complex system of NTFS permissions. Generally, network administrators prefer to use either NTFS or share permissions, not both.

Share permissions provide limited protection, but this might be sufficient on some small networks. Share permissions might also be the only option on a computer with FAT32 drives because the FAT file system does not have its own permission system.

On networks already possessing a well-planned system of NTFS permissions, share permissions are not really necessary. In this case, you can safely grant the Full Control share permission to Everyone and allow the NTFS permissions to provide security. Adding share permissions would complicate the administration process without providing any additional protection.

Configuring Volume Shadow Copies

Volume Shadow Copies is a Windows Server 2012 R2 feature that enables you to maintain previous versions of files on a server, so if users accidentally delete or overwrite files, they can access a previous copy of those files. You can implement Volume Shadow Copies only for an entire volume; you cannot select specific shares, folders, or files.

To configure a Windows Server 2012 R2 volume to create Shadow Copies, use the following procedure.

1. Open File Explorer. The File Explorer window appears.

2. In the Folders list, expand the Computer container, right-click a volume and, from the shortcut menu, select Configure Shadow Copies. The Shadow Copies dialog box appears, as shown in Figure 2-10.

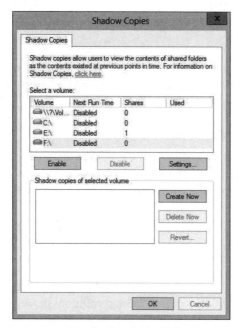

FIGURE 2-10 The Shadow Copies dialog box

3. In the Select A Volume box, choose the volume for which you want to enable Shadow Copies. By default, when you enable Shadow Copies for a volume, the system uses the following settings:

   ■ The system stores the shadow copies on the selected volume.

- The system reserves a minimum of 300 MB of disk space for the shadow copies.

- The system creates shadow copies at 7:00 A.M. and 12:00 P.M. every weekday.

4. To modify the default parameters, click Settings to open the Settings dialog box.

5. In the Storage Area box, specify the volume where you want to store the shadow copies.

6. Specify the Maximum Size for the storage area or choose the No Limit option. If the storage area becomes filled, the system begins deleting the oldest shadow copies. However, no matter how much space you allocate to the storage area, Windows Server 2012 R2 supports a maximum of 64 shadow copies for each volume.

7. Click Schedule to open the Schedule dialog box. By using the controls provided, you can modify the existing Shadow Copies tasks, delete them, or create new ones, based on the needs of your users.

8. Click OK twice to close the Schedule and Settings dialog boxes.

9. Click Enable. The system enables the Shadow Copies feature for the selected volume and creates the first copy in the designated storage area.

10. Close File Explorer.

After you complete this procedure, users can restore previous versions of files on the selected volumes from the Previous Versions tab on any file or folder's Properties sheet.

Configuring NTFS quotas

Managing disk space is a constant concern for server administrators, and one way to prevent users from monopolizing storage is to implement quotas. Windows Server 2012 R2 supports two types of storage quotas. The more elaborate of the two is implemented as part of File Server Resource Manager. The second, simpler option is *NTFS quotas*.

EXAM TIP

The objectives for the 70-410 exam specifically mention NTFS quotas, while the quotas in File Server Resource Manager are covered in the objectives for exam 70-411. Candidates should be careful to distinguish between the two types of quotas.

NTFS quotas enable administrators to set a storage limit for users of a particular volume. Depending on how you configure the quota, users exceeding the limit can either be denied disk space or just receive a warning. The space consumed by individual users is measured by the size of the files they own or create.

NTFS quotas are relatively limited in that you can only set limits at the volume level. The feature is also limited in the actions it can take in response to a user exceeding the limit. The quotas in File Server Resource Manager, by contrast, are much more flexible in the limits you can set and the responses of the program (which can send email notifications, execute commands, generate reports, or create log events.

To configure NTFS quotas for a volume, use the following procedure.

1. Open File Explorer. The File Explorer window appears.

2. In the Folders list, expand the Computer container, right-click a volume and, from the shortcut menu, select Properties. The Properties sheet for the volume appears.

3. Click the Quota tab to display the interface shown in Figure 2-11.

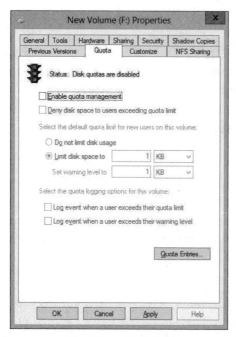

FIGURE 2-11 The Quota tab of a volume's Properties sheet

4. Select the Enable Quota Management check box to activate the rest of the controls.

5. If you want to prevent users from consuming more than their quota of disk space, select the Deny Disk Space To Users Exceeding Quota Limit check box.

6. Select the Limit Disk Space To option and specify amounts for the quota limit and the warning level.

7. Select the Log Event check boxes to control whether users exceeding the specified limits should trigger log entries.

8. Click OK to create the quota and close the Properties sheet.

9. Close File Explorer.

Configuring Work Folders

Work Folders is a Windows Server 2012 R2 feature that enables administrators to provide their users with synchronized access to their files on multiple workstations and devices while storing them on a network file server. The principle is roughly the same as Microsoft's SkyDrive service, except that the files are stored on a private Windows server instead of a cloud server on the Internet. This enables administrators to maintain control over the files, backing them up, classifying them, and/or encrypting them as needed.

EXAM TIP

Work Folders is a new feature in Windows Server 2012 R2 that has been added to the 70-410 objectives. Candidates for the revised exam should be familiar with the process of creating and configuring Work Folders on a server, though they need not dwell on the Windows 8.1 client side of the application.

To set up the Work Folders environment, you install the Work Folders role service in the File and Storage Services role on a server running Windows Server 2012 R2 and create a new type of share called a *sync share*. This installs the IIS Hostable Web Core feature, which makes it possible for the server to respond to incoming HTTP requests from Work Folders clients on the network.

On the client side, you configure Work Folders in the Windows 8.1 Control Panel, specifying the email address of the user and the location of the Work Folders on the local disk. The system also creates a system folder called Work Folders, which appears in File Explorer and in file management dialogs. When the user saves files to the Work Folders on the client system, they are automatically synchronized with the user's folder on the Work Folders server.

Users can create as many Work Folders clients as they need on different computers or other devices. After saving files to their Work Folders on their office workstations, for example, users can go home and find those files already synchronized to their home computers. In the same way, Work Folders can synchronize a user's files to a portable device at the office and the user can work on them while offline during the commute home. Arriving home and connecting to the Internet, the device synchronizes the files back to the server, so that the user finds the latest versions on the office computer the next day.

Work Folders is not designed to be a collaborative tool; it is just a means synchronizing folders between multiple devices while enabling administrators to retain control over them. It is possible to specify that Work Folders files remain encrypted during synchronization and administrators can impose security policies that force the use of lock screens and mandatory data wipes for lost machines.

Thought experiment

Creating permissions

In the following thought experiment, apply what you've learned about the objective to predict what steps you need to take. You can find answers to these questions in the "Answers" section at the end of this chapter.

You are working as a help desk administrator for a corporate network and you receive a call from a user named Leo who is requesting access to the files for a new classified project called Contoso. The Contoso files are stored in a shared folder on a file server, which is locked in a secured underground data storage facility. After verifying that the user has the appropriate security clearance for the project, you create a new group on the file server called CONTOSO_USERS and add Leo's user account to that group. Then you add the CONTOSO_USERS group to the access control list for the Contoso folder on the file server and assign the group the following NTFS permissions:

- Allow Modify
- Allow Read & Execute
- Allow List Folder Contents
- Allow Read
- Allow Write

Later, Leo calls to tell you that although he is able to access the Contoso folder and read the files stored there, he has been unable to save changes back to the server.

What is the most likely cause of the problem?

Objective summary

- Creating folder shares makes the data stored on a file server's disks accessible to network users.
- NTFS permissions enable you to control access to files and folders by specifying the tasks individual users can perform on them. Share permissions provide rudimentary access control for all the files on a network share. Network users must have the proper share and NTFS permissions to access file server shares.
- ABE applies filters to shared folders based on an individual user's permissions to the files and subfolders in the share. Simply put, users who cannot access a particular shared resource are unable to see that resource on the network.

- Offline Files is a Windows feature that enables client systems to maintain local copies of files they access from server shares.
- Volume Shadow Copies is a Windows Server 2012 R2 feature that enables you to maintain previous versions of files on a server, so if users accidentally delete or overwrite a file, they can access a copy.
- NTFS quotas enable administrators to set a storage limit for users of a particular volume.
- Work Folders is a Windows Server 2012 R2 feature that synchronizes files between multiple client devices and a file server located on a private network.

Objective review

Answer the following questions to test your knowledge of the information in this objective. You can find the answers to these questions and explanations of why each answer choice is correct or incorrect in the "Answers" section at the end of this chapter.

1. What is the maximum number of shadow copies a Windows Server 2012 R2 system can maintain for each volume?

    A. 8

    B. 16

    C. 64

    D. 128

2. Which of the following terms describes the process of granting users access to file server shares by reading their permissions?

    A. Authentication

    B. Authorization

    C. Enumeration

    D. Assignment

3. Which of the following are tasks you can perform by using the quotas in File Server Resource Manager but can't perform by using NTFS quotas? (Choose all that apply.)

    A. Send an email message to an administrator when users exceed their limits.

    B. Specify different storage limits for each user.

    C. Prevent users from consuming storage space on a volume beyond their allotted limit.

    D. Generate warnings to users when they approach their allotted storage limit.

4. In the Windows Server 2012 R2 NTFS permission system, combinations of advanced permissions are also known as _____ permissions. (Choose all that apply.)

   A. Special

   B. Basic

   C. Share

   D. Standard

5. Which of the following statements best describes the role of the security principal in file system permission assignments?

   A. The security principal in file system permission assignments is the only person who can access a file that has no permissions assigned to it.

   B. The security principal in file system permission assignments is the person responsible for creating permission policies.

   C. The security principal in file system permission assignments is the person assigning the permissions.

   D. The security principal in file system permission assignments is the person to whom the permissions are assigned.

Objective 2.2: Configure print and document services

Like the file-sharing functions discussed in the previous section, print device sharing is one of the most basic applications for which local area networks were designed.

This objective covers how to:

- Configure the Easy Print print driver
- Configure Enterprise Print Management
- Configure drivers
- Configure printer pooling
- Configure print priorities
- Configure printer permissions

Deploying a print server

Installing, sharing, monitoring, and managing a single network print device is relatively simple, but when you are responsible for dozens or even hundreds of print devices on a large enterprise network, these tasks can be overwhelming.

Understanding the Windows print architecture

It is important to understand the terms Microsoft uses when referring to the components of the network printing architecture. Printing in Microsoft Windows typically involves the following four components:

- **Print device** A *print device* is the actual hardware that produces hard-copy documents on paper or other print media. Windows Server 2012 R2 supports both local print devices, which are attached directly to computer ports, and network interface print devices, which are connected to the network either directly or through another computer.

- **Printer** In Windows, a *printer* is the software interface through which a computer communicates with a print device. Windows Server 2012 R2 supports numerous physical interfaces, including Universal Serial Bus (USB), IEEE 1394 (FireWire), parallel (LPT), serial (COM), Infrared Data Access (IrDA), Bluetooth ports, and network printing services such as LPR, Internet Printing Protocol (IPP), and standard TCP/IP ports.

- **Print server** A *print server* is a computer (or standalone device) that receives print jobs from clients and sends them to print devices that are either attached locally or connected to the network.

- **Printer driver** A *printer driver* is a device driver that converts the print jobs generated by applications into an appropriate string of commands for a specific print device. Printer drivers are designed for a specific print device and provide applications with access to all the print device's features.

> *NOTE* **PRINTING NOMENCLATURE**
>
> "Printer" and "print device" are the most commonly misused terms in the Windows printing vocabulary. Obviously, many sources use "printer" to refer to the printing hardware. However, in Windows, printer and print device are not equivalent. For example, you can add a printer to a Windows Server 2012 R2 computer without a physical print device being present. The computer can then host the printer, print server, and printer driver. These three components enable the computer to process the print jobs and store them in a print queue until the print device is available.

Understanding Windows printing

These four components work together to process the print jobs produced by Windows applications and turn them into hard-copy documents, as shown in Figure 2-12.

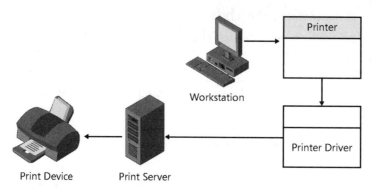

FIGURE 2-12 The Windows print architecture

Before you can print documents in Windows, you must install at least one printer. To install a printer in Windows, you must do the following:

- Select the print device's specific manufacturer and model.
- Specify the port (or other interface) the computer will use to access the print device.
- Supply a printer driver created specifically for that print device.

When you print a document in an application, you select the printer that will be the destination for the print job.

The printer is associated with a printer driver that takes the commands generated by the application and converts them into a printer control language (PCL), a language understood by the printer. PCLs can be standardized, like the PostScript language, or they can be proprietary languages developed by the print device manufacturer.

The printer driver enables you to configure the print job to use the various capabilities of the print device. These capabilities are typically incorporated into the printer's Properties sheet. For example, your word-processing application does not know if your print device is color or monochrome or if it supports duplex printing. The printer driver provides support for print device features such as these.

After the printer processes a print job, it stores the job in a print queue, known as a *spooler*. Depending on the arrangement of the printing components, the spooled jobs might be in PCL format, ready to go to the print device, or in an interim format, in which case the printer driver must process the spooled jobs into the PCL format before sending them to the device. If other jobs are waiting to be printed, a new job might wait in the spooler for some time. When the server finally sends the job to the print device, the device reads the PCL commands and produces the hard-copy document.

Windows printing flexibility

The flexibility of the Windows print architecture is manifested in the different ways you can deploy the four printing components. A single computer can perform all the roles (except for the print device, of course) or you can distribute those roles across the network. The following sections describe four fundamental configurations that are the basis of most Windows printer deployments:

- Direct printing
- Locally attached printer sharing
- Network-attached printing
- Network-attached printer sharing

You can scale these configurations up to accommodate a network of virtually any size.

DIRECT PRINTING

The simplest print architecture consists of one print device connected to one computer, also known as a locally attached print device, as shown in Figure 2-13. When you connect a print device directly to a Windows Server 2012 R2 computer and print from an application running on that system, the computer supplies the printer, printer driver, and print server functions.

FIGURE 2-13 A locally attached print device

LOCALLY ATTACHED PRINTER SHARING

In addition to printing from an application running on that computer, you can also share the printer (and the print device) with other users on the same network. In this arrangement, the computer with the locally attached print device functions as a print server. Figure 2-14 shows the other computers on the network, which are known as the print clients.

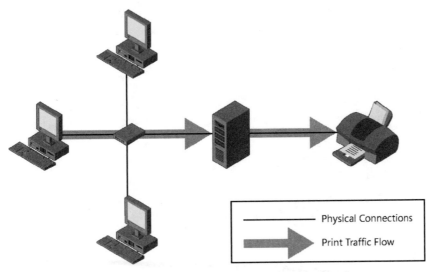

FIGURE 2-14 Sharing a locally attached printer

In the default Windows Server 2012 R2 printer-sharing configuration, each client uses its own printer and printer driver. As before, the application running on the client computer sends the print job to the printer and the printer driver renders the job, based on the capabilities of the print device.

The main advantage of this printing arrangement is that multiple users, located anywhere on the network, can send jobs to a single print device connected to a computer functioning as a print server. The downside is that processing the print jobs for many users can impose a significant burden on the print server. Although any Windows computer can function as a print server, you should use a workstation for this purpose only when you have no more than a handful of print clients to support or you have a very light printing volume.

NETWORK-ATTACHED PRINTING

The printing solutions discussed thus far involve print devices connected directly to a computer using a USB or other port. Print devices do not necessarily have to be attached to computers, however. You can connect a print device directly to the network instead. Many print device models are equipped with network interface adapters, enabling you to attach a standard network cable. Some print devices have expansion slots into which you can install a network printing adapter you have purchased separately. Finally, for print devices with no networking capabilities, standalone network print servers are available, which connect to the network and enable you to attach one or more print devices. Print devices so equipped have their own IP addresses and typically have an embedded web-based configuration interface.

With network-attached print devices, the primary deployment decision the administrator must make is to decide which computer will function as the print server. One simple (but often impractical) option is to let each print client function as its own print server, as shown in Figure 2-15. Each client processes and spools its own print jobs, connects to the print device by using a TCP (Transmission Control Protocol) port, and sends the jobs directly to the device for printing.

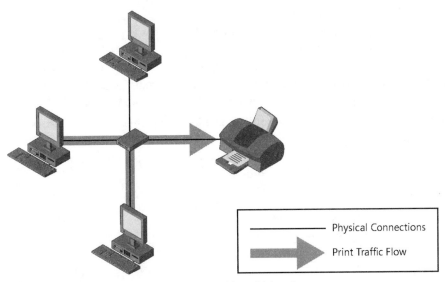

FIGURE 2-15 A network-attached print device with multiple print servers

Even individual end users with no administrative assistance will find this arrangement simple to set up. However, the disadvantages are many, including the following:

- Users examining the print queue see only their own jobs.
- Users are oblivious of the other users accessing the print device. They have no way of knowing what other jobs have been sent to the print device or how long it will be until the print device completes their jobs.
- Administrators have no way of centrally managing the print queue because each client has its own print queue.
- Administrators cannot implement advanced printing features, such as printer pools (covered later in this section) or remote administration.
- Error messages appear only on the computer that originated the job that the print device is currently processing.
- All print job processing is performed by the client computer rather than being partially offloaded to an external print server.

For these reasons, this arrangement is suitable only for small workgroup networks that do not have dedicated administrators supporting them.

NETWORK-ATTACHED PRINTER SHARING

The other, far more popular option for network-attached printing is to designate one computer as a print server and use it to service all the print clients on the network. To do this, you install a printer on one computer (which becomes the print server) and configure it to access the print device directly through a TCP port. You then share the printer, just as you would a locally attached print device, and configure the clients to access the print share.

As you can see in Figure 2-16, the physical configuration is the same as in the previous arrangement, but the logical path the print jobs take on the way to the print device is different. Instead of going straight to the print device, the jobs go to the print server, which spools them and sends them to the print device in order.

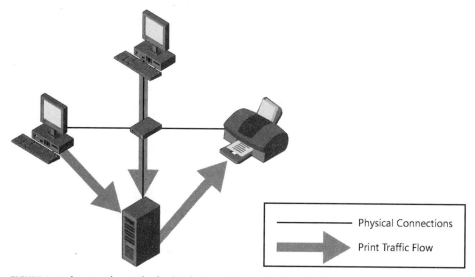

FIGURE 2-16 A network-attached print device with a single shared print server

With this arrangement, virtually all the disadvantages of the multiple print server arrangement become advantages:

- All the client jobs are stored in a single print queue, so users and administrators can see a complete list of the jobs waiting to be printed.
- Part of the job-rendering burden is shifted to the print server, returning control of the client computer to the user more quickly.
- Administrators can manage all the queued jobs from a remote location.
- Print error messages appear on all client computers.
- Administrators can implement printer pools and other advanced printing features.
- Administrators can manage security, auditing, monitoring, and logging functions from a central location.

ADVANCED PRINTING CONFIGURATIONS

Administrators can use the four configurations described in the previous sections as building blocks to create printing solutions for their networks. Many possible variations can be used to create a network printing architecture that supports your organization's needs. Some of the more advanced possibilities are as follows:

- You can connect a single printer to multiple print devices, creating what is called a *printer pool*. On a busy network with many print clients, the print server can distribute large numbers of incoming jobs among several identical print devices to provide more timely service and better fault tolerance.

- You can connect multiple print devices that support different paper forms and various paper sizes to a single printer, which will distribute jobs with different requirements to the appropriate print devices.

- You can connect multiple printers to a single print device. By creating multiple printers, you can configure different priorities, security settings, auditing, and monitoring parameters for different users. For example, you can create a high-priority printer for company executives and a lower-priority printer for junior users. This ensures that the executives' jobs get printed first, even if the printers are connected to the same print device.

Sharing a printer

Using Windows Server 2012 R2 as a print server can be simple or complex, depending on how many clients the server has to support and how much printing they do. For a home or small business network, in which a handful of users need occasional access to the printer, no special preparation is necessary. However, if the computer must support heavy printer use, hardware upgrades (such as additional disk space or system memory) might be needed.

You might also consider making the computer a dedicated print server. In addition to memory and disk space, using Windows Server 2012 R2 as a print server requires processor clock cycles, just like any other application. On a server handling heavy print traffic, other roles and applications are likely to experience substantial performance degradation. If you need a print server to handle heavy traffic, consider dedicating the computer to print server tasks only and deploying other roles and applications elsewhere.

On a Windows Server 2012 R2 computer, you can share a printer as you are installing it or at any time afterward. On older printers, you initiate the installation process by launching the Add Printer Wizard from the Devices and Printers control panel. However, most of the print devices on the market today use either a USB connection to a computer or an Ethernet or wireless connection to a network.

In the case of a USB-connected printer, you plug the print device into a USB port on the computer and turn on the device to initiate the installation process. Manual intervention is required only when Windows Server 2012 R2 does not have a driver for the print device.

For network-attached print devices, an installation program supplied with the product locates the print device on the network, installs the correct drivers, creates a printer on the computer, and configures the printer with the proper IP address and other settings.

After the printer is installed on the Windows Server 2012 R2 computer that will function as your print server, you can share it with your network clients by using the following procedure.

1. Open the Devices and Printers control panel. The Devices and Printers window appears.

2. Right-click the icon for the printer you want to share and, from the shortcut menu, select Printer Properties. The printer's Properties sheet appears.

> **NOTE PROPERTIES**
>
> The shortcut menu for every printer provides access to two Properties sheets. The Printer Properties menu item opens the Properties sheet for the printer and the Properties menu item opens the Properties sheet for the print device.

3. Click the Sharing tab.

4. Select the Share This Printer check box. The printer name appears in the Share Name text box. You can accept the default name or supply one of your own.

5. Select one or both of the following optional check boxes:

   - **Render Print Jobs On Client Computers** Minimizes the resource utilization on the print server by forcing the print clients to perform the bulk of the print processing.

   - **List In The Directory** Creates a new printer object in the Active Directory Domain Services (AD DS) database, enabling domain users to locate the printer by searching the directory. This option appears only when the computer is a member of an AD DS domain.

6. Optionally, click Additional Drivers to open the Additional Drivers dialog box. This dialog box enables you to load printer drivers for other Windows platforms, such as x86. When you install the alternate drivers, the print server automatically supplies them to clients running those operating system versions.

7. Select any combination of the available check boxes and click OK. For each check box you select, Windows Server 2012 R2 displays a Printer Drivers dialog box.

8. In each Printer Drivers dialog box, type or browse to the location of the printer drivers for the selected operating system and click OK.

9. Click OK to close the Additional Drivers dialog box.

10. Click OK to close the Properties sheet for the printer. The printer icon in the Printers control panel now includes a symbol indicating that it has been shared.

11. Close the control panel.

At this point, the printer is available to clients on the network.

Managing printer drivers

Printer drivers are the components that enable your computers to manage the capabilities of your print devices. When you install a printer on a server running Windows Server 2012 R2, you also install a driver that other Windows computers can use.

The printer drivers you install on Windows Server 2012 R2 are the same drivers that Windows workstations and other server versions use, with one stipulation. As a 64-bit platform, Windows Server 2012 R2 uses 64-bit device drivers, which are suitable for other computers running 64-bit versions of Windows. If you have 32-bit Windows systems on your network, however, you must install a 32-bit driver on the server for those systems to use.

The Additional Drivers dialog box, accessible from the Sharing tab of a printer's Properties sheet, enables you to install drivers for other processor platforms. However, you must install those drivers from a computer running on the alternative platform. In other words, to install a 32-bit driver for a printer on a server running Windows Server 2012 R2, you must access the printer's Properties sheet from a computer running a 32-bit version of Windows. You can do this by accessing the printer directly through the network by using File Explorer or by running the Print Management snap-in on the 32-bit system and using it to manage your Windows Server 2012 R2 print server.

> **NOTE INSTALLING DRIVERS**
>
> For the server to provide drivers supporting different platforms to client computers, you must make sure when installing the drivers for the same print device that they have identical names. For example, Windows Server 2012 R2 will treat "HP LaserJet 5200 PCL6" and "HP LaserJet 5200 PCL 6" as two different drivers. The names must be identical in order for the server to apply the drivers properly.

Using remote access Easy Print

When a Remote Desktop Services client connects to a server, it runs applications using the server's processor(s) and memory. However, if that client wants to print a document from one of those applications, it wants the print job to go to the print device connected to the client computer.

The component that enables Remote Desktop clients to print to their local print devices is called *Easy Print*. Easy Print takes the form of a printer driver that is installed on the server along with the Remote Desktop Session Host role service.

The Remote Desktop Easy Print driver appears automatically in the Print Management snap-in, but it is not associated with a particular print device. Instead, the driver functions as a redirector, enabling the server to access the printers on the connected clients.

On Windows Server 2012 R2, Easy Print requires no configuration other than the allowance of Remote Desktop connections or the installation of the Remote Desktop Services role. However, once it is operational, it provides the server administrator with additional access to the printers on the Remote Desktop clients.

When a Remote Desktop client connects to a server by using the Remote Desktop Connection program or the RD Web Access site, the printers installed on the client system are redirected to the server and appear in the Print Management snap-in as redirected server printers, as shown in Figure 2-17.

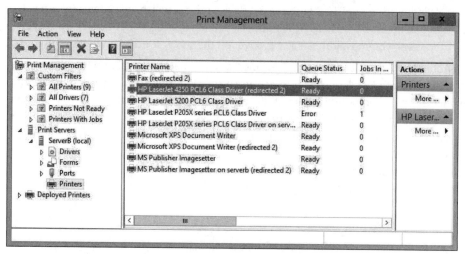

FIGURE 2-17 Printers redirected by Easy Print on a Remote Desktop server

A client running an application on the server can therefore print to a local print device using the redirected printer. Administrators can also open the Properties sheet for the redirected printer in the usual manner and then manipulate its settings.

Configuring printer security

As with folder shares, clients must have the proper permissions to access a shared printer. Printer permissions are much simpler than NTFS permissions; they dictate whether users are allowed to use the printer, manage documents submitted to the printer, or manage the properties of the printer itself. To assign permissions for a printer, use the following procedure.

1. Open Control Panel and select Hardware, Devices and Printers. The Devices and Printers window appears.

2. Right-click one of the printer icons in the window and, from the shortcut menu, select Printer Properties. The printer's Properties sheet appears.

3. Click the Security tab. The top half of the display lists all the security principals currently possessing permissions to the selected printer. The bottom half lists the permissions held by the selected security principal.

4. Click Add. The Select Users, Computers, Or Groups dialog box appears.

5. In the Enter The Object Names To Select text box, type a user or group name and click OK. The user or group appears in the Group Or User Names list.

6. Select the security principal you added and select or clear the check boxes in the bottom half of the display to Allow or Deny the user any of the basic permissions.

7. Click OK to close the Properties sheet.

8. Close Control Panel.

Like NTFS permissions, there are two types of printer permissions: basic and advanced. Each of the three basic permissions consists of a combination of advanced permissions.

Managing documents

By default, all printers assign the Allow Print permission to the Everyone special identity, which enables all users to access the printer and manage their own documents. Users who possess the Allow Manage Documents permission can manage any users' documents.

Managing documents refers to pausing, resuming, restarting, and canceling documents that are currently waiting in a print queue. Windows Server 2012 R2 provides a print queue window for every printer, which enables users to view the jobs that are currently waiting to be printed. To manage documents, use the following procedure.

1. Open Control Panel and select Hardware, Devices and Printers. The Devices and Printers window appears.

2. Right-click one of the printer icons and, from the shortcut menu, select See What's Printing. A print queue window named for the printer appears, as shown in Figure 2-18.

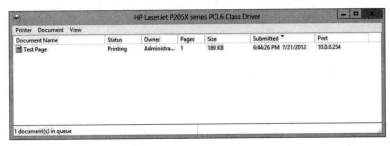

FIGURE 2-18 A Windows Server 2012 R2 print queue window

3. Select one of the menu items to perform the associated function.

4. Close the print queue window.

5. Close Control Panel.

Managing printers

Users with the Allow Manage This Printer permission can go beyond manipulating queued documents; they can reconfigure the printer itself. Managing a printer refers to altering the operational parameters that affect all users and controlling access to the printer.

Generally, most of the software-based tasks that fall under the category of managing a printer are those you perform once while setting up the printer for the first time. Day-to-day printer management is more likely to involve physical maintenance, such as clearing print jams, reloading paper, and changing toner or ink cartridges. However, the following sections examine some of the printer manager's typical configuration tasks.

Setting printer priorities

In some cases, administrators with the Manage This Printer permission might want to give certain users in your organization priority access to a print device so that when print traffic is heavy, their jobs are processed before those of other users. To do this, you must create multiple printers, associate them with the same print device, and then modify their priorities, as described in the following procedure.

1. Open Control Panel and select Hardware, Devices and Printers. The Devices and Printers window opens.

2. Right-click one of the printer icons and, from the shortcut menu, select Printer Properties. The Properties sheet for the printer appears.

3. Click the Advanced tab, as shown in Figure 2-19.

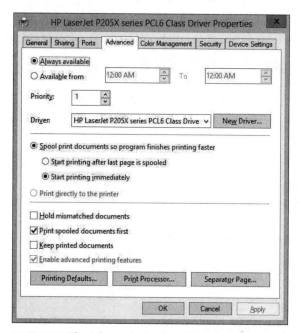

FIGURE 2-19 The Advanced tab of a printer's Properties sheet

4. Set the Priority spin box to a number representing the highest priority you want to set for the printer. Higher numbers represent higher priorities. The highest possible priority is 99.

> **NOTE PRINTER PRIORITIES**
>
> The values of the Priority spin box do not have any absolute significance; they are pertinent only in relation to one another. As long as one printer has a higher priority value than another, the server will process its print jobs first. In other words, it doesn't matter if the higher priority value is 9 or 99, as long as the lower priority value is less.

5. Click the Security tab.

6. Add the users or groups that you want to provide with high-priority access to the printer and assign the Allow Print permission to them.

7. Revoke the Allow Print permission from the Everyone special identity.

8. Click OK to close the Properties sheet.

9. Create an identical printer using the same printer driver and pointing to the same print device. Leave the Priority setting at its default value of 1 and leave the default permissions in place.

10. Rename the printers, specifying the priority assigned to each one.

11. Close Control Panel.

Inform the privileged users that they should send their jobs to the high-priority printer. All jobs sent to that printer will be processed before those sent to the other, lower-priority printer.

Creating a printer pool

As mentioned earlier, a printer pool increases the production capability of a single printer by connecting it to multiple print devices. When you create a printer pool, the print server sends each incoming job to the first print device it finds that is not busy. This effectively distributes the jobs among the available print devices, providing users with more rapid service.

To configure a printer pool, use the following procedure.

1. Open Control Panel and select Hardware, Devices and Printers. The Devices and Printers window opens.

2. Right-click one of the printer icons and, from the shortcut menu, select Printer Properties. The Properties sheet for the printer appears.

3. Click the Ports tab.

4. Select the Enable Printer Pooling check box and click OK.

5. Select all the ports to which the print devices are connected.

6. Close Control Panel.

To create a printer pool, you must have at least two identical print devices, or at least two print devices that use the same printer driver. The print devices must be in the same location because there is no way to tell which print device will process a given document. You must also connect all the print devices in the pool to the same print server. If the print server is a Windows Server 2012 R2 computer, you can connect the print devices to any viable ports.

Using the Print and Document Services role

All the printer sharing and management capabilities discussed in the previous sections are available on any Windows Server 2012 R2 computer in its default installation configuration. However, installing the Print And Document Services role on the computer provides additional tools that are particularly useful to administrators involved with network printing on an enterprise scale.

When you install the Print And Document Services role by using Server Manager's Add Roles And Features Wizard, a Select Role Services page appears, enabling you to select from the following options:

- **Print Server**   Installs the Print Management console for Microsoft Management Console (MMC), which enables administrators to deploy, monitor, and manage printers throughout the enterprise

- **Distributed Scan Server**   Enables the computer to receive documents from network-based scanners and forward them to the appropriate users

- **Internet Printing**   Creates a website that enables users on the Internet to send print jobs to shared Windows printers

- **LPD Service**   Enables UNIX clients running the line printer remote (LPR) program to send their print jobs to Windows printers

As always, Windows Server 2012 R2 adds a new icon to the Server Manager navigation pane when you install a role. The Print Services home page contains a filtered view of print-related event log entries, a status display for the role-related system services and role services, and performance counters.

The Print Management console, an administrative tool, consolidates the controls for the printing components throughout the enterprise into a single console. By using this tool, you can access the print queues and Properties sheets for all the network printers in the enterprise, deploy printers to client computers by using Group Policy, and create custom views that simplify the process of detecting print devices that need attention due to errors or depleted consumables.

Windows Server 2012 R2 installs the Print Management console when you add the Print And Document Services role to the computer. You can also install the console without the role by adding the Print And Document Services Tools feature, found under Remote Server Administration Tools, Role Administration Tools in the Add Roles And Features Wizard.

The following sections demonstrate some of the administration tasks you can perform by using the Print Management console.

Adding print servers

By default, the Print Management console displays only the local machine in its list of print servers. Each print server has four nodes beneath it, as shown in Figure 2-20, listing the drivers, forms, ports, and printers associated with that server.

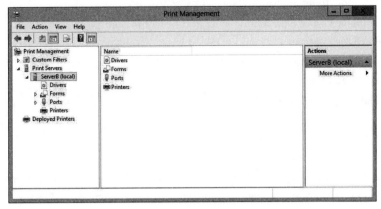

FIGURE 2-20 A print server displayed in the Print Management console

To manage other print servers and their printers, you must add them to the console by using the following procedure.

1. In Server Manager, click Tools and then click Print Management to open the Print Management console.

2. Right-click the Print Servers node and, from the shortcut menu, click Add/Remove Servers to open the Add/Remove Servers dialog box.

3. In the Specify Print Server box, click Browse. The Select Print Server dialog box opens.

4. Select the print server you want to add to the console and click Select Server. The server you selected appears in the Add Server text box in the Add/Remove Servers dialog box.

5. Click Add To List. The server you selected appears in the Print Servers list.

6. Click OK. The server appears under the Print Servers node.

7. Close the Print Management console.

You can now manage the printers associated with the server you have added to the console.

Viewing printers

One of the major difficulties for printing administrators on large enterprise networks is keeping track of dozens or hundreds of print devices, all in frequent use and all needing attention on a regular basis. Whether the maintenance required is a major repair, an ink or toner replenishment, or a paper tray refill, print devices will not get the attention they need until an administrator is aware of the problem.

The Print Management console provides multiple ways to view the printing components associated with the print servers on the network. To create views, the console takes the complete list of printers and applies various filters to it, selecting which printers to display. Under the Custom Filters node, there are four default filters, as follows:

- **All Printers**   Contains a list of all the printers hosted by all the print servers which have been added to the console
- **All Drivers**   Contains a list of all the printer drivers installed on all the print servers which have been added to the console
- **Printers Not Ready**   Contains a list of all printers that are not reporting a Ready status
- **Printers With Jobs**   Contains a list of all the printers that currently have jobs waiting in the print queue

Views such as Printer Not Ready are a useful way for administrators to identify printers that need attention without having to browse individual print servers or search through a long list of every printer on the network. In addition to these defaults, you can create your own custom filters.

Managing printers and print servers

After you have used filtered views to isolate the printers you want to examine, selecting a printer displays its status, the number of jobs currently in its print queue, and the name of the print server hosting it. If you right-click the filter in the left pane and select Show Extended View from the shortcut menu, an additional pane appears containing the contents of the selected printer's queue. You can manipulate the queued jobs just as you would from the Print Queue window in the Print Server console.

The Print Management console also enables administrators to access the configuration interface for any printer or print server appearing in any of its displays. Right-clicking a printer or print server anywhere in the console interface and then selecting Properties from the shortcut menu displays the same Properties sheet you would see on the print server computer itself. Administrators can then configure printers and print servers without having to travel to the site of the print server or establish a Remote Desktop connection to the print server.

Deploying printers with Group Policy

Configuring a print client to access a shared printer is a simple matter of browsing the network or the AD DS tree and selecting the printer. However, when you have to configure hundreds or thousands of print clients, the task becomes more complicated. AD DS helps simplify the process of deploying printers to large numbers of clients.

Publishing printers in the AD DS database enables users and administrators to search for printers by name, location, or model (if you populate the Location and Model fields in the printer object). To create a printer object in the AD DS database, you can either select the List In The Directory check box while sharing the printer or right-click a printer in the Print Management console and, from the shortcut menu, select List In Directory.

To use AD DS to deploy printers to clients, you must configure the appropriate policies in a Group Policy object (GPO). You can link a GPO to any domain, site, or organizational unit (OU) in the AD DS tree. When you configure a GPO to deploy a printer, all the users or computers in that domain, site, or OU will receive the printer connection by default when they log on.

To deploy printers with Group Policy, use the following procedure.

1. In the Print Management console, right-click a printer in the console's scope pane and, from the shortcut menu, select Deploy With Group Policy. The Deploy With Group Policy dialog box appears, as shown in Figure 2-21.

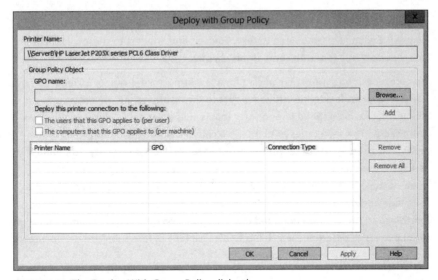

FIGURE 2-21 The Deploy With Group Policy dialog box

2. Click Browse to open the Browse For A Group Policy Object dialog box.

3. Select the GPO you want to use to deploy the printer and click OK. The GPO you selected appears in the GPO Name field.

4. Select the appropriate check box to select whether to deploy the printer to the users associated with the GPO, the computers (or both) and click Add. The new printer GPO associations appear in the table.

   Deploying the printer to the users means that all the users associated with the GPO will receive the printer connection no matter what computer they use to log on. Deploying the printer to the computers means that all the computers associated with the GPO will receive the printer connection no matter who logs on to them.

5. Click OK. A Print Management message box appears, informing you that the operation has succeeded.

6. Click OK and then click OK again to close the Deploy With Group Policy dialog box.

7. Close the Print Management console.

The next time the users running Windows Server 2008 or later and Windows Vista or later who are associated with the GPO refresh their policies or restart, they will receive the new settings and the printer will appear in the Devices and Printers control panel.

Thought experiment

Enterprise printing

In the following thought experiment, apply what you've learned about the objective to predict what steps you need to take. You can find answers to these questions in the "Answers" section at the end of this chapter.

You are a desktop support technician for a law firm with a group of 10 legal secretaries who provide administrative support to the attorneys. All the secretaries use a single, shared, high-speed laser printer that is connected to a dedicated Windows print server. The secretaries print multiple copies of large documents on a regular basis, and although the laser printer is fast, it runs almost constantly. Sometimes the secretaries have to wait 20 minutes or more after submitting a print job for their documents to reach the top of the queue. The office manager has offered to purchase additional printers for the department. However, the secretaries are accustomed to just clicking Print and don't like the idea of having to examine multiple print queues to determine which has the fewest jobs before submitting a document.

With this in mind, answer the following question.

What can you do to provide the office with a printing solution that will enable the secretaries to utilize additional printers most efficiently?

Objective summary

- Printing in Windows typically involves the following four components: print device, printer, print server, and print driver.
- The simplest form of print architecture consists of one print device connected to one computer, known as a locally attached print device. You can share this printer (and the print device) with other users on the same network.
- With network-attached print devices, the administrator's primary deployment decision is which computer will function as the print server.
- Remote Desktop Easy Print is a driver that enables Remote Desktop clients running applications on a server to redirect their print jobs back to their local print devices.
- Printer permissions are much simpler than NTFS permissions; they dictate whether users are allowed to use the printer, manage documents submitted to the printer, or manage the properties of the printer itself.
- The Print Management console is an administrative tool that consolidates the controls for the printing components throughout the enterprise into a single console.

Objective review

Answer the following questions to test your knowledge of the information in this objective. You can find the answers to these questions and explanations of why each answer choice is correct or incorrect in the "Answers" section at the end of this chapter.

1. Which of the following terms best describes the software interface through which a computer communicates with a print device?

   A. Printer

   B. Print server

   C. Printer driver

   D. Print Management console

2. You are setting up a printer pool on a computer running Windows Server 2012 R2. The printer pool contains three identical print devices. You open the Properties dialog box for the printer and select the Enable Printer Pooling option on the Ports tab. Which of the following steps must you perform next?

   A. Configure the LPT1 port to support three printers.

   B. Select or create the ports mapped to the three printers.

   C. On the Device Settings tab, configure the installable options to support two additional print devices.

   D. On the Advanced tab, configure the priority for each print device so that printing is distributed among the three print devices.

3. One of your print devices is not working properly, so you want to temporarily prevent users from sending jobs to the printer serving that device. Which of the following actions should you take?

   A. Stop sharing the printer.

   B. Remove the printer from Active Directory.

   C. Change the printer port.

   D. Rename the share.

4. You are administering a computer running Windows Server 2012 R2 configured as a print server. Users in the Marketing group report that they cannot print documents using a printer on the server. You view the permissions in the printer's properties. The Marketing group is allowed Manage Documents permission. Which of the following statements best explains why the users cannot print to the printer?

   A. The Everyone group must be granted the Manage Documents permission.

   B. The Administrators group must be granted the Manage Printers permission.

   C. The Marketing group must be granted the Print permission.

   D. The Marketing group must be granted the Manage Printers permission.

5. You are administering a print server running Windows Server 2012 R2. You want to perform maintenance on a print device physically connected to the print server. There are several documents in the print queue. You want to prevent the documents from being printed to the printer, but you don't want users to have to resubmit the documents to the printer. Which of the following statements best describes the best way to do this?

   A. Open the printer's Properties dialog box, select the Sharing tab, and select the Do Not Share This Printer option.

   B. Open the printer's Properties dialog box and select a port that is not associated with a print device.

   C. Open the printer's queue window, select the first document, and select Pause from the Document window.

   D. Open the printer's queue window and select the Pause Printing option from the Printer menu.

Objective 2.3: Configure servers for remote management

Windows Server 2012 R2 is designed to facilitate remote server management so administrators rarely, if ever, have to work directly at the server console. This conserves server resources that can better be devoted to applications and saves administrators' time.

Using Server Manager for remote management

Server Manager has been the primary server administration tool for Windows Server ever since Windows Server 2003. The most obvious improvement to the Server Manager tool in Windows Server 2012 R2 is the ability to perform administrative tasks on remote servers and on the local system.

When you log on to a GUI installation of Windows Server 2012 R2 with an administrative account, Server Manager loads automatically, displaying the Welcome tile. The Server Manager interface consists of a navigation pane on the left containing icons representing various views of server resources. Selecting an icon displays a home page in the right pane, which consists of a number of tiles containing information about the resource. The Dashboard page, which appears by default, contains, in addition to the Welcome tile, thumbnails that summarize the other views available in Server Manager. These other views include a page for the Local Server, a page for All Servers, containing any additional servers you have added to the manager, and others for server groups and role groups.

> **NOTE ADDING SERVERS**
>
> For information on adding servers to the Server Manager interface, see "Adding Servers" in Objective 1.2, "Configuring Servers."

Adding servers

The primary difference between the Windows Server 2012 R2 (and Windows Server 2012) Server Manager and previous versions is the ability to add and manage multiple servers at once. Although only the local server appears in Server Manager when you first run it, you can add other servers, enabling you to manage them together. The servers you add can be physical or virtual and can be running any version of Windows Server since Windows Server 2003. After you add servers to the interface, you can create groups containing collections of servers, such as those at a particular location or those performing a particular function. These groups appear in the navigation pane, enabling you to administer them as a single entity.

To add servers in Server Manager, use the following procedure.

1. In the navigation pane, click the All Servers icon to open the All Servers home page.

2. From the Manage menu, select Add Servers to open the Add Servers dialog box.

3. Select one of the following tabs to specify how you want to locate servers to add:

    - **Active Directory** Enables you to search for computers running specific operating systems in specific locations in the local AD DS domain

    - **DNS** Enables you to search for servers in your currently configured Domain Name System (DNS) server

    - **Import** Enables you to supply a text file containing the names or IP addresses of the servers you want to add

4. Initiate a search or upload a text file to display a list of available servers.

5. Select the servers you want to add and click the right arrow button to add them to the Selected list, as shown in Figure 2-22.

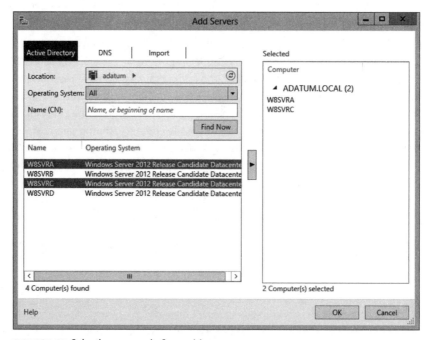

FIGURE 2-22 Selecting servers in Server Manager

6. Click OK. The servers you selected are added to the All Servers home page.

7. Close the Server Manger console.

Once you have added remote servers to the Server Manager interface, they appear on the All Servers home page. You can then access them in a variety of ways, depending on the version of Windows the remote server is running.

Managing non-domain joined servers

When you add servers that are members of an Active Directory Domain Services (AD DS) domain to the Server Manager interface, Windows Server 2012 R2 uses the standard Kerberos authentication protocol and your current domain credentials when connecting to the remote systems. You can also add servers that are not joined to an AD DS domain, but obviously, the system cannot authenticate using an AD DS account.

EXAM TIP

Candidates for the 70-410 exam should be familiar with remote management techniques for both non-domain servers and domain servers. This means using alternative authentication methods and network communication that does not rely on AD DS for server discovery.

To manage a non-domain joined server using Server Manager, you must first complete the following tasks:

- Supply administrative credentials for the non-domain joined server
- Add the non-domain joined server to the system's WS-Management TrustedHosts list

To add non-domain joined servers to Server Manager, you must use the DNS option or the Import option in the Add Servers Wizard. After creating the server entries, you must right-click each one and select Manage As from the context menu. This displays a Windows Security dialog box, in which you can supply credentials for an account with administrative privileges on the remote server.

Domain membership automatically establishes a trust relationship among the computers in the domain. To manage computers that are not in a common domain, you must establish that trust yourself by adding the computers you want to manage to the TrustedHosts list on the computer running Server Manager.

The TrustedHosts list exists on a logical drive called WSMan:; the path to the list itself is WSMan:\localhost\Client\TrustedHosts. To add a computer to the list, use the Set-Item cmdlet in Windows PowerShell. After opening a Windows PowerShell session with administrative privileges on the computer running Server Manager, use the following command to add the servers you want to manage to the list:

```
Set-Item WSMan:\localhost\Client\TrustedHosts –value <servername> –force
```

Managing Windows Server 2012 R2 servers

When you add servers running Windows Server 2012 R2 to Server Manager, you can immediately begin using the Add Roles and Features Wizard to install roles and features on any of the servers you have added.

You can also perform other administrative tasks, such as configuring network interface card (NIC) teaming and restarting the server, because Windows Remote Management (WinRM) is enabled by default on Windows Server 2012 R2.

CONFIGURING WINRM

WinRM enables administrators to manage a computer from a remote location by using tools based on Windows Management Instrumentation (WMI) and Windows PowerShell. If the default WinRM setting has been modified, or if you want to change it manually, you can do so through the Server Manager interface.

On the Local Server home page, the Properties tile contains a Remote Management indicator that specifies the server's current WinRM status. To change the WinRM state, click the Remote Management hyperlink to open the Configure Remote Management dialog box. Clearing the Enable Remote Management Of This Server From Other Computers check box disables WinRM; selecting the check box enables it.

> **NOTE USING WINDOWS POWERSHELL**
>
> To manage WinRM from a Windows PowerShell session, as in the case of a computer with a Server Core installation, use the following command:
>
> ```
> Configure-SMRemoting.exe -Get|-Enable|-Disable
> ```
>
> - **-Get** Displays the current WinRM status
> - **-Enable** Enables WinRM
> - **-Disable** Disables WinRM

CONFIGURING WINDOWS FIREWALL

If you attempt to launch MMC snap-ins targeting a remote server, such as the Computer Management console, you will receive an error because of the default Windows Firewall settings in Windows Server 2012 R2. MMC uses the Distributed Component Object Model (DCOM) for remote management instead of WinRM, and these settings are not enabled by default.

To address this problem, you must enable the following inbound Windows Firewall rules on the remote server you want to manage:

- COM+ Network Access (DCOM-In)
- Remote Event Log Management (NP-In)
- Remote Event Log Management (RPC)
- Remote Event Log Management (RPC-EPMAP)

To modify the firewall rules on the remote system, you can use any one of the following methods:

- Open the Windows Firewall with Advanced Security MMC snap-in on the remote server (if it is a Full GUI installation).
- Use the NetSecurity module in Windows PowerShell.
- Create a GPO containing the appropriate settings and apply it to the remote server.
- Run the Netsh AdvFirewall command from an administrative command prompt.

> **NOTE USING WINDOWS POWERSHELL**
>
> To configure the Windows Firewall rules required for remote server management using DCOM on a Server Core installation, you can use the following Windows PowerShell syntax:
>
> ```
> Set-NetFirewallRule –name <rule name> –enabled True
> ```
>
> To obtain the Windows PowerShell names for the preconfigured rules in Windows Firewall, use the Get-NetFirewallRule command. The resulting commands to enable the four rules listed earlier are as follows:
>
> ```
> Set-NetFirewallRule –name
>  ComPlusNetworkAccess-DCOM-In –enabled True
> Set-NetFirewallRule –name
>  RemoteEventLogSvc-In-TCP –enabled True
> Set-NetFirewallRule –name RemoteEventLogSvc-NP-In-TCP
> –enabled True
> Set-NetFirewallRule –name
>  RemoteEventLogSvc-RPCSS-In-TCP –enabled True
> ```

For the administrator interested in remote management solutions, the Group Policy method provides distinct advantages. It not only enables you to configure the firewall on the remote system without accessing the server console directly but enables you to configure the firewall on Server Core installations without having to work from the command line. Finally—and possibly most important for large networks—you can use Group Policy to configure the firewall on all the servers you want to manage at once.

To configure Windows Firewall settings by using Group Policy, use the following procedure. This procedure assumes the server is a member of an AD DS domain and has the Group Policy Management feature installed:

1. In Server Manager, open the Group Policy Management console and create a new GPO, giving it a name like *Server Firewall Configuration*.

2. Open the GPO you created using the Group Policy Management Editor.

> **MORE INFO GPOS**
>
> For more detailed information on creating GPOs and linking them to other objects, see Objective 6.1, "Create Group Policy Objects (GPOs)."

3. Browse to the Computer Configuration\Policies\Windows Settings\Security Settings \Windows Firewall with Advanced Security\Inbound Rules node.

4. Right-click Inbound Rules and, from the shortcut menu, select New Rule. The New Inbound Rule Wizard appears, displaying the Rule Type page.

5. Select the Predefined option and, in the drop-down list, select COM+ Network Access and click Next. The Predefined Rules page opens.

6. Click Next to open the Action page.

7. Leave the Allow The Connection option selected and click Finish. The rule appears in the Group Policy Management Editor console.

8. Open the New Inbound Rule Wizard again.

9. Select the Predefined option and, in the drop-down list, select Remote Event Log Management. Click Next. The Predefined Rules page opens, displaying the three rules in the Remote Event Log Management group.

10. Leave the three rules selected and click Next to open the Action page.

11. Leave the Allow The Connection option selected and click Finish. The three rules appear in the Group Policy Management Editor console.

12. Close the Group Policy Management Editor console.

13. In the Group Policy Management console, link the Server Firewall Configuration GPO you just created to your domain.

14. Close the Group Policy Management console.

The settings in the GPO you created will be deployed to your remote servers the next time they recycle or restart and you will be able to use MMC snap-ins, such as Computer Management and Disk Management, to connect to them remotely.

Managing down-level servers

The Windows Firewall rules you have to enable for remote servers running Windows Server 2012 R2 are also disabled by default on computers running earlier versions of Windows Server, so you also have to enable them there.

Unlike Windows Server 2012 R2 and Windows Server 2012, however, earlier versions of the operating system lack the WinRM support needed for them to be managed by using the new Server Manager.

By default, when you add servers running Windows Server 2008 or Windows Server 2008 R2 to the Windows Server 2012 R2 Server Manager, they appear with a manageability status that reads "Online - Verify WinRM 3.0 service is installed, running, and required firewall ports are open."

To add WinRM support to servers running Windows Server 2008 or Windows Server 2008 R2, you must download and install the following updates:

- .NET Framework 4.0
- Windows Management Framework 3.0

These updates are available from the Microsoft Download Center at the following URLs:

- *http://www.microsoft.com/en-us/download/details.aspx?id=17718*
- *http://www.microsoft.com/en-us/download/details.aspx?id=34595*

After you install the updates, the system automatically starts the Windows Remote Management service, but you must still complete the following tasks on the remote server:

- Enable the Windows Remote Management (HTTP-In) rules in Windows Firewall, as shown in Figure 2-23.

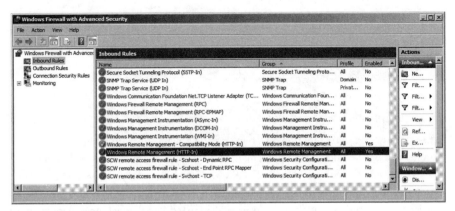

FIGURE 2-23 The Windows Remote Management rules in the Windows Firewall with Advanced Security console

- Create a WinRM listener by running the winrm quickconfig command at a command prompt with Administrative privileges.
- Enable the COM+ Network Access and Remote Event Log Management rules in Windows Firewall, as described in the previous section.

After installing the updates listed here, there are still limitations to the management tasks you can perform on earlier versions of Windows Server from a remote location. For example, you cannot use the Add Roles And Features Wizard in Server Manager to install roles and features on earlier versions of Windows Server. These servers do not appear in the server pool on the Select Destination Server page.

However, you can use Windows PowerShell to install roles and features on servers running Windows Server 2008 and Windows Server 2008 R2 remotely, as in the following procedure.

1. Open a Windows PowerShell session with Administrative privileges.

2. Establish a Windows PowerShell session with the remote computer by using the following command:

```
Enter-PSSession <remote server name> -credential <user name>
```

3. Type the password associated with the user name you specified and press Enter.

4. Display a list of the roles and features on the remote server by using the following command:

```
Get-WindowsFeature
```

5. Using the short name of the role or service as it appears in the Get-WindowsFeature display, install the component by using the following command:

```
Add-WindowsFeature <feature name>
```

6. Close the session with the remote server by using the following command:

```
Exit-PSSession
```

7. Close the Windows PowerShell window.

> **NOTE** **WINDOWS POWERSHELL**
>
> When you install a role or feature on a remote server by using Windows PowerShell, the installation does not include the role's management tools as a wizard-based installation does. However, you can install the tools along with the role or feature if you include the IncludeManagementTools parameter in the Install-WindowsFeature command line. Be aware, however, that in the case of a Server Core installation, adding the IncludeManagementTools parameter will not install any MMC snap-ins or other graphical tools.

Creating server groups

For administrators of enterprise networks, it might be necessary to add a large number of servers to Server Manager. To avoid having to work with a long scrolling list of servers, you can create server groups based on server locations, functions, or any other organizational paradigm.

When you create a server group, it appears as an icon in the navigation pane, and you can manage the servers in the group just as you would those in the All Servers group.

To create a server group, use the following procedure:

1. In Server Manager, in the navigation pane, click the All Servers icon. The All Servers home page appears.

2. From the Manage menu, select Create Server Group to open the Create Server Group dialog box, as shown in Figure 2-24.

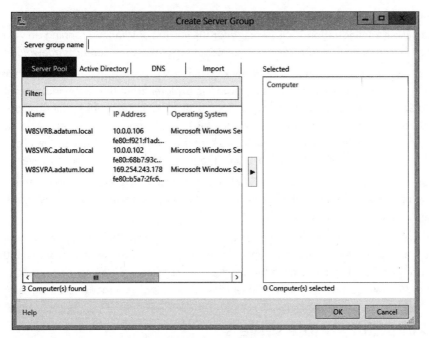

FIGURE 2-24 The Create Server Group dialog box in Server Manager

3. In the Server Group Name text box, type the name you want to assign to the server group.

4. Select one of the four tabs to choose a method for selecting servers.

5. Select the servers you want to add to the group and click the right arrow button to add them to the Selected box.

6. Click OK. A new server group icon with the name you specified appears in the navigational pane.

7. Close the Server Manager console.

Creating server groups does not affect the functions you can perform on them. You cannot, for example, perform actions on entire groups of servers. The groupings are just a means to keep a large number of servers organized and easy to locate.

Using Remote Server Administration Tools

You can manage remote servers from any computer running Windows Server 2012 R2; all the required tools are installed by default. However, administrators have found it most efficient to use their client computers to manage servers remotely (especially with the introduction of cloud-based services).

To manage Windows servers from a workstation, you must download and install the Remote Server Administration Tools package for the version of Windows running on your workstation from the Microsoft Download Center at *http://www.microsoft.com/download*.

Remote Server Administration Tools is packaged as a Microsoft Update file with an .msu extension, enabling you to deploy it easily from File Explorer, from the command prompt, or by using Software Distribution in a GPO. When you install Remote Server Administration Tools on a workstation running Windows 8 or Windows 8.1, all the tools are activated by default, unlike in previous versions that required you to turn them on by using the Windows Features control panel. You can still use the control panel to turn selected features off, however.

When you launch Server Manager on a Windows workstation, there is no local server and there are no remote servers to manage until you add some. You add servers by using the same process described in Objective 1.2.

Your access to the servers you add depends on the account you use to log on to the workstation. If an "Access denied" message appears, you can connect to the server using another account by right-clicking it and, from the shortcut menu, selecting Manage As to display a standard Windows Security dialog box, in which you can supply alternative credentials.

Working with remote servers

Once you have added remote servers to Server Manager, you can access them using a variety of remote administration tools.

Server Manager provides three basic methods for addressing remote servers, as follows:

- **Contextual tasks**   When you right-click a server in a Servers tile anywhere in Server Manager, you see a shortcut menu that provides access to tools and commands pointed at the selected server. Some of these are commands that Server Manager executes on the remote server, such as Restart Server and Windows PowerShell. Others launch tools on the local system and direct them at the remote server, such as MMC snap-ins and the Install Roles And Features Wizard. Still others modify Server Manager itself by removing servers from the interface. Other contextual tasks sometimes appear in the Tasks menus for specific panes.

- **Noncontextual tasks**   The menu bar at the top of the Server Manager console provides access to internal tasks, such as launching the Add Server Wizard and the Install Roles And Features Wizard, and the Server Manager Properties dialog box, in which you can specify the console's refresh interval.

- **Noncontextual tools**   The console's Tools menu provides access to external programs, such as MMC snap-ins and the Windows PowerShell interface, that are directed at the local system.

Thought experiment
Deploying Windows Firewall rules

In the following thought experiment, apply what you've learned about the objective to predict what steps you need to take. You can find answers to these questions in the "Answers" section at the end of this chapter.

Ralph is responsible for the 24 servers running a particular application and the servers are scattered across his company's enterprise network. Ralph wants to use Server Manager on his Windows 8 workstation to manage those servers and monitor the events that occur on them. To do this, he must enable the incoming COM+ Network Access and Remote Event Log Management rules in Windows Firewall on the servers.

Because he can't travel to the locations of all the servers and many of the sites do not have trustworthy IT personnel, Ralph has decided to use Group Policy to configure Windows Firewall on all the servers. The company's Active Directory Domain Services tree is organized geographically, which means that Ralph's servers are located in many different OUs under one domain.

With this in mind, answer the following question.

How can Ralph use Group Policy to deploy the required Windows Firewall rule settings to his 24 servers and only those servers?

Objective summary

- Windows Server 2012 R2 is designed to facilitate remote server management so administrators rarely if ever have to work directly at the server console. This conserves server resources that can better be devoted to applications.
- When you add servers running Windows Server 2012 R2 to Server Manager, you can immediately begin using the Add Roles and Features Wizard to install roles and features on any of the servers you have added.
- The Windows Firewall rules you have to enable for remote servers running Windows Server 2012 R2 are also disabled by default on computers running versions earlier than Windows Server 2012, so you also have to enable them there.
- For administrators of enterprise networks, it might be necessary to add a large number of servers to Server Manager. To avoid having to work with a long scrolling list of servers, you can create server groups based on server locations, functions, or any other organizational paradigm.
- You can manage remote servers from any computer running Windows Server 2012 R2; all the required tools are installed by default. However, the new administrative method that Microsoft is promoting urges administrators to keep servers locked away and use a workstation to manage servers from a remote location.

Objective review

Answer the following questions to test your knowledge of the information in this objective. You can find the answers to these questions and explanations of why each answer choice is correct or incorrect in the "Answers" section at the end of this chapter.

1. Which of the following tasks must you perform before you can manage a remote server running Windows Server 2012 R2 using the Computer Management snap-in?

   A. Enable WinRM on the remote server.

   B. Enable the COM+ Network Access rule on the remote server.

   C. Enable the Remote Event Log Management rules on the remote server.

   D. Install Remote Server Administration Tools on the remote server.

2. Which of the following Windows PowerShell cmdlets can you use to list the existing Windows Firewall rules on a computer running Windows Server 2012 R2? (Choose all that apply.)

   A. Get-NetFirewallRule

   B. Set-NetFirewallRule

   C. Show-NetFirewallRule

   D. New-NetFirewallRule

3. Which of the following tasks can you *not* perform remotely on a server running Windows Server 2008?

   A. Install roles by using Server Manager

   B. Install roles by using Windows PowerShell

   C. Connect to the remote server by using the Computer Management snap-in

   D. Monitor event log entries

4. Which of the following updates must you install on a server running Windows Server 2008 before you can connect to it by using Windows Server 2012 R2 Server Manager? (Choose all that apply.)

   A. .NET Framework 3.5

   B. .NET Framework 4.0

   C. Windows Management Framework 3.0

   D. Windows Server 2008 R2

5. When you run Server Manager from a Windows 8 workstation using Remote Server Administration Tools, which of the following elements do *not* appear in the default display?

   A. The Dashboard

   B. The Local Server home page

   C. The All Servers home page

   D. The Welcome tile

Answers

This section contains the solutions to the thought experiments and answers to the objective review questions in this chapter.

Objective 2.1: Thought experiment

The most likely cause of the problem is that Leo does not have sufficient share permissions for read/write access to the Contoso files. Granting the CONTOSO_USERS group the Allow Full Control share permission should enable Leo to save his changes to the Contoso files.

Objective 2.1: Review

1. **Correct answer:** C

   A. **Incorrect:** Windows Server 2012 R2 can maintain more than 8 volume shadow copies.

   B. **Incorrect:** Windows Server 2012 R2 can maintain more than 16 volume shadow copies.

   C. **Correct:** Windows Server 2012 R2 can maintain up to 64 volume shadow copies before it begins deleting the oldest data.

   D. **Incorrect:** Windows Server 2012 R2 cannot maintain 128 volume shadow copies.

2. **Correct answer:** B

   A. **Incorrect:** Authentication is the process of verifying the user's identity.

   B. **Correct:** Authorization is the process by which a user is granted access to specific resources based on the permissions he or she possesses.

   C. **Incorrect:** Access-based enumeration is a Windows feature that prevents users from seeing resources to which they do not have permissions.

   D. **Incorrect:** Assignment describes the process of granting permissions, not reading permissions.

3. **Correct answer:** A

   A. **Correct:** Using File Server Resource Manager, you can notify administrators with email messages when users exceed their allotment of storage.

   B. **Incorrect:** Using NTFS Quotas, you can create quotas for individual users that specify different storage limits.

   C. **Incorrect:** You can use NTFS quotas to prevent users from consuming storage space on a volume beyond their allotted limit.

   D. **Incorrect:** You can use NTFS quotas to generate warnings to users when they approach their allotted storage limit.

4. **Correct answers:** B, D

   A. **Incorrect:** In Windows Server versions prior to Windows Server 2012 R2, special permissions are combined to form standard permissions.

   B. **Correct:** Basic permissions are formed by creating various combinations of advanced permissions.

   C. **Incorrect:** Share permissions are a system that is separate from the NTFS permission system.

   D. **Correct:** In Windows Server versions prior to Windows Server 2012 R2, standard permissions are formed by creating various combinations of special permissions.

5. **Correct answer:** D

   A. **Incorrect:** The owner is the only person who can access a file that has no permissions assigned to it.

   B. **Incorrect:** The security principal is not the person responsible for creating an organization's permission policies.

   C. **Incorrect:** The security principal receives permissions; the security principal does not create them.

   D. **Correct:** The security principal is the user or computer to which permissions are assigned.

Objective 2.2: Thought experiment

Install additional, identical printers, connecting them to the same Windows Server 2012 R2 print server, and create a printer pool by selecting the appropriate check box on the Ports tab of the printer's Properties sheet.

Objective 2.2: Review

1. **Correct answer:** A

   A. **Correct:** In Windows, a printer is the software interface through which a computer communicates with a print device.

   B. **Incorrect:** A print server is a device that receives print jobs from clients and sends them to print devices that are either attached locally or connected to the network.

   C. **Incorrect:** A printer driver is a device driver that converts the print jobs generated by applications into an appropriate string of commands for a specific print device.

   D. **Incorrect:** The Print Management snap-in is a tool that administrators can use to manage printers all over the network.

2. **Correct answer:** B

   A. **Incorrect:** Whether the printers are pooled or not, each one must be connected to a separate port.

   B. **Correct:** To set up printer pooling, select the Enable Printer Pooling check box and select or create the ports corresponding to printers that will be part of the pool.

   C. **Incorrect:** You do not use the installable options settings to create a printer pool.

   D. **Incorrect:** Priorities have nothing to do with printer pooling.

3. **Correct answer:** A

   A. **Correct:** If you stop sharing the printer, users will no longer be able to use the print device.

   B. **Incorrect:** Removing the printer from Active Directory will prevent users from finding the printer by using a search, but they can still access it.

   C. **Incorrect:** Changing the printer port will prevent the printer from sending jobs to the print device, but it will not prevent users from sending jobs to the printer.

   D. **Incorrect:** Renaming the share can make it difficult for users to find the printer, but they can still use it when they do find it.

4. **Correct answer:** C

   A. **Incorrect:** The Manage Documents permission does not allow users to send jobs to the printer.

   B. **Incorrect:** The Manage Printers permission does not allow users to send jobs to the printer.

   C. **Correct:** The Print permission allows users to send documents to the printer; the Manage Documents permission does not.

   D. **Incorrect:** The Manage Documents permission does not allow users to send jobs to the printer.

5. **Correct answer:** D

   A. **Incorrect:** A printer that is not shared will continue to process jobs that are already in the queue.

   B. **Incorrect:** Changing the port will require the users to resubmit the jobs that were in the queue.

   C. **Incorrect:** Pausing the first document in the queue will not prevent the other queued jobs from printing.

   D. **Correct:** When you select the Pause Printing option, the documents will remain in the print queue until you resume printing. This option applies to all documents in the queue.

Objective 2.3: Thought experiment

After creating a GPO containing the required Windows Firewall settings, Ralph should create a security group containing all the 24 computer objects representing his servers. Then he should link the GPO to the company domain and use security filtering to limit the scope of the GPO to the group he created.

Objective 2.3: Review

1. **Correct answer:** B

    A. **Incorrect:** WinRM is enabled by default on Windows Server 2012 R2.

    B. **Correct:** The COM+ Network Access rule must be enabled on the remote server for MMC snap-ins to connect.

    C. **Incorrect:** The Remote Event Log Management rules are not necessary to connect to a remote server using an MMC snap-in.

    D. **Incorrect:** The remote server does not have to be running Remote Server Administration Tools.

2. **Correct answers:** A, C

    A. **Correct:** The Get-NetFirewallRule cmdlet displays a list of all the rules on a system running Windows Firewall.

    B. **Incorrect:** The Set-NetFireWallRule cmdlet is for managing specific rules, not listing them.

    C. **Correct:** The Show-NetFirewallRule cmdlet displays a list of all the rules on a system running Windows Firewall.

    D. **Incorrect:** The New-NetFireWallRule cmdlet is for creating rules, not listing them.

3. **Correct answer:** A

    A. **Correct:** You cannot install roles on a remote server running Windows Server 2008 by using Server Manager.

    B. **Incorrect:** You can install roles on a remote server running Windows Server 2008 by using Windows PowerShell.

    C. **Incorrect:** You can connect to a remote server running Windows Server 2008 by using the Computer Management console as long as you enable the COM+ Network Access rule.

    D. **Incorrect:** You can monitor event log entries on a remote server running Windows Server 2008 as long as you enable the Remote Event Log Management rules.

4. **Correct answers:** B, C

   A. Incorrect: .NET Framework 3.5 is not needed for Server Manager to connect to Windows Server 2008.

   B. Correct: .NET Framework 4.0 is needed for Server Manager to connect to Windows Server 2008.

   C. Correct: Windows Management Framework 3.0 is needed for Server Manager to connect to Windows Server 2008.

   D. Incorrect: It is not necessary to upgrade to Windows Server 2008 R2 for Server Manager to connect to Windows Server 2008.

5. **Correct answer:** B

   A. Incorrect: The Dashboard does appear in the default Server Manager display.

   B. Correct: The Local Server home page does not appear, because the local system is a workstation, not a server.

   C. Incorrect: The All Servers home page does appear in the default Server Manager display.

   D. Incorrect: The Welcome tile does appear in the default Server Manager display.

Configuring Hyper-V

The concept of virtualizing servers has, in the past several years, grown from a novel experiment to a convenient lab and testing tool to a legitimate deployment strategy for production servers. Windows Server 2012 R2 includes the Hyper-V role, which enables administrators to create virtual machines (VMs), each of which runs in its own isolated environment. VMs are self-contained units that administrators can easily move from one physical computer to another, greatly simplifying the process of deploying network applications and services.

This chapter covers some of the fundamental tasks that administrators perform to create and deploy Hyper-V servers and VMs.

Objectives in this chapter:

- Objective 3.1: Create and configure virtual machine settings
- Objective 3.2: Create and configure virtual machine storage
- Objective 3.3: Create and configure virtual networks

Objective 3.1: Create and configure virtual machine settings

Server virtualization in Windows Server 2012 R2 is based on a module called a *hypervisor*. Sometimes called a *virtual machine monitor (VMM)*, the hypervisor is responsible for abstracting the computer's physical hardware and creating multiple virtualized hardware environments, called VMs. Each VM has its own (virtual) hardware configuration and can run a separate copy of an operating system (OS). Therefore, with sufficient physical hardware and the correct licensing, a single computer running Windows Server 2012 R2 with the Hyper-V role installed can support multiple VMs, which administrators can manage as if they were standalone computers.

> *NOTE* **REMOTEFX**
> RemoteFX enables remote computers to connect Hyper-V guest VMs with an enhanced desktop experience, including graphics adapter virtualization, USB redirection, and intelligent encoding and decoding. Don't expect many questions about RemoteFX on the exam.

This objective covers how to:

- Configure dynamic memory
- Configure smart paging
- Configure Resource Metering
- Configure guest integration services
- Create and configure Generation 1 and Generation 2 VMs
- Configure and use enhanced session mode

Virtualization architectures

Virtualization products can use several different architectures to share a computer's hardware resources among VMs. The earlier type of virtualization products, including Microsoft Windows Virtual PC and Microsoft Virtual Server, requires a standard OS installed on a computer. This becomes the "host" OS. Then you install the virtualization product, which adds the hypervisor component. The hypervisor essentially runs alongside the host OS, as shown in Figure 3-1, and enables you to create as many VMs as the computer has hardware to support.

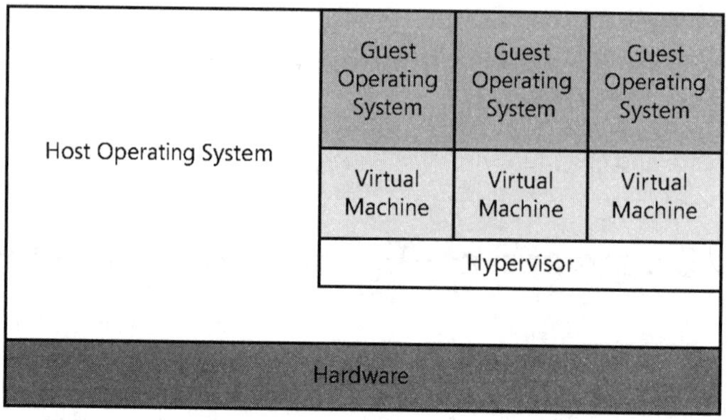

FIGURE 3-1 A hybrid VMM sharing hardware access with a host operating system

This arrangement, in which the hypervisor runs on top of a host OS, is called *Type II virtualization*. By using the Type II hypervisor, you create a virtual hardware environment for each VM. You can specify how much memory to allocate to each VM, create virtual disk drives by using space on the computer's physical drives, and provide access to peripheral devices. You then install a "guest" OS on each VM, just as if you were deploying a new computer. The host OS then shares access to the computer's processor with the hypervisor, with each taking the clock cycles it needs and passing control of the processor back to the other.

Type II virtualization can provide adequate VM performance, particularly in classroom and laboratory environments, but it does not provide performance equivalent to separate physical computers. Therefore, it is not generally recommended for high-traffic servers in production environments.

The virtualization capability built into Windows Server 2012 R2, called Hyper-V, uses a different type of architecture. Hyper-V uses Type I virtualization, in which the hypervisor is an abstraction layer that interacts directly with the computer's physical hardware—that is, without an intervening host OS. The term *hypervisor* is intended to represent the level beyond the term *supervisor*, in regard to the responsibility for allocating a computer's processor clock cycles.

The hypervisor creates individual environments called *partitions*, each of which has its own OS installed and accesses the computer's hardware via the hypervisor. Unlike Type II virtualization, no host OS shares processor time with the hypervisor. Instead, the hypervisor designates the first partition it creates as the parent partition and all subsequent partitions as child partitions, as shown in Figure 3-2.

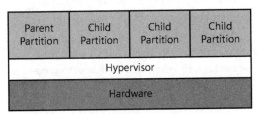

FIGURE 3-2 A Type I VMM, with the hypervisor running directly on the hardware

The parent partition accesses the system hardware through the hypervisor, just as the child partitions do. The only difference is that the parent runs the virtualization stack, which creates and manages the child partitions. The parent partition is also responsible for the subsystems that directly affect the performance of the computer's physical hardware, such as Plug and Play, power management, and error handling. These subsystems also run in the OSs on the child partitions, but they address only virtual hardware, whereas the parent, or root, partition handles the actual hardware.

> **NOTE HYPER-V**
>
> It might not seem like the Hyper-V role in Windows Server 2012 R2 provides Type I virtualization, because it requires the Windows Server OS to be installed and running. However, adding the Hyper-V role actually converts the installed instance of Windows Server 2012 R2 into the parent partition and causes the system to load the hypervisor before the OS.

Hyper-V implementations

Windows Server 2012 R2 includes the Hyper-V role only in the Standard and Datacenter editions. The Hyper-V role is required for the OS to function as a computer's primary partition, enabling it to host other VMs. No special software is required for an OS to function as a guest OS in a VM. Therefore, although Windows Server 2012 R2 Essentials does not include the Hyper-V role, it can function as a guest OS. Other guest OSs supported by Hyper-V include the current Windows workstation OSs and many other non-Microsoft server and workstation products.

Hyper-V licensing

The primary difference between the Standard and Datacenter editions of Windows Server 2012 R2 is the number of VMs they support. When you install a Windows Server 2012 R2 instance on a VM, you must have a license for it, just like when you install it on a physical machine. Purchasing the Datacenter edition allows you to license an unlimited number of VMs running Windows Server 2012 R2 on that one physical machine. The Standard license allows you to license only two virtual instances of Windows Server 2012 R2.

> **IMPORTANT READERAID HEADER**
>
> Readeraid. You might find that reports vary on the specific minimum requirements of Windows Server 2008. This is not uncommon for new operating systems because the minimum requirements change as the operating system moves from beta to the release candidate stage to the final RTM version. The requirements outlined in Table 1-1 are not finalized. You might be able to get Windows Server 2008 to install on a computer that does not meet these specifications, but the experience will be less than optimal.

Hyper-V hardware limitations

The Windows Server 2012 R2 version of Hyper-V contains massive improvements in the scalability of the system over previous versions. A Windows Server 2012 R2 Hyper-V host system can have up to 320 logical processors, supporting up to 2,048 virtual CPUs and up to 4 terabytes (TB) of physical memory.

One server can host as many as 1,024 active VMs and a single VM can have up to 64 virtual CPUs and up to 1 TB of memory.

Hyper-V can also support clusters with up to 64 nodes and 8,000 VMs.

> **NOTE WINDOWS POWERSHELL**
>
> Another major improvement in the Windows Server 2012 and Windows Server 2012 R2 versions of Hyper-V is the inclusion of a Hyper-V module for Windows PowerShell, which includes new cmdlets dedicated to the creation and management of the Hyper-V service and its VMs.

Hyper-V Server

In addition to the Hyper-V implementation in Windows Server 2012 R2, Microsoft provides a dedicated Hyper-V Server product, which is a subset of Windows Server 2012 R2. Hyper-V Server 2012 R2 includes the Hyper-V role, which it installs by default during the OS installation. With the exception of some limited File and Storage Services and Remote Desktop capabilities, the OS includes no other roles, as shown in Figure 3-3.

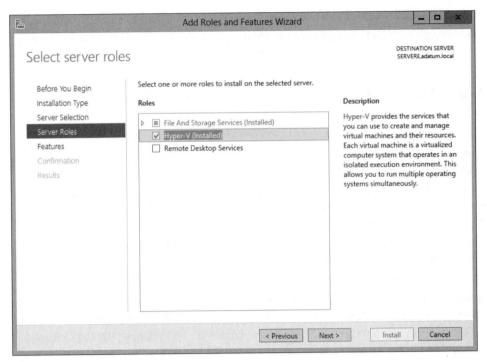

FIGURE 3-3 Roles available in Hyper-V Server

The Hyper-V Server is also limited to the Server Core interface, althoughas with all Server Core installationsit includes SCONFIG, a simple, script-based configuration interface, as shown in Figure 3-4. You can manage Hyper-V Server remotely by using Server Manager and Hyper-V Manager, just as you would any other Server Core installation.

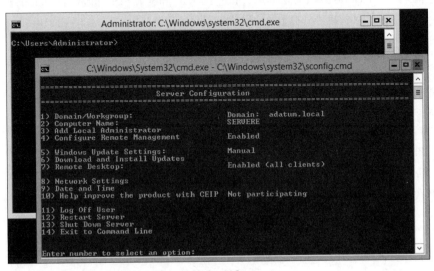

FIGURE 3-4 The Server Core interface in Hyper-V Server

Unlike Windows Server 2012 R2, Hyper-V Server is a free product, available for download from Microsoft's website. However, Hyper-V Server does not include any licenses for virtual instances. You must obtain and license all the OSs you install on the VMs you create.

Installing Hyper-V

Once you have the appropriate hardware, you can add the Hyper-V role to Windows Server 2012 R2 by using Server Manager, just as you would any other role.

Adding the Hyper-V role installs the hypervisor software, and, in the case of a full GUI installation, also installs the management tools. The primary tool for creating and managing VMs and their components on Hyper-V servers is the Hyper-V Manager console. Hyper-V Manager provides administrators with a list of all the VMs on the local host and enables administrators to configure the environments of both the servers and the individual VMs. There is also a set of Hyper-V cmdlets for Windows PowerShell that enables you to exercise complete control over VMs using that interface.

Microsoft recommends that you do not install other roles with Hyper-V. It is better to implement any other roles that you need the physical computer to perform within one of the VMs you create by using Hyper-V. In addition, you might want to consider installing Hyper-V on a computer by using the Server Core installation option. This will minimize the overhead expended on the partition. As with other roles, installing Hyper-V on Server Core excludes the graphical management tools, which you must install separately as a feature on another computer.

Before you can install the Hyper-V role on a server running Windows Server 2012 R2, you must have the appropriate hardware:

- A 64-bit processor that includes hardware-assisted virtualization. This is available in processors that include a virtualization option, such as Intel Virtualization Technology (Intel VT) or AMD Virtualization (AMD-V) technology.

- A system BIOS that supports the virtualization hardware, on which the virtualization feature has been enabled.

- Hardware-enforced Data Execution Prevention (DEP), which Intel describes as eXecute Disable (XD) and AMD describes as No eXecute (NX). This is a technology used in CPUs to segregate areas of memory. Specifically, you must enable the Intel XD bit (execute disable bit) or the AMD NX bit (no execute bit).

To install the Hyper-V role, use the following procedure.

1. In Server Manager, on the Manage menu, select Add Roles And Features. The Add Roles And Features Wizard starts, displaying the Before You Begin page.

2. Click Next to open the Select Installation Type page.

3. Leave the Role-Based Or Feature-Based Installation option selected and click Next. The Select Destination Server page opens.

4. Select the server on which you want to install Hyper-V and click Next. The Select Server Roles page opens.

5. Select the Hyper-V role. The Add Features That Are Required For Hyper-V dialog box appears.

6. Click Add Features to accept the dependencies and then click Next to open the Select Features page.

7. Click Next to open the Hyper-V page.

8. Click Next. The Create Virtual Switches page opens, as shown in Figure 3-5.

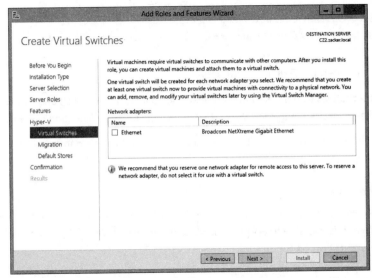

FIGURE 3-5 The Create Virtual Switches page of the Add Roles and Features Wizard

9. Select the appropriate check box for a network adapter and click Next. The Virtual Machine Migration page opens, as shown in Figure 3-6.

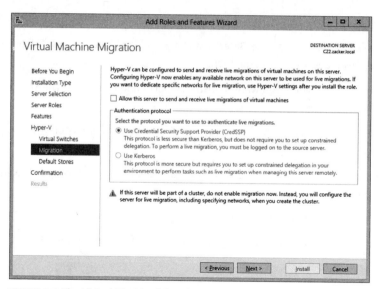

FIGURE 3-6 The Virtual Machine Migration page of the Add Roles and Features Wizard

10. Click Next to open the Default Stores page.

11. Specify alternatives to the default locations for virtual hard disk (VHD) and VM configuration files, if desired, and click Next. The Confirm Installation Selection page opens.

12. Click Install to move to the Installation Progress page as the wizard installs the role.

13. Click Close to close the wizard.

14. Restart the server.

Installing the role modifies the Windows Server 2012 R2 startup procedure so that the newly installed hypervisor is able to address the system hardware directly and then load the OS as the primary partition on top of that.

> **NOTE   USING WINDOWS POWERSHELL**
>
> You can also install the Hyper-V role by using the Install-WindowsFeature cmdlet, using the following syntax:
>
> ```
> Install-WindowsFeature –Name Hyper-V
> –ComputerName <name> -IncludeManagementTools –Restart
> ```

Using Hyper-V Manager

Once you have installed the Hyper-V role and restarted the computer, you can begin to create VMs and deploy OSs on them by using the Hyper-V Manager console, which you can access from the Tools menu in Server Manager.

Like most of the Windows Server 2012 R2 management tools, including Server Manager itself, you can use the Hyper-V Manager console to create and manage VMs on multiple servers, enabling administrators to exercise full control over their servers from a central location.

To run Hyper-V Manager on a server that does not have the Hyper-V role, you must install the Hyper-V Management Tools feature. These tools are also found in the Remote Server Administration Tools feature

Once you install and launch the Hyper-V Manager console, you can add servers to the display by right-clicking the Hyper-V Manager node in the left pane and selecting Connect To Server from the shortcut menu. The Select Computer dialog box appears, in which you can type or browse to the name of a Hyper-V server.

The Hyper-V Manager console lists all the VMs on the selected server, as shown in Figure 3-7, along with status information about each one.

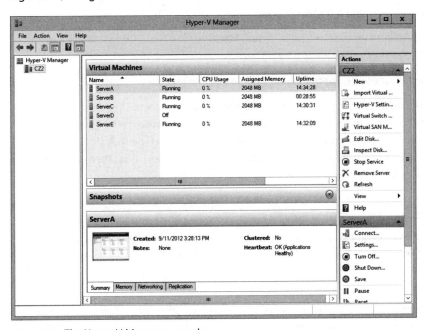

FIGURE 3-7 The Hyper-V Manager console

Creating a virtual machine

After installing Hyper-V and configuring it using Hyper-V Manager, you are ready to create VMs and install the OS on each one. By using Hyper-V Manager, you can create new VMs and define the hardware resources that the system should allocate to them. In the settings for a particular VM, depending on the physical hardware available in the computer and the limitations of the guest OS, administrators can specify the number of processors and the amount of memory allotted to a VM, install virtual network adapters, and create virtual disks by using a variety of technologies, including storage area networks (SANs).

By default, Hyper-V stores the files that make up VMs in the folders you specified on the Default Stores page during the role installation. Each VM uses the following files:

- A virtual machine configuration file in XML format with an .xml extension that contains the VM configuration information, including all settings for the VM

- One or more VHD (.vhd or .vhdx) files to store the guest OS, applications, and data for the VM

In addition, a VM can use a saved-state (.vsv) file if the machine has been placed into a saved state.

To create a new VM, use the following procedure.

1. In Server Manager, on the Tools menu, select Hyper-V Manager to open the Hyper-V Manager console.

2. In the left pane, select a Hyper-V server.

3. From the Action menu, select New, Virtual Machine. The New Virtual Machine Wizard starts, displaying the Before You Begin page.

4. Click Next to open the Specify Name And Location page.

5. In the Name text box, type a name for the VM, keeping in mind that the system will also use this name to create the VM files and folders. To create the VM files in a location other than the default, select the Store The Virtual Machine In A Different Location check box and type an alternate path in the Location text box. Then click Next. The Specify Generation page appears.

MORE INFORMATION VM GENERATIONS

For more information on the distinction between Generation 1 virtual machines and Generation 2 virtual machines, see "Creating Generation 1 and Generation 2 VMs" later in this chapter.

6. Specify whether you want to create a Generation 1 or Generation 2 virtual machine and click Next. The Assign Memory page opens.

MORE INFORMATION MEMORY

For more information on how Hyper-V uses memory, see "Allocating memory" later in this chapter.

7. In the Startup Memory text box, type the amount of memory you want the VM to use and click Next. The Configure Networking page opens, as shown in Figure 3-8.

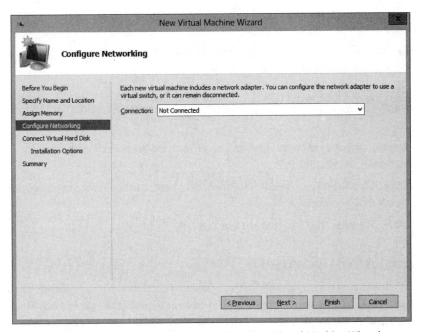

FIGURE 3-8 The Configure Networking page of the New Virtual Machine Wizard

8. From the Connection drop-down list, select a virtual switch and click Next. The Connect Virtual Hard Disk page opens, as shown in Figure 3-9.

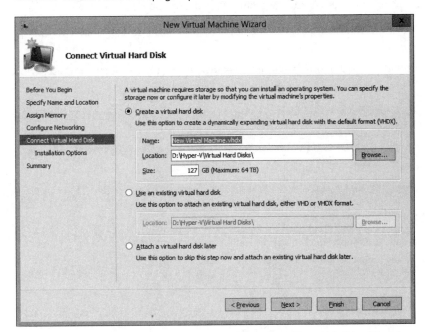

FIGURE 3-9 The Connect Virtual Hard Disk page of the New Virtual Machine Wizard

9. Leave the Create A Virtual Hard Disk option selected and type values for the following fields:

   - **Name**   Specifies the file name for the VHD, using the .vhdx format new to Windows Server 2012 R2

   - **Location**   Specifies a location for the VHD other than the default you specified on the Default Stores page

   - **Size**   Specifies the maximum size of the VHD

10. Click Next. The Installation Options page opens.

11. Leave the Install An Operating System Later Option selected and click Next. The Completing The New Virtual Machine Wizard page opens.

12. Click Finish. The wizard creates the new VM and adds it to the list of VMs in Hyper-V Manager.

The VM that this procedure creates is the equivalent of a bare-metal computer. It has all the (virtual) hardware it needs to run, but it has no software.

Each VM on a Hyper-V server consists of a collection of settings that specify the hardware resources in the machine and the configuration settings that control those resources. You can manage and modify those settings by using the Settings page for the particular VM.

Selecting a VM from the list in Hyper-V Manager displays a series of icons in the Actions pane. Clicking the Settings icon opens the Settings dialog box, shown in Figure 3-10, which is the primary configuration interface for that VM. Here, you can modify any of the settings that the New Virtual Machine Wizard configured for you.

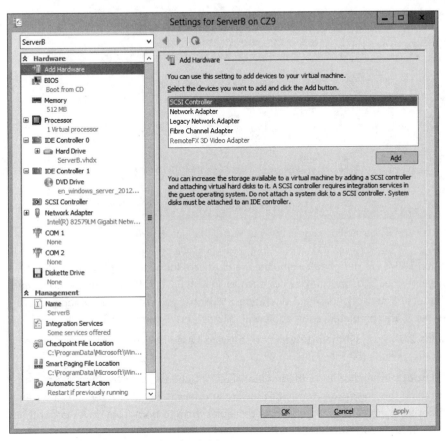

FIGURE 3-10 The Settings dialog box for a VM

Creating Generation 1 and Generation 2 VMs

In Windows Server 2012 R2, Hyper-V includes a new type of virtual machine, which it refers to as Generation 2. The VM type created by all previous versions is called Generation 1. When you create a new virtual machine in the Hyper-V manager, the New Virtual Machine Wizard includes a new page (shown in Figure 3-11) on which you specify whether you want to create a Generation 1 or Generation 2 VM. The New-VM cmdlet in Windows PowerShell also includes a new –Generation parameter.

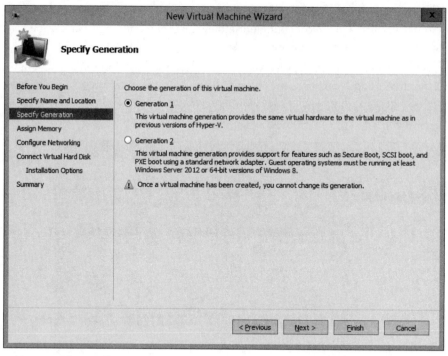

FIGURE 3-11 The Specify Generation page in the New Virtual Machine Wizard

Generation 1 VMs are designed to emulate the hardware found in a typical computer. To do this, they use drivers for specific devices, such as an AMI BIOS, an S3 graphics adapter, and an Intel chipset and network adapter. Generation 1 VMs that you create with Windows Server 2012 R2 Hyper-V are completely compatible with all previous Hyper-V versions.

Generation 2 VMs use synthetic drivers and software-based devices instead; they provide advantages that include the following:

- **UEFI boot**   Instead of using the traditional BIOS, Generation 2 VMs support Secure Boot using the Universal Extensible Firmware Interface (UEFI), which requires a system to boot from digitally signed drivers and enables them to boot from drives larger than 2 TB with GUID partition tables.

- **SCSI disks**   Generation 2 VMs omit the IDE disk controller used by Generation 1 VMs to boot the system and use a high-performance virtual SCSI controller for all disks, enabling the VMs to boot from VHDX files and support hot-disk adds and removes.

The end result is a Generation 2 virtual machine that deploys much faster than its Generation 1 counterparts and performs better as well. The limitations, however, are that Generation 2 VMs can only run the following guest operating systems:

- Windows Server 2012

- Windows Server 2012 R2

- Windows 8 64-bit

- Windows 8.1 64-bit

Installing an operating system

Once you have created a VM, you can install an OS on it. Hyper-V in Windows Server 2012 R2 supports all the following as OSs you can install in Generation 1 VMs:

- Windows Server 2012 R2
- Windows Server 2012
- Windows Server 2008 R2
- Windows Server 2008
- Windows Home Server 2011
- Windows Small Business Server 2011
- Windows Server 2003 R2
- Windows Server 2003 SP2
- Windows 8.1
- Windows 8
- Windows 7 Enterprise and Ultimate
- Windows Vista Business, Enterprise, and Ultimate SP2
- Windows XP Professional SP3
- Windows XP x64 Professional SP2
- CentOS 6.0–6.2
- Red Hat Enterprise Linux 6.0–6.2
- SUSE Linux Enterprise Server 11 SP2

NOTE GUEST OSS

This is the official list of supported guest OSs at RTM. Other OSs might also function but have not been fully tested.

One of the advantages of installing software on VMs is that there are several ways to access the installation files. A VM, by default, has a DVD drive, which can itself be physical or virtual.

When you open the Settings dialog box for a Generation 1 VM and select the DVD drive in the Hardware list, you see the interface shown in Figure 3-12. In the Media section, you can select one of the following options for the drive:

- **None** The equivalent of a drive with no disk inserted
- **Image File** Points to a disk image file with a .iso extension stored on one of the host computer's drives or on a shared network drive
- **Physical CD/DVD Drive** Links the virtual DVD drive to one of the physical DVD drives in the host computer

In a Generation 2 VM, the DVD drive supports only the None option and the Image File option, as shown in Figure 3-12. The ability to mount an image file to a virtual DVD drive is particularly useful for administrators who download OS files as disk images. Once you have mounted an installation disk, either physically or virtually, you can click Start in the Actions pane of Hyper-V Manager, which is the equivalent of turning on the VM.

Starting a VM causes the thumbnail in the Hyper-V Manager to go live, displaying the contents of the computer's screen. To display the VM's activity at full size, click Connect in the Actions pane to open a new window for the VM. You can then interact with the VM through that window, just as if you were sitting at a physical computer's console.

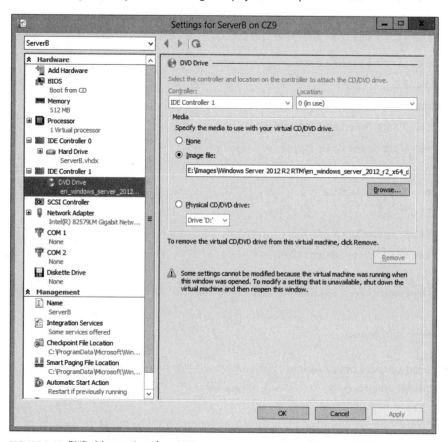

FIGURE 3-12 DVD drive settings for a VM

When the VM boots from the disk you mounted, the OS installation proceeds just as if you were using a physical computer. During the installation process, you can work with the VHD drive just as you would a physical one, creating partitions of various sizes and selecting one for the OS. When the installation is complete, the VM restarts, and you can then log on and use it in the normal manner.

Configuring Guest Integration Services

In some cases, certain Hyper-V guest OS features do not function properly using the OS's own device drivers. Hyper-V, therefore, includes a software package called Guest Integration Services, which you can install on your VMs for compatibility purposes.

Some of the functions provided by the Guest Integration Services package are as follows:

- **Operating System Shutdown** Enables the Hyper-V Manager console to remotely shut down a guest OS in a controlled manner, eliminating the need for an administrator to log on and manually shut the system down.

- **Time Synchronization** Enables Hyper-V to synchronize the OS clocks in parent and child partitions.

- **Data Exchange** Enables the Windows OSs on the parent and child partitions to exchange information, such as OS version information and fully qualified domain names.

- **Heartbeat** Implements a service in which the parent partition sends regular heartbeat signals to the child partitions, which are expected to respond in kind. A failure of a child partition to respond indicates that the guest OS has frozen or malfunctioned.

- **Backup** Enables backup of Windows VMs by using Volume Shadow Copy Services.

- **Guest Services** Enables administrators to copy files to a virtual machine without using a network connection.

The Windows Server 2012, Windows Server R2, Windows 8, and Windows 8.1 operating systems have the latest Guest Integration Services software built in, so there is no need to install the package on VMs running those OSs as guests. Earlier versions of Windows have earlier versions of the Guest Integration Services package that need to be upgraded, however, and some Windows versions do not include the package at all.

> **NOTE** **LINUX**
>
> For Linux guest OSs, you must download and install the latest release of Linux Integration Services Version 3.4 for Hyper-V from the Microsoft Download Center. As of this writing, the latest version is 3.4 and is available at *http://www.microsoft.com/en-gb/download/details.aspx?id=34603*.

To upgrade Guest Integration Services on a Windows guest OS, use the following procedure:

1. In Server Manager, on the Tools menu, select Hyper-V Manager. The Hyper-V Manager console starts.

2. In the left pane, select a Hyper-V server.

3. In the Actions pane, start the VM on which you want to install Guest Integration Services and click Connect. A Virtual Machine Connection window opens.

4. In the Virtual Machine Connection window, from the Action menu, select Insert Integration Services Setup Disk. Hyper-V mounts an image of the Guest Integration Services disk to a virtual disk drive and an Autoplay window appears.

5. Click Install Hyper-V Integration Services. A message box appears, asking you to upgrade the existing installation.

6. Click OK. The system installs the package and prompts you to restart the computer.

7. Click Yes to restart the computer.

Once you have installed or upgraded Guest Integration Services, you can enable or disable each of the individual functions by opening the Settings dialog box for the VM and selecting the Integration Services page, as shown in Figure 3-13.

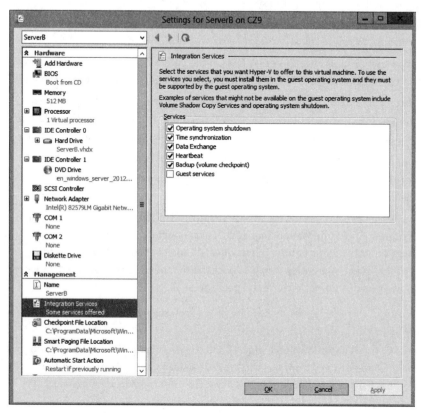

FIGURE 3-13 Integration Services settings for a VM

At this point, you are ready to configure and manage the VM just as if you were working on a physical server. This can include modifying the network configuration, enabling remote desktop, loading the appropriate roles and features, and installing applications.

Using Enhanced Session mode

In previous versions of Hyper-V, when you open a Virtual Machine Connection window in the Hyper-V Manager console, you receive mouse and keyboard connectivity plus a limited cut and paste functionality. To obtain any further access, such as audio or print functionality, you could establish a Remote Desktop Services connection to the VM, but this requires the computers to be connected to the same network, which is not always possible.

Starting in Windows Server 2012 R2, Hyper-V supports an enhanced session mode that enables the Virtual Machine Connection window to redirect any of the following local resources to VMs running Windows Server 2012 R2 or Windows 8.1:

- Display configuration
- Audio
- Printers
- Clipboard
- Smart cards
- USB devices
- Drives
- Supported Plug and Play devices

The enhanced session mode works by establishing a Remote Desktop Protocol connection between the host computer and the VM, but it does not require a standard network path because it uses VMBus instead. *VMBus* is a high-speed conduit between the various partitions running on a Hyper-V server.

Enhanced session mode is enabled by default in Windows 8.1, but in Windows Server 2012 R2, you must enable it on the Enhanced Session Mode Policy page of the Hyper-V Settings dialog box, as shown in Figure 3-14.

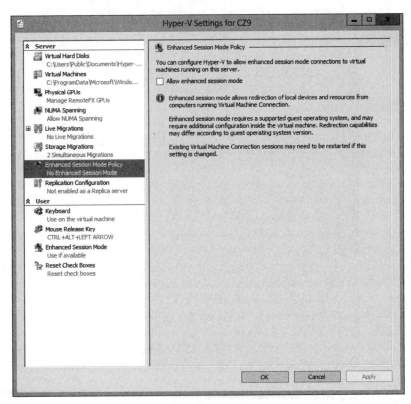

FIGURE 3-14 Enhanced Session Mode Policy settings

Allocating memory

Dynamic memory enables Hyper-V to adjust the amount of RAM allocated to VMs, depending on their ongoing requirements. Some computer components can be virtualized. You can take some disk space and create a virtual hard drive, and you can take an image file and create a virtual DVD drive. You can also create virtual network interface adapters and other components, which appear like the real thing in a VM. System memory is different, however. There is no substitute for memory, so all Hyper-V can do is take the physical memory installed in the computer and allocate it among the various VMs.

When you create a VM, you specify how much memory to allocate to the VM. Obviously, the amount of memory available for use is based on the physical memory installed in the computer.

After you have created the VM, you can modify the amount of memory allocated to it by shutting down the VM, opening its Settings dialog box, and changing the Startup RAM setting on the Memory page, as shown in Figure 3-15. This enables you to experiment with various amounts of memory, and set the optimum performance level for the system.

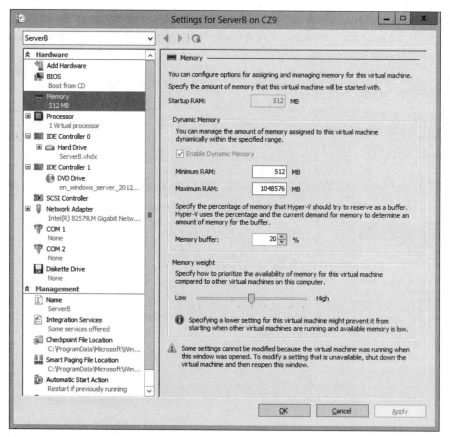

FIGURE 3-15 Memory settings for a VM

USING DYNAMIC MEMORY

In the first versions of Hyper-V, shutting down the VM was the only way to modify its memory allocation. In the Windows Server 2012 R2 version, however, you can use a feature called Dynamic Memory to automatically reallocate memory to the VM from a shared memory pool as its demands change. If a virtualized server starts to experience larger amounts of client traffic, for example, Hyper-V can increase the memory allocated to the system, and reduce it again when the traffic subsides.

To use Dynamic Memory, you must enable it by selecting the Enable Dynamic Memory check box on the VM's Memory settings page and then configure the following settings:

- **Startup RAM**   Specifies the amount of memory that you want to allocate to the VM when it starts. When you are using Dynamic Memory, this value can be the minimum amount of memory needed to boot the system.

- **Minimum RAM**   Specifies the smallest amount of memory the VM can use at any time. OSs can require more memory to start up than to run, so this value can be smaller than the Startup RAM value.

- **Maximum RAM**   Specifies the largest amount of memory that the VM can use at any time. The value can range from a low equal to the Startup RAM value to a high of 64 GB.

- **Memory Buffer**   Specifies a percentage that Hyper-V uses to calculate how much memory to allocate to the VM, compared to its actual utilization, as measured by performance counters. For example, with the Memory Buffer value set to 20 percent, a VM with applications and OS that consume 1 GB of memory will receive a dynamic allocation of 1.2 GB.

- **Memory Weight**   Specifies a relative value that specifies the priority of this VM compared to the other VMs on the same computer. When the physical memory in the computer is insufficient to allocate the full-buffered amount specified for each VM, the VMs with the highest Memory Weight settings receive priority.

> **NOTE   RAM**
>
> You can reduce the Minimum RAM, increase the Maximum RAM, or change the Memory Buffer value or the Memory Weight value at any time, but to enable or disable Dynamic Memory, you must shut down the VM.

In addition to configuring the VM settings, the guest VM must be running Windows Vista or later or Windows Server 2003 SP2 or later and have Windows Server 2012 R2 Guest Integration Services installed to use Dynamic Memory.

> **NOTE USING WINDOWS POWERSHELL**
>
> To configure the memory settings for a VM, use the Set-VMMemory cmdlet by using the following basic syntax:
>
> ```
> Set-VMMemory <VM name> -DynamicMemoryEnabled $true
> -MinimumBytes <memory> -StartupBytes <memory>
> -MaximumBytes <memory> -Priority <value> -Buffer <percentage>
> ```
>
> For example, to configure the memory settings for the VM ServerA, enabling Dynamic Memory and configuring values for all of its settings, use the following command:
>
> ```
> Set-VMMemory ServerA -DynamicMemoryEnabled $true
> -MinimumBytes 64MB
> ```

CONFIGURING SMART PAGING

Dynamic Memory was introduced in Windows Server 2008 R2 Hyper-V, but Windows Server 2012 R2 improves on the concept by adding the Minimum RAM setting. This makes it possible for Hyper-V to reduce the memory used by a VM to a level lower than that needed to start the system, reclaiming that memory for other uses.

The problem with having minimum RAM values that are lower than the startup RAM values is that it becomes possible to deplete the supply of physical memory with too many VMs running simultaneously at their minimum RAM values. If this occurs, a VM that has to restart might be unable to do so because there is not enough free memory to increase its memory allocation from its minimum RAM value to its startup RAM value.

To address this possibility, Hyper-V includes a feature called *smart paging*. If a VM has to restart and there is not enough memory available to allocate its startup RAM value, the system uses hard disk space to make up the difference and begins paging memory contents to disk.

Disk access rates are far slower than memory access rates, of course, so smart paging incurs a severe performance penalty, but the paging occurs only for as long as it takes to restart the VM and return it to its minimum RAM allocation.

Hyper-V only uses smart paging in specific conditions: when a VM must be restarted, there is no free memory available, and there are no other means available to free up the necessary memory.

You can select the Smart Paging File Location page in a VM's Setting dialog box to specify a location for the paging file. Selecting the fastest possible hard drive is recommended.

Configuring resource metering

Resource metering is a Windows PowerShell–based feature in Windows Server 2012 R2 Hyper-V that enables administrators to document VM usage by using a variety of criteria. There are various reasons why organizations might want to track the use of VMs. For large corporations, it might be a matter of internal accounting and controlling ongoing expenses, such as wide area network (WAN) bandwidth. For service providers, it might be necessary to bill customers based on the VM resources they use.

Resource metering uses Windows PowerShell cmdlets to track a variety of performance metrics for individual VMs, including the following:

- CPU utilization
- Minimum, maximum, and average memory utilization
- Disk space utilization
- Incoming and outgoing network traffic

Resource metering statistics remain consistent, even when you transfer VMs between host systems by using Live Migration or move VHD files between VMs.

To use resource metering, you must first enable it for the specific VM that you want to monitor by using the Enable-VMResourceMetering cmdlet with the following syntax:

```
Enable-VMResourceMetering –VMName <name>
```

Once you have enabled metering, you can display a statistical report at any time by using the Measure-VM cmdlet with the following syntax:

```
Measure-VM –VMName <name>
```

In addition to metering resources for entire VMs, administrators can also create resource pools that enable them to monitor specific VM components, such as processors, memory, network adapters, and VHDs. You create a resource pool by using the New-VMResourcePool cmdlet and then enable metering for the pool by using Enable-VMResourceMetering.

By using techniques such as pipelining, administrators can use the resource metering cmdlets to gather data on VM performance and export it to applications or data files.

 Thought experiment

Configuring virtual machine memory

In the following thought experiment, apply what you've learned about this objective to predict what steps you need to take. You can find answers to these questions in the "Answers" section at the end of this chapter.

Alice has a computer with 8 GB of memory installed and running Windows Server 2012 R2, which she has configured as a Hyper-V server. After creating eight VMs, each with a startup RAM value of 1,024 MB, Alice is having trouble getting all eight VMs to boot. What settings can she modify to resolve the problem without changing the startup RAM value?

Objective summary

- Virtualization is a process that adds a layer of abstraction between actual, physical hardware and the system making use of it. Instead of having the server access the computer's hardware directly, an intervening component called a hypervisor creates a VM environment, and the server OS runs in that environment.

- Virtualization is the process of deploying and maintaining multiple instances of an OS, called VMs, on a single computer.

- Microsoft Hyper-V is a hypervisor-based virtualization system for x64 computers starting with Windows Server 2008. The hypervisor is installed between the hardware and the OS and is the main component that manages the virtual computers.

- For licensing purposes, Microsoft refers to each VM that you create on a Hyper-V server as a virtual instance. Each Windows Server 2012 R2 version includes licenses for a set number of virtual instances; you must purchase additional licenses to license additional instances.

- To keep a small footprint and minimal overhead, Hyper-V Server contains only the Windows Hypervisor, Windows Server driver model, and virtualization components.

- Hyper-V in Windows Server 2012 R2 supports two types of VMs: Generation 1 and Generation 2. Generation 1 VMs are designed to emulate the hardware found in a typical computer and are compatible with previous versions of Hyper-V. Generation 2 VMs use synthetic drivers and software-based devices instead and can only run on the Windows Server 2012 R2 Hyper-V.

- Windows Server 2012 R2 Hyper-V supports an enhanced session mode that enables the Virtual Machine Connection window to redirect a variety of local resources to VMs running Windows Server 2012 R2 or Windows 8.1.

Objective review

Answer the following questions to test your knowledge of the information in this objective. You can find the answers to these questions and explanations of why each answer choice is correct or incorrect in the "Answers" section at the end of this chapter.

1. Which of the following statements about Type I and Type II virtualization are true? (Choose all that apply.)

    A. In Type I virtualization, the hypervisor runs on top of a host OS.

    B. In Type I virtualization, the hypervisor runs directly on the computer hardware.

    C. In Type II virtualization, the hypervisor runs on top of a host OS.

    D. In Type II virtualization, the hypervisor runs directly on the computer hardware.

2. Which of the following types of server virtualization provides the best performance for high-traffic servers in production environments?

   A. Type I virtualization

   B. Type II virtualization

   C. Presentation virtualization

   D. RemoteApp

3. Which of the following Microsoft operating systems includes a license that enables you to license an unlimited number of virtual instances?

   A. Hyper-V Server

   B. Windows Server 2012 R2 Datacenter

   C. Windows Server 2012 R2 Standard

   D. Windows Server 2012 R2 Foundation

4. Which of the following Hyper-V features make it possible for a VM to function with a minimum RAM value that is lower than the startup RAM value? (Choose all that apply.)

   A. Smart paging

   B. Dynamic Memory

   C. Memory Weight

   D. Guest Integration Services

5. When you install the Hyper-V role on a server running Windows Server 2012 R2, the instance of the OS on which you installed the role is converted to what system element?

   A. The hypervisor

   B. The Virtual Machine Monitor

   C. The parent partition

   D. A child partition

6. Which of the following statements about Generation 1 and Generation 2 virtual machines are true? (Choose all that apply.)

   A. You must create a Generation 1 VM before you can create a Generation 2 VM.

   B. Generation 2 VMs deploy faster than Generation 1 VMs.

   C. Generation 2 VMs only support Windows 8.1 and Windows Server 2012 R2 as guest operating systems.

   D. Generation 2 VMs use the same device drivers as Generation 1 VMs.

Objective 3.2: Create and configure virtual machine storage

When you create a VM in Windows Server 2012 R2 Hyper-V, you emulate all the components that you typically find in a physical computer. When you virtualize memory, as discussed in Objective 3.1, "Create and configure virtual machine settings," you take a portion of the physical memory in the computer and dedicate it to a VM. The same is true with hard disk space. Hyper-V uses a specialized VHD format to package part of the space on a physical disk and make it appear to the VM as though it is a physical hard disk drive.

When you create a new Generation 1 VM in Hyper-V, the wizard creates a virtual storage subsystem that consists of two Integrated Drive Electronics (IDE) controllers and one Small Computer Systems Interface (SCSI) controller. The IDE controllers host the VM's system drive and its DVD drive. Like their physical equivalents, each IDE controller can host two devices, so you can create two additional virtual drives and add them to the system.

The SCSI controller in the default Generation 1 VM configuration is unpopulated, and you can create additional drives and add them to that controller to provide the VM with additional storage. In a Generation 2 VM, the system and DVD drives are connected to the default SCSI controller and there is no IDE alternative.

In a VM of either generation, you can also create additional SCSI controllers and add drives to them. By creating multiple drives and controllers, Hyper-V makes it possible to construct virtual storage subsystems that emulate almost any physical storage solution you might devise.

> **This objective covers how to:**
> - Create VHDs and VHDX
> - Configure differencing drives
> - Modify VHDs
> - Configure pass-through disks
> - Manage checkpoints
> - Implement a virtual Fibre Channel adapter
> - Configure storage Quality of Service (QoS)

Virtual disk formats

Windows Server 2012 R2 Hyper-V supports the original VHD disk image file and the new VHDX format. The original VHD format was created by a company called Connectix for its Virtual PC product. Microsoft later acquired the product and used the VHD format for all its subsequent virtualization products, including Hyper-V. There are three types of VHD files, as follows:

- **Fixed hard disk image**   An image file of a specified size in which all the disk space required to create the image is allocated during its creation. Fixed disk images can be wasteful in terms of storage because they can contain large amounts of empty space, but they are also efficient from a performance standpoint because there is no overhead due to dynamic expansion.

- **Dynamic hard disk image**   An image file with a specified maximum size, which starts small and expands as needed to accommodate the data the system writes to it. This option conserves disk space but can negatively affect performance.

- **Differencing hard disk image**   A child image file associated with a specific parent image. The system writes all changes made to the data on the parent image file to the child image, to manage disk space or to facilitate a rollback at a later time.

VHD images are limited to maximum size of 2 TB and are compatible with all versions of Hyper-V and Microsoft Type II hypervisor products, such as Virtual Server and Virtual PC. Windows Server 2012 introduced an updated version of the format, which uses a VHDX filename extension.

VHDX image files can be as large as 64 TB, and they also support 4-KB logical sector sizes to provide compatibility with new 4-KB native drives. VHDX files can also use larger block sizes (up to 256 MB), which enable administrators to fine-tune the performance level of a virtual storage subsystem to accommodate specific applications and data file types. However, VHDX files are not backward compatible and can only be read by Windows Server 2012, Windows Server 2012 R2, Windows 8, and Windows 8.1 Hyper-V servers. If migrating your VMs from Windows Server 2012 R2 to an older version of Hyper-V is even a remote possibility, you should continue using the VHD file format.

Creating virtual disks

Windows Server 2012 R2 Hyper-V provides several ways to create virtual disk files. You can create them as part of a VM or create them at another time and add them to a VM. The graphical interface in Hyper-V Manager provides access to most of the VHD parameters, but the Windows PowerShell cmdlets included in Windows Server 2012 R2 provide the most granular control over the disk image format.

Creating a virtual disk with a VM

The New Virtual Machine Wizard includes a Connect Virtual Hard Disk page with which you can add a single disk to your new VM. The options for this disk are relatively limited and consist of the following:

- **Create A Virtual Hard Disk**   Enables you to specify the name, location, and size of a new VHD. The wizard only allows you to create a dynamically expanding disk using the VHDX format, but you can also create fixed and differencing VHDX disks using Windows PowerShell.

- **Use An Existing Virtual Hard Disk**   Enables you to specify the location of an existing VHD or VHDX disk, which the VM will presumably use as its system disk.
- **Attach A Virtual Hard Disk Later**   Prevents the wizard from adding any virtual disks to the VM configuration. The assumption is that you will manually add a disk later, before you start the VM.

The object of this wizard page is to create the disk on which you will install the VM's OS or to select an existing disk on which an OS is already installed. The disk the wizard creates is always a dynamically expanding one connected to IDE Controller 0 on a Generation 1 VM or connected to the SCSI Controller on a Generation 2 VM.

> **NOTE VHDS**
>
> It has become a common practice for Microsoft to release evaluation copies of its products as preinstalled VHD files as an alternative to the traditional installable disk images. After downloading one of these files, you can create a VM on a Hyper-V server and select the Use An Existing Virtual Hard Disk option to mount the VHD as its system drive.

Creating a new virtual disk

You can create a VHD file at any time without adding it to a VM by using the New Virtual Hard Disk Wizard in Hyper-V Manager. To create a new virtual disk, use the following procedure.

1.   In Server Manager, on the Tools menu, select Hyper-V Manager. The Hyper-V Manager console opens.

2.   In the left pane, select a Hyper-V server.

3.   From the Action menu, select New, Hard Disk to start the New Virtual Hard Disk Wizard, displaying the Before You Begin page.

4.   Click Next to open the Choose Disk Format page.

5.   Select one of the following disk format options:
     - **VHD**   Creates an image no larger than 2 TB, using the highly compatible VHD format
     - **VHDX**   Creates an image up to 64 TB, using the new VHDX format

6.   Click Next to open the Choose Disk Type page.

7.   Select one of the following disk type options:
     - **Fixed Size**   Creates a disk of a specific size, allocating all of the space at once
     - **Dynamically Expanding**   Creates a disk that can grow to the maximum size you specify as you add data
     - **Differencing**   Creates a child drive that will contain changes made to a specified parent drive

8. Click Next. The Specify Name And Location page opens.

9. Specify a file name for the disk image in the Name text box and, if desired, specify a location for the file other than the server default. Click Next to open the Configure Disk page.

10. For fixed and dynamically expanding disks, select and configure one of the following options:

   ■ **Create A New Blank Virtual Hard Disk**   Specifies the size (or the maximum size) of the disk image file to create

   ■ **Copy The Contents Of The Specified Physical Disk**   Enables you to select one of the physical hard disks in the computer and copy its contents to the new disk image

   ■ **Copy The Contents Of The Specified Virtual Hard Disk**   Enables you to select an existing virtual disk file and copy its contents to the new disk image

11. Click Next. The Completing The New Virtual Hard Disk Wizard page opens.

12. Click Finish.

The wizard creates the new image disk and saves it to the specified location.

NOTE **USING WINDOWS POWERSHELL**

You can create new VHD files by using Windows PowerShell, which gives you more control than is available through the graphical interface. To create a new disk image, use the New-VHD cmdlet with the following basic syntax:

```
New-VHD -Path c:\filename.vhd|c:\filename.vhdx
-Fixed|-Dynamic|-Differencing -SizeBytes <size>
[-BlockSizeBytes <block size>]
[-LogicalSectorSizeBytes 512|4096] [-ParentPath <pathname>]
```

When using the cmdlet to create a disk image, the extension you specify for the filename determines the format (VHD or VHDX); also, you can specify the block size and the logical sector size for the image, two things you cannot do in the GUI. For example, the following command creates a 400-GB fixed VHDX image file with a logical sector size of 4 KB:

```
New-VHD -Path c:\diskfile.vhdx -Fixed
-SizeBytes 400GB -LogicalSectorSizeBytes 4096
```

Adding virtual disks to virtual machines

Creating virtual disk image files as a separate process enables administrators to exercise more control over their capabilities, but after creating the VHD or VHDX files, you must add them to a VM for them to be useful.

To add a hard disk drive to a physical computer, you must connect it to a controller; the same is true with a VM in Hyper-V. When you open the Settings dialog box for a Generation 1 VM in its default configuration, you see three controllers labeled IDE Controller 0, IDE Controller 1, and SCSI Controller. These correspond to the controllers you might find in a typical physical server computer.

Each IDE controller can support two devices and the default VM configuration uses one channel on IDE Controller 0 for the system hard disk and one channel on IDE controller 1 for the system's DVD drive. If you did not create a virtual disk as part of the new Virtual Machine Wizard—that is, if you chose the Attach A Virtual Hard Disk Later option—then you must add a hard disk image to IDE Controller 0 to use as a system drive. A Generation 1 VM cannot boot from the SCSI controller.

To add an existing virtual system drive to a VM, use the following procedure.

1. In Server Manager, on the Tools menu, select Hyper-V Manager to open the Hyper-V Manager console.

2. In the left pane, select a Hyper-V server.

3. Select a VM and, in the Actions pane, select Settings. The Settings dialog box for the VM appears.

4. Select IDE Controller 0, as shown in Figure 3-16.

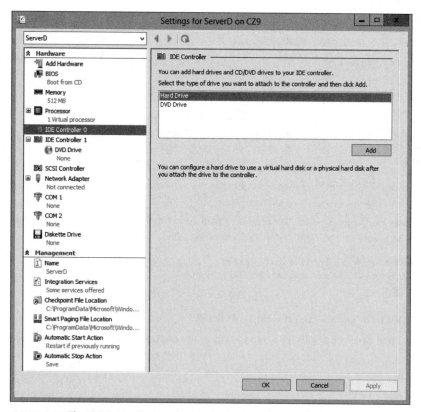

FIGURE 3-16 The IDE Controller interface in the Settings dialog box

5. In the IDE Controller box, select Hard Drive and click Add. The Hard Drive page opens, as shown in Figure 3-17.

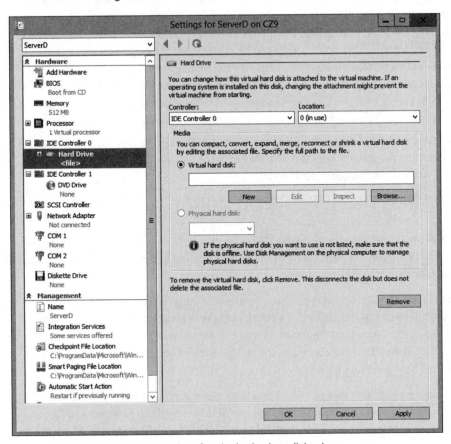

FIGURE 3-17 The Hard Drive interface in the Settings dialog box

6. In the Controller drop-down and the Location drop-down, select the IDE controller and the channel you want to use for the hard disk.

7. With the Virtual Hard Disk option selected, click Browse and select the disk image file you want to add.

8. Click OK to close the Settings dialog box.

Although you cannot use a SCSI drive as the system disk in a Generation 1 VM, you can add virtual data disks to the SCSI controller. In Generation 2 VMs, you must create a SCSI system disk to boot the machine. . Unlike the IDE connectors, which support only two devices each, a SCSI connector in Hyper-V can support up to 64 drives. You can also add multiple SCSI controllers to a VM, providing almost unlimited scalability for your virtual storage subsystem.

Creating differencing disks

A 1differencing disk enables you to preserve an existing virtual disk image file in its original state while mounting it in an operating system and even modifying its contents. For example, when building a laboratory setup, you can create a baseline system by installing a clean copy of an OS on a new virtual disk and configuring the environment to fit your needs. Then you can create a new child-differencing disk using your baseline image as the parent. All subsequent changes you make to the system will then be written to the differencing disk while the parent remains untouched. You can experiment on the test system as you wish, knowing that you can revert to your baseline configuration by just creating a new differencing disk.

You can create multiple differencing disks that point to the same parent image, enabling you to populate a lab network with as many VMs as you need, which saves disk space and eliminates the need to repeatedly install the OS.

To create a cloned version of a baseline installation with a differencing disk, use the following procedure.

1. **Install and configure the baseline VM**   Create a new VM with a new disk image file and install a guest OS on it. Configure the OS as needed and install any roles, features, applications, or services you need.

2. **Generalize the parent image**   Open an elevated command prompt on the baseline system and run the Sysprep.exe utility with the appropriate parameters for your requirements. Sysprep configures the system to assign itself a new, unique security ID (SID) the next time the computer starts. This enables you to create multiple cloned systems from a single disk image.

3. **Create a parent disk image**   Once you have generalized the baseline installation, you no longer need the original VM. You can delete everything except the VHD or VHDX file containing the disk image. This will become your parent image. Open the Properties sheet for the image file and set the read-only flag to ensure that the baseline does not change.

4. **Create a differencing disk**   By using the New Virtual Hard Disk Wizard or the New-VHD cmdlet for Windows PowerShell, create a new differencing disk pointing to the baseline image you created and prepared earlier as the parent image.

5. **Create a cloned VM**   Create a new VM and, on the Connect Virtual Hard Disk page, attach the differencing disk you just created to it by using the Use An Existing Virtual Hard Disk option.

You can then proceed to create additional cloned VMs with differencing disks that all use the same parent. Each one can function independently and the parent disk will remain unchanged.

When you create a differencing drive by using the New Virtual Hard Disk Wizard, selecting the Differencing option on the Choose Disk Type page causes the Configure Disk page to appear as shown in Figure 3-18. In the Location text box, specify the name of the file that you want to use as the parent image.

In the same way, if you create the differencing disk by using Windows PowerShell, you must run the New-VHD cmdlet with the –Differencing parameter and the –ParentPath parameter, specifying the location of the parent disk.

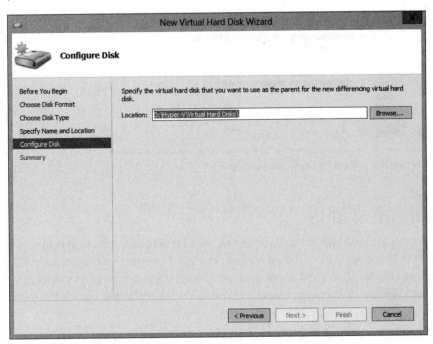

FIGURE 3-18 The Configure Disk page in the New Virtual Hard Disk Wizard

Configuring pass-through disks

This objective has thus far been concerned primarily with VHDs, areas of space on a physical disk drive allocated for use by VMs. However, it is also possible for VMs to access physical disks directly.

A pass-through disk is a type of virtual disk that points to a physical disk drive installed on the host computer. When you add a hard drive to any of the controllers in a VM, you have the option of selecting a physical hard disk as opposed to a virtual one.

To add a physical hard disk to a VM, the VM must have exclusive access to it. This means that you must first take the disk offline in the parent OS by using the Disk Management snap-in, as shown in Figure 3-19, or the Diskpart.exe utility. Once the disk is offline, it will be available for selection in the Physical Hard Disk drop-down list.

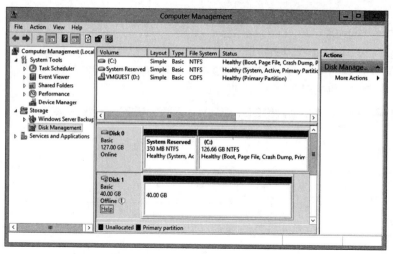

FIGURE 3-19 An offline disk in the Disk Management snap-in

Modifying virtual disks

Windows Server 2012 R2 and Hyper-V provide several ways for administrators to manage and manipulate VHD images without mounting them in a VM. Once you have created a VHD, whether you have attached it to a VM or not, you can manage it by using the Edit Virtual Hard Disk Wizard in Hyper-V Manager. To edit an existing VHD or VHDX file, use the following procedure.

1. In Server Manager, on the Tools menu, select Hyper-V Manager to open the Hyper-V Manager console.

2. In the left pane, select a Hyper-V server.

3. In the Actions pane, select Edit Disk. The Edit Virtual Hard Disk Wizard starts, displaying the Before You Begin page.

4. Click Next to open the Locate Disk page.

5. Type or browse to the name of the VHD or VHDX file you want to open and click Next. The Choose Action page appears.

6. Select one of the following functions:

   - **Compact**   Reduces the size of a dynamically expanding or differencing disk by deleting empty space while leaving the disk's capacity unchanged

   - **Convert**   Changes the type of format of a disk by copying the data to a new disk image file

   - **Expand**   Increases the capacity of the disk by adding empty storage space to the image file

- **Shrink** Reduces the capacity of the disk by deleting empty storage space from the file

- **Merge** Combines the data on a differencing disk with that of the parent disk to form a single composite image file

7. Click Next to open the Completing The Edit Virtual Hard Disk Wizard page.

8. Complete any new pages presented by the wizard as a result of your selection and click Finish.

The options that appear on the wizard's Choose Action page depend on the current status of the image file you select. For example, the Merge option only appears if you choose a differencing disk, and the Shrink option does not appear unless there is free space in the file that the wizard can delete.

In addition to these disk-editing functions provided by Hyper-V Manager, it is possible to use the Disk Management snap-in on the Hyper-V host to mount a VHD or VHDX file as a drive and access its contents, just as if it were a physical disk.

To mount a VHD file, use the following procedure.

1. In Server Manager, on the Tools menu, select Computer Management to open the Computer Management console.

2. In the left pane, select Disk Management. The Disk Management snap-in opens.

3. From the Action menu, select Attach VHD. The Attach Virtual Hard Disk dialog box appears.

4. In the Location text box, type or browse to the image disk file you want to attach and click OK. The disk appears in the Disk Management interface.

5. Close the Computer Management console.

At this point, you can work with the virtual disk and its contents using any standard tools, just as you would a physical hard disk drive. To detach the VHD, you use the same procedure and select Detach VHD from the Action menu.

Creating checkpoints

In Hyper-V, a *checkpoint* is a captured image of the state, data, and hardware configuration of a VM at a particular moment in time. Creating checkpoints is a convenient way for administrators to revert a VM to a previous state at will. For example, if you create a checkpoint just before applying a system update, and the update is somehow problematic, you can apply the checkpoint and return the VM to the state in which it was before you applied the update.

EXAM TIP

Prior to Windows Server 2012 R2, the checkpoints in Hyper-V were known as snapshots. Checkpoints function in exactly the same way as snapshots; only the name is changed. You can expect to see either term on the 70-410 exam.

Creating a checkpoint is as simple as selecting a running VM in Hyper-V Manager and selecting Checkpoint from the Actions pane. The system creates a checkpoint file with an AVHD or AVHDX extension, in the same folder as the VHD file, and adds the checkpoint to the Hyper-V Manager display, as shown in Figure 3-20.

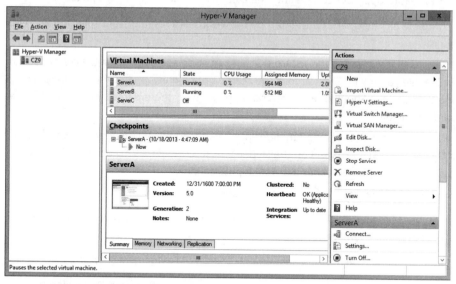

FIGURE 3-20 A checkpoint in Hyper-V Manager

Checkpoints are a useful tool for administrators implementing a test environment in Hyper-V, but they are not recommended for heavy use in production environments. In addition to consuming disk space, the presence of checkpoints can reduce the overall per-formance of a VM's disk subsystem. Administrators also should not use checkpoints on VMs containing databases—such as those created by SQL Server, Exchange, or Windows domain controllers—because the checkpointing process does not account for the current state of the database, and corruption might occur.

Configuring Storage Quality of Service (QoS)

Because it is common for there to be more than one virtual hard disk hosted by a single physical hard disk, it is possible for one virtual disk to monopolize the input/output capacity of a physical disk, causing the other virtual disks to slow down. To help prevent this, Windows Server 2012 R2 enables you to control the *Quality of Service (QoS)* for a given virtual hard disk.

QoS management in Hyper-V takes the form of controls that enables you to specify the minimum and maximum input/output operations per second (IOPS) for a disk. To configure storage QoS, open the Settings dialog box for a VM, expand a hard drive component, and select Advanced Features to display the Advanced Features page shown in Figure 3-21.

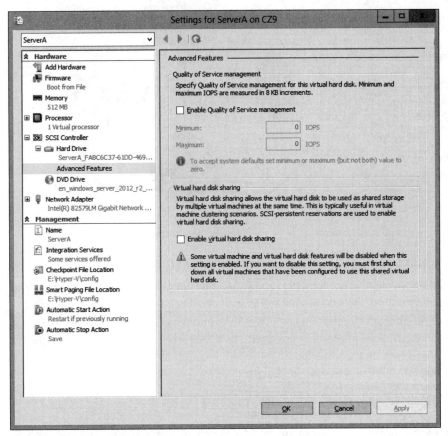

FIGURE 3-21 Storage Quality of Service controls in Hyper-V Manager

After selecting the Enable Quality of Service Management check box, you can specify Minimum IOPS values and Maximum IOPS values for the disk in 8 KB increments.

Connecting to a storage area network (SAN)

At its most basic level, a *storage area network (SAN)* is simply a network dedicated to high-speed connections between servers and storage devices. Instead of installing disk drives into servers or connecting them by using an external SCSI bus, a SAN consists of one or more drive arrays equipped with network interface adapters, which you connect to your servers by using standard twisted pair or fiber optic network cables. A SAN-connected server, therefore, typically has at least two network adapters, one for the standard local area network (LAN) connection and one for the SAN, as shown in Figure 3-22.

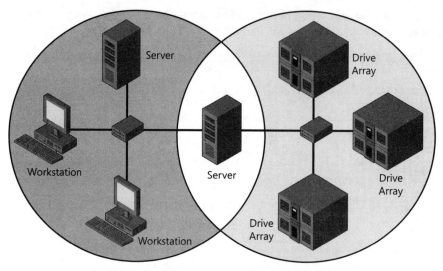

FIGURE 3-22 A server connected to a SAN

The advantages of SANs are many. By connecting the storage devices to a network instead of to the servers themselves, you avoid the limitations imposed by the maximum number of devices you can connect directly to a computer. SANs also provide added flexibility in their communications capabilities. Because any device on a SAN can conceivably communicate with any other device on the same SAN, high-speed data transfers can occur in any of the following ways:

- **Server to storage**   Servers can access storage devices over the SAN just as if they were connected directly to the computer.
- **Server to server**   Servers can use the SAN to communicate directly with one another at high speeds to avoid flooding the LAN with traffic.
- **Storage to storage**   Storage devices can communicate among themselves without server intervention, for example, to perform backups from one medium to another or to mirror drives on different arrays.

Although a SAN is not in itself a high-availability technology, you can make it one by connecting redundant servers to the same network, as shown in Figure 3-23, enabling them to access the same data storage devices. If one server should fail, another can assume its roles by accessing the same data. This is called *server clustering*.

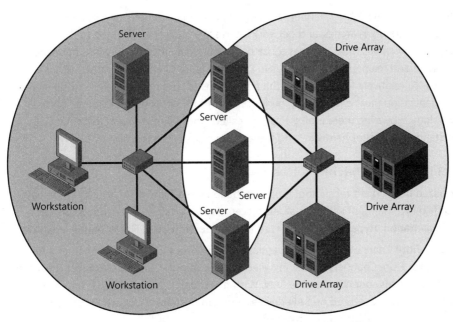

FIGURE 3-23 Multiple servers connected to a SAN

Because they use standard networking technologies, SANs can also greatly extend the distances between servers and storage devices. You can design a SAN that spans different rooms, different floors, or even different buildings, just as you would a standard computer network.

Servers and storage devices cannot exchange SCSI commands over a SAN connection the way they do when the devices are directly connected using a SCSI cable. To communicate over a SAN, servers and storage devices map their SCSI communications onto another protocol, such as Fibre Channel.

Using Fibre Channel

Fibre Channel is a versatile SAN communications technology supporting various network media, transmission speeds, topologies, and upper-level protocols. Its primary disadvantage is that it requires specialized hardware that can be extremely expensive.

> **MORE INFORMATION** **FIBRE CHANNEL**
>
> The nonstandard spelling of the word *fibre* in Fibre Channel is deliberate, to distinguish the term from fiber optic. Fibre Channel can run on either twisted-pair copper cables or it can run on optical cables, whereas the spelling *fiber* always refers to an optical medium.

Installing a traditional Fibre Channel SAN entails building an entirely new network with its own special medium, switches, and network interface adapters. In addition to the hardware costs, which can easily be 10 times those of a traditional Ethernet network, there are also installation and maintenance expenses to consider. Fibre Channel is a rather esoteric technology, with relatively few experts in the field. To install and maintain a Fibre Channel SAN, an organization must either hire experienced staff or train existing personnel on the new technology. However, there is also a variant called Fibre Channel over Ethernet (FCoE) that uses standard Ethernet hardware and is therefore much less expensive.

Connecting virtual machines to a SAN

The specialized networking technologies used to build Fibre Channel SANs have, in the past, made it difficult to use them with virtualized servers. However, since the Windows Server 2012 implementation, Hyper-V has supported the creation of virtual Fibre Channel adapters.

A Hyper-V Fibre Channel adapter is essentially a pass-through device that enables a VM to access a physical Fibre Channel adapter installed in the computer, and through that, to access the external resources connected to the SAN. With this capability, applications running on VMs can access data files stored on SAN devices and administrators can use VMs to create server clusters with shared storage subsystems.

To support virtual Fibre Channel connectivity, the physical Fibre Channel host bus adapter(s) in the host computer must have drivers that explicitly support virtual Fibre Channel. This support is relatively rare, but more manufacturers are expected to update their drivers to provide the necessary support. Your SAN must also be able to address its connected resources by using logical unit numbers (LUNs).

Assuming you have the appropriate hardware and software installed on the host computer, you implement the Fibre Channel capabilities in Hyper-V by first creating a virtual SAN by using the Virtual SAN Manager, accessible from Hyper-V Manager. When you create the virtual SAN, the World Wide Node Names (WWNNs) and World Wide Port Names (WWPNs) of your host bus adapter appear, as shown in Figure 3-24.

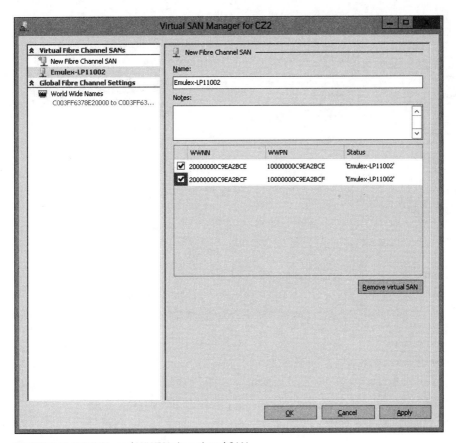

FIGURE 3-24 WWNNs and WWPNs in a virtual SAN

The next step is to add a Fibre Channel adapter to a VM from the Add Hardware page in the Settings dialog box. When you do this, the virtual SAN you created earlier is available on the Fibre Channel Adapter page, shown in Figure 3-25. Hyper-V virtualizes the SAN and makes the WWNNs and WWPNs available to the VM.

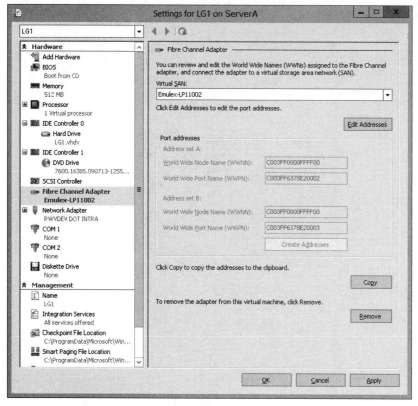

FIGURE 3-25 A Fibre Channel adapter in a VM

Thought experiment
Creating a VHD

In the following thought experiment, apply what you've learned about this objective to predict what steps you need to take. You can find answers to these questions in the "Answers" section at the end of this chapter.

Ed wants to create a new VHD file on his Hyper-V server by using Windows Power-Shell. He runs the Get-Disk cmdlet and receives the following results:

Number	Friendly Name		Operational Status	Total Size	Partition Style
0	WDC	WD5003ABYX-18WERA0	Online	465.76 GB	MBR
1	WDC	WD1002FAEX-00Z3A0	Online	931.51 GB	GPT

What command should Ed use to create a new 500-GB fixed VHD for his Server A VM, in the Windows Server 2012 R2 format, using data from the 465-GB drive on his computer, and a 4,096-byte sector size?

Objective summary

- Hyper-V uses a specialized VHD format to package part of the space on a physical disk and make it appear to the VM as though it is a physical hard disk drive.
- A dynamic hard disk image is an image file with a specified maximum size, which starts small and expands as needed to accommodate the data the system writes to it.
- A differencing hard disk image is a child image file associated with a specific parent image. The system writes all changes made to the operating system to the child image, to facilitate a rollback at a later time.
- VHDX image files in Windows Server 2012 R2 can be as large as 64 TB, and they also support 4-KB logical sector sizes to provide compatibility with new 4-KB native drives.
- A pass-through disk is a type of virtual disk that points to a physical disk drive installed on the host computer.
- In Hyper-V, a checkpoint is a captured image of the state, data, and hardware configuration of a VM at a particular moment in time.
- QoS management in Hyper-V takes the form of controls that enable you to specify the minimum and maximum input/output operations per second (IOPS) for a disk.
- The specialized networking technologies used to build Fibre Channel SANs have, in the past, made it difficult to use them with virtualized servers. However, Windows Server 2012 R2 Hyper-V supports the creation of virtual Fibre Channel adapters.

Objective review

Answer the following questions to test your knowledge of the information in this objective. You can find the answers to these questions and explanations of why each answer choice is correct or incorrect in the "Answers" section at the end of this chapter.

1. Which of the following statements about VHDX files is *not* true?

   A. VHDX files can be as large as 64 TB.

   B. VHDX files can only be opened by computers running Windows Server 2012 and Windows Server 2012 R2.

   C. VHDX files support larger block sizes than VHD files.

   D. VHDX files support 4-KB logical sectors.

2. Which of the following must be true about a pass-through disk?

   A. A pass-through disk must be offline in the guest OS that will access it.

   B. A pass-through disk must be offline in the parent partition of the Hyper-V server.

   C. A pass-through disk can only be connected to a SCSI controller.

   D. A pass-through disk must be added to a VM with the Disk Management snap-in.

3. The Merge function only appears in the Edit Virtual Hard Disk Wizard under which of the following conditions?

   A. When you select a VHDX file for editing

   B. When you select two or more disks for editing

   C. When you select a disk with free space available in it

   D. When you select a differencing disk for editing

4. Which of the following are valid reasons *not* to take checkpoints of VMs? (Choose all that apply.)

   A. Checkpoints can consume a large amount of disk space.

   B. Each checkpoint requires a separate copy of the VM's memory allocation.

   C. Each checkpoint can take several hours to create.

   D. The existence of checkpoints slows down VM performance.

5. Which of the following is *not* required to add a Fibre Channel adapter to a Hyper-V VM?

   A. You must create a Fibre Channel virtual SAN.

   B. You must have a physical Fibre Channel adapter installed in the host computer.

   C. You must have a Fibre Channel adapter driver that supports virtual networking.

   D. You must have a SCSI cable connecting the Fibre Channel adapter to the storage devices.

Objective 3.3: Create and configure virtual networks

Networking is a critical part of creating a VM infrastructure. Depending on your network plan, the VMs you create on a Windows Server 2012 R2 Hyper-V server can require communication with other VMs, with the computers on your physical network, and with the Internet.

When you build a network out of physical computers, you install a network interface adapter in each one and connect it to a hardware switch. The same principle is true in a Hyper-V environment, except that you use virtual components instead of physical ones. Each VM you create has at least one virtual network adapter and you can connect that adapter to a virtual switch. This enables you to connect the VMs on your Hyper-V server in various network configurations that either include or exclude the systems on your physical network.

You can create multiple virtual switches on a Hyper-V server and multiple network adapters in each VM. This enables you to create a flexible networking environment that is suitable for anything from a laboratory or classroom network to a production environment. In addition, Windows Server 2012 R2 has added the ability to create extensions for virtual switches so that software developers can enhance their capabilities.

Creating virtual switches

A *virtual switch*, like its physical counterpart, is a device that functions at Layer 2 of the Open Systems Interconnect (OSI) reference model. A switch has a series of ports, each of which is connected to a computer's network interface adapter. Any computer connected to the switch can transmit data to any other computer connected to the same switch.

Unlike physical switches, the virtual switches created by Hyper-V can have an unlimited number of ports, so administrators don't have to be concerned about connecting switches together or about uplinks and crossover circuits.

Creating the default virtual switch

The Windows Server 2012 R2 Add Roles and Features Wizard provides the opportunity to create virtual switches when you install the Hyper-V role. When you install Hyper-V on a server running Windows Server 2012 R2, the Create Virtual Switches page provides you with the opportunity to create a virtual switch for each of the physical network adapters installed in the host computer. These switches enable VMs to participate on the networks to which the physical adapters are connected.

When you create a virtual switch, the networking configuration in the host OS on the parent partition changes. The new virtual switch appears in the Network Connections window, and if you examine its properties, you can see that the switch is bound to the operating system's TCP/IP client, as shown in Figure 3-26.

Meanwhile, Hyper-V also changes the properties of original network connection representing the physical network interface adapter in the computer. The physical network adapter is now bound only to the virtual switch, as shown in Figure 3-27.

As a result, the computer's physical network configuration, in which its network adapter is connected to an external physical switch, is overlaid by the virtual network configuration created by Hyper-V. In this virtual configuration, the virtual switch is connected to the physical switch and the network adapter in the host OS is connected to the virtual switch. The internal virtual network and the external physical network are joined into a single LAN, just as if you connected two physical switches.

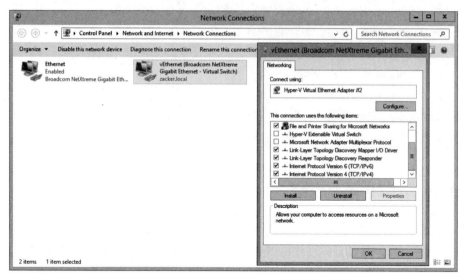

FIGURE 3-26 A virtual switch and its properties, displayed in the host OS

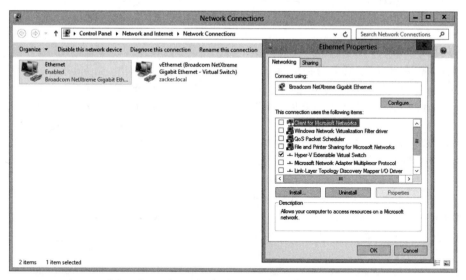

FIGURE 3-27 A network interface adapter in the host OS, bound to a virtual switch

Once Hyper-V has created the virtual switch and made these configuration changes, any new VMs that administrators choose to connect to the virtual switch become part of this conjoined network, as do any physical computers connected to the physical network through an external switch.

This type of virtual switch is, in Hyper-V terminology, an external network switch because it provides connections external to the Hyper-V environment. This is typically the preferred arrangement for a production network in which Hyper-V VMs provide and consume services for the entire network.

For example, a VM connected to this switch will automatically obtain an IP address from a Dynamic Host Configuration Protocol (DHCP) server on the physical network, if there is one. As an alternative, you could configure a VM as a DHCP server and let it provide addresses to all of the systems on the network, virtual or physical.

Perhaps more important, this arrangement can also enable your VMs to access the Internet by using the router and DNS servers on the external network. The VMs can then download OS updates from servers on the Internet, just as external machines often do.

There are situations in which this type of virtual switch is inappropriate. If you are creating a laboratory network for product testing or a classroom network, you might not want it to be accessible to or from the external network. In these cases, you must create a different type of virtual switch by using the Virtual Switch Manager in Hyper-V Manager.

Creating a new virtual switch

Hyper-V in Windows Server 2012 R2 supports three types of switches, which you must create in the Virtual Switch Manager before you can connect VMs to them.

To create a new virtual switch, use the following procedure.

1. In Server Manager, on the Tools menu, select Hyper-V Manager to open the Hyper-V Manager console.

2. In the left pane, select a Hyper-V server.

3. From the Actions pane, select Virtual Switch Manager. The Virtual Switch Manager dialog box for the Hyper-V server opens, as shown in Figure 3-28.

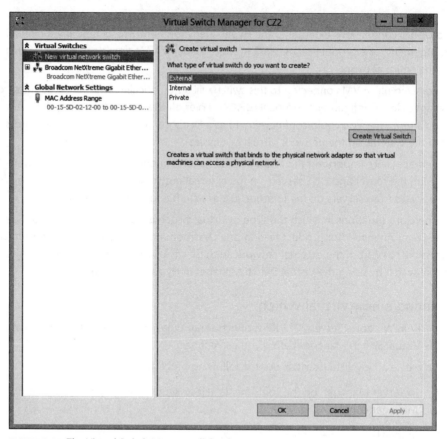

FIGURE 3-28 The Virtual Switch Manager dialog box

4. In the Create Virtual Switch section, select one of the following switch types:

- **External** The virtual switch is bound to the networking protocol stack in the host OS and connected to a physical network interface adapter in the Hyper-V server. VMs running on the server's parent and child partitions can all access the physical network to which the physical adapter is connected.

- **Internal** An internal network switch is bound to a separate instance of the networking protocol stack in the host OS, independent from the physical network interface adapter and its connected network. VMs running on the server's parent and child partitions can all access the virtual network implemented by the virtual switch; the host OS on the parent partition can access the physical network through the physical network interface adapter, but the VMs on the child partitions cannot access the physical network through the physical adapter.

- **Private** A private network switch exists only in the Hyper-V server and is accessible only to the VMs running on the child partitions. The host OS on the parent partition can access the physical network through the physical network interface adapter, but it cannot access the virtual network created by the virtual switch.

5. Click Create Virtual Switch to open the Virtual Switch Properties page.

6. Configure the following options, if desired:

   - **Allow Management Operating System To Share This Network Adapter**   Selected by default when you create an external virtual switch, clearing this check box excludes the host OS from the physical network while allowing access to the child VMs.

   - **Enable Single Root I/O Virtualization (SR-IOV)**   Enables you to create an external virtual switch that is associated with a physical network adapter capable of supporting SR-IOV. This option is only available when creating a new virtual switch; you cannot modify an existing virtual switch to use this option.

   - **Enable Virtual LAN Identification For Management Operating System**   If your host computer is connected to a physical switching infrastructure that uses virtual LANs (VLANs) to create separate subnets, you can select this check box and enter a VLAN identifier to associate the virtual switch with a particular VLAN on your physical network.

7. Click OK. The new virtual switch appears in the left pane, in the list of virtual switches.

You can create additional virtual switches as needed. You can create only one external switch for each physical network adapter in the computer, but you can create multiple internal or private switches to create as many virtual networks as you need.

> ***NOTE*   USING WINDOWS POWERSHELL**
>
> To create a new virtual switch by using Windows PowerShell, use the New-VMSwitch cmdlet with the following basic syntax:
>
> ```
> New-VMSwitch <switch name> -NetAdapterName <adapter name>
> [-SwitchType Internal|Private]
> ```
>
> For example, to create an external switch called LAN Switch, you would use the following command:
>
> ```
> New-VMSwitch "LAN Switch" -NetAdapterName "Ethernet"
> ```

Configuring MAC addresses

Every network interface adapter has a *Media Access Control (MAC) address*—sometimes called a hardware address—that uniquely identifies the device on the network. On physical network adapters, the MAC is assigned by the manufacturer and permanently entered in the adapter's firmware. The MAC address is a 6-byte hexadecimal value, the first three bytes of which are an organizationally unique identifier (OUI) that specifies the manufacturer, and the last three bytes of which identify the adapter itself.

The MAC address is essential to the operation of a LAN, so the virtual network adapters on a Hyper-V server need to have them. The server has at least one real MAC address, provided in its physical network adapter, but Hyper-V cannot use that one address for all the virtual adapters connecting VMs to the network.

Instead, Hyper-V creates a pool of MAC addresses during the installation of the role and it assigns addresses from this pool to VMs as you create them. To view or modify the MAC address pool for the Hyper-V server, you open the Virtual Switch Manager and, under Global Network Settings, select MAC Address Range, as shown in Figure 3-29.

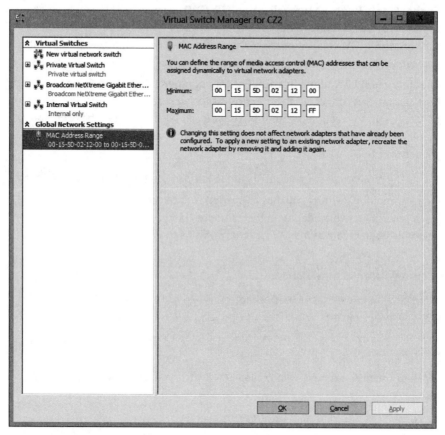

FIGURE 3-29 The MAC Address Range in the Virtual Switch Manager

The first three bytes of the MAC address range are always 00-15-5D, which is an OUI registered by Microsoft. The fourth and fifth bytes of the MAC address are the last two bytes of the IP address assigned to the server's physical network adapter, converted to hexadecimal notation. The sixth and last byte of the MAC address contains the range of values from 00 to FF, which provides 256 possible addresses.

The Hyper-V server assigns the MAC addresses to the network adapters in VMs as administrators create the adapters. The adapters retain their MAC addresses permanently or until the adapter is removed from the VM. The server reclaims any unused addresses and reuses them.

The default pool of 256 addresses is expected to be sufficient for most Hyper-V VM configurations, but if it is not, you can modify the Minimum and Maximum values to enlarge the pool. To prevent address duplication, you should change the second-to-last byte only, making it into a range of addresses like the last byte.

For example, the range illustrated in the figure provides 256 addresses with the following values:

00-15-1D-02-12-00 to 00-15-1D-02-12-FF

Modifying only the least significant digit, as in the following values, increases the pool from 256 to 4,096:

00-15-1D-02-10-00 to 00-15-1D-02-1F-FF

> **WARNING MAC ADDRESSES**
>
> When you modify the MAC address pool and you have other Hyper-V servers on your network, you must be careful not to create an overlap situation in which duplicate MAC addresses can occur or networking problems can result.

Creating virtual network adapters

Once you have created virtual switches in Hyper-V Manager, you can connect VMs to them by creating and configuring virtual network adapters. When you create a new VM, the default configuration includes one virtual network adapter. The New Virtual Machine Wizard includes a Configure Networking page, on which you can select one of the virtual switches you have created.

If you have created only the default external virtual switch when installing Hyper-V, then connecting a VM to that switch joins the system to the physical network. If you want to create additional network adapters in your VMs, you must use the following procedure.

1. In Server Manager, on the Tools menu, select Hyper-V Manager to open the Hyper-V Manager console.

2. In the left pane, select a Hyper-V server.

3. In the Virtual Machines list, select a VM and, in the Actions pane, click Settings. The Settings dialog box for the VM appears.

4. In the Add Hardware list, select Network Adapter and click Add. A new adapter appears in the Hardware list, as shown in Figure 3-307.

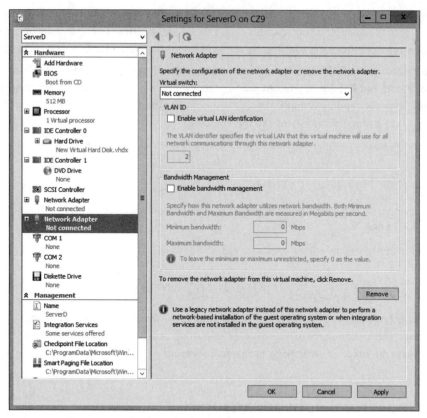

FIGURE 3-30 A new network adapter in the Settings dialog box

5. In the Virtual Switch drop-down list, select the switch to which you want to connect the network adapter.

6. If your host computer is connected to a physical switching infrastructure that uses VLANs to create separate subnets, you can select the Enable Virtual LAN Identification check box and enter a VLAN identifier to associate the network adapter with a particular VLAN on your physical network.

7. To control the amount of network bandwidth allocated to the network adapter, select the Enable Bandwidth Management check box and supply values for the Minimum Bandwidth and Maximum Bandwidth settings.

8. Click OK. The settings are saved to the VM configuration.

You can create up to 12 network adapters on a Windows Server 2012 R2 Hyper-V server: eight synthetic and four emulated.

Synthetic adapters and emulated adapters

Selecting the Network Adapter option on the Add Hardware page creates what is known in Hyper-V terminology as a synthetic network adapter. Hyper-V supports two types of network and storage adapters: synthetic and emulated (sometimes called legacy).

A *synthetic adapter* is a purely virtual device that does not correspond to a real-world product. Synthetic devices in a VM running on a child partition communicate with the parent partition by using a high-speed conduit called the VMBus.

The virtual switches you create in Hyper-V reside in the parent partition and are part of a component called the network Virtualization Service Provider (VSP). The synthetic network adapter in the child partition is a Virtualization Service Client (VSC). The VSP and the VSC are both connected to the VMBus, which provides interpartition communications, as shown in Figure 3-31. The VSP, in the parent partition, provides the VSC, in the child partition, with access to the physical hardware in the host computer; that is, the physical network interface adapter.

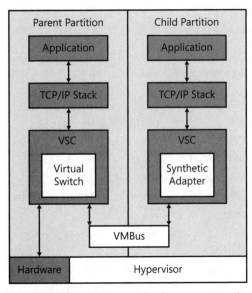

FIGURE 3-31 Synthetic network adapters communicate by using the VMBus

Because they have access to the hardware through the VMBus, synthetic adapters provide a much higher level of performance than the alternative, emulated adapters. Synthetic adapters are implemented as part of the Guest Integration Services package that runs on supported guest OSs. The main drawback of synthetic network adapters is that they are not operational until the OS is loaded on the VM.

An *emulated adapter*—sometimes called a *legacy adapter*—is a standard network adapter driver that communicates with the parent partition by making calls directly to the hypervisor, which is external to the partitions, as shown in Figure 3-32. This communication method is substantially slower than the VMBus used by the synthetic network adapters and is therefore less desirable.

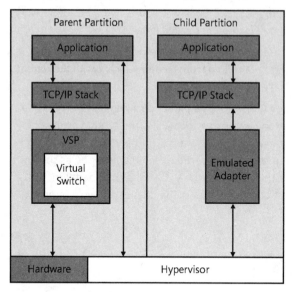

FIGURE 3-32 Emulated network adapters communicate by using the hypervisor

To install an emulated adapter, you use the same procedure described earlier, except that you select Legacy Network Adapter from the Add Hardware list. Unlike synthetic adapters, emulated adapters load their drivers before the OS, so it is possible to boot the VM by using the Preboot eXecution Environment (PXE) and then deploy an OS over the network.

This is one of two scenarios in which using an emulated adapter is preferable to using a synthetic adapter. The other is when you are installing an OS on your VMs that does not have a Guest Integration Services package available for it.

Configuring hardware acceleration settings

Some physical network interface adapters have features that are designed to improve performance by offloading certain functions from the system processor to components built into the adapter itself. Hyper-V includes support for some of these features, as long as the hardware in the physical network adapter supports them properly.

When you expand a network adapter in the Settings dialog box of a VM, you gain access to the Hardware Acceleration page. On this page, you can configure the following hardware acceleration settings:

- **Enable Virtual Machine Queue** *Virtual machine queue (VMQ)* is a technique that stores incoming packets intended for VMs in separate queues on the physical network adapter and delivers them directly to the VMs, bypassing the processing normally performed by the virtual switch on the parent partition.

- **Enable IPsec Task Offloading** Uses the components on the network adapter to perform some of the cryptographic functions required by IPsec. You can also specify the maximum number of security associations you want the adapter to be able to calculate.
- **Single-Root I/O Virtualization** Enables the virtual adapter to take advantage of the SR-IOV capabilities of the physical adapter.

Configuring advanced network adapter features

The Advanced Features page provides additional options for supporting network adapter capabilities, as follows:

- **Static MAC Address** By default, virtual network adapters receive a dynamically assigned MAC address from the Hyper-V server. However, you can opt to create a static MAC address by using this option. The only requirement is that no other adapter, virtual or physical, on the same network uses the same address.
- **Enable MAC Address Spoofing** When enabled, the port in the virtual switch to which the virtual network adapter is connected can send and receive packets that contain any MAC address. The virtual switch port can also learn of new MAC addresses and add them to its forwarding table.
- **Enable DHCP Guard** Prevents the adapter from processing messages sent by rogue DHCP servers.
- **Port Mirroring Mode** Enables the adapter to forward all the packets it receives over the network to another virtual adapter for analysis by using an application such as Network Monitor.
- **NIC Teaming** Enables the adapter to add its bandwidth to that of other adapters in the same guest OS in a NIC teaming arrangement.

Configuring NIC teaming in a virtual network environment

As explained in objective 1.2, "Configuring Servers," *NIC teaming* is a Windows feature that enables administrators to join multiple network adapters into a single entity for performance enhancement or fault tolerance purposes. Hyper-V virtual machines can also take advantage of NIC teaming, but they are limited to teams of only two, as opposed to the host operating system, which can have teams of up to 64 NICs.

To use NIC teaming in Hyper-V, you must complete three basic tasks, as follows:

1. Create the NIC team in the Windows Server 2012 R2 host operating system.
2. In Hyper-V Manager, create an external virtual switch using the NIC team.
3. Configure the network adapter in a virtual machine to connect to the virtual switch representing the NIC team.

Creating the NIC team

NIC teams must consist of physical network interface adapters, so before you can use a NIC team in a virtual machine, you must create it in the host operating system. After installing two NICs in the computer, you can create a NIC team with Server Manager in the usual manner, using the settings shown in Figure 3-33. Creating the team installs the Microsoft Network Adapter Multiplexor Driver, which appears as one of the components of the network connection representing the team.

FIGURE 3-33 The NIC Teaming dialog box

Creating the team virtual switch

Once you have created the NIC team, you can open the Virtual Switch Manager and create a new virtual switch by selecting the External network option and choosing Microsoft Network Adapter Multiplexor Driver from the drop-down list, as shown in Figure 3-34.

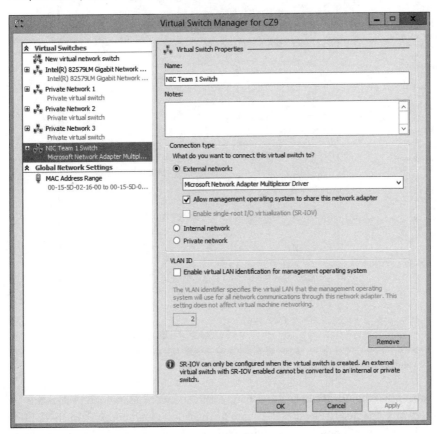

FIGURE 3-34 The Virtual Switch Properties settings for a NIC team switch

Configuring a NIC team virtual network adapter

To configure a virtual machine to use a NIC team, you must use the Settings dialog box to modify the properties for a virtual network adapter, configuring it to use the team switch you created in the previous section, as shown in Figure 3-35.

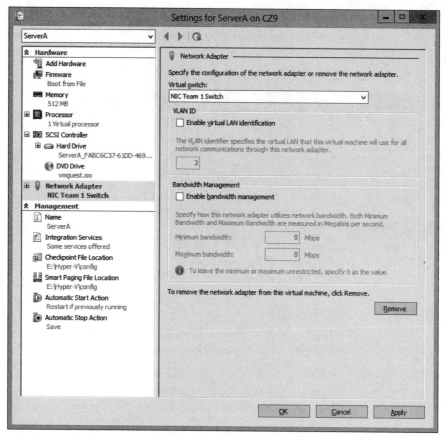

FIGURE 3-35 The Network Adapter settings for a NIC team adapter

Finally, you must open the Advanced Features page for the network adapter and select the Enable The Network Adapter To Be Part Of A Team In The Guest Operating System check box. At this point, the NIC team is operational for the virtual machine. You can unplug one of the network cables and the system will maintain its connection to the network.

Creating virtual network configurations

Hyper-V makes it possible to extend nearly any existing physical network configuration into its virtual space or create a completely separated and isolated network within the Hyper-V environment.

The basic default configuration of a Hyper-V VM connects its network adapter to an external virtual switch, thus attaching the guest OS on the VM to the outside network. The VM can then take advantage of services running on the outside network and send traffic through routers to other networks, including the Internet.

This type of arrangement can enable administrators to consolidate many physical servers into VMs on a single Hyper-V server, providing them all with access to the entire network.

There is no distinction here between the physical network and the virtual one in the Hyper-V space.

Extending a production network into virtual space

Keep in mind that a Hyper-V server can have multiple physical network adapters installed in it, which might be connected to different networks to separate traffic or they might be connected to the same network to increase available bandwidth. You might also have adapters dedicated to SAN connections for shared storage and server clustering.

Microsoft recommends the use of at least two physical network adapters in a Hyper-V server, with one adapter servicing the parent partition and the other connected to the child partitions. When you have more than two physical adapters in the server, you can create separate external virtual network switches for the physical adapters and connect each one to a separate VM.

Creating an isolated network

For testing and evaluation purposes or for classroom situations, administrators might want to create isolated network environments. By creating internal or private virtual switches, you can create a network that exists only within the Hyper-V space, with or without the parent partition included.

An isolated network such as this has limitations, however. If you want to install the guest OSs by using Windows Deployment Services or configure the VMs by using DHCP, you must install and configure those services on your private network. The guest OSs also do not have access to the Internet, which prevents them from downloading OS updates. In this case, you must deploy appropriate substitutes on the private network.

One way to provide your systems with updates is to install two network adapters on each of your VMs, connecting one to a private switch and one to an external switch. This enables the VMs to access the Internet and the private network.

Another method for creating an isolated network is to use VLANs. This is particularly helpful if you have VMs on different Hyper-V servers that you want to add to the isolated network. By connecting the network adapters to an external switch and configuring them with the same VLAN identifier, you can create a network within a network, which isolates the VLAN from other computers. You can, for example, deploy a DHCP server on your VLAN without it interfering with the other DHCP servers in your production environment.

Thought experiment

Configuring Hyper-V networking

In the following thought experiment, apply what you've learned about this objective to predict what steps you need to take. You can find answers to these questions in the "Answers" section at the end of this chapter.

Ralph has a Windows Server 2012 R2 Hyper-V server with one physical network adapter and one external virtual switch connected to that adapter. This arrangement enables the VMs on the server to automatically download OS updates from the Internet. However, Ralph wants to use the VMs on the Hyper-V server on an isolated test network on which he can evaluate new software products. The test network must have its own DHCP server that does not interfere with the DHCP server on the production network.

How can Ralph create the test network he needs for his VMs without changing the configuration that provides the machines with Internet access?

Objective summary

- Networking is a critical part of creating a VM infrastructure. Depending on your network plan, the VMs you create on a Windows Server 2012 R2 Hyper-V server can require communication with other VMs, with the computers on your physical network, and with the Internet.

- A virtual switch, like its physical counterpart, is a device that functions at Layer 2 of the OSI reference model. A switch has a series of ports, each of which is connected to a computer's network interface adapter. Any computer connected to the switch can transmit data to any other computer connected to the same switch.

- Hyper-V in Windows Server 2012 R2 supports three types of switches: external, internal, and private, which you must create in the virtual Switch Manager before you can connect VMs to them.

- Every network interface adapter has a MAC address—sometimes called a hardware address—that uniquely identifies the device on the network.

- Once you have created virtual switches in Hyper-V Manager, you can connect VMs to them by creating and configuring virtual network adapters.

- Selecting the Network Adapter option on the Add Hardware page creates what is known in Hyper-V terminology as a synthetic network adapter. Hyper-V supports two types of network and storage adapters: synthetic and emulated (sometimes called legacy).

- NIC teaming is a Windows feature that enables administrators to join multiple network adapters into a single entity for performance enhancement or fault tolerance purposes.

Objective review

Answer the following questions to test your knowledge of the information in this objective. You can find the answers to these questions and explanations of why each answer choice is correct or incorrect in the "Answers" section at the end of this chapter.

1. Which of the following are valid reasons for using an emulated network adapter rather than a synthetic one? (Choose all that apply.)

   A. You want to install the guest OS by using a Windows Deployment Services server.

   B. There is no Guest Integration Services package available for the guest OS you plan to use.

   C. The manufacturer of your physical network adapter has not yet provided a synthetic network adapter driver.

   D. The emulated network adapter provides better performance.

2. Which of the following statements is *not* true about synthetic network adapters?

   A. Synthetic adapters communicate with the parent partition by using the VMBus.

   B. Synthetic adapters require the Guest Integration Services package to be installed on the guest OS.

   C. Synthetic adapters provide faster performance than emulated adapters.

   D. Synthetic adapters can start the child VM by using a PXE network boot.

3. What is the maximum number of ports supported by a Hyper-V virtual switch?

   A. 8

   B. 256

   C. 4,096

   D. Unlimited

4. Which of the following virtual switch types does *not* enable guest OSs to communicate with the parent partition?

   A. External

   B. Internal

   C. Private

   D. Isolated

5. How many dynamically assigned MAC addresses can a Hyper-V server provide by default?

   A. 8

   B. 256

   C. 4,096

   D. Unlimited

Answers

This section contains the solutions to the thought experiments and answers to the objective review questions in this chapter.

Objective 3.1: Thought experiment

Alice can enable Dynamic Memory on each of the eight VMs and set the minimum RAM value on each to 512 MB. This will enable each VM to start with 1,024 MB of memory and then reduce its footprint, allowing the next machine to start.

Objective 3.1: Review

1. **Correct answers:** B, C

    A. **Incorrect:** In Type I virtualization, the hypervisor does not run on top of a host OS.

    B. **Correct:** A Type I hypervisor runs directly on the computer hardware.

    C. **Correct:** A Type II hypervisor runs on top of a host OS.

    D. **Incorrect:** In Type II virtualization, the hypervisor does not run directly on the computer hardware.

2. **Correct answer:** A

    A. **Correct:** Type I virtualization provides the best performance because the hypervisor runs directly on the computer hardware and does not have the overhead of a host OS.

    B. **Incorrect:** Type II virtualization provides poorer performance than Type I because of the need to share processor time with the host OS.

    C. **Incorrect:** Presentation virtualization is the term used to describe the Remote Desktop Services functionality in Windows. It is not designed for virtualizing servers.

    D. **Incorrect:** RemoteApp is a technology for virtualizing individual applications and deploying them by using Remote Desktop Services.

3. **Correct answer:** B

    A. **Incorrect:** Hyper-V Server does not include a license for any virtual instances.

    B. **Correct:** Windows Server 2012 R2 Datacenter edition includes a license that enables you to create an unlimited number of virtual instances.

    C. **Incorrect:** Windows Server 2012 R2 Standard edition includes a license that enables you to create two virtual instances.

    D. **Incorrect:** Windows Server 2012 R2 Foundation edition does not include support for Hyper-V.

4. **Correct answers:** A, B, D

   A. **Correct:** Smart paging enables a VM to restart even if the amount of RAM specified as the startup value is unavailable. Smart paging causes the system to use disk space as a temporary substitute for memory during a system restart.

   B. **Correct:** Dynamic Memory enables you to specify a minimum RAM value that is smaller than the startup RAM value, but Smart paging enables the system to function with those parameters.

   C. **Incorrect:** Windows Memory Weight controls the allocation of memory among VMs, but it does not affect the ability of a system to start.

   D. **Correct:** Guest Integration Services is required for a guest OS to use Dynamic Memory.

5. **Correct answer:** C

   A. **Incorrect:** The instance of the OS on which you install Hyper-V does not become the hypervisor.

   B. **Incorrect:** The instance of the OS on which you install Hyper-V does not become the VMM.

   C. **Correct:** The instance of the OS on which you install the Hyper-V role becomes the parent partition.

   D. **Incorrect:** The instance of the OS on which you install the Hyper-V role does not become the child partition.

6. **Correct answer:** B

   A. **Incorrect:** You can create a new Generation 1 or Generation 2 virtual machine at any time.

   B. **Correct:** Because they use improved and synthetic drivers, Generation 2 VMs deploy faster than Generation 1 VMs.

   C. **Incorrect:** Generation 2 VMs can run Windows Server 2012, Windows Server 2012 R2, Windows 8, or Windows 8.1 as a guest operating system.

   D. **Incorrect:** Generation 2 VMs use improved and synthetic drivers, as compared to the legacy drivers in Generation 1 VMs.

Objective 3.2: Thought experiment

Ed should use the following Windows PowerShell command to create the VHD.

```
New-VHD -Path c:\servera.vhdx -Fixed -SizeBytes 500GB -LogicalSectorSizeBytes 4096 -
SourceDisk 0
```

Objective 3.2: Review

1. **Correct answer:** B

A. **Incorrect:** VHDX files can be as large as 64 TB, whereas VHD files are limited to 2 TB.

B. **Correct:** Windows Server 2012, Windows Server 2012 R2, Windows 8, and Windows 8.1 can all open VHDX files.

C. **Incorrect:** VHDX files support block sizes as large as 256 MB.

D. **Incorrect:** VHDX files can support the 4,096-byte block sizes found on some newer drives.

2. **Correct answer:** B

A. **Incorrect:** A pass-through disk must be online in the guest OS that will access it.

B. **Correct:** A pass-through disk must be offline in the parent container so that the guest OS can have exclusive access to it.

C. **Incorrect:** A pass-through disk can be connected to any type of controller.

D. **Incorrect:** You do not use the Disk Management snap-in to add a pass-through disk to a VM; you use Hyper-V Manager.

3. **Correct answer:** D

A. **Incorrect:** You can merge VHD or VHDX disks.

B. **Incorrect:** You can only select one disk for editing.

C. **Incorrect:** There is no free space requirement when merging a disk.

D. **Correct:** The Merge function appears only when you select a differencing disk for editing. The object of the function is to combine the data in the differencing disk with that of the parent.

4. **Correct answers:** A, D

A. **Correct:** Checkpoints consume disk space that could be better used for other purposes.

B. **Incorrect:** Checkpoints do not require a duplicate memory allocation.

C. **Incorrect:** Under typical conditions, checkpoints do not take several hours to create.

D. **Correct:** The Hyper-V server must locate and process checkpoints each time it accesses a VM's disk drives, slowing down its performance.

5. **Correct answer:** D

A. **Incorrect:** You must create a Fibre Channel SAN before you can add a Fibre Channel adapter to a VM.

B. Incorrect: You must have a physical Fibre Channel adapter before you can create virtual Fibre Channel components.

C. Incorrect: The driver for your physical Fibre Channel adapter must support virtual networking.

D. Correct: SCSI cables are not required for Fibre Channel installations.

Objective 3.3: Thought experiment

Ralph can create an isolated test environment without changing the virtual switch configuration by selecting the Enable Virtual LAN Identification check box on the network adapter in each VM and specifying the same VLAN identifier for each VM he wants on the test network.

Objective 3.3: Review

1. **Correct answers:** A, B

   A. Correct: A Windows Deployment Server installation requires the network adapter to support PXE, which emulated adapters do, but synthetic adapters do not.

   B. Correct: Synthetic adapter drivers are installed as part of the Guest Integration Services package; if there is no package for the guest OS, then there are no synthetic drivers.

   C. Incorrect: Synthetic adapter drivers are not provided by hardware manufacturers.

   D. Incorrect: Synthetic adapters provide better performance than emulated adapters.

2. **Correct answer:** D

   A. Incorrect: Synthetic adapters use the faster VMBus for communications with the parent partition; emulated adapters must use calls to the hypervisor.

   B. Incorrect: Synthetic adapter drivers are installed as part of the Guest Integration Services package on the guest OS.

   C. Incorrect: Because of their more efficient communication with the parent partition, synthetic adapters perform better than emulated adapters.

   D. Correct: Synthetic network adapters load with the Guest Integration Services on the guest OS, which prevents them from supporting PXE.

3. **Correct answer:** D

   A. Incorrect: Switches limited to eight connections would be insufficient for many Hyper-V installations.

B. Incorrect: Hyper-V switches are not limited to 256 connections.

C. Incorrect: Hyper-V switches are not limited to 4,096 connections.

D. Correct: Hyper-V virtual switches can support an unlimited number of connections.

4. **Correct answer:** C

A. Incorrect: External switches enable the guest OSs to communicate with the outside network and the parent partition.

B. Incorrect: Internal switches enable the guest OSs to communicate with the parent partition but not with the outside network.

C. Correct: Private switches enable the guest OSs to communicate with one another but not with the outside network or the parent partition.

D. Incorrect: Isolated is not a technical term referring to a type of virtual switch.

5. **Correct answer:** B

A. Incorrect: A pool of eight MAC addresses would be insufficient for many Hyper-V installations.

B. Correct: A Hyper-V server provides a pool of 256 MAC addresses by default. You can create more by modifying the default address range.

C. Incorrect: Hyper-V, by default, dedicates only one byte of the MAC address to a dynamic value, which is not enough to support 4,096 addresses.

D. Incorrect: Hyper-V creates a finite pool of MAC addresses by specifying minimum and maximum address values.

CHAPTER 4

Deploying and configuring core network services

This chapter discusses the vital infrastructure services that nearly every network must implement. Every computer on a TCP/IP network must have at least one Internet Protocol (IP) address and most networks today use the Dynamic Host Configuration Protocol (DHCP) to assign those addresses. To simplify resource access on the Internet and to locate Active Directory Domain Services (AD DS) domain controllers, TCP/IP computers must have access to a Domain Name System (DNS) server. Windows Server 2012 R2 includes all these services and provides the tools to manage them.

Objectives in this chapter:

- Objective 4.1: Configure IPv4 and IPv6 addressing
- Objective 4.2: Deploy and configure Dynamic Host Configuration Protocol (DHCP) service
- Objective 4.3: Deploy and configure DNS service

Objective 4.1: Configure IPv4 and IPv6 addressing

Server administrators must be familiar with the basic principles of the IPv4 and IPv6 address spaces. This section reviews those principles and describes the usual process for designing IPv4 and IPv6 addressing strategies.

This objective covers how to:

- Configure IP address options
- Configure subnetting
- Configure supernetting
- Configure interoperability between IPv4 and IPv6
- Configure ISATAP
- Configure Teredo

IPv4 addressing

As you probably know, The IPv4 address space consists of 32-bit addresses, notated as four 8-bit decimal values from 0 to 255 and separated by periods (for example, 192.168.43.100). This is known as *dotted-decimal notation* and the individual 8-bit decimal values are called *octets* or *bytes*.

Each address consists of network bits, which identify a network, and host bits, which identify a particular device on that network. To differentiate the network bits from the host bits, each address must have a subnet mask.

A subnet mask is another 32-bit value consisting of binary 1 bits and 0 bits. When compared to an IP address, the bits corresponding to the 1s in the mask are the network bits, and the bits corresponding to the 0s are the host bits. Thus, if the 192.168.43.100 address mentioned earlier has a subnet mask of 255.255.255.0 (which in binary form is 11111111.11111111.11111111.00000000), the first three octets (192.168.43) identify the network and the last octet (100) identifies the host.

IPv4 classful addressing

Because the subnet mask associated with IP addresses can vary, the number of bits used to identify the network and the host can also vary.

The original IP standard defines three classes of IP addresses, which support networks of different sizes, as shown in Figure 4-1.

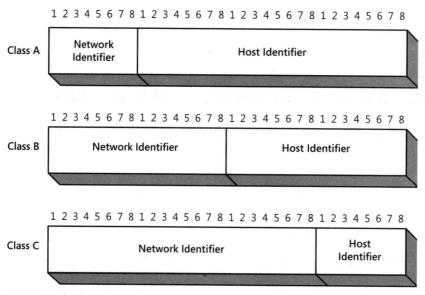

FIGURE 4-1 The three IPv4 address classes

The number of networks and hosts supported by each of the address classes are listed in Table 4-1.

TABLE 4-1 IPv4 address classes

IP Address Class	Class A	Class B	Class C
First bit values (binary)	0	10	110
First byte values (decimal)	1–127	128–191	192–223
Number of network identifier bits	8	16	24
Number of host identifier bits	24	16	8
Number of possible networks	126	16,384	2,097,152
Number of possible hosts	16,777,214	65,534	254

> **NOTE ADDITIONAL CLASSES**
>
> In addition to Classes A, B, and C, the IP standard defines Class D and Class E. Class D addresses begin with the bit values 1110 and Class E addresses begin with 11110. The Internet Assigned Numbers Authority (IANA) has allocated Class D addresses for use as multicast identifiers. A *multicast address* identifies a group of computers on a network, all of which possess a similar trait. Multicast addresses enable TCP/IP applications to send traffic to computers that perform specific functions (such as all the routers on the network), even if they're located on different subnets. Class E addresses are defined as experimental and are as yet unused.

The "First bit values" row in the table specifies the binary values that the first one, two, or three bits of an address in each class must have. Early TCP/IP implementations used these bit values instead of a subnet mask to determine the class of an address. The binary values of the first bits of each address class limit the possible decimal values for the first byte of the address. For example, because the first bit of a Class A address must be 0, the possible binary values of the first byte in a Class A address range from 00000001 to 01111111, which in decimal form are values ranging from 1 to 127. Thus, in the classful addressing system, when you see an IP address in which the first byte is a number from 1 to 127, you know that this is a Class A address.

In a Class A address, the network identifier is the first eight bits of the address and the host identifier is the remaining 24 bits. Thus, there are only 126 possible Class A networks (network identifier 127 is reserved for diagnostic purposes), but each network can have as many as 16,777,214 network interface adapters on it. Class B and Class C addresses devote more bits to the network identifier, which means they support a greater number of networks, but at the cost of having fewer host identifier bits. This trade-off reduces the number of hosts that can be created on each network.

The values in Table 4-1 for the number of hosts each address class supports might appear low. For example, an 8-bit binary number can have 256 (that is, 2^8) possible values, not 254, as shown in the table for the number of hosts on a Class C address. The value 254 is used because the original IP addressing standard states that you can't assign the "all zeros" or "all ones" addresses to individual hosts. The "all zeros" address identifies the local network, not a specific host, and the "all ones" identifier always signifies a broadcast address. You cannot assign either value to an individual host. Therefore, to calculate the number of possible network or host addresses you can create with a given number of bits, you use the formula 2^x-2, where x is the number of bits.

Classless Inter-Domain Routing

When IP was developed, no one imagined that the 32-bit address space would ever be exhausted. In the early 1980s, there were no networks that had 65,536 computers, never mind 16 million, and no one worried about the wastefulness of assigning IP addresses based on these classes.

Because of that wastefulness, classful addressing was gradually obsolesced by a series of subnetting methods, including variable length subnet masking (VLSM) and eventually *Classless Inter-Domain Routing (CIDR)*. CIDR is a subnetting method that enables administrators to place the division between the network bits and the host bits anywhere in the address, not just between octets. This makes it possible to create networks of almost any size.

CIDR also introduces a new notation for network addresses. A standard dotted-decimal address representing the network is followed by a forward slash and a numeral specifying the size of the network-identifying prefix. For example, 192.168.43.0/24 represents a single Class C network that uses a 24-bit network identifier, leaving the other 8 bits for up to 254 host identifiers. Each of those hosts would receive an address from 192.168.43.1 to 192.168.43.254, using the subnet mask 255.255.255.0.

However, by using CIDR, an administrator can subnet this address further by allocating some of the host bits to create subnets. To create subnets for four offices, for example, the administrator can take two of the host identifier bits, changing the network address in CIDR notation to 192.168.43.0/26. Because the network identifier is now 26 bits, the subnet masks for all four networks will now be 11111111.11111111.11111111.11000000 in binary form, or 255.255.255.192 in standard decimal form. Each of the four networks will have up to 62 hosts, using the IP address ranges shown in Table 4-2.

TABLE 4-2 Sample CIDR 192.168.43.0/26 networks

Network Address	Starting IP Address	Ending IP Address	Subnet Mask
192.168.43.0	192.168.43.1	192.168.43.62	255.255.255.192
192.168.43.64	192.168.43.65	192.168.43.126	255.255.255.192
192.168.43.128	192.168.43.129	192.168.43.190	255.255.255.192
192.168.43.192	192.168.43.193	192.168.43.254	255.255.255.192

If the administrator needs more than four subnets, changing the network address to 192.168.43.0/28 adds two more bits to the network address for a maximum of 16 subnets, each of which can support up to 14 hosts. The subnet mask for these networks would therefore be 255.255.255.240.

Public and private IPv4 addressing

For a computer to be accessible from the Internet, there must be an IP address that is both registered and unique, either on the server or a device providing access to it, such as a NAT router. All web servers on the Internet have registered addresses, as do all other types of Internet servers.

The IANA is the ultimate source for all registered addresses. Managed by the Internet Corporation for Assigned Names and Numbers (ICANN), this organization allocates blocks of addresses to regional Internet registries (RIR), which, in turn, allocate smaller blocks to Internet service providers (ISPs). An organization that wants to host a server on the Internet typically obtains a registered address from an ISP.

Registered IP addresses are not necessary for workstations that merely access resources on the Internet. If organizations used registered addresses for all their workstations, the IPv4 address space would have been depleted long ago. Instead, organizations typically use private IP addresses for their workstations. Private IP addresses are blocks of addresses that are allocated specifically for private network use. Anyone can use these addresses without registering them, but they cannot make computers using private addresses accessible from the Internet without using a specialized technology such as network address translation (NAT).

The three blocks of addresses allocated for private use are as follows:

- 10.0.0.0/8
- 172.16.0.0/12
- 192.168.0.0/16

Most enterprise networks use addresses from these blocks for their workstations. It doesn't matter if multiple organizations use the same addresses, because the workstations are never directly connected to the same network.

IPv4 subnetting

In most cases, enterprise administrators use addresses in one of the private IP address ranges to create the subnets they need. If you are building a new enterprise network from scratch, you can choose any one of the private address blocks and make things easy on yourself by subnetting along the octet boundaries.

For example, you can take the 10.0.0.0/8 private IP address range and use the entire second octet as a subnet ID. This enables you to create up to 256 subnets with as many as 65,536 hosts on each one. The subnet masks for all the addresses on the subnets will be 255.255.0.0 and the network addresses will proceed as follows:

- 10.0.0.0/16
- 10.1.0.0/16

- 10.2.0.0/16
- 10.3.0.0/16
- ...
- 10.255.0.0/16

When you are working on an existing network, the subnetting process is likely to be more difficult. You might, for example, be given a relatively small range of addresses and be asked to create a certain number of subnets from them. To do this, you use the following procedure.

1. Determine how many subnet identifier bits you need to create the required number of subnets.

2. Subtract the subnet bits you need from the host bits and add them to the network bits.

3. Calculate the subnet mask by adding the network and subnet bits in binary form and converting the binary value to decimal.

4. Take the least significant subnet bit and the host bits, in binary form, and convert them to a decimal value.

5. Increment the network identifier (including the subnet bits) by the decimal value you calculated to determine the network addresses of your new subnets.

Using the example earlier in this chapter, if you take the 192.168.43.0/24 network address and allocate two extra bits for the subnet ID, you get a binary subnet mask value of 11111111.11111111.11111111.11000000 (255.255.255.192 in decimal form, as noted earlier).

The least significant subnet bit plus the host bits gives you a binary value of 1000000, which converts to a decimal value of 64. Therefore, if you know that the network address of your first subnet is 192.168.43.0, the second subnet must be 192.168.43.64, the third 192.168.43.128, and the fourth 192.168.43.192, as shown in Table 4-2.

Supernetting

In addition to simplifying network notation, CIDR also makes possible a technique called IP address aggregation or supernetting, which can help reduce the size of Internet routing tables. A supernet is a combination of contiguous networks that all contain a common CIDR prefix. When an organization possesses multiple contiguous networks that can be expressed as a supernet, it is possible to list those networks in a routing table by using only one entry instead of many.

For example, if an organization has the following five subnets, standard practice would be to create a separate routing table entry for each one.

- 172.16.43.0/24
- 172.16.44.0/24
- 172.16.45.0/24

- 172.16.46.0/24

- 172.16.47.0/24

To create a supernet encompassing all five of these networks, you must isolate the bits they have in common. When you convert the network addresses from decimal to binary, you get the following values:

```
172.16.43.0    10101100.00010000.00101011.00000000
172.16.44.0    10101100.00010000.00101100.00000000
172.16.45.0    10101100.00010000.00101101.00000000
172.16.46.0    10101100.00010000.00101110.00000000
172.16.47.0    10101100.00010000.00101111.00000000
```

In binary form, you can see that all five addresses have the same first 21 bits. Those 21 bits become the network identifier of the supernet address, as follows:

```
10101100.00010000.00101
```

After zeroing out the host bits to form the network address and converting the binary number back to decimal form, as follows, the resulting supernet address is 172.16.40.0/21.

```
10101100.00010000.00101000.00000000     172.16.40.0/21
```

This one network address can replace the original five in routing tables duplicated throughout the Internet. This is just one example of a technique that administrators can use to combine dozens or even hundreds of subnets into single routing table entries.

Assigning IPv4 addresses

In addition to understanding how IP addressing works, a network administrator must be familiar with the methods for deploying IP addresses to the computers on a network.

To assign IPv4 addresses, there are three basic methods:

- Manual configuration

- Dynamic Host Configuration Protocol (DHCP)

- Automatic Private IP Addressing (APIPA)

The advantages and disadvantages of these methods are discussed in the following sections.

MANUAL IPV4 ADDRESS CONFIGURATION

Configuring a TCP/IP client manually is neither difficult nor time-consuming. Most operating systems provide a graphical interface that enables you to enter an IPv4 address, a subnet mask, and various other TCP/IP configuration parameters. To configure IP address settings in Windows Server 2012 R2, you use the Internet Protocol Version 4 (TCP/IPv4) Properties sheet, as shown in Figure 4-2.

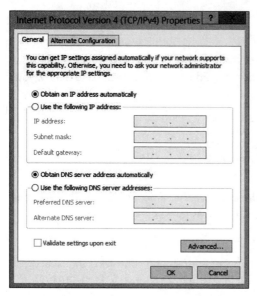

FIGURE 4-2 The Internet Protocol Version 4 (TCP/IPv4) Properties sheet

When you select the Use The Following IP Address option, you can configure the following IP address options:

- **IP Address**   Specifies the IP address on the local subnet that will identify the network interface in the computer
- **Subnet Mask**   Specifies the mask associated with the local subnet
- **Default Gateway**   Specifies the IP address of a router on the local subnet, which the system will use to access destinations on other networks
- **Preferred DNS Server**   Specifies the IP address of the DNS server the system will use to resolve host names into IP addresses

The primary problem with manual configuration is that a task requiring two minutes for one workstation requires several hours for 100 workstations and several days for 1,000. Manually configuring all but the smallest networks is impractical, and not just because it is slow. You must also track the IPv4 addresses you assign and make sure each system has an address that is unique. This can present formidable logistical challenges, which is why few network administrators choose this option.

DYNAMIC HOST CONFIGURATION PROTOCOL (DHCP)

DHCP is an application-layer protocol that together enable administrators to dynamically allocate IP addresses from a pool. Computers equipped with DHCP clients automatically contact a DHCP server when they start, and the server assigns them unique addresses and all the other configuration parameters the server is configured to provide.

The DHCP server provides addresses to clients on a leased basis, and after a predetermined interval, each client either renews its address or releases it back to the server for reallocation. DHCP not only automates the address assignment process but also keeps track of the addresses it assigns, preventing address duplication on the network.

> **NOTE** **DHCP ADDRESS ALLOCATION**
>
> For more information on DHCP, see Objective 4.2, "Configuring Servers."

AUTOMATIC PRIVATE IP ADDRESSING (APIPA)

APIPA is the name assigned by Microsoft to a DHCP failover mechanism used by all the current Microsoft Windows operating systems. On Windows computers, the DHCP client is enabled by default. If, after several attempts, a system fails to locate a DHCP server on the network, APIPA takes over and automatically assigns an address on the 169.254.0.0/16 network to the computer.

For a small network that consists of only a single local area network (LAN), APIPA is a simple and effective alternative to installing a DHCP server. However, for installations consisting of multiple LANs connected by routers, administrators must take more positive control over the IP address assignment process. This usually means deploying one or more DHCP servers in some form.

IPv6 addressing

As most administrators know, IPv6 is designed to increase the size of the IP address space, thus providing addresses for many more devices than IPv4. The 128-bit address size of IPv6 allows for 2^{128} possible addresses—which is over 54 million addresses for each square meter of the Earth's surface.

In addition to providing more addresses, IPv6 will also reduce the size of the routing tables in the routers scattered around the Internet. This is because the size of the addresses provides for more than the two levels of subnetting currently possible with IPv4.

Introducing IPv6

IPv6 addresses are different from IPv4 addresses in many ways other than length. Instead of the four 8-bit decimal numbers separated by periods that IPv4 uses, IPv6 addresses use a notation called colon-hexadecimal format, which consists of eight 16-bit hexadecimal numbers separated by colons, as follows:

`XX:XX:XX:XX:XX:XX:XX:XX`

Each *X* represents eight bits (or one byte), which in hexadecimal notation is represented by two characters, as in the following example:

`21cd:0053:0000:0000:e8bb:04f2:003c:c394`

CONTRACTING IPV6 ADDRESSES

When an IPv6 address has two or more consecutive 8-bit blocks of zeros, you can replace them with a double colon, as follows (but you can use only one double colon in any IPv6 address):

`21cd:0053::e8bb:04f2:003c:c394`

You can also remove the leading zeros in any block where they appear, as follows:

`21cd:53::e8bb:4f2:3c:c394`

EXPRESSING IPV6 NETWORK ADDRESSES

There are no subnet masks in IPv6. Network addresses use the same slash notation as CIDR to identify the network bits. In this example, the network address is notated as follows:

`21cd:53::/64`

This is the contracted form for the following network address:

`21cd:0053:0000:0000/64`

IPv6 address types

There are no broadcast transmissions in IPv6, and therefore no broadcast addresses, as in IPv4. IPv6 supports three types of transmissions, as follows:

- **Unicast**   Provides one-to-one transmission service to individual interfaces, including server farms sharing a single address
- **Multicast**   Provides one-to-many transmission service to groups of interfaces identified by a single multicast address
- **Anycast**   Provides one-to-one-of-many transmission service to groups of interfaces, only the nearest of which (measured by the number of intermediate routers) receives the transmission

> **NOTE   IPV6 SCOPES**
>
> In IPv6, the scope of an address refers to the size of its functional area. For example, the scope of a global unicast is unlimited; that is, the entire Internet. The scope of a link-local unicast is the immediate link; that is, the local network. The scope of a unique local unicast consists of all the subnets within an organization.

IPv6 also supports several address types, as described in the following sections.

GLOBAL UNICAST ADDRESSES

A global unicast address is the equivalent of a registered IPv4 address, routable worldwide and unique on the Internet.

LINK-LOCAL UNICAST ADDRESSES

In IPv6, systems that assign themselves an address automatically create a link-local unicast address, which is essentially the equivalent of an APIPA address in IPv4. All link-local addresses have the same network identifier: a 10-bit prefix of 1111111010 followed by 54 zeros, resulting in the following network address:

`fe80:0000:0000:0000/64`

In its more compact form, the link-local network address is as follows:

`fe80::/64`

Because all link-local addresses are on the same network, they are not routable, and systems possessing them can only communicate with other systems on the same link.

UNIQUE LOCAL UNICAST ADDRESSES

Unique local unicast addresses are the IPv6 equivalent of the 10.0.0.0/8, 172.16.0.0/12, and 192.168.0.0/16 private network addresses in IPv4. Like the IPv4 private addresses, unique local addresses are routable within an organization. Administrators can also subnet them as needed to support an organization of any size.

> *NOTE* **DEPRECATED IPV6 ADDRESSES**
>
> Many sources of IPv6 information continue to list site-local unicast addresses as a valid type of unicast, with a function similar to that of the private IPv4 network addresses. For various reasons, site-local unicast addresses have been deprecated, and although their use is not forbidden, their functionality has been replaced by unique local unicast addresses.

MULTICAST ADDRESSES

Multicast addresses always begin with a value of 11111111 in binary, or ff in hexadecimal.

ANYCAST ADDRESSES

The function of an anycast address is to identify the routers within a given address scope and send traffic to the nearest router, as determined by the local routing protocols. Organizations can use anycast addresses to identify a particular set of routers in the enterprise, such as those that provide access to the Internet. To use anycasts, the routers must be configured to recognize the anycast addresses as such.

Assigning IPv6 addresses

The processes by which administrators assign IPv6 addresses to network computers are similar to those in IPv4. As with IPv4, a Windows computer can obtain an IPv6 address by three possible methods:

- **Manual allocation** A user or administrator manually supplies an address and other information for each network interface.

- **Self-allocation** The computer creates its own address by using a process called stateless address autoconfiguration.

- **Dynamic allocation** The computer solicits and receives an address from a DHCPv6 server on the network.

MANUAL IPV6 ADDRESS ALLOCATION

For the enterprise administrator, manual allocation of addresses is even more impractical in IPv6 than in IPv4 because of the length of the addresses involved. However, it is possible, and the procedure for doing so in Windows Server 2012 R2 is the same as that for IPv4, except that you open the Internet Protocol Version 6 (TCP/IPv6) Properties sheet, as shown in Figure 4-3.

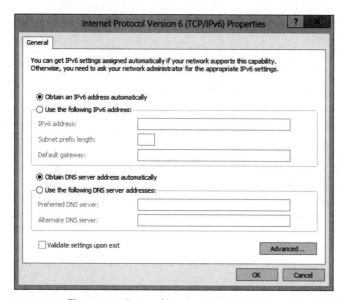

FIGURE 4-3 The Internet Protocol Version 6 (TCP/IPv6) Properties sheet

Because of the difficulties of working with IPv6 addresses manually, the following two options are far more prevalent.

STATELESS IPV6 ADDRESS AUTOCONFIGURATION

When a Windows computer starts, it initiates the stateless address autoconfiguration process, during which it assigns each interface a link-local unicast address. This assignment always occurs, even when the interface is to receive a global unicast address later. The link-local address enables the system to communicate with the router on the link, which provides additional instructions.

The steps of the stateless address autoconfiguration process are as follows.

1. **Link-local address creation** The IPv6 implementation on the system creates a link-local address for each interface by using the fe80::/64 network address and generating

an interface ID, either by using the interface's media access control (MAC) address or a pseudorandom generator.

2. **Duplicate address detection**   Using the IPv6 Neighbor Discovery (ND) protocol, the system transmits a Neighbor Solicitation message to determine if any other computer on the link is using the same address and listens for a Neighbor Advertisement message sent in reply. If there is no reply, the system considers the address to be unique on the link. If there is a reply, the system must generate a new address and repeat the procedure.

3. **Link-local address assignment**   When the system determines that the link-local address is unique, it configures the interface to use that address. On a small network consisting of a single segment or link, this might be the interface's permanent address assignment. On a network with multiple subnets, the primary function of the link-local address assignment is to enable the system to communicate with a router on the link.

4. **Router advertisement solicitation**   The system uses the ND protocol to transmit Router Solicitation messages to the all routers multicast address. These messages compel routers to transmit the Router Advertisement messages more frequently.

5. **Router advertisement**   The router on the link uses the ND protocol to transmit Router Advertisement messages to the system, which contain information on how the autoconfiguration process should proceed. The Router Advertisement messages typically supply a network prefix, which the system will use with its existing interface ID to create a global or unique local unicast address. The messages might also instruct the system to initiate a stateful autoconfiguration process by contacting a specific DHCPv6 server. If there is no router on the link, as determined by the system's failure to receive Router Advertisement messages, then the system must attempt to initiate a stateless autoconfiguration process.

6. **Global or unique local address configuration**   Using the information it receives from the router, the system generates a suitable address that is routable, either globally or within the enterprise, and configures the interface to use it. If so instructed, the system might also initiate a stateful autoconfiguration process by contacting the DHCPv6 server specified by the router and obtaining a global or unique local address from that server, along with other configuration settings.

DYNAMIC HOST CONFIGURATION PROTOCOL V6

If you are an enterprise administrator with a multisegment network, it will be necessary to use unique local or global addresses for internetwork communication, so you will need either routers that advertise the appropriate network prefixes or DHCPv6 servers that can supply addresses with the correct prefixes.

The Remote Access role in Windows Server 2012 R2 supports IPv6 routing and advertising, and the DHCP Server role supports IPv6 address allocation.

Subnetting IPv6 Addresses

As with IPv4, administrators can create a hierarchy of subnets using IPv6 addresses. However, in IPv6, no subnet masks are needed because there are ample bits in the network identifier to create a subnet identifier without having to borrow from the host bits.

The format for an IPv6 global unicast address divides the 128 bits into the following three sections:

- **Global routing prefix**   A 48-bit field beginning with the 001 FP value, the hierarchical structure of which is left up to the regional Internet registry (RIR)
- **Subnet ID**   A 16-bit field that organizations can use to create an internal hierarchy of subnets
- **Interface ID**   A 64-bit field identifying a specific interface on the network

When you obtain an IPv6 network address from an ISP or an RIR, you typically get the global routing prefix, commonly known as a "/48". You are then left with the subnet ID field to use for subnetting the network as you wish. Some possible subnetting options are as follows:

- **One-level subnet**   By setting all subnet ID bits to 0, all the computers in the organization are part of a single subnet.
- **Two-level subnet**   By creating a series of 16-bit values, you can split the network into as many as 65,536 subnets. This is the functional equivalent of IPv4 subnetting, but with a much larger subnet address space.
- **Multi-level subnet**   By allocating specific numbers of subnet ID bits, you can create multiple levels of subnets, sub-subnets, and sub-sub-subnets, suitable for an enterprise of almost any size.

For example, consider a large international enterprise with its subnet ID divided as follows:

- **Country (4 bits)**   Creates up to 16 subnets representing the countries in which the organization has offices
- **State (6 bits)**   Creates up to 64 sub-subnets within each country, representing states, provinces, or other geographical divisions
- **Office (2 bits)**   Creates up to four sub-sub-subnets within each state or province, representing offices located in various cities
- **Department (4 bits)**   Creates up to 16 sub-sub-sub-subnets within each office, representing the various departments or divisions.

Thus, to create a subnet ID for a particular office, you need to assign values for each field. To use the value 1 for the United States, the Country bits of the subnet ID would be as follows:

```
0001------------
```

To create a binary state designation for Alaska using the value 49 , the State field would appear as follows:

```
----110001------
```

For the second office in Alaska, use the value 2 for the Office bits, as follows:

----------10----

For the Sales department in the office, use the value 9 for the Department bits, as follows:

------------1001

The resulting value for the subnet ID, in binary form, would therefore be as follows:

0001110001101001

In hexadecimal form, that would be 1c69.

Because the organization that owns the prefix wholly controls the subnet ID, enterprise administrators can adjust the number of levels in the hierarchy and the number of bits dedicated to each level as needed.

Planning an IP transition

Many enterprise administrators are so comfortable working with IPv4 addresses that they are hesitant to change. Network Address Translation (NAT) and CIDR have been excellent stopgaps to the depletion of the 32-bit IP address space for years, and many would like to see them continue as such. However, the IPv6 transition, long a specter on the horizon, is now approaching at frightening speed, and it is time for administrators not familiar with the new technologies to catch up.

The networking industry—and particularly the Internet—has made huge investments in IPv4 technologies; replacing them with IPv6 has been a gradual process. In fact, it is a gradual process that was supposed to have begun in earnest over 10 years ago. However, many administrators don't replace their IPv4 equipment unless it stops working. Unfortunately, the day when that equipment stops working is approaching rapidly. So, although it might not yet be time to embrace IPv6 exclusively, administrators should have the transition in mind as they design their networks and make their purchasing decisions.

> **NOTE IPV4 ADDRESS EXHAUSTION**
>
> The exhaustion of the IANA unallocated address pool occurred on January 31, 2011. One of the RIRs, the Asia Pacific Network Information Center (APNIC), was depleted on April 15, 2011, and the other RIRs are expected to follow.

Enterprise administrators can do as they wish within the enterprise itself. If all the network devices in the organization support IPv6, they can begin to use IPv6 addresses at any time. However, the Internet is still firmly based on IPv4, and will continue to be for several years. Therefore, the transition from IPv4 to IPv6 must be a gradual project that includes a period of support for both IP versions.

Now, and in the immediate future, administrators must work under the assumption that the rest of the world is using IPv4, so you must implement a mechanism for transmitting your

IPv6 traffic over an IPv4 connection. Eventually, the situation will be reversed. Most of the world will be running IPv6 and the remaining IPv4 technologies will have to transmit their older traffic over new links.

Using a dual IP stack

The simplest and most obvious method for transitioning from IPv4 to IPv6 is to run both. This is what all current versions of Windows do, going back as far as Windows Server 2008 and Windows Vista.

By default, these operating systems install both IP versions and use them simultaneously. Even if you had never heard of IPv6 until today, your computers are likely already using it and have IPv6 link-local addresses that you can see by running the ipconfig /all command.

The network layer implementations in Windows are separate, so you configure them separately. For both IPv4 and IPv6, you can choose to configure the address and other settings manually or use autoconfiguration.

Because Windows supports both IP versions, the computers can communicate with TCP/IP resources running either IPv4 or IPv6. However, an enterprise network includes other devices, most notably routers, which might not yet support IPv6. The Internet is also almost completely based on IPv4.

Beginning immediately, administrators should make sure that any network layer equipment they purchase includes support for IPv6. Failure to do so will almost certainly cost them later.

Tunneling

Right now, there are many network services that are IPv4-only and comparatively few that require IPv6. Those IPv6 services are coming, however.

The DirectAccess remote networking feature in Windows Server 2012 R2 and Windows 8.1 is an example of an IPv6 technology and much of its complexity is due to the need to establish IPv6 connections over the IPv4 Internet.

The primary method for transmitting IPv6 traffic over an IPv4 network is called *tunneling*. Tunneling, in this case, is the process by which a system encapsulates an IPv6 datagram within an IPv4 packet, as shown in Figure 4-4. The system then transmits the IPv4 packet to its destination, with none of the intermediate systems aware of the packet's contents.

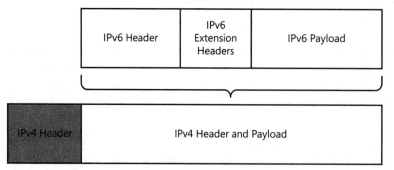

FIGURE 4-4 IPv6 traffic encapsulated inside an IPv4 datagram

Tunneling can work in a variety of configurations, depending on the network infrastructure, including router-to-router, host-to-host, router-to-host, and host-to-router. However, the most common configuration is router-to-router, as in the case of an IPv4-only connection between an IPv6 branch office and an IPv6 home office, as shown in Figure 4-5.

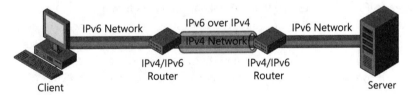

FIGURE 4-5 Two IPv6 networks connected by an IPv4 tunnel

The two routers support both IPv4 and IPv6 and the local networks at each site use IPv6. However, the link connecting the two sites is IPv4-only. By creating a tunnel between the routers in the two offices, they can exchange IPv6 traffic as needed by using their IPv4 interfaces. Computers at either site can send IPv6 traffic to the other site and the routers are responsible for encapsulating the IPv6 data in IPv4 packets for the trip through the tunnel.

Windows supports several different tunneling methods, both manual and automatic, as described in the following sections.

CONFIGURING TUNNELS MANUALLY

It is possible to manually create semipermanent tunnels that carry IPv6 traffic through an IPv4-only network. When a computer running Windows Server 2012 R2 or Windows 8.1 is functioning as one end of the tunnel, you can use the following command:

```
netsh interface ipv6 add v6v4tunnel "interface" localaddress remoteaddress
```

In this command, interface is a friendly name you want to assign to the tunnel you are creating; localaddress and remoteaddress are the IPv4 addresses forming the two ends of the tunnel. An example of an actual command would be as follows:

```
netsh interface ipv6 add v6v4tunnel "tunnel" 206.73.118.19 157.54.206.43
```

CONFIGURING TUNNELS AUTOMATICALLY

There are also a number of mechanisms that automatically create tunnels over IPv4 connections. These are technologies designed to be temporary solutions during the transition from IPv4 to IPv6. All of them include a mechanism for expressing an IPv4 address in the IPv6 format. The IPv4-to-IPv6 transition technologies that Windows supports are described in the following sections.

6TO4

The 6to4 mechanism essentially incorporates the IPv4 connections in a network into the IPv6 infrastructure by defining a method for expressing IPv4 addresses in IPv6 format and encapsulating IPv6 traffic into IPv4 packets.

ISATAP

Intra-Site Automatic Tunnel Addressing Protocol (ISATAP) is an automatic tunneling protocol used by the Windows workstation operating systems that emulates an IPv6 link by using an IPv4 network.

ISATAP also converts IPv4 addresses into the IPv6 link-layer address format, but it uses a different method than 6to4. ISATAP does not support multicasting, so it cannot locate routers in the usual manner by using the Neighbor Discovery protocol. Instead, the system compiles a potential routers list (PRL) by using DNS queries and sends Router Discovery messages to them on a regular basis by using Internet Control Message Protocol version 6 (ICMPv6).

TEREDO

To use 6to4 tunneling, both endpoints of the tunnel must have registered IPv4 addresses. However, on many networks, the system that would function as the endpoint is located behind a NAT router, and therefore has an unregistered address. In such a case, the only registered address available is assigned to the NAT router itself, and unless the router supports 6to4 (which many don't), it is impossible to establish the tunnel.

Teredo is a mechanism that addresses this shortcoming by enabling devices behind non-IPv6 NAT routers to function as tunnel endpoints. To do this, Teredo encapsulates IPv6 packets within transport-layer User Datagram Protocol (UDP) datagrams rather than network-layer IPv4 datagrams, as 6to4 does.

For a Teredo client to function as a tunnel endpoint, it must have access to a Teredo server, with which it exchanges Router Solicitation messages and Router Advertisement messages to determine whether the client is located behind a NAT router.

To initiate communications, a Teredo client exchanges null packets called *bubbles* with the desired destination, using the Teredo servers at each end as intermediaries. The function of the bubble messages is to create mappings for both computers in each other's NAT routers.

Thought experiment
Subnetting IPv4 addresses

In the following thought experiment, apply what you've learned about this objective to predict what steps you need to take. You can find answers to these questions in the "Answers" section at the end of this chapter.

The enterprise administrator has assigned Arthur the network address 172.16.8.0/24 for the branch office network that he is constructing. Arthur calculates that this gives him 254 (2^8) IP addresses, which is enough for his network, but he has determined that he needs six subnets with at least 10 hosts on each one.

With this in mind, answer the following questions.

1. How can Arthur subnet the address he has been given to satisfy his needs?

2. What IP addresses and subnet masks will the computers on his branch office network use?

Objective summary

- The IPv4 address space consists of 32-bit addresses, notated as four 8-bit decimal values from 0 to 255 separated by periods, as in the example 192.168.43.100. This is known as dotted-decimal notation and the individual 8-bit decimal values are called octets or bytes.

- Because the subnet mask associated with IP addresses can vary, the number of bits used to identify the network and the host can also vary. The original IP standard defines three address classes for assignment to networks, which support different numbers of networks and hosts.

- Because of its wastefulness, classful addressing was gradually made obsolete by a series of subnetting methods, including VLSM and eventually CIDR.

- When a Windows computer starts, it initiates the IPv6 stateless address autoconfiguration process, during which it assigns each interface a link-local unicast address.

- The simplest and most obvious method for transitioning from IPv4 to IPv6 is to run both, and this is what all current versions of Windows do.

- The primary method for transmitting IPv6 traffic over an IPv4 network is called tunneling. Tunneling is the process by which a system encapsulates an IPv6 datagram within an IPv4 packet.

Objective review

Answer the following questions to test your knowledge of the information in this objective. You can find the answers to these questions and explanations of why each answer choice is correct or incorrect in the "Answers" section at the end of this chapter.

1. Which of the following is the primary method for transmitting IPv6 traffic over an IPv4 network?

    A. Subnetting

    B. Tunneling

    C. Supernetting

    D. Contracting

2. Which of the following is the IPv6 equivalent to a private IPv4 address?

    A. Link-local unicast address

    B. Global unique unicast address

    C. Unique local unicast address

    D. Anycast address

3. Which of the following is an automatic tunneling protocol used by Windows operating systems that are located behind NAT routers?

   A. Teredo

   B. 6to4

   C. ISATAP

   D. APIPA

4. Which type of IP address must a system have to be visible from the Internet?

   A. Registered

   B. Binary

   C. Class B

   D. Subnetted

5. Which of the following subnet mask values would you use when configuring a TCP/IP client with an IPv4 address on the 172.16.32.0/19 network?

   A. 255.224.0.0

   B. 255.240.0.0

   C. 255.255.224.0

   D. 255.255.240.0

   E. 255.255.255.240

Objective 4.2: Configure servers

A server is rarely ready to perform all the tasks you have planned for it immediately after installation. Typically, some postinstallation configuration is required, and further configuration changes might become necessary after the server is in service.

This objective covers how to:

- Create and configure scopes
- Configure a DHCP reservation
- Configure DHCP options
- Configure client and server for PXE boot
- Configure DHCP relay agent
- Authorize DHCP server

Understanding DHCP

DHCP is a service that automatically configures the IP address and other TCP/IP settings on network computers by assigning addresses from a pool (called a *scope*) and reclaiming them when their leases expire.

Aside from being a time-consuming chore, manually configuring TCP/IP clients can result in typographical errors that cause addressing conflicts that interrupt network communications. DHCP prevents these errors and provides many other advantages, including automatic assignment of new addresses when computers are moved from one subnet to another and automatic reclamation of addresses that are no longer in use.

DHCP consists of three components, as follows:

- A DHCP service, which responds to client requests for TCP/IP configuration settings
- A DHCP client, which issues requests to servers and applies the TCP/IP configuration settings it receives to the local computer
- A DHCP communications protocol, which defines the formats and sequences of the messages exchanged by DHCP clients and servers

All the Microsoft Windows operating systems include DHCP client capabilities, and all the server operating systems (including Windows Server 2012 R2) include the Microsoft DHCP Server role.

The DHCP standards define three different IP address allocation methods:

- **Dynamic allocation**   The DHCP server assigns an IP address to a client computer from a scope for a specified length of time. Each client must periodically renew the lease to continue using the address. If the client allows the lease to expire, the address is returned to the scope for reassignment to another client.
- **Automatic allocation**   The DHCP server permanently assigns an IP address to a client computer from a scope. Once the DHCP server assigns the address to the client, the only way to change it is to manually reconfigure the computer.
- **Manual allocation**   The DHCP server permanently assigns a specific IP address to a specific computer on the network. In the Microsoft DHCP server, manually allocated addresses are called reservations.

In addition to IP addresses, DHCP can provide clients with values for the other parameters needed to configure a TCP/IP client, including a subnet mask, default gateway, and DNS server addresses. The object is to eliminate the need for any manual TCP/IP configuration on a client system. For example, the Microsoft DHCP server includes more than 50 configuration parameters, which it can deliver along with the IP address, even though Windows clients can only use a subset of those parameters.

DHCP communications use eight types of messages, each of which uses the same basic packet format. DHCP traffic is carried within standard UDP/IP datagrams, using port 67 at the server and port 68 at the client.

DHCP options

All DHCP messages include an options field, which is a catch-all area designed to carry the various parameters (other than the IP address) used to configure the client system's TCP/IP stack. Some of the most commonly-used options are described in the following sections.

THE DHCP MESSAGE TYPE OPTION

The DHCP Message Type option identifies the overall function of the DHCP message and is required in all DHCP packets. The DHCP communication protocol defines eight message types, as follows:

- **DHCPDISCOVER**   Used by clients to request configuration parameters from a DHCP server
- **DHCPOFFER**   Used by servers to offer IP addresses to requesting clients
- **DHCPREQUEST**   Used by clients to accept or renew an IP address assignment
- **DHCPDECLINE**   Used by clients to reject an offered IP address
- **DHCPACK**   Used by servers to acknowledge a client's acceptance of an offered IP address
- **DHCPNAK**   Used by servers to reject a client's acceptance of an offered IP address
- **DHCPRELEASE**   Used by clients to terminate an IP address lease
- **DHCPINFORM**   Used by clients to obtain additional TCP/IP configuration parameters from a server

BOOTP VENDOR INFORMATION EXTENSIONS

These options include many of the basic TCP/IP configuration parameters used by most client systems, such as the following:

- **Subnet Mask**   Specifies which bits of the IP address identify the host system and which bits identify the network where the host system resides
- **Router**   Specifies the IP address of the router (or default gateway) on the local network segment the client should use to transmit to systems on other network segments
- **Domain Name Server**   Specifies the IP addresses of the servers the client will use for DNS name resolution
- **Host Name**   Specifies the DNS host name the client will use
- **Domain Name**   Specifies the name of the DNS domain on which the system will reside

> **NOTE BOOTP**
>
> The Bootstrap Protocol (BOOTP) is the predecessor to DHCP. The two are largely compatible; the primary difference is that BOOTP allocates IP addresses permanently, and not by leasing them.

DHCP EXTENSIONS

These options are used to provide parameters that govern the DHCP lease negotiation and renewal processes.

- **Requested IP Address**   Used by the client to request a particular IP address from the server
- **IP Address Lease Time**   Specifies the duration of a dynamically allocated IP address lease
- **Server Identifier**   Specifies the IP address of the server involved in a DHCP transaction; used by the client to address unicasts to the server
- **Parameter Request List**   Used by the client to send a list of requested configuration options (identified by their code numbers) to the server
- **Message**   Used to carry an error message from the server to the client in a DHCPNAK message
- **Renewal (T1) time value**   Specifies the time period that must elapse before an IP address lease enters the renewing state
- **Rebinding (T2) time value**   Specifies the time period that must elapse before an IP address lease enters the rebinding state

DHCP communications

To design a DHCP strategy for an enterprise network and deploy it properly requires an understanding of the communications that occur between DHCP clients and servers. In Windows computers, the DHCP client is enabled by default, although it is not mentioned by name in the interface. The Obtain An IP Address Automatically option in the Internet Protocol Version 4 (TCP/IPv4) Properties sheet and the Obtain An IPv6 Address Automatically option in the Internet Protocol Version 6 (TCP/IPv6) Properties sheet control the activation of the client for IPv4 and IPv6, respectively.

DHCP LEASE NEGOTIATION

DHCP communication is always initiated by the client, as shown in Figure 4-6, and proceeds as follows:

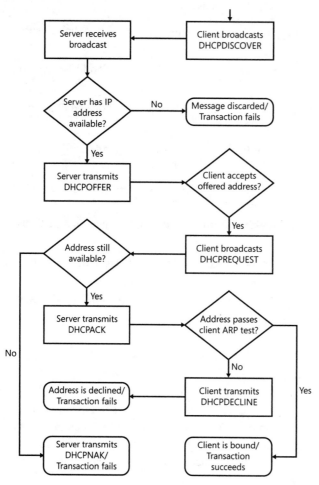

FIGURE 4-6 The DHCP IP address assignment process

1. When a computer boots for the first time with the DHCP client active, the client generates a series of DHCPDISCOVER messages to solicit an IP address assignment from a DHCP server and broadcasts them on the local network.

2. All DHCP servers receiving the DHCPDISCOVER broadcast messages generate DHCPOFFER messages containing an IP address and other TCP/IP configuration parameters and transmit them to the client.

3. After a specified period, the client accepts one of the offered addresses by broadcasting a DHCPREQUEST message containing the address of the offering server.

4. When the offering server receives the DHCPREQUEST message, it adds the offered IP address and other settings to its database.

5. The server transmits a DHCPACK message to the client, acknowledging the completion of the process. If the server cannot complete the assignment, it transmits a DHCPNAK message to the client and the process restarts.

6. As a final test, the client broadcasts the offered IP address using the Address Resolution Protocol (ARP) to ensure that no other system on the network is using it. If the client receives no response to the ARP broadcast, the DHCP transaction is completed. If another system responds to the ARP message, the client discards the IP address and transmits a DHCPDECLINE message to the server, nullifying the transaction. The client then restarts the process.

DHCP LEASE RENEWAL

By default, the DHCP Server service in Windows Server 2012 R2 uses dynamic allocation, leasing IP addresses to clients for eight-day periods. At periodic intervals during the lease, the client attempts to contact the server to renew the lease, as shown in Figure 4-7, by using the following procedure:

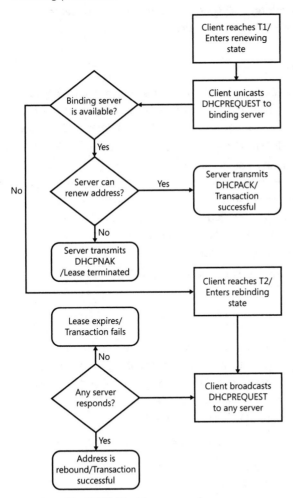

FIGURE 4-7 The DHCP IP address renewal process

1. When the DHCP client reaches the 50 percent point of the lease's duration (called the *renewal time value* or *T1 value*), the client begins generating unicast DHCPREQUEST messages and transmitting them to the DHCP server holding the lease.

2. If the server does not respond by the time the client reaches the 87.5 percent point of the lease's duration (called the rebinding time value or T2 value), the client begins transmitting its DHCPREQUEST messages as broadcasts in an attempt to solicit an IP address assignment from any DHCP server on the network.

3. If the server receives the DHCPREQUEST message from the client, it responds with either a DHCPACK message, which approves the lease renewal request, or a DHCPNAK message, which terminates the lease. If the client receives no responses to its DHCPREQUEST messages by the time the lease expires, or if it receives a DHCPNAK message, the client releases its IP address. All TCP/IP communication then ceases, except for the transmission of DHCPDISCOVER broadcasts.

Deploying a DHCP server

DHCP servers operate independently, so you must install the service and configure scopes on every computer that will function as a DHCP server. The DHCP Server service is packaged as a role in Windows Server 2012 R2, which you can install by using the Add Roles And Features Wizard, accessible from the Server Manager console.

When you install the DHCP Server role on a computer that is a member of an Active Directory Domain Services domain, the DHCP Server is automatically authorized to allocate IP addresses to clients that are members of the same domain. If the server is not a domain member when you install the role, and you join it to a domain later, you must manually authorize the DHCP server in the domain by right-clicking the server node in the DHCP console and, from the shortcut menu, selecting Authorize.

After installing the DHCP Server role, you must configure the service by creating a scope before it can serve clients.

Creating a scope

A scope is a range of IP addresses on a particular subnet that are selected for allocation by a DHCP server. In Windows Server versions prior to Windows Server 2012, you can create a scope as you install the DHCP Server role. However, in Windows Server 2012 and Windows Server 2012 R2, the procedures are separate. To create a scope by using the DHCP snap-in for Microsoft Management Console (MMC), use the following procedure.

1. In Server Manager, click Tools, DHCP. The DHCP console opens.

2. Expand the server node and the IPv4 node.

3. Right-click the IPv4 node and, from the shortcut menu, select New Scope. The New Scope Wizard opens, displaying the Welcome page.

4. Click Next. The Scope Name page opens.

5. Type a name for the scope into the Name text box and click Next. The IP Address Range page opens, as shown in Figure 4-8.

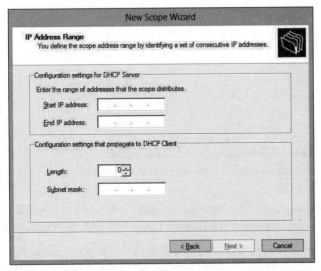

FIGURE 4-8 Configuring the IP Address Range page in the DHCP console

6. In the Start IP Address text box, type the first address in the range of addresses you want to assign. In the End IP Address box, type the last address in the range.

7. In the Subnet Mask text box, type the mask value for the subnet on which the scope will operate and click Next. The Add Exclusions And Delay page opens.

8. In the Start IP Address and End IP Address text boxes, specify a range of addresses you want to exclude from the scope. Then click Next to open the Lease Duration page.

9. Specify the length of the leases for the addresses in the scope and click Next. The Configure DHCP Options page opens.

10. Select Yes, I Want To Configure These Options Now and click Next. The Router (Default Gateway) page opens, as shown in Figure 4-9.

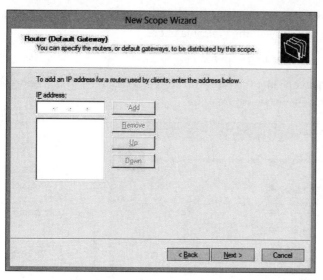

FIGURE 4-9 Configuring the Router (Default Gateway) page in the DHCP console

11. In the IP Address text box, specify the address of a router on the subnet served by the scope and click Add. Then click Next. The Domain Name And DNS Servers page opens.

12. In the Server Name text box, type the name of a DNS server on the network and click Resolve or type the address of a DNS server in the IP Address text box and click Add. Then click Next. The WINS Servers page opens.

13. Click Next to open the Activate Scope page.

14. Select Yes, I Want To Activate This Scope Now and click Next. The Completing The New Scope Wizard page opens.

15. Click Finish to close the wizard.

16. Close the DHCP console.

Once you have created the scope, all the DHCP clients on the subnet you identified can obtain their IP addresses and other TCP/IP configuration settings via DHCP. You can also use the DHCP console to create additional scopes for other subnets.

Configuring DHCP options

The New Scope Wizard enables you to configure a few of the most commonly used DHCP options as you create a new scope, but you can always configure the many other options at a later time.

The Windows DHCP server supports two kinds of options:

- **Scope Options** Options supplied only to DHCP clients receiving addresses from a particular scope

- **Server Options** Options supplied to all DHCP clients receiving addresses from the server

The Router option is a typical example of a scope option because a DHCP client's default gateway address must be on the same subnet as its IP address. The DNS Servers option is typically a server option, because DNS servers do not have to be on the same subnet, and networks often use the same DNS servers for all their clients.

All the options supported by the Windows DHCP server can be either scope or server options, and the process of configuring them is basically the same. To configure a scope option, right-click the Scope Options node and, from the shortcut menu, select Configure Options. This opens the Scope Options dialog box, which provides appropriate controls for each of the available options (see Figure 4-10).

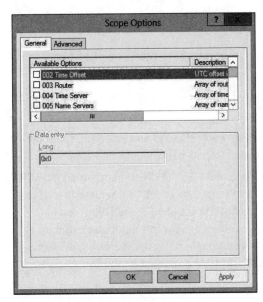

FIGURE 4-10 The Scope Options dialog box

Right-clicking the Server Options node enables you to open the Server Options dialog box, which behaves the same way as the Scope Options dialog box.

Creating a reservation

Although DHCP is an excellent TCP/IP configuration solution for most of the computers on a network, there are a few for which it is not. DHCP servers themselves, for example, need static IP addresses.

Because the DHCP dynamic allocation method allows for the possibility that a computer's IP address could change, it is not appropriate for these particular roles. However, it is possible to assign addresses to these computers by using DHCP, using manual, instead of dynamic, allocation.

In a Windows DHCP server, a manually allocated address is called a *reservation*. You create a reservation by expanding the scope node, right-clicking the Reservations node, and, from the shortcut menu, selecting New Reservation. The New Reservation dialog box opens, as shown in Figure 4-11.

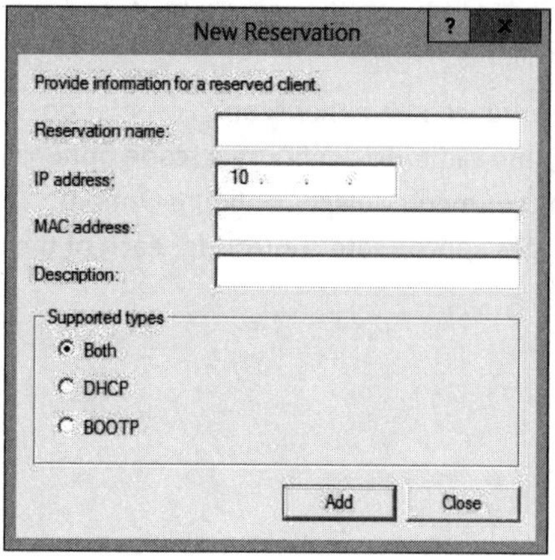

FIGURE 4-11 Creating a reservation

In this dialog box, you specify the IP address you want to assign and associate it with the client computer's MAC address, which is hard-coded into its network interface adapter.

It is also possible to manually configure the computer's TCP/IP client, but creating a DHCP reservation ensures that all your IP addresses are managed by your DHCP servers. In a large enterprise, where various administrators might be dealing with DHCP and TCP/IP configuration issues, the IP address that one technician manually assigns to a computer might be included in a DHCP scope by another technician, resulting in potential addressing conflicts. Reservations create a permanent record of the IP address assignment on the DHCP server.

Using PXE

The Windows operating systems include a DHCP client that can configure the local IP address and other TCP/IP settings of computers with an operating system already installed. However, it is also possible for a bare metal computer—that is, a computer with no operating system installed—to use DHCP.

The *Preboot eXecution Environment (PXE)* is a feature built into many network interface adapters that enables them to connect to a DHCP server over the network and obtain TCP/IP client settings, even when there is no operating system on the computer. Administrators typically use this capability to automate the operating system deployment process on large fleets of computers.

In addition to configuring the IP address and other TCP/IP client settings on the computer, the DHCP server can supply the workstation with an option specifying the location of a boot file that the system can download and use to start the computer and initiate a Windows operating system installation. A PXE-equipped system downloads boot files by using the

Trivial File Transfer Protocol (TFTP), a simplified version of the FTP protocol that requires no authentication.

Windows Server 2012 R2 includes a role called *Windows Deployment Services (WDS)*, which enables administrators to manage image files that remote computers can use to start up and install Windows. For a PXE adapter to access WDS images, the DHCP server on the network must have a custom PXEClient option (option 60) configured with the location of the WDS server on the network.

The PXE client on the workstation typically needs no configuration, with the possible exception of an alteration of the boot device order so that the computer attempts a network boot before using the local devices.

In a properly configured WDS deployment of Windows 8.1, the client operating system deployment process proceeds as follows:

1. The client computer starts and, finding no local boot device, attempts to perform a network boot.

2. The client computer connects to a DHCP server on the network, from which it obtains a DHCPOFFER message containing an IP address and other TCP/IP configuration parameters, plus the 060 PXEClient option, containing the name of a WDS server.

3. The client connects to the WDS server and is supplied with a boot image file, which it downloads by using TFTP.

4. The client loads Windows PE and the WDS client from the boot image file onto a RAM disk (a virtual disk created out of system memory) and displays a boot menu containing a list of the install images available from the WDS server.

5. The user on the client computer selects an install image from the boot menu, and the operating system installation process begins. From this point, the setup process proceeds just like a manual installation.

> **MORE INFO**   **WINDOWS DEPLOYMENT SERVICES**
>
> For more information on using WDS, see Objective 1.1, "Deploy and manage server images," in Exam 70-411, "Administering Windows Server 2012 R2."

Deploying a DHCP relay agent

Because they rely on broadcast transmissions, DHCPv4 clients can access DHCP servers only on the local network, under normal circumstances. However, it is possible to create a DHCP infrastructure in which one server provides addresses for multiple subnets. To do this, you must install a DHCP relay agent on every subnet that does not have a DHCP server on it. Many routers are capable of functioning as DHCP relay agents, but in situations where they are not, you can configure a Windows Server 2012 R2 computer to function as a relay agent by using the following procedure.

1. In Server Manager, using the Add Roles And Features Wizard, install the Remote Access role, including the Routing role service.

2. Click Open The Getting Started Wizard. The Configure Remote Access Getting Started Wizard opens.

3. Click Deploy VPN Only. The Routing And Remote Access console appears.

4. Right-click the server node and, on the shortcut menu, select Configure And Enable Routing And Remote Access. The Routing And Remote Access Server Setup Wizard appears.

5. Click Next to bypass the Welcome page. The Configuration page opens, as shown in Figure 4-12.

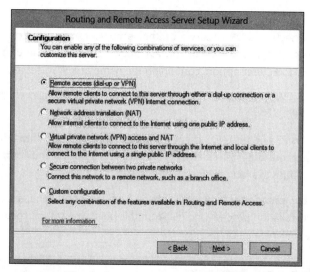

FIGURE 4-12 The Configuration page of the Routing and Remote Access Server Setup Wizard

6. Select Custom Configuration and click Next. The Custom Configuration page opens.

7. Select the LAN Routing check box and click Next. The Completing The Routing And Remote Access Server Setup Wizard page opens.

8. Click Finish. A Routing and Remote Access message box appears, prompting you to start the service.

9. Click Start Service.

10. Expand the IPv4 node. Then, right-click the General node and, in the shortcut menu, select New Routing Protocol. The New Routing Protocol dialog box appears.

11. Select DHCP Relay Agent and click OK. A DHCP Relay Agent node appears, subordinate to the IPv4 node.

12. Right-click the DHCP Relay Agent node and, on the shortcut menu, select New Interface. The New Interface For DHCP Relay Agent dialog box appears.

13. Select the interface to the subnet on which you want to install the relay agent and click OK. The DHCP Relay Properties sheet for the interface appears.

14. Leave the Relay DHCP Packets check box selected, and configure the following settings, if needed.

- **Hop-Count Threshold**   Specifies the maximum number of relay agents through which DHCP messages can pass before being discarded. The default value is 4 and the maximum value is 16. This setting prevents DHCP messages from being relayed endlessly around the network.

- **Boot Threshold**   Specifies the time interval (in seconds) that the relay agent should wait before forwarding each DHCP message it receives. The default value is 4 seconds. This setting enables you to control which DHCP server processes the clients for a particular subnet.

15. Click OK.

16. Right-click the DHCP Relay Agent node and, on the shortcut menu, select Properties. The DHCP Relay Agent Properties sheet appears, as shown in Figure 4-13.

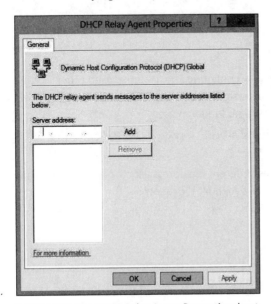

FIGURE 4-13 The DHCP Relay Agent Properties sheet

17. Type the IP address of the DHCP server to which you want the agent to relay messages and click Add. Repeat this step to add additional servers, if necessary.

18. Click OK.

19. Close the Routing And Remote Access console.

At this point, the server is configured to relay DHCP messages to the server addresses you specified.

Thought experiment

Configuring DHCP servers

In the following thought experiment, apply what you've learned about this objective to predict what steps you need to take. You can find answers to these questions in the "Answers" section at the end of this chapter.

After deploying a large number of wireless laptop computers on the network, Ralph, the IT director at Contoso, Ltd., decides to use DHCP to enable the laptop users to move from one subnet to another without having to manually reconfigure their IP addresses. Soon after the DHCP deployment, however, Ralph notices that some of the IP address scopes are being depleted, resulting in some computers being unable to connect to a new subnet.

With this in mind, answer the following question.

What can Ralph do to resolve this problem without altering the network's subnetting?

Objective summary

- DHCP is a service that automatically configures the IP address and other TCP/IP settings on network computers by assigning addresses from a pool (called a scope) and reclaiming them when they are no longer in use.

- DHCP consists of three components: a DHCP service, a DHCP client, and a DHCP communications protocol.

- The DHCP standards define three different IP address allocation methods: dynamic allocation, automatic allocation, and manual allocation.

Objective review

Answer the following questions to test your knowledge of the information in this objective. You can find the answers to these questions and explanations of why each answer choice is correct or incorrect in the "Answers" section at the end of this chapter.

1. Which of the following terms best describes the component that enables DHCP clients to communicate with DHCP servers on other subnets?

   A. Forwarder

   B. Resolver

   C. Scope

   D. Relay agent

2. Which of the following message types is *not* used during a successful DHCP address assignment?

   A. DHCPDISCOVER

   B. DHCPREQUEST

   C. DHCPACK

   D. DHCPINFORM

3. Which of the following DHCP address allocation types is the equivalent of a reservation in Windows Server 2012 R2?

   A. Dynamic allocation

   B. Automatic allocation

   C. Manual allocation

   D. Hybrid allocation

4. Which of the following network components are typically capable of functioning as DHCP relay agents?

   A. Windows 8.1 computers

   B. Routers

   C. Switches

   D. Windows Server 2012 R2 computers

5. Which of the following TCP/IP parameters is typically deployed as a scope option in DHCP?

   A. DNS Server

   B. Subnet Mask

   C. Lease Duration

   D. Default Gateway

Objective 4.3: Deploy and configure the DNS service

DNS is a crucial element of both Internet and Active Directory communications. All TCP/IP communication is based on IP addresses. Each computer on a network has at least one network interface, which is called a host in TCP/IP parlance, and each host has an IP address that is unique on that network. Every datagram transmitted by a TCP/IP system contains the IP address of the sending computer and the IP address of the intended recipient. However, when users access a shared folder on the network or a website on the Internet, they usually do so by specifying or selecting a host name, not an IP address. This is because names are far easier to remember and use than IP addresses.

> **This objective covers how to:**
> - Configure Active Directory integration of primary zones
> - Configure forwarders
> - Configure Root Hints
> - Manage DNS cache
> - Create A and PTR resource records

Understanding the DNS architecture

For TCP/IP systems to use these friendly host names, they must have a way to discover the IP address associated with the name. In the early days of TCP/IP networking, each computer had a list of names and their equivalent IP addresses, called a host table. At that time, the small number of computers on the fledgling Internet made the maintenance and distribution of a single host table practical.

Today, there are millions of computers on the Internet, and the idea of maintaining and distributing a single file containing names for all of them is absurd. Instead of using the host table stored on every computer, TCP/IP networks today use DNS servers to convert host names into IP addresses. This conversion process is referred to as name resolution.

At its core, the DNS is still a list of names and their equivalent IP addresses, but the methods for creating, storing, and retrieving those names are very different from those in a host table. DNS consists of three elements:

- **The DNS namespace** The DNS standards define a tree-structured namespace in which each branch of the tree identifies a domain. Each domain contains a collection of resource records that contain host names, IP addresses, and other information. Query operations are attempts to retrieve specific resource records from a particular domain.

- **Name servers** A DNS server is a service running on a server computer that maintains information about the domain tree structure and (sometimes) contains authoritative information about one or more specific domains in that structure. The application is capable of responding to queries for information about the domains for which it is the authority and also of forwarding queries about other domains to other name servers. This enables any DNS server to access information about any domain in the tree.

- **Resolvers** A *resolver* is a client program that generates DNS queries and sends them to a DNS server for fulfillment. A resolver has direct access to at least one DNS server and can also process referrals to direct its queries to other servers when necessary.

In its most basic form, the DNS name resolution process consists of a resolver submitting a name resolution request to its designated DNS server. When the server does not possess information about the requested name, it forwards the request to another DNS server on the network. The second server generates a response containing the IP address of the requested name and returns it to the first server, which relays the information to the resolver, as shown in Figure 4-14. In practice, however, the DNS name resolution process can be considerably more complex, as you will learn in the following sections.

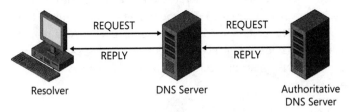

FIGURE 4-14 DNS servers relaying requests and replies to other DNS servers

DNS communications

Although all Internet applications use DNS to resolve host names into IP addresses, this name resolution process is easiest to see when you're using a web browser to access an Internet site. When you type a URL containing a DNS name (for example, www.microsoft.com) into the browser's Address box and press the Enter key, if you look quickly enough, you might be able to see a message that says something like "Finding Site: www.microsoft.com." Then, a few seconds later, you might see a message that says "Connecting to," followed by an IP address. It is during this interval that the DNS name resolution process occurs.

From the client's perspective, the procedure that occurs during these few seconds consists of the application using the built-in DNS resolver to send a query message to its designated DNS server that contains the name to be resolved. The server then replies with a message containing the IP address corresponding to that name. Using the supplied address, the application can then transmit a message to the intended destination. It is only when you examine the DNS server's role in the process that you see how complex the procedure really is.

To better explain the relationships among the DNS servers for various domains in the namespace, the following procedure diagrams the Internet name resolution process.

1. A user on a client system specifies the DNS name of an Internet server in an application such as a web browser. The application generates an application programming

interface (API) call to the resolver on the client system and the resolver creates a DNS recursive query message containing the server name, which it transmits to the DNS server identified in computer's TCP/IP configuration, as shown in Figure 4-15.

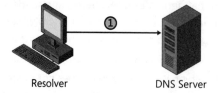

Resolver   DNS Server

FIGURE 4-15 The client resolver sending a name resolution request to its DNS server

2. The client's DNS server, after receiving the query, checks its resource records to see if it is the authoritative source for the zone containing the requested server name. If it is not, which is typical, the DNS server generates an iterative query and submits it to one of the root name servers, as shown in Figure 4-16. The root name server examines the name requested by the client's DNS server and consults its resource records to identify the authoritative servers for the name's top-level domain. The root name server then transmits a reply to the client's DNS server that contains a referral to the top-level domain server IP addresses.

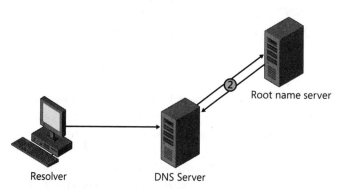

Root name server

Resolver   DNS Server

FIGURE 4-16 The client's DNS server forwarding the request to a root name server

3. The client's DNS server, now in possession of the top-level domain server address for the requested name, generates a new iterative query and transmits it to the top-level domain server, as shown in Figure 4-17. The top-level domain server examines the second-level domain in the requested name and transmits a referral containing the addresses of authoritative servers for that second-level domain back to the client's DNS server.

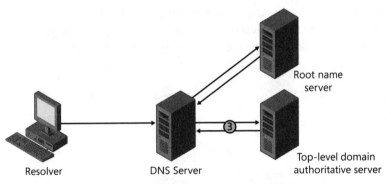

FIGURE 4-17 The client's DNS server forwarding the request to a top-level domain server

> ***NOTE* COMBINING STEPS**
>
> In the DNS name resolution process just described, the process of resolving the top-level and second-level domain names is portrayed in separate steps. However, this is often not the case. The most commonly used top-level domains (such as com, net, and org) are actually hosted by the root name servers. This eliminates one referral from the name resolution process.

4. The client's DNS server generates another iterative query and transmits it to the second-level domain server, as shown in Figure 4-18. If the second-level domain server is the authority for the zone containing the requested name, it consults its resource records to determine the IP address of the requested system and transmits it in a reply message back to that client's DNS server.

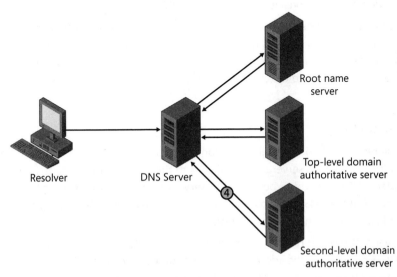

FIGURE 4-18 The client's DNS server forwarding the request to a second-level domain server

5. The client's DNS server receives the reply from the authoritative server and transmits the IP address back to the resolver on the client system, as shown in Figure 4-19. The resolver relays the address to the application, which can then initiate IP communications with the system specified by the user.

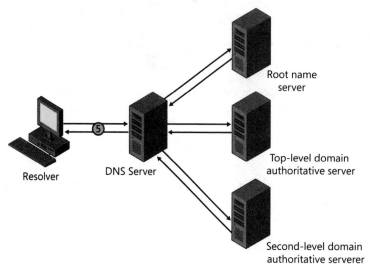

FIGURE 4-19 The client's DNS server responding to the client resolver

Depending on the name the client is trying to resolve, this process can be simpler or considerably more complex than the one shown here. On one hand, if the client's DNS server is the authority for the domain in which the requested name is located, no other servers or iterative requests are necessary. On the other hand, if the requested name contains three or more levels of domains, additional iterative queries might be necessary.

This procedure also assumes a successful completion of the name resolution procedure. If any of the authoritative DNS servers queried returns an error message to the client's DNS server stating, for example, that one of the domains in the name does not exist, then this error message is relayed back to the client and the name resolution process is said to have failed.

DNS server caching

The DNS name resolution process might seem long and complex, but in many cases it isn't necessary for the client's DNS server to send queries to the servers for each domain specified in the requested DNS name. This is because DNS servers are capable of retaining the information they learn about the DNS namespace in the course of their name resolution procedures and storing it in a cache on the local hard drive.

A DNS server that receives requests from clients, for example, caches the IP addresses of the requested systems and the addresses for authoritative servers of particular domains. The next time a client requests the resolution of a previously resolved name, the server can respond immediately with the cached information. In addition, if a client requests another name in one of the same domains, the server can send a query directly to an authoritative server for that domain rather than to a root name server. Thus, the names in commonly accessed domains generally resolve quickly because one of the servers along the line has information about the domain in its cache, whereas names in obscure domains take longer, because the entire request/referral process is needed.

Caching is a vital element of the DNS architecture because it reduces the number of requests sent to the root name and top-level domain servers, which, being at the top of the DNS tree, are the most likely to act as a bottleneck for the whole system. However, caches must be purged eventually, and there is a fine line between effective and ineffective caching.

Because DNS servers retain resource records in their caches, it can take hours or even days for changes made in an authoritative server to be propagated around the Internet. During this period, users might receive incorrect information in response to a query. If information remains in server caches too long, then the changes administrators make to the data in their DNS servers take too long to propagate around the Internet. If caches are purged too quickly, then the number of requests sent to the root name and top-level domain servers increases precipitously.

The amount of time that DNS data remains cached on a server is called its *time to live (TTL)*. Unlike most data caches, the TTL is not specified by the administrator of the server where the cache is stored. Instead, the administrators of each authoritative DNS server specify how long the data for the resource records in their domains or zones should be retained in the servers where it is cached. This enables administrators to specify a TTL value based on the volatility of their server data. On a network where changes in IP addresses or the addition of new resource records is frequent, a lower TTL value increases the likelihood that clients will receive current data. On a network that rarely changes, a longer TTL value minimizes the number of requests sent to the parent servers of your domain or zone.

To modify the TTL value for a zone on a Windows Server 2012 R2 DNS server, right-click the zone, open the Properties sheet, and click the Start Of Authority (SOA) tab, as shown in Figure 4-20. On this tab, you can modify the TTL for this record setting from its default value of one hour.

FIGURE 4-20 Viewing the Start Of Authority (SOA) tab on a DNS server's Properties sheet

Client-side resolver caching

The client resolver on Windows systems also contains a caching mechanism, which stores resolved IP addresses and also HOSTS file information on a local drive. When a client enounters a name that needs to be resolved into an IP address, it checks its local cache first, before sending a request to its DNS server.

DNS referrals and queries

The process by which one DNS server sends a name resolution request to another DNS server is called a referral. Referrals are essential to the DNS name resolution process.

As you noticed in the process described earlier, the DNS client's primary involvement in the name resolution process is sending one query and receiving one reply. The client's DNS server might have to send referrals to several servers before it reaches the one that has the information it needs.

DNS servers recognize two types of name resolution requests, as follows:

- **Recursive query** In a recursive query, the DNS server receiving the name resolution request takes full responsibility for resolving the name. If the server possesses information about the requested name, it replies immediately to the requestor. If the server has no information about the name, it sends referrals to other DNS servers until it obtains the information it needs. TCP/IP client resolvers always send recursive queries to their designated DNS servers.

- **Iterative query** In an iterative query, the server that receives the name resolution request immediately responds with the best information it possesses at the time. DNS servers use iterative queries when communicating with each other. In most cases, it would be improper to configure one DNS server to send a recursive query to another DNS server. The only time a DNS server sends recursive queries to another server is in the case of a special type of server called a forwarder, which is specifically configured to interact with other servers in this way.

DNS forwarders

One of the scenarios in which DNS servers send recursive queries to other servers is when you configure a server to function as a forwarder. On a network running several DNS servers, you might not want all the servers sending queries to other DNS servers on the Internet. If the network has a relatively slow connection to the Internet, for example, several servers transmitting repeated queries might use too much of the available bandwidth.

To prevent this, the Windows Server 2012 R2 DNS server enables you to configure one server to function as the forwarder for all Internet queries generated by the other servers on the network. Any time a server has to resolve the DNS name of an Internet system and fails to find the needed information in its cache, it transmits a recursive query to the forwarder, which is then responsible for sending its own iterative queries over the Internet connection. Once the forwarder resolves the name, it sends a reply back to the original DNS server, which relays it to the client.

To configure forwarders on a Windows Server 2012 R2 DNS server, right-click the server node, open the Properties sheet, and click the Forwarders tab, as shown in Figure 4-21. On this tab, you can add the names and addresses of the servers that you want your server to use as forwarders.

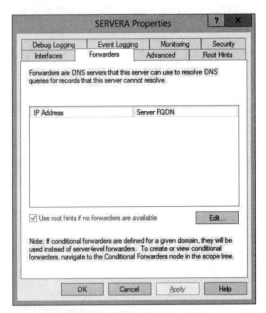

FIGURE 4-21 The Forwarders tab on a DNS server's Properties sheet

The Windows Server 2012 R2 DNS server also supports *conditional forwarding*, which enables administrators to specify different server IP addresses for specific domain names. When the server receives a name resolution request, it checks the domain name in the request against its list of forwarders and passes the request to another server only if the domain appears in the list. By using this feature, organizations with multiple internal domains can resolve names throughout the enterprise without having to send requests to servers on the Internet.

Reverse name resolution

The name resolution process described earlier is designed to convert DNS names into IP addresses. However, there are occasions when it is necessary for a computer to convert an IP address into a DNS name. This is called a *reverse name resolution*.

Because the domain hierarchy is organized according to domain names, there is no apparent way to resolve an IP address into a name by using iterative queries, except by forwarding the reverse name resolution request to every DNS server on the Internet in search of the requested address, which is obviously impractical.

To overcome this problem, the developers of the DNS created a special domain called in-addr.arpa, specifically designed for reverse name resolution. The in-addr.arpa second-level domain contains four additional levels of subdomains. Each of the four levels consists of subdomains that are named using the numerals 0 to 255. For example, beneath in-addr.arpa, there are 256 third-level domains, which have names ranging from 0.in-addr.arpa to 255.in-addr.arpa. Each of those 256 third-level domains has 256 fourth-level domains beneath it, also numbered from 0 to 255, and each fourth-level domain has 256 fifth-level domains, as shown in Figure 4-22. Each of those fifth-level domains can have up to 256 hosts in it, also numbered from 0 to 255.

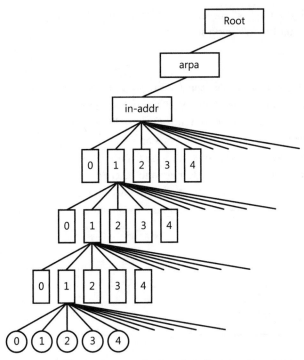

FIGURE 4-22 The DNS reverse lookup domain

By using this hierarchy of subdomains, it is possible to express the first three bytes of an IP address as a DNS domain name and to create a resource record named for the fourth byte in the appropriate fifth-level domain. For example, to resolve the IP address 192.168.89.34 into a name, a DNS server would locate a domain called 89.168.192.in-addr.arpa in the usual manner and read the contents of a resource record named 34 in that domain.

> **NOTE   REVERSE LOOKUP ADDRESSES**
>
> In the in-addr.arpa domain, the IP address is reversed in the domain name because IP addresses have the least pertinent bit (that is, the host identifier) on the right, but DNS fully qualified domain names (FQDNs) have the host name on the left.

Deploying a DNS server

The process of deploying a DNS server on a Windows Server 2012 R2 computer is just a matter of installing the DNS Server role by using the Add Roles And Features Wizard in Server Manager. The actual installation requires no additional input; there are no additional pages in the wizard and no role services to select.

Once you install the DNS Server role, the computer is ready to perform caching-only name resolution services for any clients that have access to it. The role also installs the DNS Manager console, which you use to configure the DNS server's other capabilities. To configure the server to perform other services, consult the following sections.

Creating zones

A zone is an administrative entity you create on a DNS server to represent a discrete portion of the DNS namespace. Administrators typically divide the DNS namespace into zones to store them on different servers and to delegate their administration to different people. Zones always consist of entire domains and/or subdomains. You can create a zone that contains multiple domains as long as those domains are contiguous in the DNS namespace. For example, you can create a zone containing a parent domain and its child, because they are directly connected, but you cannot create a zone containing two child domains without their common parent, because the two children are not directly connected, as shown in Figure 4-23.

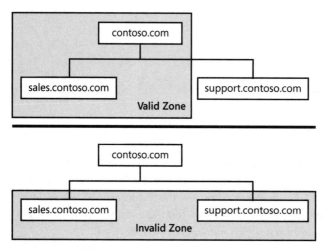

FIGURE 4-23 Valid zones must consist of contiguous domains

You can divide the DNS namespace into multiple zones and host them on a single DNS server if you want, although there is usually no persuasive reason to do so. The DNS server in Windows Server 2012 R2 can support as many as 200,000 zones on a single server, although it is hard to imagine a scenario that would require that many. In most cases, an administrator creates multiple zones on a server and then delegates most of them to other servers, which then become responsible for hosting them.

Every zone consists of a zone database, which contains the resource records for the domains in that zone. The DNS server in Windows Server 2012 R2 supports three zone types, which specify where the server stores the zone database and what kind of information it contains. These zone types are as follows:

- **Primary zone** Creates a primary zone that contains the master copy of the zone database, where administrators make all changes to the zone's resource records. If the zone is not stored in Active Directory , the server creates a primary master zone database file on the local drive. This is a simple text file that is compliant with most non-Windows DNS server implementations.

- **Secondary zone**   Creates a duplicate of a primary zone on another server. The secondary zone contains a backup copy of the primary master zone database file, stored as an identical text file on the server's local drive. You can only update the resource records in a secondary zone by replicating the primary master zone database file, by using a process called a zone transfer.

- **Stub zone**   Creates a copy of a primary zone that contains the key resource records that identify the authoritative servers for the zone. The stub zone forwards or refers requests. When you create a stub zone, you configure it with the IP address of the server that hosts the zone from which you created the stub. When the server hosting the stub zone receives a query for a name in that zone, it either forwards the request to the host of the zone or replies with a referral to that host, depending on whether the query is recursive or iterative.

DNS was designed long before Active Directory, so most of the Internet relies on primary and secondary zones using text-based database files. The most common DNS server implementation on the Internet is a UNIX program called BIND that uses these databases.

However, for DNS servers supporting internal domains, especially AD DS domains, using the Windows DNS server to create a primary zone and store it in Active Directory is the recommended procedure. When you store the zone in the AD DS database, you do not have to create secondary zones or perform zone transfers, because AD DS takes the responsibility for replicating the data, and whatever backup solution you use to protect Active Directory also protects the DNS data.

EXAM TIP

Exam 70-410 covers only the process of creating a primary zone stored in Active Directory. The procedures for creating text-based primary and secondary zones and configuring zone transfers are covered on Exam 70-411, "Administering Windows Server 2012 R2," in Objective 3.1, "Configure DNS zones."

USING ACTIVE DIRECTORY–INTEGRATED ZONES

When you are running the DNS server service on a computer that is an Active Directory Domain Services domain controller and you store the zone in Active Directory while creating a zone in the New Zone Wizard, the server does not create a zone database file. Instead, the server stores the DNS resource records for the zone in the AD DS database. Storing the DNS database in Active Directory provides a number of advantages, including ease of administration, conservation of network bandwidth, and increased security.

In Active Directory–integrated zones, the zone data is replicated automatically to other domain controllers, along with all other Active Directory data. Active Directory uses a multiple master replication system so that copies of the database are updated on all domain controllers in the domain. You can modify the DNS resource records on any writable domain controller hosting a copy of the zone data, and Active Directory will automatically update all the other domain controllers. You don't have to create secondary zones or manually configure zone transfers, because Active Directory performs all database replication activities.

By default, Windows Server 2012 R2 replicates the data for a primary zone stored in Active Directory to all the other domain controllers running the DNS server in the same AD DS domain where the zone is stored. You can also modify the scope of zone database replication to keep copies on all domain controllers throughout the enterprise or on all domain controllers in the AD DS domain, regardless of whether they are running the DNS server. You can also create a custom replication scope that copies the zone database to the domain controllers you specify.

Active Directory conserves network bandwidth by replicating only the DNS data that has changed since the last replication and by compressing the data before transmitting it over the network. The zone replications also use the full security capabilities of Active Directory, including encryption and Kerberos-based authentication, which are considerably more robust than those of file-based zone transfers. The protection provided by Active Directory is also automatic and invisible to the administrator, unlike the process of encrypting file-based zone transfers using IPsec.

CREATING AN ACTIVE DIRECTORY ZONE

To create a new primary zone and store it in Active Directory, use the following procedure.

1. In Server Manager on a domain controller, click Tools, DNS to open the DNS Manager console.

2. Expand the server node and select the Forward Lookup Zones folder.

3. Right-click the Forward Lookup Zones folder and, from the shortcut menu, select New Zone. The New Zone Wizard starts.

4. Click Next to bypass the Welcome page and open the Zone Type page.

5. Leave the Primary Zone option and the Store The Zone In Active Directory (Available Only If DNS Server Is A Domain Controller) check box selected and click Next. The Active Directory Zone Replication Scope page opens.

6. Click Next. The Zone Name page opens.

7. Specify the name you want to assign to the zone in the Zone Name text box and click Next. The Dynamic Update page opens.

8. Select one of the following options:

   - Allow Only Secure Dynamic Updates
   - Allow Both Nonsecure And Secure Dynamic Updates
   - Do Not Allow Dynamic Updates

9. Click Next. The Completing the New Zone Wizard page opens.

10. Click Finish. The wizard creates the zone.

11. Close the DNS Manager console.

To create a primary zone in Active Directory with Windows PowerShell, you use the Add-DnsServerPrimaryZone cmdlet, as shown in the following example.

```
Add-DnsServerPrimaryZone -Name "zonename.adatum.com" -ReplicationScope "Domain"
-PassThru
```

Once you have created a primary zone, you can proceed to create resource records that specify the names of the hosts on the network and their equivalent IP addresses.

Creating resource records

When you run your own DNS server, you create a resource record for each host name that you want to be accessible by the rest of the network.

There are several different types of resource records used by DNS servers, the most important of which are as follows:

- **SOA (Start of Authority)**   Indicates that the server is the best authoritative source for data concerning the zone. Each zone must have an SOA record and only one SOA record can be in a zone.

- **NS (Name Server)**   Identifies a DNS server functioning as an authority for the zone. Each DNS server in the zone (whether primary master or secondary) must be represented by an NS record.

- **A (Address)**   Provides a name-to-address mapping that supplies an IPv4 address for a specific DNS name. This record type performs the primary function of the DNS: converting names to addresses.

- **AAAA (Address)**   Provides a name-to-address mapping that supplies an IPv6 address for a specific DNS name. This record type performs the primary function of the DNS: converting names to addresses.

- **PTR (Pointer)**   Provides an address-to-name mapping that supplies a DNS name for a specific address in the in-addr.arpa domain. This is the functional opposite of an A record, used for reverse lookups only.

- **CNAME (Canonical Name)**   Creates an alias that points to the canonical name (that is, the "real" name) of a host identified by an A record. Administrators use CNAME records to provide alternative names by which systems can be identified.

- **MX (Mail Exchanger)**   Identifies a system that will direct email traffic sent to an address in the domain to the individual recipient, a mail gateway, or another mail server.

EXAM TIP

Exam 70-410 covers only the process of creating A and PTR resource records. The procedures for creating other resource record types are covered on Exam 70-411, "Administering
Windows Server 2012 R2," in Objective 3.2, "Configure DNS records."

To create a new Address resource record, use the following procedure.

1. Log on to Windows Server 2012 R2 using an account with Administrative privileges.
   The Server Manager window opens.

2. Click Tools, DNS to open the DNS Manager console.

3. Expand the server node and select the Forward Lookup Zones folder.

4. Right-click the zone in which you want to create the record and, from the shortcut
   menu, select New Host (A or AAAA). The New Host dialog box appears, as shown in
   Figure 4-24.

FIGURE 4-24 Configuring the New Host dialog box

5. In the Name text box, type the host name for the new record. The FQDN for the
   record appears.

6. In the IP Address text box, type the IPv4 or IPv6 address associated with the
   host name.

7. Select the following check boxes, if necessary:

   - **Create Associated Pointer (PTR) Record**   Creates a reverse name lookup
     record for the host in the in-addr.arpa domain

   - **Allow Any Authenticated User To Update DNS Records With The Same
     Owner Name**   Enables users to modify their own resource records

8. Click Add Host. The new resource record is created in the zone you selected.

9. Close the DNS Manager console.

To create a PTR record for a new host, you can select the Create Associated Pointer (PTR) Record check box in the New Host dialog box, but that will only be effective if a reverse look-up zone already exists on the server. To create the zone, follow the same procedure described earlier, this time selecting the Reverse Lookup Zones folder.

When you elect to create an IPv4 reverse lookup zone, a Reverse Lookup Zone Name page opens, like the one shown in Figure 4-25, in which you supply the Network ID that the wizard will use to create the zone.

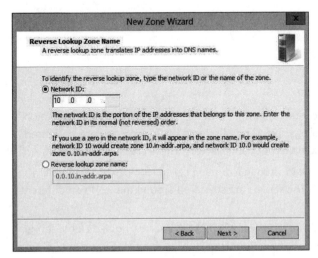

FIGURE 4-25 Configuring the Reverse Lookup Zone Name page in the New Zone Wizard

Once the zone is created, you can either create PTR records along with A or AAAA records or create a new PTR record by using the New Resource Record dialog box.

Configuring DNS server settings

Once you have installed a DNS server and created zones and resource records on it, there are many settings you can alter to modify its behavior. The following sections describe some of these settings.

CONFIGURING ACTIVE DIRECTORY DNS REPLICATION

To modify the replication scope for an Active Directory–integrated zone, open the zone's Properties sheet in the DNS Manager console and, on the General tab, click Change for Replication: All DNS Servers In The Active Directory Domain to display the Change Zone Replication Scope dialog box, shown in Figure 4-26. The options are the same as those in the New Zone Wizard.

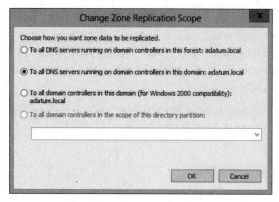

FIGURE 4-26 The Change Zone Replication Scope dialog box

CONFIGURING ROOT HINTS

Most DNS servers must be able to contact the root name servers to initiate name resolution processes. Most server implementations, including Microsoft DNS Server, are preconfigured with the names and addresses of multiple root name servers. These are called *Root Hints*.

The 13 root name server names are located in a domain called root-servers.net and are named using letters of the alphabet. The servers are scattered around the world on different subnets to provide fault tolerance.

To modify the Root Hints on a Windows Server 2012 R2 DNS server, right-click the server node, open the Properties sheet, and click the Root Hints tab, as shown in Figure 4-27. On this tab, you can add, edit, or remove Root Hints from the list provided.

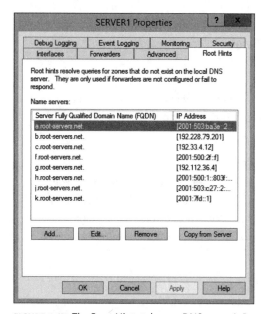

FIGURE 4-27 The Root Hints tab on a DNS server's Properties sheet

Thought experiment
Controlling DNS traffic

In the following thought experiment, apply what you've learned about this objective to predict what steps you need to take. You can find answers to these questions in the "Answers" section at the end of this chapter.

Alice is an enterprise administrator for Wingtip Toys, which has recently expanded its Customer Service division by adding 100 workstations. All the workstations on the company network are configured to use a server on the perimeter network as their primary DNS server and a server on their ISP's network as a secondary server. As a result of the expansion, Internet performance has slowed noticeably and a Network Monitor trace indicates that there is a disproportionate amount of DNS traffic on the link between the perimeter network and the ISP's network.

With this in mind, answer the following question.

What are two ways that Alice can reduce the amount of DNS traffic passing over the Internet connection?

Objective summary

- DHCP is a service that automatically configures the IP address and other TCP/IP settings on network computers by assigning addresses from a pool (called a scope) and reclaiming them when they are no longer in use.
- TCP/IP networks today use DNS servers to convert host names into IP addresses. This conversion process is referred to as name resolution.
- DNS consists of three elements: the DNS namespace, name servers, and resolvers.
- The hierarchical nature of the DNS namespace is designed to make it possible for any DNS server on the Internet to locate the authoritative source for any domain name by using a minimum number of queries.
- In a recursive query, the DNS server receiving the name resolution request takes full responsibility for resolving the name. In an iterative query, the server that receives the name resolution request immediately responds with the best information it possesses at the time.
- For Internet name resolution purposes, the only functions required of the DNS server are the ability to process incoming queries from resolvers and send its own queries to other DNS servers on the Internet.

Objective review

Answer the following questions to test your knowledge of the information in this objective. You can find the answers to these questions and explanations of why each answer choice is correct or incorrect in the "Answers" section at the end of this chapter.

1. Which of the following resource record types contains the information a DNS server needs to perform reverse name lookups?

   A. A

   B. CNAME

   C. SOA

   D. PTR

2. Which of the following would be the correct FQDN for a resource record in a reverse lookup zone if the computer's IP address is 10.75.143.88?

   A. 88.143.75.10.in-addr.arpa

   B. 10.75.143.88.in-addr.arpa

   C. in-addr.arpa.88.143.75.10

   D. arpa.in-addr.10.75.143.88

3. Which of the following is *not* one of the elements of DNS?

   A. Resolvers

   B. Relay agents

   C. Name servers

   D. Namespace

4. In which of the following DNS transactions does the querying system generate a recursive query?

   A. A DNS client sends the server name www.adatum.com to its designated DNS server for resolution.

   B. A client's DNS server sends a request to a root domain server to find the authoritative server for the com top-level domain.

   C. A client's DNS server sends a request to the com top-level domain server to find the authoritative server for the adatum.com domain.

   D. A client's DNS server sends a request to the adatum.com domain server to find the IP address associated with the server name www.

5. Which of the following contains the controls used to modify DNS name caching?

   A. The Forwarders tab of a server's Properties sheet

   B. The Start of Authority (SOA) tab of a zone's Properties sheet

   C. The Root Hints tab of a server's Properties sheet

   D. The New Zone Wizard

Answers

This section contains the solutions to the thought experiments and answers to the objective review questions in this chapter.

Objective 4.1: Thought experiment

Arthur can subnet the address he has been given by using four host bits to give him 16 subnets with up to 14 hosts on each. The computers will use a subnet mask of 255.255.255.240 and IP address ranges as follows:

172.16.8.1 - 172.16.8.14
172.16.8.17 - 172.16.8.30
172.16.8.33 - 172.16.8.46
172.16.8.49 - 172.16.8.62
172.16.8.65 - 172.16.8.78
172.16.8.81 - 172.16.8.94
172.16.8.97 - 172.16.8.110
172.16.8.113 - 172.16.8.126
172.16.8.129 - 172.16.8.142
172.16.8.145 - 172.16.8.158
172.16.8.161 - 172.16.8.174
172.16.8.177 - 172.16.8.190
172.16.8.193 - 172.16.8.206
172.16.8.209 - 172.16.8.222
172.16.8.225 - 172.16.8.238
172.16.8.241 - 172.16.8.254

Objective 4.1: Review

1. **Correct answer:** B

   A. **Incorrect:** Subnetting is a technique for creating administrative divisions on a network; it does not transmit IPv6 traffic over an IPv4 network.

   B. **Correct:** Tunneling is a method for encapsulating IPv6 traffic within IPv4 datagrams.

   C. **Incorrect:** Supernetting is a method for combining consecutive subnets into a single entity.

   D. **Incorrect:** Contracting is a method for shortening IPv6 addresses.

2. **Correct answer:** C

   A. **Incorrect:** Link-local unicast addresses are self-assigned by IPv6 systems. They are therefore the equivalent of APIPA addresses on IPv4.

   B. **Incorrect:** A global unicast address is the equivalent of a registered IPv4 address, routable worldwide and unique on the Internet.

   C. **Correct:** Unique local unicast addresses are the IPv6 equivalent of the 10.0.0.0/8, 172.16.0.0/12, and 192.168.0.0/16 private network addresses in IPv4.

   D. **Incorrect:** The function of an anycast address is to identify the routers within a given address scope and send traffic to the nearest router.

3. **Correct answer:** A

   A. **Correct:** Teredo is a mechanism that enables devices behind non-IPv6 NAT routers to function as tunnel endpoints.

   B. **Incorrect:** 6to4 incorporates the IPv4 connections in a network into the IPv6 infrastructure by defining a method for expressing IPv4 addresses in IPv6 format and encapsulating IPv6 traffic into IPv4 packets.

   C. **Incorrect:** Intra-Site Automatic Tunnel Addressing Protocol (ISATAP) is an automatic tunneling protocol used by the Windows workstation operating systems that emulates an IPv6 link using an IPv4 network.

   D. **Incorrect:** APIPA is an automatic IPv4 address self-assignment process. It has nothing to do with tunneling.

4. **Correct answer:** A

   A. **Correct:** For an address to be visible from the Internet, it must be registered with the IANA.

   B. **Incorrect:** Binary is a system of numbering that can be used to express any IP address.

   C. **Incorrect:** All address classes can be visible or invisible to the Internet.

   D. **Incorrect:** Subnetted addresses can be visible or invisible to the Internet.

5. **Correct answer:** C

   A. **Incorrect:** In binary form, the mask 255.224.0.0 is 11111111.11100000.00000000. 00000000, which contains only 11 network identifier bits.

   B. **Incorrect:** In binary form, the mask 255.240.0.0 is 11111111.11110000.00000000. 00000000, which contains only 12 network identifier bits.

   C. **Correct:** In binary form, the mask 255.255.224.0 is 11111111.11111111.11100000. 00000000, which contains 19 network identifier bits.

   D. **Incorrect:** In binary form, the mask 255.255.240.0 is 11111111.11111111.11110000. 00000000, which contains 20 network identifier bits.

   E. **Incorrect:** In binary form, the mask 255.255.255.240 is 11111111.11111111. 11111111.11110000, which contains 28 network identifier bits.

Objective 4.2: Thought experiment

Roger can reduce the duration of the IP address leases in his scopes so that abandoned addresses will be available to clients more quickly.

Objective 4.2: Review

1. **Correct answer:** D

   A. **Incorrect:** A forwarder is a DNS server that accepts recursive queries from other servers.

   B. **Incorrect:** A resolver is a DNS client component.

   C. **Incorrect:** A scope is a range of IP addresses that a DHCP server is configured to allocate.

   D. **Correct:** A relay agent is a software module that receives DHCP broadcast messages and forwards them to a DHCP server on another subnet.

2. **Correct answer:** D

   A. **Incorrect:** The DHCP address assignment process begins when the DHCP client generates DHCPDISCOVER messages and broadcasts them on the local network.

   B. **Incorrect:** The client eventually stops broadcasting and signals its acceptance of one of the offered addresses by generating a DHCPREQUEST message.

   C. **Incorrect:** When the server offering the accepted IP address receives the DHCPREQUEST message, it transmits a DHCPACK message to the client, acknowledging the completion of the process.

   D. **Correct:** The DHCPINFORM message type is not used during an IP address assignment.

3. **Correct answer:** C

   A. **Incorrect:** Dynamic allocation is when the DHCP server assigns an IP address to a client computer from a scope for a specified length of time.

   B. **Incorrect:** Automatic allocation is when the DHCP server permanently assigns an IP address to a client computer from a scope.

   C. **Correct:** Manual allocation is when the DHCP server permanently assigns a specific IP address to a specific computer on the network. In the Windows Server 2012 R2 DHCP server, manually allocated addresses are called reservations.

   D. **Incorrect:** Hybrid is a DHCP infrastructure type, not a type of address allocation.

4. **Correct answers:** B, D

   A. **Incorrect:** Windows 8.1 cannot function as a LAN router, and it therefore cannot function as a DHCP relay agent.

   B. **Correct:** Most IP routers have DHCP relay agent capabilities built into them. If the routers connecting your subnets are so equipped, you can use them as relay agents, eliminating the need for a DHCP server on each subnet.

   C. **Incorrect:** Switches are data-link layer devices and are designed to communicate with devices on the same subnet. A DHCP relay agent requires access to two subnets.

   D. **Correct:** If your routers cannot function as DHCP relay agents, you can use the relay agent capability built into the Windows server operating systems. In Windows Server 2012 R2, the DHCP relay agent capability is built into the Remote Access role.

5. **Correct answer:** D

   A. **Incorrect:** In most cases, all the computers on a network will use the same DNS server, so it is more convenient to deploy its address once by using a server option than to deploy it as a scope option on every scope.

   B. **Incorrect:** The subnet mask is automatically included with every address lease and therefore does not have to be deployed as a scope option or a server option.

   C. **Incorrect:** The lease duration option is automatically included with every address lease and therefore does not have to be deployed as a scope option or a server option.

   D. **Correct:** The default gateway must be a router on the same subnet as the IP addresses the DHCP server is allocating. Therefore, the gateway address is different for every scope and must be deployed as a scope option.

Objective 4.3: Thought experiment

1. Alice can configure the DNS server on the perimeter network to use the ISP's DNS server as a forwarder.

2. Alice can configure the workstations to use the ISP's DNS server as their primary DNS server.

Objective 4.3: Review

1. **Correct answer:** D

   A. **Incorrect:** A resource record contains information for forward name lookups, not reverse name lookups.

   B. **Incorrect:** CNAME resource records contain alias information for A records. They are not used for reverse name lookups.

   C. **Incorrect:** SOA records specify that a server is the authoritative source for a zone. They are not used for reverse name lookups.

   D. **Correct:** PTR records contain the information needed for the server to perform reverse name lookups.

2. **Correct answer:** A

   A. **Correct:** To resolve the IP address 10.75.143.88 into a name, a DNS server would locate a domain called 143.75.10.in-addr.arpa in the usual manner and read the contents of a resource record named 88 in that domain.

   B. **Incorrect:** The least significant bits in the IP address (that is, 88) should come first in the FQDN.

   C. **Incorrect:** The top-level domain used for reverse lookups is arpa. Therefore, arpa must be the last and most significant name in a reverse lookup FQDN.

   D. **Incorrect:** The top-level domain used for reverse lookups is arpa. Therefore, arpa must be the last and most significant name in a reverse lookup FQDN.

3. **Correct answer:** B

   A. **Incorrect:** Resolvers are client programs that generate DNS queries and send them to a DNS server for fulfillment.

   B. **Correct:** Relay agents are router devices that enable DHCP clients to communicate with servers on other networks.

   C. **Incorrect:** Name servers are applications running on server computers that maintain information about the domain tree structure.

   D. **Incorrect:** DNS consists of a tree-structured namespace in which each branch of the tree identifies a domain.

4. **Correct answer:** A

   A. **Correct:** When a client sends a name resolution query to its DNS server, it uses a recursive request so that the server will take on the responsibility for resolving the name.

   B. **Incorrect:** A DNS server seeking the server for a top-level domain uses iterative, not recursive, queries.

   C. **Incorrect:** A DNS server seeking the server for a second-level domain uses iterative, not recursive, queries.

   D. **Incorrect:** A DNS server requesting a server name resolution from an authoritative server uses iterative, not recursive, queries.

5. **Correct answer:** B

   A. **Incorrect:** The Forwarders tab is where you specify the addresses of servers that will have your server's recursive queries.

   B. **Correct:** The Start of Authority (SOA) tab of a zone's Properties sheet contains the Minimum (Default) TTL setting that controls DNS name caching for the zone.

   C. **Incorrect:** The Root Hints tab is where you specify the addresses of the root name servers on the Internet.

   D. **Incorrect:** The New Zone Wizard does not enable you to modify name caching settings.

CHAPTER 5

Installing and administering Active Directory

A directory service is a repository of information about the resources—hardware, software, and human—that are connected to a network. Users, computers, and applications throughout the network can access the repository for a variety of purposes, including user authentication, configuration data storage, and even simple white pages–style information lookups. Active Directory Domain Services (AD DS) is the directory service that Microsoft first introduced in Windows 2000 Server, and Microsoft has upgraded it in each successive server operating system release, including Windows Server 2012 R2.

This chapter covers some of the fundamental tasks that administrators perform to install and manage AD DS.

Objectives in this chapter

- Objective 5.1: Install domain controllers
- Objective 5.2: Create and manage Active Directory users and computers
- Objective 5.3: Create and manage Active Directory groups and organizational units (OUs)

Objective 5.1: Install domain controllers

AD DS is a directory service that enables administrators to create organizational divisions called *domains*. A domain is a logical container of network components, hosted by at least one server designated as a domain controller. The domain controllers for each domain replicate their data among themselves for fault tolerance and load balancing purposes.

This objective covers how to:

- Add or remove a domain controller from a domain
- Upgrade a domain controller
- Install Active Directory Domain Services (AD DS) on a Server Core installation
- Deploy Active Directory infrastructure as a service (IaaS) in Windows Azure
- Install a domain controller from Install from Media (IFM)
- Resolve DNS SRV record registration issues
- Configure a global catalog server

Deploying Active Directory Domain Services

To create a new domain or to add a domain controller to an existing domain, you must install the Active Directory Domain Services role on a Windows Server 2012 R2 computer and then run the Active Directory Domain Services Configuration Wizard.

To use a Windows Server 2012 R2 computer as a domain controller, you should configure it to use static IP addresses, not addresses supplied by a Dynamic Host Configuration Protocol (DHCP) server. In addition, if you are creating a domain in an existing forest or adding a domain controller to an existing domain, you must configure the computer to use the Domain Name System (DNS) server that hosts the existing forest or domain, at least during the Active Directory promotion.

Installing the Active Directory Domain Services role

Although it does not actually convert the computer into a domain controller, installing the Active Directory Domain Services role prepares the computer for the conversion process.

To install the role, use the following procedure.

1. In Server Manager, from the Manage menu, select Add Roles And Features. The Add Roles And Features Wizard starts, displaying the Before You Begin page.

2. Click Next. The Select Installation Type page opens.

3. Leave the Role-Based Or Feature-Based Installation option selected and click Next to open the Select Destination Server page.

4. Select the server that you want to promote to a domain controller and click Next. The Select Server Roles page opens.

5. Select the Active Directory Domain Service role. The Add Features That Are Required For Active Directory Domain Services dialog box opens.

6. Click Add Features to accept the dependencies and then click Next. The Select Features page opens.

7. Click Next. The Active Directory Domain Services page opens, displaying information about the role.

8. Click Next. A Confirm Installation Selections page opens.

9. Select from the following optional functions, if desired:

   - **Restart The Destination Server Automatically If Desired** Causes the server to restart automatically when the installation is completed, if the selected roles and features require it

   - **Export Configuration Settings** Creates an XML script documenting the procedures performed by the wizard, which you can use to install the same configuration on another server using Windows PowerShell

   - **Specify An Alternate Source Path** Specifies the location of an image file containing the software needed to install the selected roles and features

10. Click Install, which displays the Installation Progress page. Once the role has been installed, a Promote This Server To A Domain Controller link appears.

11. Leave the wizard open.

> *NOTE* **DCPROMO.EXE**
>
> The Dcpromo.exe program from previous version of Windows Server has been deprecated in favor of the Server Manager domain controller installation process documented in the following sections. However, it is still possible to automate AD DS installations by running Dcpromo.exe with an answer file. You can also use Windows PowerShell to install a domain controller.

Once you have installed the role, you can run the Active Directory Domain Services Installation Wizard. The wizard procedure varies, depending on what the function of the new domain controller will be. The following sections describe the procedures for the most common types of domain controller installations.

Creating a new forest

When beginning a new AD DS installation, the first step is to create a new forest, which you do by creating the first domain in the forest, the forest root domain.

To create a new forest, use the following procedure.

1. On the Installation Progress page that appears at the end of the Active Directory Domain Services role installation procedure, click the Promote This Server To A Domain Controller hyperlink. The Active Directory Domain Services Configuration Wizard starts, displaying the Deployment Configuration page.

2. Select the Add A New Forest option, as shown in Figure 5-1, and, in the Root Domain Name text box, type the name of the domain you want to create.

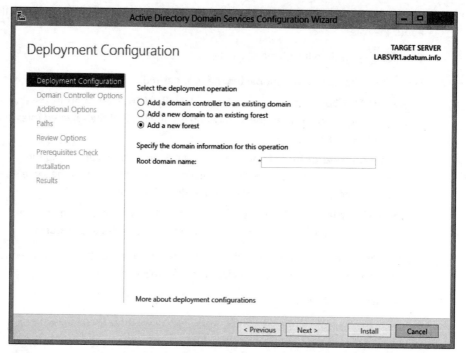

FIGURE 5-1 The Deployment Configuration page of the Active Directory Domain Services Configuration Wizard

3. Click Next. The Domain Controller Options page opens, as shown in Figure 5-2.

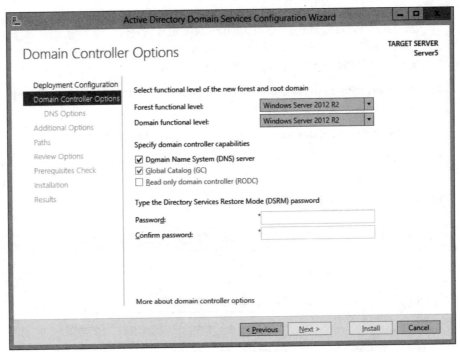

FIGURE 5-2 The Domain Controller Options page of the Active Directory Domain Services Configuration Wizard

4. If you plan to add domain controllers running earlier versions of Windows Server to this forest, select the earliest Windows version you plan to install from the Forest Functional Level drop-down list.

5. If you plan to add domain controllers running earlier versions of Windows Server to this domain, select the earliest Windows version you plan to install from the Domain Functional Level drop-down list.

6. If you do not already have a DNS server on your network, leave the Domain Name System (DNS) Server check box selected. If you have a DNS server on the network, and the domain controller is configured to use that server for DNS services, then clear the check box.

> **NOTE   DOMAIN CONTROLLER OPTIONS**
>
> The Global Catalog (GC) and Read Only Domain Controller (RODC) options are unavailable because the first domain controller in a new forest must be a Global Catalog server and it cannot be a read-only domain controller.

7. In the Password and Confirm Password text boxes, type the password you want to use for Directory Services Restore Mode (DSRM) and click Next. The DNS Options page opens, displaying a warning that a delegation for the DNS server cannot be created, because the DNS Server service is not installed yet.

8. Click Next to open the Additional Options page, which displays the NetBIOS equivalent of the domain name you specified.

9. Modify the name, if desired, and click Next to open the Paths page.

10. Modify the default locations for the AD DS files, if desired, and click Next. The Review Options page opens.

11. Click Next to open the Prerequisites Check page, as shown in Figure 5-3.

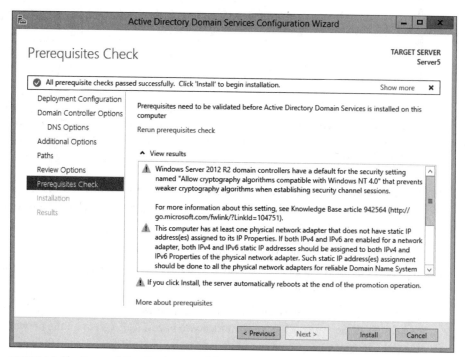

FIGURE 5-3 The Prerequisites Check page of the Active Directory Domain Services Configuration Wizard.

12. The wizard performs a number of environment tests to determine if the system can function as a domain controller. The results can appear as cautions, which enable the procedure to continue, or as warnings, which require you to perform certain actions before the server can be promoted. Once the system has passed all the prerequisite checks, click Install. The wizard creates the new forest and configures the server to function as a domain controller.

13. Restart the computer.

With the forest root domain in place, you can create additional domain controllers in that domain or add new domains to the forest.

Adding a domain controller to an existing domain

Every Active Directory domain should have a minimum of two domain controllers.

To add a domain controller to an existing Windows Server 2012 R2 domain, use the following procedure.

1. On the Installation Progress page that appears at the end of the Active Directory Domain Services role installation procedure, click the Promote This Server To A Domain Controller hyperlink. The Active Directory Domain Services Configuration Wizard starts, displaying the Deployment Configuration page.

2. Select the Add A Domain Controller To An Existing Domain option and click Select.

3. If you are not logged on to an existing domain in the forest, a Credentials For Deployment Operation dialog box opens, in which you must supply administrative credentials for the domain to proceed. After you are authenticated, the Select A Domain From The Forest dialog box opens.

4. Select the domain to which you want to add a domain controller and click OK. The selected domain name appears in the Domain field.

5. Click Next. The Domain Controller Options page, shown in Figure 5-4, opens.

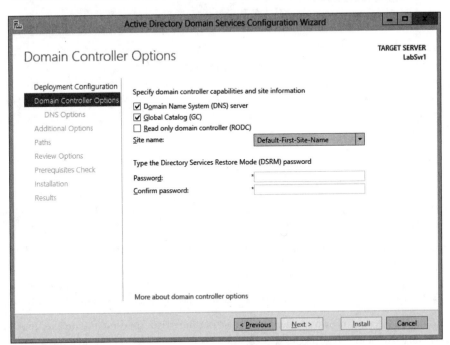

FIGURE 5-4 The Domain Controller Options page of the Active Directory Domain Services Configuration Wizard

6. If you want to install the DNS Server service on the computer, leave the Domain Name System (DNS) Server check box selected. Otherwise, the domain will be hosted on the DNS server the computer is configured to use.

7. Leave the Global Catalog (GC) check box selected if you want the computer to function as a global catalog server. This is essential if you will be deploying the new domain controller at a site that does not already have a GC server.

8. Select the Read Only Domain Controller (RODC) check box, if desired, to create a domain controller that administrators cannot use to modify AD DS objects.

9. In the Site Name drop-down list, select the site where the domain controller will be located.

10. In the Password and Confirm Password text boxes, type the password you want to use for Directory Services Restore Mode (DSRM) and click Next to move to the Additional Options page, shown in Figure 5-5.

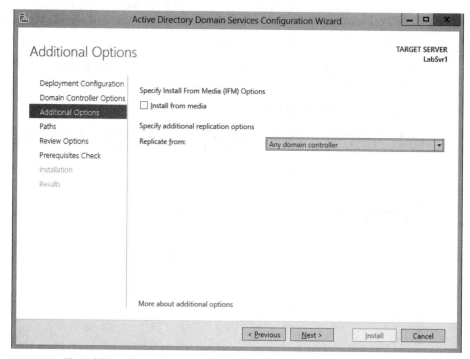

FIGURE 5-5 The Additional Options page of the Active Directory Domain Services Configuration Wizard

11. To use the Install From Media option, select the Install From Media check box.

12. In the Replicate From drop-down list, select the existing domain controller that the server should use as a data source. Then click Next to open the Paths page.

13. Modify the default locations for the AD DS files, if desired, and click Next. The Review Options page opens.

14. Click Next to move to the Prerequisites Check page.

15. Once the system has passed all the prerequisite checks, click Install. The wizard configures the server to function as a domain controller.

16. Restart the computer.

The domain controller is now configured to service the existing domain. AD DS replication between the two will begin automatically.

Creating a new child domain in a forest

Once you have a forest with at least one domain, you can add a child domain beneath any existing domain. The process of creating a new child domain is similar to that of creating a new forest, except that the Deployment Configuration page of the Active Directory Domain Services Configuration Wizard requires you to specify the parent domain beneath which you want to create a child, as shown in Figure 5-6.

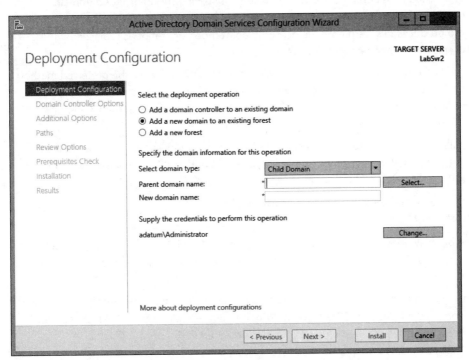

FIGURE 5-6 The Deployment Configuration page of the Active Directory Domain Services Configuration Wizard

Installing AD DS on Server Core

In Windows Server 2012 R2, it is possible to install AD DS on a computer running the Server Core installation option and promote the system to a domain controllerall by using Windows PowerShell.

In Windows Server 2008 and Windows Server 2008 R2, the accepted method for installing AD DS on a computer using the Server Core installation option is to create an answer file and load it from the command prompt by using the Dcpromo.exe program with the /unattend parameter.

In Windows Server 2012 R2, running Dcpromo.exe with no parameters no longer launches the Active Directory Domain Services Configuration Wizard, but administrators who have already invested considerable time in developing answer files for unattended domain controller installations can continue to execute them from the command prompt, although doing so produces this warning: "The dcpromo unattended operation is replaced by the ADDSDeployment module for Windows PowerShell."

For AD DS installations on Server Core, Windows PowerShell is now the preferred method. As with the wizard-based installation, the Windows PowerShell procedure occurs in two phases: first, you must install the Active Directory Domain Services role; then, you must promote the server to a domain controller.

Installing the Active Directory Domain Services role by using Windows PowerShell is no different from installing any other role. In an elevated Windows PowerShell session, use the following command:

```
Install-WindowsFeature –name AD-Domain-Services
-IncludeManagementTools
```

Like other Windows PowerShell role installations, the Install-WindowsFeature cmdlet does not install the management tools for the role, unless you include the –IncludeManagement-Tools parameter in the command.

Once you have installed the role, promoting the server to a domain controller is somewhat more complicated. The ADDSDeployment Windows PowerShell module includes separate cmdlets for the three deployment configurations covered in the previous sections:

- Install-ADDSForest
- Install-ADDSDomainController
- Install-ADDSDomain

Each of these cmdlets has many possible parameters to support the many configuration options you find in the Active Directory Domain Services Configuration Wizard. In its simplest form, the following command would install a domain controller for a new forest called adatum.com:

```
Install-ADDSForest -DomainName "adatum.com"
```

The defaults for all of the cmdlet's other parameters are the same as those in the Active Directory Domain Services Configuration Wizard. Running the cmdlet with no parameters steps through the options, prompting you for values. You can also display basic syntax information by using the Get-Help command, as shown in Figure 5-7.

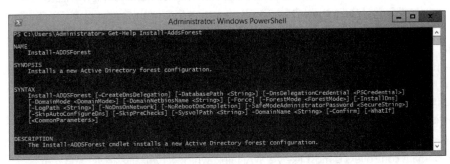

FIGURE 5-7 Syntax for the Install-ADDSForest cmdlet in Windows PowerShell

Another way to perform a complex installation by using Windows PowerShell is to use a computer running Windows Server 2012 R2 with the full GUI option to generate a script. Begin by running the Active Directory Domain Services Configuration Wizard, configuring all the options with your desired settings. When you reach the Review Option page, click View Script to display the Windows PowerShell code for the appropriate cmdlet, as shown in Figure 5-8.

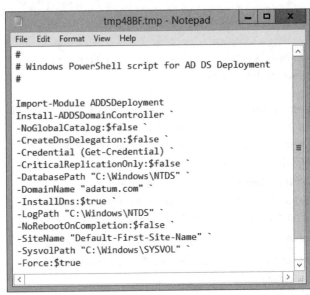

FIGURE 5-8 An installation script generated by the Active Directory Domain Services Configuration Wizard

This feature works as it does because Server Manager is actually based on Windows PowerShell, so the script contains the cmdlets and parameters that are running when the wizard performs an installation. You can also use this scripting capability with the Install-ADDSDomainController cmdlet to deploy multiple domain controllers for the same domain.

Using Install from Media (IFM)

Earlier in this objective, in the procedure for installing a replica domain controller, the Additional Options page of the Active Directory Domain Services Configuration Wizard included an Install From Media check box. This is an option that enables administrators to streamline the process of deploying replica domain controllers to remote sites.

Usually, installing a domain controller to an existing domain creates the AD DS database structure, but there is no data in it until the server is able to receive replication traffic from the other domain controllers. When the domain controllers for a particular domain are well connected, such as by LAN, replication occurs almost immediately after the new domain controller is installed, and is entirely automatic.

When installing a domain controller at a remote location, however, the connection to the other domain controllers is most likely a WAN link, which is typically slower and more expensive than a LAN connection. In this case, the initial replication with the other domain controllers can be much more of a problem. The slow speed of the WAN link might cause the replication to take a long time, and it might also flood the connection, delaying regular traffic. If the domain controllers are located in different AD DS sites without an appropriate site link, no replication will occur until an administrator creates and configures the required links.

> **NOTE REPLICATION**
>
> The first replication that occurs after the installation of a new domain controller is the only one that requires the servers to exchange a complete copy of the AD DS database. In subsequent replications, the domain controllers only exchange information about the objects and attributes that have changed since the last replication.

By using a command-line tool called Ntdsutil.exe, administrators can avoid these problems by creating domain controller installation media that includes a copy of the AD DS database. By using this media when installing a remote domain controller, the data is installed along with the database structure and a full replication is not necessary.

To create IFM media, you must run the Ntdsutil.exe program on a domain controller running the same version of Windows that you intend to deploy. The program is interactive, requiring you to enter a sequence of commands like the following:

- **Ntdsutil**   Launches the program
- **Activate instance ntds**   Focuses the program on the installed AD DS instance
- **Ifm**   Switches the program into IFM mode

- **Create Full|RODC <*path name*>**   Creates media for either a full read/write domain controller or a read-only domain controller and saves it to the folder specified by the path name variable

> *NOTE*   **NTDSUTIL.EXE PARAMETERS**
>
> The Ntdsutil.exe create command also supports parameters that include the contents of the SYSVOL volume with the AD DS data. The Windows Server 2012 R2 version of the program adds a nodefrag parameter that speeds up the media creation process by skipping the defragmentation.

When you execute these commands, the Ntdsutil.exe program creates a snapshot of the AD DS database, mounts it as a volume to defragment it, and then saves it to the specified folder along with a copy of the Windows Registry, as shown in Figure 5-9.

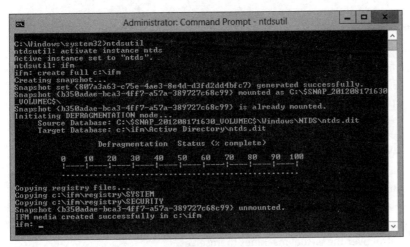

FIGURE 5-9 An Ntdsutil.exe command sequence

Once you have created the IFM media, you can transport it to the servers you intend to deploy as domain controllers by using any convenient means. To use the media, you run the Active Directory Domain Services Configuration Wizard in the usual way, select the Install From Media check box and specify the path to the location of the folder.

Upgrading Active Directory Domain Services

Introducing Windows Server 2012 R2 onto an existing AD DS installation is easier than it has ever been in previous versions of the operating system.

There are two ways to upgrade an AD DS infrastructure. You can upgrade the existing down-level domain controllers to Windows Server 2012 R2 or you can add a new Windows Server 2012 R2 domain controller to your existing environment.

There are few upgrade paths to Windows Server 2012 R2. You can upgrade a Windows Server 2008 or Windows Server 2008 R2 domain controller to Windows Server 2012 R2, but no earlier versions are upgradable.

In the past, if you wanted to add a new domain controller to an existing AD DS installation based on previous Windows versions, you had to run a program called Adprep.exe to upgrade the domains and forest. Depending on the complexity of the installation, this could involve logging on to various domain controllers using different credentials, locating different versions of Adprep.exe, and running the program several times using the /domainprep parameter for each domain and the /forestprep parameter for the forest.

In Windows Server 2012 R2, the Adprep.exe functionality has been fully incorporated into Server Manager in the Active Directory Domain Services Configuration Wizard. When you install a new Windows Server 2012 R2 domain controller, you only have to supply appropriate credentials; the wizard takes care of the rest.

> **NOTE GROUP MEMBERSHIPS**
>
> To install the first Windows Server 2012 R2 domain controller onto a down-level AD DS installation, you must supply credentials for a user who is a member of the Enterprise Admins and Schema Admins groups and a member of the Domain Admins group in the domain that hosts the schema master.

Deploying Active Directory IaaS on Windows Azure

In addition to running Windows Server 2012 R2 on physical computers and locally hosted virtual machines, Microsoft's Windows Azure service enables administrators to create virtual machines using leased cloud resources provided by Microsoft. This capability, called *Infrastructure as a Service (IaaS)*, enables administrators to run applications in the cloud while maintaining full control over the virtual machines themselves.

Windows Azure resources can be self-contained in the cloud and administrators can create a virtualized AD DS forest to organize and manage them. It is also possible to configure Windows Azure resources as an extension to the existing physical and virtual resources hosted on a private network. For example, after creating a virtual network in the Windows Azure cloud and connecting it to your private network with a site-to-site link using a virtual private networking (VPN) device, you can create a Windows Server 2012 R2 virtual machine in the cloud and configure it as a domain controller for an existing domain.

The process of installing AD DS on a Windows Azure virtual machine and promoting it to a domain controller is no different from that of a private network server. You use the Add Roles And Features Wizard to install the AD DS role and then use the Active Directory Domain Services Configuration Wizard to configure the domain controller. The complicated part of the process is the configuration of the virtual network infrastructure to allow communication between the cloud network and your physical network.

Windows Azure is an ideal platform for AD DS domain controller replicas because it provides IP address consistency in a new way. Windows Azure virtual machines must obtain IP addresses from DHCP serversyou cannot assign static IP addresses to thembut unlike standard DHCP address leases that can expire, causing the address to change, a cloud VM retains its IP address lease for its lifetime.

> **NOTE AD DS AND WINDOWS AZURE AD**
>
> You can install Active Directory Domain Services on any Windows Azure VM running Windows Server. AD DS is part of the operating system and requires no special resources other than those needed to provision the virtual machine, such as sufficient disk space for the AD DS database. However, there is also a cloud service called Windows Azure Active Directory (Windows Azure AD) that can provide identity and access management within the cloud. Although the two can interact, Windows Azure AD is not the same as the AD DS service supplied with Windows Server 2012 R2

Removing a domain controller

With the deprecation of Dcpromo.exe, the process of demoting a domain controller has changed and is not immediately intuitive.

To remove a domain controller from an AD DS installation, you must begin by running the Remove Roles And Features Wizard, as shown in the following procedure.

1. In Server Manager, launch the Remove Roles And Features Wizard and remove the Active Directory Domain Services role and its accompanying features. A Validation Results dialog box opens, as shown in Figure 5-10.

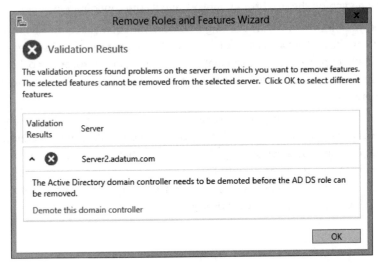

FIGURE 5-10 The Validation Results dialog box of the Remove Roles And Features Wizard

2. Click the Demote This Domain Controller hyperlink. The Active Directory Domain Services Configuration Wizard starts, displaying the Credentials page.

3. Select the Force The Removal Of This Domain Controller check box and click Next to open the New Administrator Password page.

4. In the Password and Confirm Password text boxes, type the password you want the server to use for the local Administrator account after the demotion. Then click Next. The Review Options page opens.

5. Click Demote. The wizard demotes the domain controller and restarts the system.

6. Log on using the local Administrator password you specified earlier.

7. Launch the Remove Roles And Features Wizard again and repeat the process of removing the Active Directory Domain Services role and its accompanying features.

8. Close the wizard and restart the server.

> **NOTE USING WINDOWS POWERSHELL**
>
> To demote a domain controller by using Windows PowerShell, use the following command:
>
> ```
> Uninstall-ADDSDomainController -ForceRemoval
> -LocalAdministratorPassword <password> -Force
> ```

Configuring the global catalog

The global catalog is an index of all the AD DS objects in a forest that prevents systems from having to perform searches among multiple domain controllers. The importance of the global catalog varies depending on the size of your network and its site configuration.

For example, if your network consists of a single domain, with domain controllers that are all located at one site and are well connected, the global catalog serves little purpose other than universal group searches. You can make all your domain controllers global catalog servers if you wish. The searches will be load balanced and the replication traffic will likely not overwhelm the network.

However, if your network consists of multiple domains, with domain controllers located at multiple sites connected by WAN links, then the global catalog configuration is critical. If possible, you do not want users performing AD DS searches that must reach across slow, expensive WAN links to contact domain controllers at other sites. Placing a global catalog server at each site is recommended in this case. The initial replication might generate a lot of traffic, but the savings in the long run should be significant.

When you promote a server to a domain controller, you have the option of making the domain controller a global catalog server. If you decline to do so at that time, you can make any domain controller a global catalog server by using the following procedure.

1. In Server Manager, on the Tools menu, select Active Directory Sites And Services. The Active Directory Sites And Services console opens.

2. Expand the site where the domain controller you want to function as a global catalog server is located. Then expand the Servers folder and select the server you want to configure.

3. Right-click the NTDS Settings node for the server and, from the shortcut menu, select Properties to open the NTDS Settings Properties sheet.

4. Select the Global Catalog check box and click OK.

5. Close the Active Directory Sites And Services console.

Troubleshooting DNS SRV registration failure

DNS is essential to the operation of Active Directory Domain Services. To accommodate directory services such as AD DS, a special DNS resource record was created that enables clients to locate domain controllers and other vital AD DS services.

When you create a new domain controller, one of the most important parts of the process is the registration of the server in the DNS. This automatic registration is the reason an AD DS forest must have access to a DNS server that supports the Dynamic Updates standard defined in Request for Comments (RFC) 2136.

If the DNS registration process fails, then computers on the network will not be able to locate that domain controller, the consequences of which can be serious. Computers will be unable to use that domain controller to join the domain, existing domain members might be unable to log on, and other domain controllers will be unable to replicate with it.

DNS problems are, in most cases, due to general networking faults or DNS client configuration error. The first steps you should take are to try pinging the DNS server and to make sure that the TCP/IP client configuration has the correct addresses for the DNS servers it should be using.

To confirm that a domain controller has been registered in the DNS, open a command prompt window with Administrative privileges and enter the following command:

```
dcdiag /test:registerindns /dnsdomain:<domain name> /v
```

Thought experiment

Designing an Active Directory infrastructure

In the following thought experiment, apply what you've learned about this objective to predict what steps you need to take. You can find answers to these questions in the "Answers" section at the end of this chapter.

Robert is designing a new Active Directory Domain Services infrastructure for a company called Litware, Inc., which has its headquarters in New York and two additional offices in London and Tokyo. The London office consists only of sales and marketing staff; it does not have its own IT department. The Tokyo office is larger, with representatives from all the company departments, including a full IT staff. The Tokyo office is connected to the headquarters using a 64-Kbps demand-dial link, and the London office has a 512-Kbps frame relay connection. The company has registered the litware.com domain name, and Robert has created a subdomain called inside.litware.com for use by Active Directory.

Based on this information, design an Active Directory infrastructure for Litware, Inc. that is as economical as possible, specifying how many domains to create, what to name them, how many domain controllers to install, and where to install them. Explain each of your decisions.

Objective summary

- A directory service is a repository of information about the resources—hardware, software, and human—that are connected to a network. Active Directory is the directory service that Microsoft first introduced in Windows 2000 Server, which has been upgraded in each successive server operating system release, including Windows Server 2012 R2.

- When you create your first domain on an Active Directory network, you are in essence creating the root of a domain tree. You can populate the tree with additional domains, as long as they are part of the same contiguous namespace.

- When beginning a new AD DS installation, the first step is to create a new forest, which you do by creating the first domain in the forest, the forest root domain.

- In Windows Server 2012 R2, it is now possible to install AD DS on a computer running the Server Core installation option and promote the system to a domain controller, all by using Windows PowerShell.

- IFM is a feature that enables administrators to streamline the process of deploying replica domain controllers to remote sites.

- There are two ways to upgrade an AD DS infrastructure. You can upgrade the existing down-level domain controllers to Windows Server 2012 R2 or you can add a new Windows Server 2012 R2 domain controller to your existing installation.
- The global catalog is an index of all the AD DS objects in a forest that prevents systems from having to perform searches among multiple domain controllers.
- DNS is essential to the operation of AD DS. To accommodate directory services such as AD DS, a special DNS resource record was created that enables clients to locate domain controllers and other vital AD DS services.

Objective review

Answer the following questions to test your knowledge of the information in this objective. You can find the answers to these questions and explanations of why each answer choice is correct or incorrect in the "Answers" section at the end of this chapter.

1. Which of the following cannot contain multiple Active Directory domains?

   A. Organizational units

   B. Sites

   C. Trees

   D. Forests

2. What are the two basic classes of Active Directory objects?

   A. Resource

   B. Leaf

   C. Domain

   D. Container

3. Which of the following is *not* true about an object's attributes?

   A. Administrators must manually supply information for certain attributes.

   B. Every container object has, as an attribute, a list of all the other objects it contains.

   C. Leaf objects do not contain attributes.

   D. Active Directory automatically creates the globally unique identifier (GUID).

4. Which of the following is *not* a reason you should try to create as few domains as possible when designing an Active Directory infrastructure?

   A. Creating additional domains increases the administrative burden of the installation.

   B. Each additional domain you create increases the hardware costs of the Active Directory deployment.

   C. Some applications might have problems working in a forest with multiple domains.

   D. You must purchase a license from Microsoft for each domain you create.

5. Which of the following does an Active Directory client use to locate objects in another domain?

    A. DNS

    B. Global Catalog

    C. DHCP

    D. Site Link

Objective 5.2: Create and manage Active Directory users and computers

Users and computers are the basic leaf objects that populate the branches of the AD DS tree. Creating and managing these objects are everyday tasks for most AD DS administrators.

> **This objective covers how to:**
> - Automate the creation of Active Directory accounts
> - Create, copy, configure, and delete users and computers
> - Configure templates
> - Perform bulk Active Directory operations
> - Configure user rights
> - Offline domain join
> - Manage inactive and disabled accounts

Creating user objects

The user account is the primary means by which people using an AD DS forest access resources. Resource access for individuals takes place through their individual user accounts. To gain access to the network, prospective network users must authenticate to a network with a specific user account.

Authentication is the process of confirming a user's identity by using a known value such as a password, a smart card, or a fingerprint. When a user supplies a name and password, the authentication process validates the credentials supplied in the logon against information that has been stored within the AD DS database. Do not confuse authentication with authorization, which is the process of confirming that an authenticated user has the correct permissions to access one or more network resources.

There are two types of user accounts on systems running Windows Server 2012 R2, as follows:

- **Local users** These accounts can only access resources on the local computer and are stored in the local Security Account Manager (SAM) database on the computer where they reside. Local accounts are never replicated to other computers and do not provide domain access. This means that a local account configured on one server cannot be used to access resources on a second server; you would need to configure a second local account in that case.

- **Domain users** These accounts can access AD DS or network-based resources, such as shared folders and printers. Account information for these users is stored in the AD DS database and replicated to all domain controllers within the same domain. A subset of the domain user account information is replicated to the global catalog, which is then replicated to other global catalog servers throughout the forest.

User creation tools

One of the most common tasks for administrators is the creation of Active Directory user objects. Windows Server 2012 R2 includes several tools you can use to create objects. The specific tool you use depends on how many objects you need to create, the time frame available for the creation of these groups, and any special circumstances, such as importing users from an existing database.

When creating a single user, administrators can use Active Directory Administrative Center or the Active Directory Users And Computers console. However, when you need to create multiple users in a short time frame or you have an existing database from which to import these objects, you will want to use a more efficient tool. Windows Server 2012 R2 provides a number of tools you can choose based on what you want to accomplish. The following list describes the most commonly used methods for creating multiple users and groups. These tools are detailed in the upcoming sections.

- **Dsadd.exe** The standard command-line tool for creating AD DS leaf objects, which you can use with batch files to create AD DS objects in bulk

- **Windows PowerShell** The Windows maintenance tool that enables you to create object creation scripts of nearly unlimited complexity

- **Comma-Separated Value Directory Exchange (CSVDE.exe)** A command-line utility that can create new AD DS objects by importing information from a comma-separated value (.csv) file

- **LDAP Data Interchange Format Directory Exchange (LDIFDE.exe)** Like CSVDE, but with more functionality, LDIFDE is a utility that can import AD DS information and use it to add, delete, or modify objects, in addition to modifying the schema, if necessary

These tools all have their roles in network administration; it is up to the administrator to select the best tool to suit his or her skill set and the particular situation.

The following sections examine various scenarios for using these tools to create user objects.

Creating single users

For some administrators, creating individual user accounts is a daily task and there are many ways to go about it. Windows Server 2012 R2 has redesigned the Active Directory Administrative Center (ADAC) application, first introduced in Windows Server 2008 R2, to fully incorporate new features such as the Active Directory Recycle Bin and fine-grained password policies. You can also use the tool to create and manage AD DS user accounts

To create a single user account by using the Active Directory Administrative Center, use the following procedure.

1. In Server Manager, on the Tools menu, select Active Directory Administrative Center. The Active Directory Administrative Center console opens.

2. In the left pane, find the domain in which you want to create the user object and select a container in that domain.

3. In the Tasks pane, under the container name, click New, User to open the Create User window, as shown in Figure 5-11.

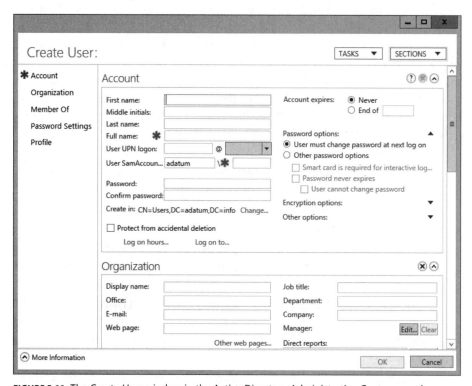

FIGURE 5-11 The Create User window in the Active Directory Administrative Center console

4. Type the user's name in the Full Name field and an account name in the User SamAccountName Logon field.

5. Type an initial password for the user in the Password field and the Confirm password field.

6. Supply information for any of the optional fields on the page you wish.

7. Click OK. The user object appears in the container.

8. Close the Active Directory Administrative Center console.

Administrators who are more comfortable with the familiar Active Directory Users And Computers console can still use it to create user objects by using the New Object – User Wizard, as shown in Figure 5-12.

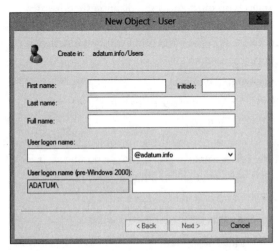

FIGURE 5-12 The New Object - User Wizard in the Active Directory Users And Computers console

For administrators working on Server Core installations or who are more comfortable with the command line, it is also possible to create user objects without a graphical interface.

USING DSADD.EXE

For administrators more comfortable with the traditional command prompt, the Dsadd.exe program can create new user objects by using the syntax shown in Figure 5-13.

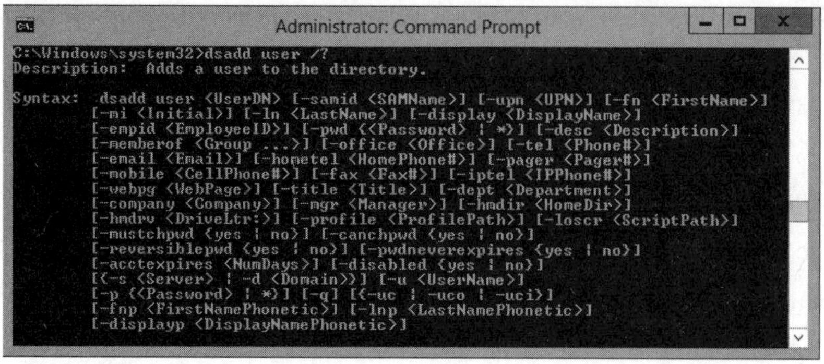

FIGURE 5-13 Syntax of the Dsadd.exe program

To create a user by using the Dsadd.exe utility, you must know the distinguished name (DN) for the user and the user's login ID, also known as the SAM account name attribute within AD DS. The distinguished name of an object signifies its location within the Active Directory structure. For example, in the distinguished name:

cn=Elizabeth Andersen,ou=Research,dc=adatum,dc=com

the cn refers to the common name for Elizabeth Andersen's user account, which resides in the Research OU, which resides in the adatum.com domain.

Each object has a unique DN, but this DN can change if you move the object to different locations within the Active Directory structure. For example, if you create an additional layer of OUs representing offices in different cities, the previous DN might change to:

cn=Elizabeth Andersen,ou=Research,ou=Baltimore,dc=adatum,dc=com

even though it is the same user object with the same rights and permissions.

The SAM account name refers to each user's login name—the portion to the left of the @ within a User Principal Name—which is eander in eander@adatum.com. The SAM account name must be unique across a domain.

When you have both these items, you can create a user with the Dsadd.exe utility by using the following syntax:

```
dsadd user <distinguished name> –samid <SAM account name>
```

For example, in its simplest form, you can create the account for Elizabeth Andersen referenced earlier as follows:

```
dsadd user
cn="Elizabeth Andersen,ou=Research,dc=adatum,dc=com"
–samid eander
```

You can also add attribute values by using the Dsadd.exe tool. The following command adds some of the most common attributes to the user object:

```
Dsadd.exe user
"CN=Elizabeth Andersen,OU=Research,DC=adatum,DC=local"
-samid "eander"
-fn "Elizabeth"
-ln "Andersen"
-disabled no
-mustchpwd yes
-pwd "Pa$$w0rd"
```

USING WINDOWS POWERSHELL

Microsoft is placing increased emphasis on Windows PowerShell as a server management tool, and provides a cmdlet called New-ADUser, which you can use to create a user account and configure any or all of the attributes associated with it. The New-ADUser cmdlet has many parameters, as shown in Figure 5-14, to enable access to all the user object's attributes.

FIGURE 5-14 Syntax of the New-ADUser cmdlet

For example, to create a new user object for Elizabeth Andersen in an organizational unit (OU) called Research, you could use the New-ADUser cmdlet with the following parameters:

```
new-ADUser
-Name "Elizabeth Andersen"
-SamAccountName "eander"
-GivenName "Elizabeth"
-SurName "Andersen"
-path 'OU=Research,DC=adatum,dc=local'
-Enabled $true
-AccountPassword "Pa$$w0rd"
-ChangePasswordAtLogon $true
```

The –Name and –SamAccountName parameters are required to identify the object. The –path parameter specifies the location of the object in the AD DS hierarchy. The –Enabled parameter ensures that the account is active.

Creating user templates

In some cases, administrators have to create single users on a regular basis, but the user accounts contain so many attributes that creating them individually is time-consuming.

One way to speed up the process of creating complex user objects is to use the New-ADUser cmdlet or the Dsadd.exe program and retain your commands in a script or batch file. However, if you prefer a graphical interface, you can do roughly the same thing by creating a user template.

A user template is a standard user object containing boilerplate attribute settings. When you want to create a new user with those settings, just copy the template to a new user object and change the name and any other attributes that are unique to the user.

To create a user template by using the Active Directory Users And Computers console, use the following procedure.

1. In Server Manager, on the Tools menu, select Active Directory Users And Computers. The Active Directory Administrative Users And Computers console appears.

2. Create a user object with the name Default Template, clearing the User Must Change Password At Next Logon check box and selecting the Account Is Disabled check box.

3. Open the user's Properties sheet and modify the attributes on the various tabs with values common to all the users you will be creating.

To use the template, right-click the Default Template user object and, from the shortcut menu, select Copy. The Copy Object – User Wizard starts, as shown in Figure 5-15.

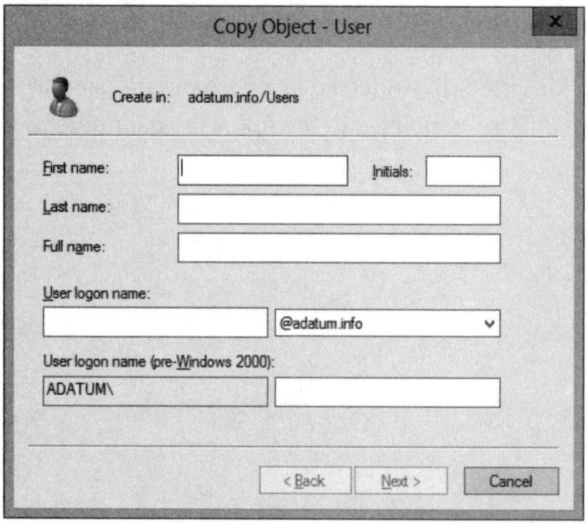

FIGURE 5-15 The Copy Object – User Wizard

Enter the required unique information for the user and clear the Account Is Disabled check box before clicking OK. The wizard creates a new user object with a subset of the attributes you configured in the template.

Creating multiple users

Administrators sometimes have to create hundreds or thousands of user objects, making the single object creation procedures impractical. The previous sections described the procedures for creating single users and group objects by using the GUI and some of the available command-line tools in Windows Server 2012 R2. The following sections examine some of the mechanisms for automating the creation of large numbers of Active Directory objects.

USING CSVDE.EXE

Applications such as Microsoft Excel can generate lists of users, with their accompanying information, to add to the AD DS database. In these cases, you can export information from the applications by saving it to a file in CSV format. CSV format also can be used to import information into and export it from other third-party applications.

A CSV file is a plain text file that consists of recordseach on a separate linewhich are divided into fields, separated by commas. The format is a way to save database information in a universally understandable way.

The CSVDE.exe command-line utility enables administrators to import or export Active Directory objects. It uses a CSV file that is based on a header record, which identifies the attribute contained in each comma-delimited field. The header record is just the first line of the text file that uses proper attribute names. To be imported into AD DS, the attribute names in the CSV file must match the attributes allowed by the Active Directory schema. For example, if you have a list of people and telephone numbers you want to import as users into the Active Directory database, you will need to create a header record that accurately reflects the object names and attributes you want to create. Review the following attributes that are commonly used for creating user accounts.

- **dn** Specifies the distinguished name of the object so that the object can be properly placed in Active Directory
- **samAccountName** Populates the SAM account field
- **objectClass** Specifies the type of object to be created, such as user, group, or OU
- **telephoneNumber** Populates the Telephone Number field
- **userPrincipalName** Populates the User Principal Name field

As you create your CSV file, you must order the data to reflect the sequence of the attributes in the header record. If fields and data are out of order, you will either encounter an error when running the CSVDE.exe utility or you might get inaccurate results in the created objects. The following example of a header record uses the previously listed attributes to create a user object.

```
dn,samAccountName,userPrincipalName,telephoneNumber,objectClass
```

A data record conforming to this header record would then appear as follows:

```
"cn=Elizabeth Andersen,ou=Research,dc=adatum,dc=com",eander,eander@adatum.com,586-555-1234,user
```

After you have added a record for each account you want to create, save the file using .csv as the extension. You then use the following command syntax to run the CSVDE.exe program and import the file:

```
csvde.exe -i -f <filename.csv>
```

The -i switch tells CSVDE.exe that this operation will import data. The -f switch is used to specify the .csv file containing the records to be imported.

USING LDIFDE.EXE

LDIFDE.exe is a utility that has the same basic functionality as CSVDE.exe and provides the ability to modify existing records in Active Directory. For this reason, LDIFDE.exe is a more flexible option. Consider an example where you have to import 200 new users into your AD DS structure. In this case, you can use CSVDE.exe or LDIFDE.exe to import the users. However, you can use LDIFDE.exe to modify or delete the objects later, whereas CSVDE.exe does not provide this option.

You can use any text editor to create the LDIFDE.exe input file, which is formatted according to the LDAP Data Interchange Format (LDIF) standard. The format for the data file containing the object records you wish to create is significantly different from that of CSVDE. exe. The following example shows the syntax for a data file to create the same user account discussed in the CSVDE.exe example.

```
dn: "cn=Elizabeth Andersen,ou=Research,dc=adatum,dc=com"
changetype: add
ObjectClass: user
SAMAccountName: eander
UserPrincipalName: eander@adatum.com
telephoneNumber: 586-555-1234
```

Using LDIFDE.exe, you can specify one of three actions that will be performed with the LDIF file:

- **Add**   Creates new objects by using the LDIF records
- **Modify**   Modifies existing object attributes by using the LDIF records
- **Delete**   Deletes existing objects by using the LDIF records

After creating the data file and saving it using the .ldf file extension, use the following syntax to execute the LDIFDE.exe program:

```
ldifde -i -f <filename.ldf>
```

The next example illustrates the LDIF syntax to modify the telephone number of an existing user object. Note that the hyphen in the last line is required for the file to function correctly.

```
dn: "cn=Elizabeth Andersen,ou=Research,dc=adatum,dc=com"
changetype: modify
replace: telephoneNumber
telephoneNumber: 586-555-1111
-
```

USING WINDOWS POWERSHELL

It is also possible to use CSV files to create user objects with Windows PowerShell by using the Import-CSV cmdlet to read the data from the file and piping it to the New-ADUser cmdlet. To insert the data from the file into the correct user object attributes, use the New-ADUser cmdlet parameters to reference the field names in the CSV file's header record.

An example of a bulk user creation command would be as follows:

```
Import-CSV users.csv | foreach
{New-ADUser -SamAccountName $_.SamAccountName
-Name $_.Name -Surname $_.Surname
-GivenName $_.GivenName -Path "OU=Research,DC=adatum,DC=COM" -AccountPassword Pa$$w0rd
-Enabled $true}
```

Creating computer objects

Because an AD DS forest uses a centralized directory, there has to be some means of tracking the actual computers that are part of the domain. To do this, Active Directory uses computer accounts, which are realized in the form of computers objects in the Active Directory database. You might have a valid Active Directory user account and a password, but if your computer is not represented by a computer object, you cannot log on to the domain using that system.

Computer objects are stored in the Active Directory hierarchy just like user objects are; they possess many of the same capabilities, such as the following:

- Computer objects consist of properties that specify the computer's name, where it is located, and who is permitted to manage it.
- Computer objects inherit group policy settings from container objects such as domains, sites, and OUs.
- Computer objects can be members of groups and inherit permissions from group objects.

When a user attempts to log on to an Active Directory domain, the client computer establishes a connection to a domain controller to authenticate the user's identity. Before the user authentication occurs, the two computers perform a preliminary authentication by using their respective computer objects to ensure that both systems are part of the domain. The NetLogon service running on the client computer connects to the same service on the domain controller, and then each one verifies that the other system has a valid computer account. When this validation is completed, the two systems establish a secure communications channel between them, which they can then use to begin the user authentication process.

The computer account validation between the client and the domain controller is a genuine authentication process using account names and passwords, just as when a user authenticates to the domain. The difference is that the passwords used by the computer accounts are generated automatically and kept hidden. Administrators can reset computer accounts, but they do not have to supply passwords for them.

What this means for administrators is that, in addition to creating user accounts in the domain, they also have to make sure that the network computers are part of the domain. Adding a computer to an AD DS domain consists of two steps:

- **Creating a computer account**   You create a computer account by creating a new computer object in Active Directory and assigning the name of an actual computer on the network.

- **Joining the computer to the domain**   When you join a computer to the domain, the system contacts a domain controller, establishes a trust relationship with the domain, locates (or creates) a computer object corresponding to the computer's name, alters its security identifier (SID) to match that of the computer object, and modifies its group memberships.

How these steps are performed and who performs them depends on the way in which you deploy computers on your network. There are many ways to create new computer objects, and how administrators elect to do this depends on several factors, including the number of objects they need to create, where they will be when creating the objects, and what tools they prefer to use.

Generally speaking, you create computer objects when you deploy new computers in the domain. Once a computer is represented by an object and joined to the domain, any user in the domain can log on from that computer. For example, you do not have to create new computer objects or rejoin computers to the domain when employees leave the company and new hires start using their computers. However, if you reinstall the operating system on a computer, you must create a new computer object for it (or reset the existing one), because the newly installed computer will have a different SID.

The creation of a computer object must always occur before the corresponding computer can join the domain, although it might not appear that way. There are two basic strategies for creating Active Directory computer objects, which are as follows:

- Create the computer objects in advance by using an Active Directory tool, so that the computers can locate the existing objects when they join the domain.

- Begin the joining process first and let the computer create its own computer object.

In either case, the computer object exists before the joining takes place. In the second strategy, the joining process appears to begin first, but the computer creates the object before the actual joining process begins.

When there are a number of computers to deploy, particularly in different locations, administrators can conceivably create the computer objects in advance. For large numbers of computers, it is even possible to automate the computer object creation process by using command-line tools and batch files, although many use a third-party tool for this task. The following sections examine the tools you can use for computer object creation.

Creating computer objects by using Active Directory Users And Computers

As with user objects, you can create computer objects by using the Active Directory Users And Computers console. To create computer objects in an Active Directory domain by using the Active Directory Users And Computers console or by using any tool, you must have the appropriate permissions for the container in which the objects will be located.

By default, the Administrators group has permission to create objects anywhere in the domain, and the Account Operators group has the special permissions needed to create computer objects in and delete them from the Computers container and from any new OUs you create. Members of the Domain Admins and Enterprise Admins groups can also create computer objects anywhere. An administrator can also explicitly delegate control of containers to particular users or groups, enabling them to create computer objects in those containers.

The process of creating a computer object in Active Directory Users And Computers is similar to that of creating a user object. You select the container in which you want to place the object and, from the Action menu, select New, Computer. The New Object – Computer Wizard starts, as shown in Figure 5-16.

FIGURE 5-16 The New Object – Computer Wizard

The Properties sheet for Computer objects in the Active Directory Users and Computers console shows relatively few attributes and, in most cases, you will likely just supply them with a name, which can be up to 64 characters long. This name must match the name of the computer joined with the object.

Creating computer objects by using Active Directory Administrative Center

As with users, you can also create computer objects in the Active Directory Administrative Center. To create a computer object, you choose a container and then select New, Computer from the Tasks list to open the Create Computer dialog box.

Creating computer objects by using Dsadd.exe

As with users, the graphical tools provided with Windows Server 2012 R2 are good for creating and managing single objects, but many administrators turn to the command line when they have to create multiple objects.

The Dsadd.exe utility enables you to create computer objects from the command line, just as you created user objects earlier in this lesson. You can create a batch file of Dsadd. exe commands to generate multiple objects in one process. The basic syntax for creating a computer object by using Dsadd.exe is as follows:

```
dsadd computer <ComputerDN>
```

The <ComputerDN> parameter specifies a distinguished name for the new computer object you want to create. The DNs use the same format as those in CSV files, as discussed earlier.

Creating computer objects by using Windows PowerShell

Windows PowerShell includes the New-ADComputer cmdlet, which you can use to create computer objects with the following basic syntax. This cmdlet creates computer objects, but it does not join them to a domain.

```
new-ADComputer -Name <computer name> -path <distinguished name>
```

Managing Active Directory objects

Once you have created user and computer objects, you can manage them and modify them in many of the same ways by which you created them.

Double-clicking any object in the Active Directory Administrative Center or the Active Directory Users And Computers console opens the Properties sheet for that object. The windows appear different, but they contain the same information and provide the same ability to alter the object attributes.

Managing multiple users

When managing domain user accounts, there are likely to be times when you have to make the same changes to multiple user objects, and modifying each one individually would be a tedious chore.

In these instances, it is possible to modify the properties of multiple user accounts simultaneously by using the Active Directory Administrative Center or the Active Directory Users And Computers console. You just select several user objects by holding down the Ctrl key as you click each user and then select Properties. A Properties sheet opens, containing the attributes you can manage for the selected objects simultaneously, as shown in Figure 5-17.

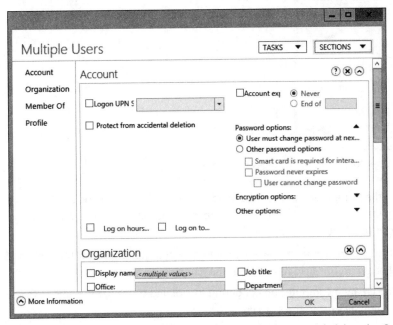

FIGURE 5-17 A Multiple Users Properties sheet in Active Directory Administrative Center

Joining computers to a domain

The process of joining a computer to a domain must occur from the computer itself and be performed by a member of the computer's local Administrators group. After logging on, you join a computer running Windows Server 2012 R2 to a domain from the Computer Name tab in the System Properties sheet. You can access the System Properties sheet from Server Manager, by clicking the Computer name or domain hyperlink on the server's Properties tile, from the Control Panel.

On a computer that is not joined to a domain, the Computer Name tab displays the name assigned to the computer during the operating system installation and the name of the workgroup to which the system currently belongs (which is WORKGROUP, by default). To join the computer to the domain, click Change to display the Computer Name/Domain Changes dialog box shown in Figure 5-18.

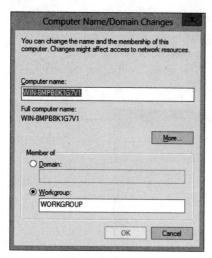

FIGURE 5-18 The Computer Name/Domain Changes dialog box

In this dialog box, the Computer Name field enables you to change the name assigned to the computer during installation. Depending on whether you have already created a computer object, observe the following precautions:

- To join a domain in which you have already created a computer object for the system in AD DS, the name on this field must match the name of the object exactly.
- If you intend to create a computer object during the joining process, the name in this field must not already exist in the domain.

When you select the Domain option and enter the name of the domain the computer will join, the computer establishes contact with a domain controller for the domain and a second Computer Name Changes dialog box opens, prompting you for the name and password of a domain user account with permission to join the computer to the domain.

Once you have authenticated with the domain controller, the computer is welcomed to the domain and you are instructed to restart the computer.

JOINING A DOMAIN BY USING NETDOM.EXE

It is also possible to use the Netdom.exe command-line utility to join a computer to a domain. The syntax for the command is as follows:

```
netdom join <computername> /Domain:<DomainName>
[/UserD:<User> /PasswordD:<UserPassword>] [/OU:OUDN]
```

CREATING COMPUTER OBJECTS WHILE JOINING

You can join a computer to a domain whether or not you have already created a computer object for it. Once the computer authenticates to the domain controller, the domain controller scans the Active Directory database for a computer object with the same name as the computer. If it does not find a matching object, the domain controller creates one in the default container (usually the Computers container), using the name supplied by the computer.

For the computer object to be created automatically in this manner, one would expect that the user account you specify when connecting to the domain controller must have object creation privileges for the Computers container, such as membership in the Administrators group. However, this is not always the case.

Domain users can also create computer objects through an interesting, indirect process. The Default Domain Controllers Policy Group Policy object (GPO) grants a user right called Add Workstations To The Domain (as shown in Figure 5-19) to the Authenticated Users special identity. This means that any user who is successfully authenticated to Active Directory is permitted to join up to 10 workstations to the domain and create 10 associated computer objects, even if the user does not possess explicit object creation permissions.

FIGURE 5-19 The Default Domain Controllers Policy user rights assignments

JOINING A DOMAIN WHILE OFFLINE

It is typical for administrators to join computers to domains while the computers are connected to the network and have access to a domain controller. However, there are situations in which administrators might want to set up computers without access to a domain controller, such as a new branch office installation. In these cases, it is possible to perform an offline domain join by using a command-line program called Djoin.exe.

The offline domain join procedure requires you to run the Djoin.exe program twice, first on a computer with access to a domain controller and then on the computer to be joined. When connected to the domain controller, the program gathers computer account metadata for the system to be joined and saves it to a file. The syntax for this phase of the process is as follows:

```
djoin /provision /domain <domain name>
/machine <computer name> /savefile <filename.txt>
```

You then transport the metadata file to the computer to be joined and run Djoin.exe again, specifying the name of the file. The program saves the metadata from the file to the computer, so that the next time it has access to a domain controller, the system is automatically joined to the domain. The syntax for the second phase of the process is as follows:

```
djoin /requestODJ /loadfile <filename.txt>
/windowspath %SystemRoot% /localos
```

Managing disabled accounts

Disabling a user account prevents anyone from using it to log on to the domain until an administrator with the appropriate permissions enables it again. You can disable user accounts manually, to prevent their use while preserving all their attributes, but it is also possible for a domain controller to automatically disable them. For example, repeated violations of password policy settings can disable an account to prevent intruders from making further attack attempts.

To disable or enable a user or computer account in Active Directory Administrative Center or Active Directory Users And Computers, just right-click the object and select Disable or Enable from the shortcut menu. You can also disable and enable multiple accounts by selecting multiple objects and right-clicking.

To disable or enable a user or computer account by using Windows PowerShell, use the following cmdlet syntax:

```
Disable-ADAccount -Identity <account name>
Enable-ADAccount -Identity <account name>
```

Thought experiment
Creating user objects

In the following thought experiment, apply what you've learned about this objective to predict what steps you need to take. You can find answers to these questions in the "Answers" section at the end of this chapter.

You are a network administrator who is in the process of building an Active Directory network for a company called Fabrikam, Inc., and you have to create user objects for the 75 users in the Inside Sales department. You have already created the fabrikam.com domain and an OU called Inside Sales for this purpose. The Human Resources department has provided you with a list of the users' names and has instructed you to create the account names by using the first initial and the last name. Each user object must also have the value Inside Sales in the Department property and Fabrikam, Inc. in the Company property. Using the first name in the list, Oliver Cox, as an example, which of the following command-line formats would enable you to create the 75 user objects with the required property values?

A. dsadd "Oliver Cox" -samid ocox –company "Fabrikam, Inc." –dept "Inside Sales"

B. dsadd user CN=Oliver Cox,CN=Inside Sales,DC=fabrikam,DC=com -samid ocox –company Fabrikam, Inc. –dept Inside Sales

C. dsadd –company "Fabrikam, Inc." -samid ocox –dept "Inside Sales" "CN=Oliver Cox,CN=Inside Sales,DC=fabrikam,DC=com"

D. dsadd user "CN=Oliver Cox,CN=Inside Sales,DC=fabrikam,DC=com" -samid ocox –company "Fabrikam, Inc." –dept "Inside Sales"

Objective summary

- The user account is the primary means by which people using an AD DS forest access resources.

- One of the most common tasks for administrators is the creation of Active Directory user objects. Windows Server 2012 R2 includes several tools you can use to create objects.

- Windows Server 2012 R2 has redesigned the Active Directory Administrative Center (ADAC) application, first introduced in Windows Server 2008 R2, to fully incorporate new features such as the Active Directory Recycle Bin and fine-grained password policies. You can also use the tool to create and manage AD DS user accounts.

- For applications in which you can have a number of users, with their accompanying information, to add to the AD DS database, you can export information from the applications by saving it to a file in CSV format.

- LDIFDE.exe is a utility that has the same basic functionality as CSVDE.exe and provides the ability to modify existing records in Active Directory.

- Because an AD DS forest uses a centralized directory, there has to be some means of tracking the actual computers that are part of the domain. To do this, Active Directory uses computer accounts, which are realized in the form of computer objects in the Active Directory database.

- The process of joining a computer to a domain must occur at the computer itself and be performed by a member of the computer's local Administrators group.

- It is possible to perform an offline domain join by using a command-line program called Djoin.exe.

Objective review

Answer the following questions to test your knowledge of the information in this objective. You can find the answers to these questions and explanations of why each answer choice is correct or incorrect in the "Answers" section at the end of this chapter.

1. Which of the following can be used to add, delete, or modify objects in Active Directory, in addition to modifying the schema if necessary?

    A. DCPROMO

    B. LDIFDE

    C. CSVDE

    D. NSLOOKUP

2. When using CSVDE, what is the first line of the text file that uses proper attribute names?

   A. Header row

   B. Header record

   C. Name row

   D. Name record

3. Which of the following utilities are used to perform an offline domain join?

   A. net join

   B. join

   C. djoin

   D. dconnect

4. Which of the following is *not* a type of user account that can be configured in Windows Server 2012 R2?

   A. Local accounts

   B. Domain accounts

   C. Network accounts

   D. Built-in accounts

5. Which of the following are the two built-in user accounts created automatically on a computer running Windows Server 2012 R2?

   A. Network

   B. Interactive

   C. Administrator

   D. Guest

Objective 5.3: Create and manage Active Directory groups and organizational units (OUs)

OUs can be nested to create a design that enables administrators to take advantage of the natural inheritance of the Active Directory hierarchy. You should limit the number of OUs that are nested, because too many levels can slow the response time to resource requests and complicate the application of Group Policy settings.

When you first install Active Directory Domain Services, there is only one OU in the domain, by default: the Domain Controllers OU. All other OUs must be created by an AD administrator.

There is another type of container object found in a domain, which is actually called a container. For example, a newly created domain has several container objects in it, including one called Users, which contains the domain's predefined users and groups, and another called Computers, which contains the computer objects for all the systems joined to the domain except for domain controllers.

Unlike with OUs, you cannot assign Group Policy settings to container objects. You also cannot create new container objects by using the standard Active Directory administration tools, such as the Active Directory Users And Computers console. You can create container objects by using scripts, but there is no compelling reason to do so. OUs are the preferred method of subdividing a domain.

This objective covers how to:
- Configure group nesting
- Convert groups (including security, distribution, universal, domain local, and domain global)
- Manage group membership using Group Policy
- Enumerate group membership
- Delegate the creation and management of Active Directory objects
- Manage default Active Directory containers
- Create, copy, configure, and delete groups and OUs

Creating OUs

OUs are the simplest type of object to create in the AD DS hierarchy. You only have to supply a name for the object and define its location in the Active Directory tree.

To create an OU object by using the Active Directory Administrative Center, use the following procedure.

1. In Server Manager, on the Tools menu, select Active Directory Administrative Center to open the Active Directory Administrative Center console.

2. In the left pane, right-click the object beneath which you want to create the new OU and, from the shortcut menu, select New, Organizational Unit. The Create Organizational Unit window opens, as shown in Figure 5-20.

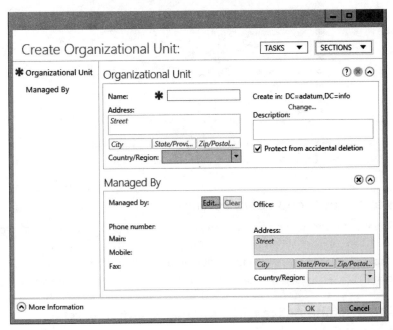

FIGURE 5-20 The Create Organizational Unit window in Active Directory Administrative Center

3. In the Name field, type a name for the OU and add any optional information you desire.

4. Click OK. The OU object appears in the object you selected.

5. Close the Active Directory Administrative Center console.

Creating an OU in the Active Directory Users And Computers console works in roughly the same way, although the New Object – Organizational Unit dialog box looks different. Once you have created an OU, you can double-click it to open its Properties sheet, where you can modify its attributes, or right-click it and select Move to open the Move dialog box, as shown in Figure 5-21.

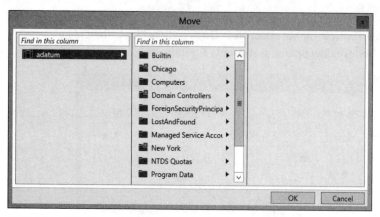

FIGURE 5-21 The Move dialog box in Active Directory Administrative Center

Using OUs to assign Group Policy settings

One of the main reasons for creating an OU is to assign different Group Policy settings to a particular collection of objects. When you assign Group Policy settings to an OU, every object contained in that OU receives those settings, including other OUs. This enables administrators to deploy Group Policy settings to only part of a domain, rather than the entire domain.

Using OUs to delegate Active Directory management tasks

Creating OUs enables you to implement a decentralized administration model, in which others manage portions of the AD DS hierarchy, without affecting the rest of the structure.

Delegating authority at a site level affects all domains and users within the site. Delegating authority at the domain level affects the entire domain. However, delegating authority at the OU level affects only that OU and its subordinate objects. By granting administrative authority over an OU structure, as opposed to an entire domain or site, you gain the following advantages:

- **Minimal number of administrators with global privileges**   By creating a hierarchy of administrative levels, you limit the number of people who require global access.
- **Limited scope of errors**   Administrative mistakes such as a container deletion or group object deletion affect only the respective OU structure.

The Delegation of Control Wizard provides a simple interface you can use to delegate permissions for domains, OUs, and containers. AD DS has its own system of permissions, much like those of NTFS and printers. The Delegation of Control Wizard is essentially a front-end interface that creates complex combinations of permissions based on specific administrative tasks.

The wizard interface enables you to specify the users or groups to which you want to delegate management permissions and the specific tasks you wish them to be able to perform. You can delegate predefined tasks or create custom tasks that enable you to be more specific.

To delegate administrative control over an OU, use the following procedure.

1. From Server Manager, open the Active Directory Users And Computers console, right-click the object over which you want to delegate control and click Delegate Control. The Delegation of Control Wizard starts, displaying the Welcome page.

2. Click Next to move to the Users Or Groups page.

3. Click Add To open the Select Users, Computers, Or Groups dialog box.

4. Type the name of the user or group to which you want to delegate control of the object and click OK. The user or group appears in the Selected Users And Groups list.

5. Click Next. The Tasks To Delegate page opens, with the following options:

   - **Delegate The Following Common Tasks**   Enables you to choose from a list of predefined tasks

   - **Create A Custom Task To Delegate**   Enables you to be more specific about the task delegation

6. Select Create A Custom Task To Delegate and click Next. The Active Directory Object Type page opens, displaying the following options:

   - **This Folder, Existing Objects In This Folder, And Creation Of New Objects In This Folder**   Delegates control of the container, including all its current and future objects

   - **Only The Following Objects In The Folder**   Enables you to select specific objects to be controlled. You can select Create Selected Objects In This Folder to allow selected object types to be created, or select Delete Selected Objects In This Folder to allow selected object types to be deleted

7. Select This Folder, Existing Objects In This Folder, And Creation Of New Objects In This Folder and click Next. The Permissions page opens.

8. Set the delegated permissions according to your needs for the user or group to which you are delegating control. You can combine permissions from the following three options:

   - **General**   Displays general permissions, which are equal to those displayed on the Security tab in an object's properties

   - **Property-specific**   Displays permissions that apply to specific attributes or properties of an object

   - **Creation/deletion of specific child objects**   Displays permissions that apply to creation and deletion permissions for specified object types

9. Click Next to open the Completing The Delegation of Control Wizard page.

10. Click Finish.

11. Close the Active Directory Users And Computers console.

In this procedure, you granted permissions over a portion of Active Directory to a specified administrator or group of administrators. Although you can use the Delegation of Control Wizard to grant permissions, you cannot use it to modify or remove permissions. To perform these tasks, you must use the interface provided on the Security tab in the AD DS object's Properties sheet.

> **NOTE   ADVANCED VIEW**
>
> By default, the Security tab does not appear in an OU's Properties sheet in the Active Directory Users And Computers console. To display the tab, you must select Advanced Features from the console's View menu.

Working with groups

Since the early days of the Microsoft server operating system, administrators have used groups to manage network permissions. Groups enable administrators to assign permissions to multiple users simultaneously. A group can be defined as a collection of user or computer accounts that functions as a security principal, in much the same way that a user does.

In Windows Server 2012 R2, when a user logs on to Active Directory, an access token is created that identifies the user and that user's group memberships. Domain controllers use this access token to verify a user's permissions when the user attempts to access a local or network resource. By using groups, administrators can grant multiple users the same permission level for resources on the network. If, for example, you have 25 users in the graphics department who need access to a color printer, you can either assign each user the appropriate permissions for the printer or you can create a group containing the 25 users and assign the appropriate permissions to the group. By using a group object to access a resource, you have accomplished the following:

- When users need access to the printer, you can just add them to the group. Once added, the users receive all permissions assigned to this group. Similarly, you can remove users from the group when you want to revoke their access to the printer.

- Administrators only have to make one change to modify the level of access to the printer for all the users. Changing the group's permissions changes the permission level for all group members. Without the group, you would have to modify all 25 user accounts individually.

> **NOTE   ACCESS TOKENS**
>
> Users' access tokens are only generated when they first log on to the network from their workstation. If you add users to a group, they will need to log off and log back on again for that change to take effect.

Users can be members of more than one group. In addition, groups can contain other Active Directory objects, such as computers, and other groups in a technique called group nesting. Group nesting describes the process of configuring one or more groups as members of another group. For example, consider a company that has two groups: marketing and graphic design. Graphic design group members have access to a high-resolution color laser printer. If the marketing group members also need access to the printer, you can just add the marketing group as a member of the graphic design group. This gives the marketing group members the same permission to the color laser printer as the members of the graphic design group.

Group types

There are two group classifications in Windows Server 2012 R2: group type and group scope. Group type defines how a group is used within Active Directory.

The two Windows Server 2012 R2 group types are as follows:

- **Distribution groups** Nonsecurity-related groups created for the distribution of information to one or more persons
- **Security groups** Security-related groups created for granting resource access permissions to multiple users

Active Directory–aware applications can use distribution groups for nonsecurity-related functions. For example, Microsoft Exchange uses distribution groups to send messages to multiple users. Only applications that are designed to work with Active Directory can make use of distribution groups in this manner.

Groups that you use to assign permissions to resources are referred to as security groups. Administrators make users who need access to the same resource members of a security group. They then grant the security group permission to access the resource. After you create a group, you can convert it from a security group to a distribution group, or vice versa, at any time.

Group scopes

In addition to security and distribution group types, several group scopes are available within Active Directory. The group scope controls which objects the group can contain, limiting the objects to the same domain or permitting objects from remote domains, and also controls the location in the domain or forest where the group can be used. Group scopes available in an Active Directory domain include domain local groups, global groups, and universal groups.

DOMAIN LOCAL GROUPS

Domain local groups can have any of the following as members:

- User accounts
- Computer accounts
- Global groups from any domain in the forest
- Universal groups
- Domain local groups from the same domain

You use domain local groups to assign permissions to resources in the same domain as the domain local group. Domain local groups can make permission assignment and maintenance easier to manage.

GLOBAL GROUPS

Global groups can have any of the following as members:

- User accounts
- Computer accounts
- Other global groups from the same domain

You can use global groups to grant or deny permissions to any resource located in any domain in the forest. You accomplish this by adding the global group as a member of a domain local group that has the desired permissions. Global group memberships are replicated only to domain controllers within the same domain. Users with common resource needs should be members of a global group to facilitate the assignment of permissions to resources. You can change the membership of the global group as frequently as necessary to provide users with the necessary resource permissions.

UNIVERSAL GROUPS

Universal groups can have any of the following as members:

- User accounts
- Computer accounts
- Global groups from any domain in the forest
- Other universal groups

Universal groups, like global groups, can organize users according to their resource access needs. You can use them to provide access to resources located in any domain in the forest by using domain local groups.

You can also use universal groups to consolidate groups and accounts that either span multiple domains or span the entire forest. A key point in the application and utilization of universal groups is that group memberships in universal groups should not change frequently, because universal groups are stored in the global catalog. Changes to universal group membership lists are replicated to all global catalog servers throughout the forest. If these changes occur frequently, the replication process can consume a significant amount of bandwidth, especially on relatively slow and expensive WAN links.

Nesting groups

As discussed earlier, group nesting is the term used when groups are added as members of other groups. For example, when you make a global group a member of a universal group, it is said to be nested within the universal group.

Group nesting reduces the number of times you need to assign permissions to users in different domains in a multidomain forest. For example, if you have multiple child domains in your AD DS hierarchy, and the users in each domain need access to an enterprise database application located in the parent domain, the simplest way to set up access to this application is as follows.

1. Create global groups in each domain that contain all users needing access to the enterprise database.

2. Create a universal group in the parent domain. Include each location's global group as a member.

3. Add the universal group to the required domain local group to assign the necessary permission to access and use the enterprise database.

This traditional approach to group nesting in AD DS is often referred to by using the mnemonic AGUDLP: you add Accounts to Global groups, add those global groups to Universal groups, add universal groups to Domain Local groups, and, finally, assign Permissions to the domain local groups.

Administrators can use the same method to create their own domain local groups, to which they will delegate administrative tasks and user rights for particular OUs. Then, after creating global groups (or universal groups for forest-wide assignments) and adding them to the domain local groups, the structure is in place.

Creating groups

The procedure for creating groups in Active Directory Administrative Center or Active Directory Users And Computers is nearly identical to that for creating OUs. When you create a group, you must specify a name for the group object. The name you select can be up to 64 characters long and must be unique in the domain. You must also choose a group type and a group scope. Figure 5-22 shows the Create Group window in Active Directory Administrative Center.

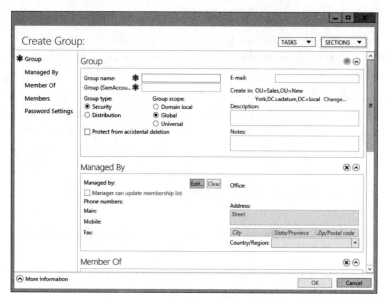

FIGURE 5-22 Creating a group in Active Directory Administrative Center

The New Object – Group dialog box in Active Directory Users And Computers looks slightly different, but contains the same basic controls.

Although the graphical AD DS utilities are a convenient tool for creating and managing groups individually, they are not the most efficient method for creating large numbers of security principals. The command-line tools included with Windows Server 2012 R2 enable you to create and manage groups in large numbers by using batch files or other types of scripts. Some of these tools are discussed in the following sections.

CREATING GROUPS FROM THE COMMAND LINE

You can use the Dsadd.exe tool to create new user objects, and you can also use the program to create group objects. The basic syntax for creating group objects with Dsadd.exe is as follows:

```
dsadd group <GroupDN> [parameters]
```

The <GroupDN> parameter is a DN for the new group object you want to create. The DNs use the same format as those in CSV files.

By default, Dsadd.exe creates global security groups, but you can use command-line parameters to create groups with other types and scopes and to specify members and memberships for the groups and other group object properties. The most commonly used command-line parameters are as follows:

- **-secgrp yes|no** Specifies whether the program should create a security group (yes) or a distribution group (no). The default value is yes.

- **-scope l|g|u**   Specifies whether the program should create a domain local (l), global (g), or universal (u) group. The default value is g.
- **-samid <SAMName>**   Specifies the SAM name for the group object.
- **-desc <description>**   Specifies a description for the group object.
- **-memberof <GroupDN>**   Specifies the DNs of one or more groups of which the new group should be made a member.
- **-member <GroupDN>**   Specifies the DNs of one or more objects that should be made members of the new group.

For example, to create a new group called Sales in the Users container and make the Administrator user a member, you would use the following command:

```
dsadd group "CN=Sales,CN=Users,DC=adatum,DC=com"
-member "CN=Administrator,CN=Users,DC=adatum,DC=com"
```

To create a new group object by using Windows PowerShell, you use the New-ADGroup cmdlet, with the following syntax:

```
New-ADGroup
-Name <group name>
-SamAccountName <SAM name>
-GroupCategory Distribution|Security
-GroupScope DomainLocal|Global|Universal
-Path <distinguished name>
```

For example, to create a global security group called Sales in the Chicago OU, you would use the following command:

```
New-ADGroup -Name Sales -SamAccountName Sales
-GroupCategory Security -GroupScope Global
-Path "OU=Chicago,DC=Adatum,DC=Com"
```

Managing group memberships

Unlike the Active Directory Administrative Center, which enables you to specify a group's members as you create the group, in Active Directory Users And Computers you must create the group object first, and then add members to it.

To add members to a group, select it in the console and, from the Action menu, select Properties to open the group's Properties sheet and then select the Members tab.

On the Members tab, you can add objects to the group's membership list, and on the Member Of tab, you can add the group to the membership list of another group. For both these tasks, you use the standard Select Users, Contacts, Computers, Service Accounts, Or Groups dialog box to choose objects.

Once you enter or find the objects you want to add, click OK to close the Properties sheet and add the objects to the group's membership list.

MANAGE GROUP MEMBERSHIP BY USING GROUP POLICY

It is also possible to control group memberships by using Group Policy. When you create Restricted Groups policies, you can specify the membership for a group and enforce it, so that changes made to the membership will be reversed during the next policy refresh.

To create Restricted Groups policies, use the following procedure.

1. From Server Manager, open the Group Policy Management Console, create a new GPO and link it to your domain.

2. Open the GPO in the Group Policy Management Editor and browse to the Computer Configuration\Policies\Windows Settings\Security Settings\Restricted Groups folder, as shown in Figure 5-23.

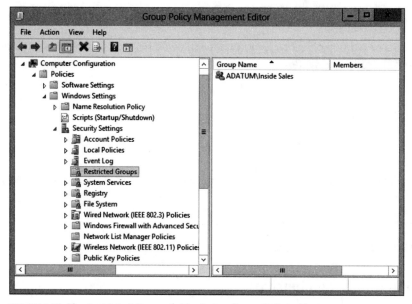

FIGURE 5-23 The Restricted Groups folder in the Group Policy object

3. Right-click the Restricted Groups folder and, from the shortcut menu, select Add Group to open the Add Group dialog box.

4. Type or browse to add a group object and click OK. The group appears in the Restricted Groups folder and a Properties sheet for the policy appears, as shown in Figure 5-24.

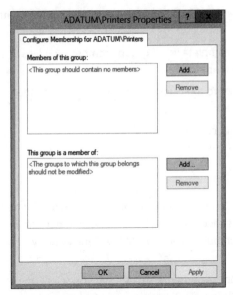

FIGURE 5-24 The Properties sheet for a Restricted Groups policy

5. Click one or both of the Add buttons to add objects that should be members of the group or other groups of which the group should be a member.

6. Click OK.

7. Close the Group Policy Management Editor and Group Policy Management consoles.

The members you specify for a group in a Restricted Groups policy are the only members permitted to remain in that group. The policy does not prevent administrators from modifying the group membership by using other tools, but the next time the system refreshes its group policy settings, the group membership list will be overwritten by the policy.

MANAGING GROUP OBJECTS BY USING DSMOD.EXE

Dsmod.exe enables you to modify the properties of existing group objects from the Windows Server 2012 R2 command prompt. By using this program, you can perform tasks such as adding members to a group, removing them from a group, and changing a group's type and scope. The basic syntax for Dsmod.exe is as follows:

```
dsmod group <GroupDN> [parameters]
```

The most commonly used command-line parameters for Dsmod.exe are as follows:

- **-secgrp yes|no**   Sets the group type to security group (yes) or distribution group (no).
- **-scope l|g|u**   Sets the group scope to domain local (l), global (g), or universal (u).
- **-addmbr <members>**   Adds members to the group. Replace members with the DNs of one or more objects.

- **-rmmbr \<members>** Removes members from the group. Replace members with the DNs of one or more objects.

- **-chmbr \<members>** Replaces the complete list of group members. Replace members with the DNs of one or more objects.

For example, to add the Administrator user to the Guests group, you would use the following command:

```
dsmod group "CN=Guests,CN=Builtin,DC=adatum,DC=com"
-addmbr "CN=Administrator,CN=Users,DC=adatum,DC=com"
```

Converting groups

As group functions change, you might need to change a group object's type. To change the type of a group, open the group's Properties sheet in the Active Directory Administrative Center or the Active Directory Users And Computers console. On the General tab, you can modify the Group Type option and click OK.

The process for changing the group's scope is the same, except that you select one of the Group Scope options on the General tab. The AD DS utilities only enable you to perform permissible scope changes. Table 5-1 lists the scope changes that are permitted.

TABLE 5-1 Active Directory Group Scope conversion restrictions

	To Domain Local	**To Global**	**To Universal**
From Domain Local	Not applicable	Not permitted	Permitted only when the domain local group does not have other domain local groups as members
From Global	Not permitted	Not applicable	Permitted only when the global group is not a member of another global group
From Universal	No restrictions	Permitted only when the universal group does not have other universal groups as members	Not applicable

Deleting a group

As with user objects, each group object that you create in AD DS has a unique, nonreusable SID. Windows Server 2012 R2 uses the SID to identify the group and the permissions assigned to it.

When you delete a group, Windows Server 2012 R2 does not use the same SID for that group again, even if you create a new group with the same name as the one you deleted. Therefore, you cannot restore the access permissions you assigned to resources by re-creating a deleted group object. You must add the newly re-created group as a security principal in the resource's access control list (ACL) again.

When you delete a group, you delete only the group object and the permissions and rights specifying that group as the security principal. Deleting a group does not delete the objects that are members of the group.

Thought Experiment
Creating groups

In the following thought experiment, apply what you've learned about this objective to predict what steps you need to take. You can find answers to these questions in the "Answers" section at the end of this chapter.

The enterprise network for the Fabrikam Corporation consists of a forest root domain called fabrikam.com and two child domains called east.fabrikam.com and west.fabrikam.com. There are four department managers with user accounts in the fabrikam.com domain and two each in the east.fabrikam.com and west.fabrikam.com domains. Each of the three domains has a global group with the domain's managers as members. You want all of the members of these groups to be able to access a common set of resources in the fabrikam.com domain, while still segregating the managers' abilities to access resources in domains other than their own. How should you configure the groups to provide the desired functionality?

Objective summary

- Adding OUs to your Active Directory hierarchy is easier than adding domains; you don't need additional hardware, and you can easily move or delete an OU as necessary.

- When you want to grant a collection of users permission to access a network resource, such as a file system share or a printer, you cannot assign permissions to an OU; you must use a security group instead. Although they are container objects, groups are not part of the Active Directory hierarchy in the same way that domains and OUs are.

- Creating OUs enables you to implement a decentralized administration model, in which others manage portions of the AD DS hierarchy, without affecting the rest of the structure.

- Groups enable administrators to assign permissions to multiple users simultaneously. A group can be defined as a collection of user or computer accounts that functions as a security principal, in much the same way that a user does.

- In Active Directory, there are two types of groups: security and distribution. There are also three group scopes: domain local, global, and universal.

- Group nesting is the term used when groups are added as members of other groups.

- It is possible to control group memberships by using Group Policy. When you create Restricted Groups policies, you can specify the membership for a group and enforce it.

Objective review

Answer the following questions to test your knowledge of the information in this objective. You can find the answers to these questions and explanations of why each answer choice is correct or incorrect in the "Answers" section at the end of this chapter.

1. Which of the following groups are used to consolidate groups and accounts that span either multiple domains or the entire forest?

   A. Global

   B. Domain local

   C. Built-in

   D. Universal

2. Which of the following is *not* a correct reason for creating an OU?

   A. To create a permanent container that cannot be moved or renamed

   B. To duplicate the divisions in your organization

   C. To delegate administration tasks

   D. To assign different Group Policy settings to a specific group of users or computers

3. Which of the following group scope modifications are never permitted? (Choose all that apply.)

   A. Global to universal

   B. Global to domain local

   C. Universal to global

   D. Domain local to universal

4. In a domain running at the Windows Server 2012 R2 domain functional level, which of the following security principals can be members of a global group? (Choose all that apply.)

   A. Users

   B. Computers

   C. Universal groups

   D. Global groups

5. You are attempting to delete a global security group in the Active Directory Users And Computers console but the console will not let you complete the task. Which of the following could possibly be causes for the failure? (Choose all that apply.)

   A. There are still members in the group.

   B. One of the group's members has the group set as its primary group.

   C. You do not have the proper permissions for the container in which the group is located.

   D. You cannot delete global groups from the Active Directory Users And Computers console.

Answers

This section contains the solutions to the thought experiments and answers to the objective review questions in this chapter.

Objective 5.1: Thought experiment

Robert should install Active Directory on a domain controller in the New York headquarters, creating a forest root domain called hq.inside.litware.com. Because the London office is well connected, but lacks its own IT staff, he can install a read-only domain controller for the hq.inside.litware.com domain there, so that the London users can authenticate by using a local domain controller. For the Tokyo office, which is not as well connected and has its own IT staff, the design should call for two domain controllers hosting a separate domain in the same forest, called tokyo.inside.litware.com. This will provide the Tokyo users with local domain controller access and minimize the amount of replication traffic passing over the demand-dial link between the New York and Tokyo offices.

Objective 5.1: Review

1. **Correct answer:** A

   A. **Correct:** In AD DS, you can subdivide a domain into OUs and populate it with objects, but you cannot create domains within OUs.

   B. **Incorrect:** A site can contain multiple domains.

   C. **Incorrect:** A tree can contain multiple domains.

   D. **Incorrect:** A forest can contain multiple domains.

2. **Correct answers:** B, D

   A. **Incorrect:** There is no object class called resource.

   B. **Correct:** There are two basic classes of objects: container objects and leaf objects. A leaf object cannot have subordinate objects.

   C. **Incorrect:** A domain is a specific object type, not a general classification.

   D. **Correct:** There are two basic classes of objects: container objects and leaf objects. A container object is one that can have other objects subordinate to it.

3. **Correct answer:** C

   A. **Incorrect:** Some attributes are created automatically, whereas administrators must supply information for other attributes manually.

   B. **Incorrect:** A container object has, as one of its attributes, a list of all the other objects it contains.

   C. **Correct:** Leaf objects have attributes that contain information about the specific resource the object represents.

   D. **Incorrect:** Some attributes are created automatically, such as the globally unique identifier (GUID) that the domain controller assigns to each object when it creates it.

4. **Correct answer:** D

   A. **Incorrect:** Each domain in an Active Directory installation is a separate administrative entity. The more domains you create, the greater the number of ongoing administration tasks you have to perform.

   B. **Incorrect:** Every domain requires its own domain controllers, so each additional domain you create increases the overall hardware and maintenance costs of the deployment.

   C. **Incorrect:** Applications might have problems working in a multidomain forest.

   D. **Correct:** No special Microsoft licenses are needed for domains.

5. **Correct answer:** B

   A. **Incorrect:** DNS is used for searches within a domain.

   B. **Correct:** To locate an object in another domain, Active Directory clients perform a search of the global catalog first. This search provides the client with the information it needs to search for the object in the specific domain that contains it.

   C. **Incorrect:** DHCP does not provide search capabilities.

   D. **Incorrect:** Site link objects do not provide search capabilities.

Objective 5.2: Thought experiment

Correct answer: D. Answer A is incorrect because the user command is missing and because the user's name is not expressed in distinguished name (DN) format. Answer B is incorrect because the command-line variables containing spaces are not surrounded by quotation marks. Answer C is incorrect because the user command is missing and because the –company and –dept parameters appear before the DN.

Objective 5.2: Review

1. **Correct answer:** B

   A. **Incorrect:** Dcpromo, now deprecated in Windows Server 2012 R2, is a tool used to promote and demote Active Directory domain controllers.

   B. **Correct:** Like CSVDE.exe, the LDAP Data Interchange Format Directory Exchange (LDIFDE.exe) utility can be used to import or export Active Directory information. It can be used to add, delete, or modify objects in Active Directory, in addition to modifying the schema, if necessary.

   C. **Incorrect:** CSVDE.exe can create Active Directory objects from information in CSV files, but it cannot modify existing objects.

   D. **Incorrect:** NSLOOKUP is a DNS name resolution utility. It cannot create AD DS objects.

2. **Correct answer:** B

   A. **Incorrect:** The first line of the CSV file is the header record, not the header row.

   B. **Correct:** The CSVDE command-line utility enables an administrator to import or export AD DS objects. It uses a .csv file that is based on a header record, which describes each part of the data. A header record is just the first line of the text file that uses proper attribute names.

   C. **Incorrect:** The first line of the CSV file is the header record, not the name row.

   D. **Incorrect:** The first line of the CSV file is the header record, not the name record.

3. **Correct answer:** C

   A. **Incorrect:** You cannot perform an offline domain join by using the net join command.

   B. **Incorrect:** You cannot perform an offline domain join by using the join command.

   C. **Correct:** You can perform an offline domain join on a computer running Windows Server 2012 R2 by using the Djoin.exe utility.

   D. **Incorrect:** You cannot perform an offline domain join by using the dconnect command.

4. **Correct answer:** C

   A. **Incorrect:** Local accounts can be created and configured in Windows Server 2012 R2.

   B. **Incorrect:** Domain accounts can be created and configured in Windows Server 2012 R2.

   C. **Correct:** There are three types of user accounts in Windows Server 2012 R2: local accounts, domain accounts, and built-in user accounts.

   D. **Incorrect:** Built-in accounts can be configured, but not created in Windows Server 2012 R2.

5. **Correct answers:** C, D

   A. **Incorrect:** There is no Network account in Windows Server 2012 R2.

   B. **Incorrect:** There is no Interactive account in Windows Server 2012 R2.

   C. **Correct:** By default, the two built-in user accounts created on a computer running Windows Server 2012 R2 are the Administrator account and the Guest account.

   D. **Correct:** By default, the two built-in user accounts created on a computer running Windows Server 2012 R2 are the Administrator account and the Guest account.

Objective 5.3: Thought experiment

Correct answer: Create a universal group in the fabrikam.com domain and add all three global groups to this universal group. Then create a domain local group in the fabrikam.com domain and add the universal group to this domain local group. Finally, assign the permissions needed to access the common resources to the domain local group.

Objective 5.3: Review

1. **Correct answer:** D

   A. **Incorrect:** Global groups cannot contain users from other domains.

   B. **Incorrect:** Domain local groups cannot have permissions for resources in other domains.

   C. **Incorrect:** Built-in groups have no inherent cross-domain qualities.

   D. **Correct:** Universal groups, like global groups, are used to organize users according to their resource access needs. You can use them to organize users to facilitate access to any resource located in any domain in the forest through the use of domain local groups. Universal groups are used to consolidate groups and accounts that span either multiple domains or the entire forest.

2. **Correct answer:** A

   A. **Correct:** The reasons for creating an OU include duplicating organizational divisions, assigning Group Policy settings, and delegating administration. You can easily move or rename an OU as necessary.

   B. **Incorrect:** Duplicating organizational divisions is a viable reason for creating an OU.

   C. **Incorrect:** Delegating administration tasks is a viable reason for creating an OU.

   D. **Incorrect:** Assigning Group Policy settings is a viable reason for creating an OU.

3. **Correct answer:** B

   A. **Incorrect:** Global to universal group conversions are sometimes permitted.

   B. **Correct:** Global to domain local group conversions are never permitted.

   C. **Incorrect:** Universal to global group conversions are sometimes permitted.

   D. **Incorrect:** Domain local to universal group conversions are sometimes permitted.

4. **Correct answers:** A, B, D

   A. **Correct:** Users can be security principals in a global group.

   B. **Correct:** Computers can be security principals in a global group.

   C. **Incorrect:** Universal groups cannot be security principals in a global group.

   D. **Correct:** Global groups can be security principals in a global group.

5. **Correct answers:** B, C

   A. **Incorrect:** It is possible to delete a group that has members.

   B. **Correct:** If any member sets the group as its primary group, then the system does not permit the group to be deleted.

   C. **Correct:** You must have the appropriate Active Directory permissions for the container in which the group is located to delete it.

   D. **Incorrect:** It is possible to delete groups by using the Active Directory Users and Groups console.

CHAPTER 6

Creating and managing Group Policy

Group Policy is a mechanism for controlling and deploying operating system settings to computers all over your network. Group Policy consists of user and computer settings for the various Microsoft Windows operating systems, which the systems implement during computer startup and shutdown and user logon and logoff. You can configure one or more Group Policy Objects (GPOs) and then use a process called linking to associate them with specific Active Directory Domain Services (AD DS) objects. When you link a GPO to a container object, all the objects in that container receive the settings you configured in the GPO. You can link multiple GPOs to a single AD DS container or link one GPO to multiple containers throughout the AD DS hierarchy.

This chapter covers some of the fundamental tasks that administrators perform to create and deploy Group Policy settings.

Objectives in this chapter:

- Objective 6.1: Create Group Policy Objects (GPOs)
- Objective 6.2: Configure security policies
- Objective 6.3: Configure application restriction policies
- Objective 6.4: Configure Windows Firewall

Objective 6.1: Create Group Policy Objects

Although the name Group Policy Object implies that policies are linked directly to groups, this is not the case. GPOs can be linked to sites, domains, and organizational units (OUs) to apply settings to all users and computers within AD DS containers. However, an advanced technique named security filtering enables you to apply GPO settings to one or more users or groups within a container by selectively granting the Apply Group Policy and Read permissions to one or more users or security groups.

The administrative benefits of GPOs are probably their greatest contribution to network efficiency. Administrators find that Group Policy implementation helps them achieve centralized management. The following list identifies administrative benefits to Group Policy implementation:

- Administrators have control over centralized configuration of user settings, application installation, and desktop configuration.

- Centralized administration of user files eliminates the need for and cost of trying to recover files from a damaged drive.

- The need to manually make security changes on each computer is reduced by the automated, rapid deployment of new settings through Group Policy.

This objective covers how to:
- Configure a Central Store
- Manage starter GPOs
- Configure GPO links
- Configure multiple local group policies
- Configure security filtering

Understanding Group Policy Objects

GPOs contain all the Group Policy settings that administrators wish to deploy to user and computer objects within a domain, site, or OU. To deploy a GPO, an administrator must associate it with a container. This association is achieved by linking the GPO to the desired AD DS domain, site, or OU object. Administrative tasks for Group Policy include creating GPOs, specifying where to store them, and managing the AD DS links.

There are three types of GPOs: local GPOs, nonlocal GPOs, and starter GPOs.

Local GPOs (LGPOs)

All Windows operating systems have support for *local GPOs*, sometimes known as LGPOs. Windows versions since Windows Server 2008 R2 and Windows Vista can support multiple local GPOs. This support enables administrators to specify a different local GPO for administrators and to create specific GPO settings for one or more local users configured on a workstation. This ability is particularly valuable for computers in public locations such as libraries and kiosks, when they are not part of an Active Directory infrastructure. Older Windows releases can support only one local GPO and the settings in that local GPO apply to all users who log on to the computer.

Local GPOs contain fewer options than domain GPOs. They do not support folder redirection or Group Policy software installation. Fewer security settings are available. When a local and a nonlocal (Active Directory–based) GPO have conflicting settings, the nonlocal GPO settings overwrite the local GPO settings.

Nonlocal GPOs

Nonlocal GPOs are created in AD DS and linked to sites, domains, and OUs. Once linked to a container, the settings in the GPO are applied to all users and computers within that container by default.

Starter GPOs

Starter GPOs were introduced in Windows Server 2008. A *starter GPO* is essentially a template for the creation of domain GPOs based on a standard collection of settings. When you create a new GPO from a starter GPO, all the settings in the starter GPO are automatically copied to the new GPO as its default settings.

Configuring a Central Store

In Windows Server 2008 and Windows Vista, Microsoft replaced the token-based administrative template (ADM) files used with previous versions of Group Policy with an XML-based file format (ADMX). Administrative templates are the files defining the registry-based settings that appear in GPOs.

Earlier Windows versions created a copy of the ADM files for each GPO administrators created and placed them in the SYSVOL volume of a domain controller. A large Active Directory installation could easily have dozens of GPOs and each copy of the ADM files required 4 MB of storage. The result was a condition called SYSVOL bloat, in which there were hundreds of megabytes of redundant information stored on SYSVOL volumes, which had to be replicated to all the domain controllers for the domain.

To address this problem, Group Policy tools can now access the ADMX files from a Central Store, a single copy of the ADMX files stored on domain controllers. To use a Central Store, you must create the appropriate folder in the SYSVOL volume on a domain controller.

By default, tools such as the Group Policy Management Console (GPMC) save the ADMX files to the \\%*systemroot*%\PolicyDefinitions folder, which on most computers is C:\Windows\PolicyDefinitions. To create a Central Store, you must copy the entire PolicyDefinitions folder to the same location as the Group Policy templates; that is, %*systemroot*%\SYSVOL\sysvol\<domain name>\Policies, on a domain controller, or, in universal naming convention (UNC) notation, \\< *domain name* >\SYSVOL\< *domain name* >\Policies.

Using the Group Policy Management Console

The Group Policy Management Console is the Microsoft Management Console (MMC) snap-in that administrators use to create GPOs and manage their deployment to AD DS objects. The Group Policy Management Editor is a separate snap-in that opens GPOs and enables you to modify their settings.

There are several different ways of working with these two tools, depending on what you want to accomplish. You can create a GPO and then link it to a domain, site, or OU, or you can create and link a GPO in a single step. Windows Server 2012 R2 implements the tools as the Group Policy Management feature and installs them automatically with the AD DS role. You can install the feature manually on a member server by using the Add Roles And Features Wizard in Server Manager. The Group Policy Management tools are also included in the Remote Server Administration Tools package for Windows workstations.

Creating and linking nonlocal GPOs

If you decide to leave the default Windows GPOs unaltered, the first steps in deploying your own customized Group Policy settings are to create one or more new GPOs and link them to appropriate AD DS objects.

To use the Group Policy Management Console to create a new GPO and link it to an OU object in AD DS, use the following procedure.

1. Open the Active Directory Administrative Center and create an OU called Sales in your domain.

2. In Server Manager, from the Tools menu, select Group Policy Management. The Group Policy Management Console appears, as shown in Figure 6-1.

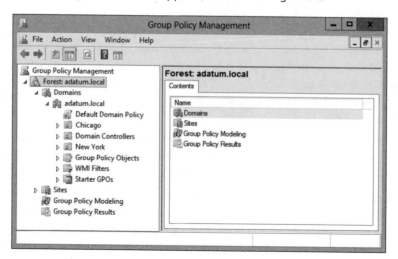

FIGURE 6-1 The Group Policy Management Console

3. Expand the forest container and browse to your domain. Then expand the domain container and select the Group Policy Objects folder. The GPOs that currently exist in the domain appear on the Contents tab.

4. Right-click the Group Policy Objects folder and, from the shortcut menu, select New. The New GPO dialog box appears.

5. In the Name text box, type a name for the new GPO and click OK. The new GPO appears in the Contents list.

6. In the left pane, right-click the domain, site, or OU object to which you want to link the new GPO and, from the shortcut menu, select Link An Existing GPO. The Select GPO dialog box appears.

7. Select the GPO you want to link to the object and click OK. The GPO appears on the object's Linked Group Policy Objects tab, as shown in Figure 6-2.

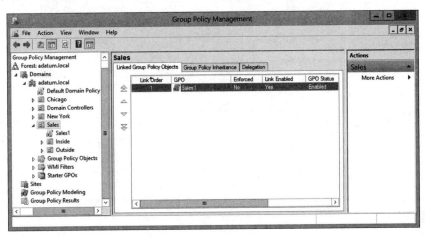

FIGURE 6-2 The Linked Group Policy Objects tab

8. Close the Group Policy Management Console.

You can also create and link a GPO to an Active Directory container in a single step, by right-clicking an object and selecting Create A GPO In This Domain And Link It Here from the shortcut menu.

If you link a GPO to a domain object, it applies to all users and computers in the domain. On a larger scale, if you link a GPO to a site that contains multiple domains, the Group Policy settings are applied to all the domains and the child objects beneath them. This process is referred to as *GPO inheritance*.

Using security filtering

Linking a GPO to a container causes all the users and computers in that container to receive the GPO settings by default. This is because creating the link grants the Read and Apply Group Policy permissions for the GPO to the users and computers in the container.

More precisely, the system grants the permissions to the Authenticated Users special identity, which includes all the users and computers in the domain. However, by using a technique named security filtering, you can modify the default permission assignments so that only certain users and computers receive the permissions and, consequently, the settings in the GPO.

To modify the default security filtering configuration for a GPO, select it in the left pane of the Group Policy Management Console, as shown in Figure 6-3. In the Security Filtering area, you can use the Add button or the Remove button to replace the Authenticated Users special identity with specific user, computer, or group objects. Of the users and computers in the container to which the GPO is linked, only those you select in the Security Filtering pane will receive the settings from the GPO.

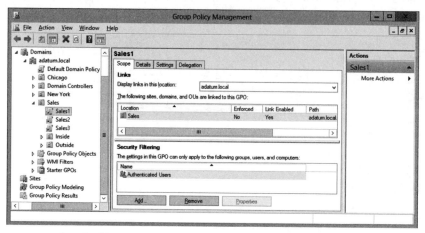

FIGURE 6-3 Security filtering in the Group Policy Management Console

Managing starter GPOs

Starter GPOs are essentially templates that you can use to create multiple GPOs with the same set of baseline Administrative Templates settings. You create and edit starter GPOs just as you would any other GPO. In the Group Policy Management Console, you right-click the Starter GPOs folder and, from the shortcut menu, select New to create a blank starter GPO. You can then open the starter GPO in the Group Policy Management Editor and configure any settings you want to carry over to the new GPOs you create from it.

> **NOTE USING STARTER GPOS**
>
> When you view the Starter GPOs node in the Group Policy Management Console for the first time, a message appears, prompting you to create the Starter GPOs folder by clicking a button.

Once you have created and edited your starter GPOs, you can create new GPOs from them in multiple ways. You can right-click a starter GPO and select New GPO From Starter GPO from the shortcut menu, or you can create a new GPO in the usual manner described earlier and select the starter GPO you want to use in the Source Starter GPO drop-down list. You can also use the New-GPO cmdlet in Windows PowerShell. This copies the settings from the starter GPO to the new GPO, which you can continue to edit from there.

Configuring Group Policy settings

Group Policy settings enable you to customize the configuration of a user's desktop, environment, and security settings. The settings are divided into two subcategories: Computer Configuration and User Configuration. The subcategories are referred to as Group Policy nodes. A node is just a parent structure that holds all related settings. In this case, the node is specific to computer configurations and user configurations.

Group Policy nodes provide a way to organize the settings according to where they are applied. The settings you define in a GPO can be applied to client computers, users, or member servers and domain controllers. The application of the settings depends on the container to which you link the GPO. By default, all objects within the container to which you link the GPO are affected by the GPO's settings.

The Computer Configuration and User Configuration nodes contain three subnodes, or extensions, that further organize the available Group Policy settings. Within the Computer Configuration and User Configuration nodes, the subnodes are as follows:

- **Software Settings**   The Software Settings folder located under the Computer Configuration node contains Software Installation settings that apply to all users who log on to a domain using any computer affected by the GPO. The Software Settings folder located under the User Configuration node contains Software Installation settings that are applied to all users designated by the Group Policy, regardless of the computer from which they log on.

- **Windows Settings**   The Windows Settings folder located under the Computer Configuration node contains security settings and scripts that apply to all users who log on to AD DS from that specific computer. The Windows Settings folder located under the User Configuration node contains settings related to folder redirection, security settings, and scripts that apply to specific users.

- **Administrative Templates**   Windows Server 2012 R2 includes thousands of Administrative Template policies, which contain all registry-based policy settings. Administrative Templates are files with the .admx extension. They are used to generate the user interface for the Group Policy settings that you can set by using the Group Policy Management Editor.

To work with Administrative Template settings, you must understand the three different states of each policy setting. These three states are as follows:

- **Not Configured**   No modification to the registry from its default state occurs as a result of the policy. Not Configured is the default setting for the majority of GPO settings. When a system processes a GPO with Not Configured settings, the registry keys affected by the settings are not modified or overwritten, whatever their current value.

- **Enabled**   The policy function is explicitly activated in the registry, whatever its previous state.

- **Disabled**   The policy function is explicitly deactivated in the registry, whatever its previous state.

Understanding these states is critical when you are working with Group Policy inheritance and multiple GPOs. If a policy setting is disabled in the registry by default and you have a lower-priority GPO that explicitly enables that setting, you must configure a higher-priority GPO to disable the setting if you want to restore it to its default. Applying the Not Configured state will not change the setting, leaving it enabled.

Creating multiple local GPOs

Computers that are members of an AD DS domain benefit from a great deal of flexibility when it comes to Group Policy configuration. Standalone (non–AD DS) systems can achieve some of that flexibility as long as they are running at least Windows Vista or Windows Server 2008 R2. These operating systems enable administrators to create multiple local GPOs that provide different settings for users, based on their identities.

Windows systems supporting multiple local GPOs have three layers of Group Policy support, as follows:

- **Local Group Policy**   Identical to the single local GPO supported by older operating system versions, the Local Group Policy layer consists of both computer settings and user settings and applies to all system users, administrative or not. This is the only local GPO that includes computer settings, so to apply Computer Configuration policies, you must use this GPO.

- **Administrators and Nonadministrators Group Policy**   This layer consists of two GPOs: one that applies to members of the local Administrators group and one that applies to all users who are not members of the local Administrators group. Unlike the Local Group Policy GPO, this layer does not include computer settings.

- **User-specific Group Policy**   This layer consists of GPOs that apply to specific local user accounts created on the computer. These GPOs can apply to individual users only, not to local groups. These GPOs also do not have computer configuration settings.

Windows applies the local GPOs in the order listed here. The Local Group Policy settings are applied first, then either the Administrators GPO or the Non-Administrators GPO, and, finally, any user-specific GPOs. As with nonlocal GPOs, the settings processed later can overwrite any earlier settings with which they conflict.

In the case of a system that is also a member of a domain, the three layers of local GPO processing come first, followed by the standard order of nonlocal Group Policy application.

To create local GPOs, you use the Group Policy Object Editor, which is an MMC snap-in provided on all Windows computers specifically for the management of local GPOs, as in the following procedure.

1.   Open the Run dialog box and, in the Open text box, type **mmc** and click OK. An empty MMC console opens.

2.   Click File, Add/Remove Snap-In to open the Add Or Remove Snap-Ins dialog box.

3. From the Available Snap-Ins list, select Group Policy Object Editor and click Add. The Select Group Policy Object page opens.

4. To create the local Group Policy GPO, click Finish. To create a secondary or tertiary GPO, click Browse. The Browse For A Group Policy Object dialog box opens.

5. Click the Users tab, as shown in Figure 6-4.

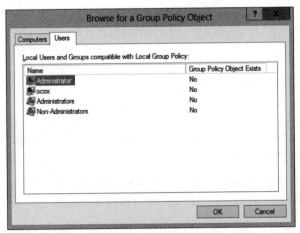

FIGURE 6-4 The Users tab of the Browse For A Group Policy Object dialog box

> **NOTE MULTIPLE LOCAL GPOS**
>
> Windows computers that do not support multiple local GPOs lack the Users tab in the Browse For A Group Policy Object dialog box. This includes domain controllers and computers running Windows versions prior to Windows Vista and Windows Server 2008 R2.

6. To create a secondary GPO, select either Administrators or Non-Administrators and click OK. To create a tertiary GPO, select a user and click OK. The GPO appears on the Select Group Policy Object page.

7. Click Finish. The snap-in appears in the Add Or Remove Snap-Ins dialog box.

8. Click OK. The snap-in appears in the MMC console.

9. Click File, Save As. A Save As combo box appears.

10. Type a name for the console to save it in the Administrative Tools program group.

11. Close the MMC console.

You can now open this console whenever you need to configure the settings in the GPO you created.

Thought experiment

Implementing Group Policy

In the following thought experiment, apply what you've learned about this objective to predict what steps you need to take. You can find answers to these questions in the "Answers" section at the end of this chapter.

After a recent incident in which an employee left the company with a substantial amount of confidential data, the IT director has given Alice the task of implementing Group Policy settings that prevent all users except administrators and members of the Executives group from installing any USB devices.

Alice creates a GPO called Device Restrictions for this purpose and links it to the company's single domain object. The GPO contains the following settings from the Computer Configuration\Policies\Administrative Templates\System\Device Installation\Device Installation Restrictions folder:

- Allow administrators to override Device Installation Restriction policies–Enabled
- Prevent installation of devices not described by other policy settings–Enabled

What else must Alice do to satisfy the requirements of her assignment?

Objective summary

- Group Policy consists of user and computer settings that can be implemented during computer startup and user logon. These settings can be used to customize the user environment, to implement security guidelines, and to assist in simplifying user and desktop administration.
- In AD DS, Group Policies can be assigned to sites, domains, and OUs. By default, there is one local policy per computer. Local policy settings are overwritten by Active Directory policy settings.
- The Group Policy Management console is the tool used to create and modify GPOs and their settings.

Objective review

Answer the following questions to test your knowledge of the information in this objective. You can find the answers to these questions and explanations of why each answer choice is correct or incorrect in the "Answers" section at the end of this chapter.

1. Which of the following types of files do Group Policy tools access from a Central Store by default?

    A. ADM files

    B. ADMX files

    C. Group Policy Objects

    D. Security templates

2. Which of the following local GPOs takes precedence on a system with multiple local GPOs?

    A. Local Group Policy

    B. Administrators Group Policy

    C. Non-Administrators Group Policy

    D. D. User-specific Group Policy

3. Which of the following techniques can be used to apply GPO settings to a specific group of users in an OU?

    A. GPO linking

    B. B. Administrative templates

    C. C. Security filtering

    D. D. Starter GPOs

4. Which of the following statements best describes the function of a starter GPO?

    A. A starter GPO functions as a template for the creation of new GPOs.

    B. A starter GPO is the first GPO applied by all Active Directory clients.

    C. A starter GPO uses a simplified interface for elementary users.

    D. A starter GPO contains all the settings found in the default Domain Policy GPO.

5. When you apply a GPO with a value of Not Configured for a particular setting to a system on which that same setting is disabled, what is the result?

    A. The setting remains disabled.

    B. The setting is changed to Not Configured.

    C. The setting is changed to Enabled.

    D. The setting generates a conflict error.

Objective 6.2: Configure security policies

One of the primary aims of Group Policy is to provide centralized management of security settings for users and computers. Most of the settings that pertain to security are found in the Windows Settings folder within the Computer Configuration node of a GPO. You can use security settings to govern how users are authenticated to the network, the resources they are permitted to use, group membership policies, and events related to user and group actions recorded in the event logs. Policy settings in the Computer Configuration node apply to a computer; it does not matter who is logging on to it. There are more Computer Configuration security settings than settings you can apply to a specific user.

> **This objective covers how to:**
> - Configure User Rights Assignment
> - Configure Security Options settings
> - Configure Security templates
> - Configure Audit Policy
> - Configure Local Users and Groups
> - Configure User Account Control (UAC)

Defining local policies

Local policies enable administrators to set user privileges on the local computer that govern what users can do on the computer and determine if the system should track user activities in an event log. Tracking events that take place on the local computer, a process referred to as auditing, is another important part of monitoring and managing activities on a computer running Windows Server 2012 R2.

The Local Policies node of a GPO, found under Security Settings, has three subordinate nodes: Audit Policy, User Rights Assignment, and Security Options. As discussed in each of the following sections, keep in mind that local policies are local to a computer. When they are part of a GPO in Active Directory, they affect the local security settings of computer accounts to which the GPO is applied.

Planning and configuring an audit policy

The Audit Policy section of a GPO enables administrators to log successful and failed security events, such as logon events, account access, and object access. You can use auditing to track both user activities and system activities. Planning to audit requires that you determine the computers to be audited and the types of events you wish to track.

When you consider events to audit, such as account logon events, you must decide whether you wish to audit successful logon attempts, failed logon attempts, or both. Tracking successful events enables you to determine how often users access network resources. This information can be valuable when planning your resource usage and budgeting for new resources. Tracking failed events can help you determine when security breaches occur or are attempted. For example, if you notice frequent failed logon attempts for a specific user account, you might want to investigate further. The policy settings available for auditing are shown in Figure 6-5.

When an audited event occurs, Windows Server 2012 R2 writes an event to the security log on the domain controller or the computer where the event took place. If it is a logon attempt or other Active Directory–related event, the event is written to the domain controller. If it is a computer event, such as a floppy drive access, the event is written to the local computer's event log.

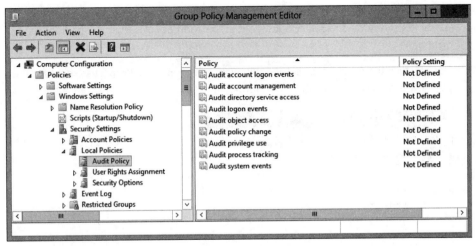

FIGURE 6-5 Audit Policies in the default domain policy

You must decide which computers, resources, and events you want to audit. It is important to balance the need for auditing against the potential information overload that would be created if you audited every possible type of event. The following guidelines can help you to plan your audit policy:

- **Audit only pertinent items** Determine the events you want to audit and consider whether it is more important to track successes or failures of these events. You should only plan to audit events that will help you gather network information.

- **Archive security logs to provide a documented history** Keeping a history of event occurrences can provide you with documentation you can use to support the need for additional resources based on past usage.

- **Configure the size of your security logs carefully** You need to plan the size of your security logs based on the number of events that you anticipate logging. You can configure the Event Log Policy settings under the Computer Configuration\Windows Settings\Security Settings\Event Log node of a GPO.

Implementation of your plan requires that you specify the categories to be audited and, if necessary, configure objects for auditing. To configure an audit policy, use the following procedure.

1. In Server Manager, on the Tools menu, select Group Policy Management to open the Group Policy Management console.

2. Expand the forest container and browse to your domain. Then expand the domain container and select the Group Policy Objects folder. The GPOs that currently exist in the domain appear on the Contents tab.

3. Right-click the Default Domain Policy GPO and click Edit. A Group Policy Management Editor window for this policy opens.

4. Browse to the Computer Configuration\Policies\Windows Settings\Security Settings \Local Policies node and select Audit Policy. The audit policy settings appear in the right pane.

5. Double-click the Audit Policy setting you want to modify. The Properties sheet for the policy you chose opens, as shown in Figure 6-6.

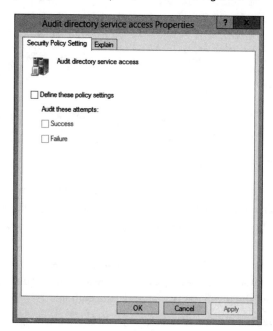

FIGURE 6-6 The Properties sheet for a policy setting

6. Select the Define These Policy Settings check box.

7. Select the appropriate check boxes to audit Success, Failure, or both.

8. Click OK to close the setting's Properties sheet.

9. Close the Group Policy Management Editor and the Group Policy Management console.

You have now configured an audit policy in the default domain policy GPO, which will be propagated to all the computers in the domain during the next policy refresh.

Configuring objects for auditing is necessary when you have configured either of the two following event categories:

- **Audit Directory Service Access**   This event category logs user access to Active Directory objects, such as other user objects or OUs.

- **Audit Object Access**   This event category logs user access to files, folders, registry keys, and printers.

Each of these event categories requires additional setup steps, in which you open the Properties sheet for the object to be audited and specify the security principals or the files and folders for which you want to audit access.

> **NOTE AUDITING OPTIONS**
>
> Beginning in Windows Server 2008, new options became available for AD DS auditing that indicate that a change has occurred and provide the old value and the new value. For example, if you change a user's description from Marketing to Training, the Directory Services Event Log will record two events containing the original value and the new value.

Assigning user rights

As shown in Figure 6-7, the User Rights Assignment settings in Windows Server 2012 R2 are extensive and include settings that pertain to rights users need to perform system-related tasks.

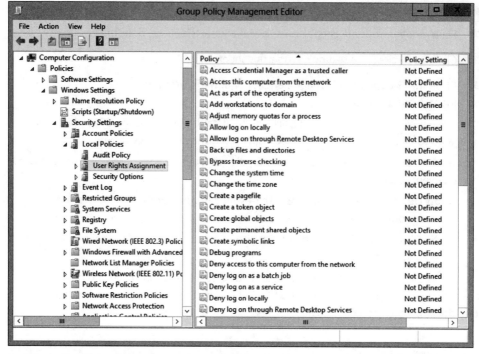

FIGURE 6-7 User Rights Assignment settings in a GPO

For example, a user logging on locally to a domain controller must have the Allow Log On Locally right assigned to his or her account or be a member of one of the following AD DS groups: Account Operators, Administrators, Backup Operators, Print Operators, or Server Operators.

These group memberships enable users to log on locally because Windows Server 2012 R2 assigns the Allow Log On Locally user right to those groups in the Default Domain Controllers Policy GPO by default.

Other similar settings included in this collection are related to user rights associated with system shutdown, taking ownership privileges of files or objects, restoring files and directories, and synchronizing directory service data.

Configuring security options

The Security Options node in a GPO, shown in Figure 6-8, includes security settings related to interactive logon, digital signing of data, restrictions for access to floppy and CD-ROM drives, unsigned driver installation behavior, and logon dialog box behavior.

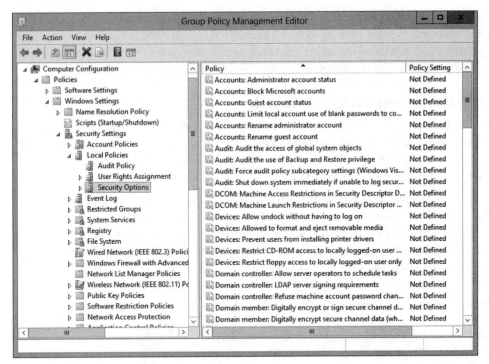

FIGURE 6-8 The Security Options node in a GPO

The Security Options category also includes options to configure authentication and communication security within Active Directory.

Using security templates

A *security template* is a collection of configuration settings stored as a text file with an .inf extension. Security templates can contain many of the same security parameters as GPOs. However, security templates present these parameters in a unified interface, enable you to save your configurations as files, and simplify the process of deploying them when and where they are needed.

The settings that you can deploy by using security templates include many of the security policies covered in this objective, including audit policies, user rights assignments, security options, event log policies, and restricted groups. By itself, a security template is a convenient way to configure the security of a single system. When you combine security templates with Group Policy or scripting, they enable administrators to maintain the security of networks consisting of hundreds or thousands of computers running various versions of Microsoft Windows.

By using these tools together, administrators can create complex security configurations and mix and match those configurations for each of the various roles computers serve in their organizations. When deployed across a network, security templates enable you to implement consistent, scalable, and reproducible security settings throughout the enterprise.

Using the Security Templates console

Security templates are plain text files that contain security settings in a variety of formats, depending on the nature of the individual settings. Although it is possible to work with security template files directly by using any text editor, Windows Server 2012 R2 provides a graphical interface that makes the job much easier.

To create and manage security templates, you use the Security Templates snap-in for MMC. You can also download and install the Security Compliance Manager (SCM) tool from the Microsoft website; this tool provides similar functionality plus a collection of system security baselines. By default, the Windows Server 2012 R2 Administrative Tools menu does not include an MMC containing the Security Templates snap-in, so you have to create one yourself by using the MMC Add Or Remove Snap-Ins dialog box. When you create a new template, the console provides an interface like the one shown in Figure 6-9.

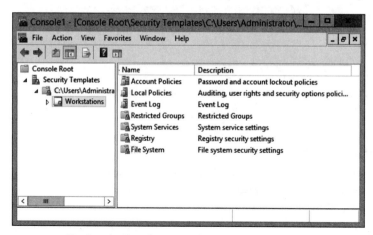

FIGURE 6-9 The Security Templates snap-in

The left pane of the Security Templates snap-in points to a default folder in which the console stores the template files you create by default. The snap-in interprets any file in this folder with an .inf extension as a security template, even though the extensions do not appear in the console.

When you create a new template in the console, you see a hierarchical display of the policies in the template and their current settings. Many of the policies are identical to those in a GPO, both in appearance and function. You can modify the policies in each template just as you would those in a GPO.

Creating security templates

To create a new security template from scratch, use the following procedure.

1. Open the Run dialog box and, in the Open text box, type **mmc** and click OK. An empty MMC appears.

2. Click File, Add/Remove Snap-In to open the Add Or Remove Snap-Ins dialog box.

3. From the Available Snap-Ins list, select Security Templates and click Add. The snap-in appears in the Add Or Remove Snap-Ins dialog box.

4. Click OK. The snap-in appears in the MMC.

5. Click File, Save As. A Save As combo box appears.

6. Type a name for the console to save it in the Administrative Tools program group.

7. Expand the Security Templates node.

8. Right-click the security template search path and, from the shortcut menu, select New Template. A dialog box appears.

9. In the Template name field, type a name for the template and click OK. The new template appears in the console. Leave the console open.

When you create a blank security template, there are no policies defined in it. Applying the blank template to a computer will have no effect on it.

Working with security template settings

Security templates contain many of the same settings as GPOs, so you are already familiar with some of the elements of a template. For example, security templates contain the same local policy settings described earlier in this chapter; the templates are just a different way to configure and deploy those policies. Security templates also provide a means for configuring the permissions associated with files, folders, registry entries, and services.

Security templates have more settings than Local Computer Policy, because a template includes options for both standalone computers and computers that are participating in a domain.

Importing security templates into GPOs

The simplest way to deploy a security template on multiple computers simultaneously is to import the template into a GPO. Once you import the template, the template settings become part of the GPO, and the network's domain controllers deploy them to all the computers affected by that GPO. As with any Group Policy deployment, you can link a GPO to any domain, site, or OU object in the Active Directory tree. The settings in the GPO are then inherited by all the container and leaf objects subordinate to the object you selected.

To import a security template into a GPO, use the following procedure.

1. In Server Manager, on the Tools menu, select Group Policy Management. The Group Policy Management console appears.

2. Expand the forest container and browse to your domain. Then expand the domain container and select the Group Policy Objects folder. The GPOs that currently exist in the domain appear on the Contents tab.

3. Right-click the GPO into which you want to import the template and click Edit. A Group Policy Management Editor window for this policy opens.

4. Browse to the Computer Configuration\Policies\Windows Settings\Security Settings node. Right-click the Security Settings node and, from the shortcut menu, select Import Policy. The Import Policy From dialog box appears.

5. Browse to the security template file you want to import and click Open. The policy settings in the template are copied to the GPO.

6. Close the Group Policy Management Editor and Group Policy Management console.

Configuring local users and groups

Windows Server 2012 R2 provides two separate interfaces for creating and managing local user accounts: the User Accounts control panel and the Local Users and Groups snap-in for MMC, which is included in the Computer Management console. Both of these interfaces provide access to the same Security Account Manager (SAM) where the user and group information is stored, so any changes you make using one interface will appear in the other.

Microsoft designed the User Accounts control panel and the Local Users And Groups snap-in for computer users with different levels of expertise, and they provide different degrees of access to the SAM, as follows:

- **User Accounts**   Provides a simplified interface with limited access to user accounts. By using this interface, you can create local user accounts and modify their basic attributes, but you cannot create groups or manage group memberships (except for that of the Administrators group).

- **Local Users And Groups**   Provides full access to local users and groups and all their attributes.

Using the User Accounts control panel

Windows Server 2012 R2 creates two local user accounts during the operating system installation process: the Administrator account and the Guest account. The setup program prompts the installer for an Administrator password during the installation, and the Guest account is disabled by default.

Once the installation process is completed, the system restarts. Because only the Administrator account is available, the computer logs on using that account. This account has administrative privileges, so at this point you can create additional user accounts or modify the existing ones.

> **NOTE CREATING LOCAL USERS**
>
> You can only create new user accounts in the control panel on Windows Server 2012 R2 computers that are part of a workgroup. When you join a computer to an AD DS domain, you must use the Local Users And Groups snap-in to create new local user accounts. Domain controllers have no local user or group accounts.

By default, the User Accounts control panel creates standard accounts. To grant a local user administrative capabilities, you must change the account type by using the interface shown in Figure 6-10.

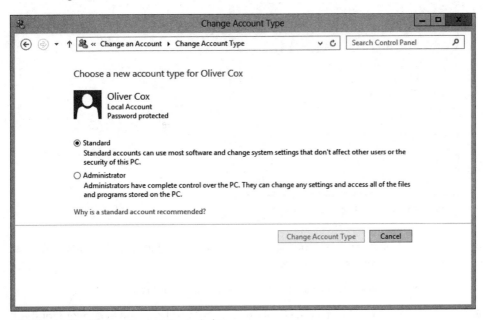

FIGURE 6-10 The Change Account Type window

What the User Accounts control panel refers to as an account type is actually a group membership. Selecting the Standard option adds the user account to the local Users group, whereas selecting the Administrator option adds the account to the Administrators group.

Using the Local Users And Groups snap-in

By default, the Local Users And Groups snap-in is part of the Computer Management console. However, you can also load the snap-in by itself or create your own MMC with any combination of snap-ins you wish.

To create a local user account with the Local Users And Groups snap-in, use the following procedure.

1. In Server Manager, on the Tools menu, select Computer Management to open the Computer Management console.

2. Expand the Local Users And Groups node and click Users to view a list of the current local users.

3. Right-click the Users folder and, from the shortcut menu, select New User. The New User dialog box opens, as shown in Figure 6-11.

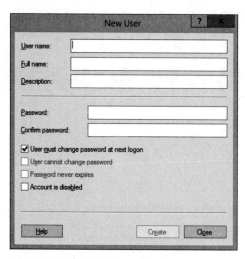

FIGURE 6-11 The New User dialog box

4. In the User Name text box, type the name you want to assign to the user account. This is the only required field in the dialog box.

5. Specify a Full Name and a Description for the account if desired.

6. In the Password text box and the Confirm Password text box, type a password for the account if desired.

7. Select or clear the four check boxes to control the following functions:

   - **User Must Change Password At Next Logon** Selecting this check box forces the new user to change the password after logging on for the first time.

   - **User Cannot Change Password** Selecting this check box prevents the user from changing the account password.

   - **Password Never Expires** Selecting this check box prevents the existing password from ever expiring.

   - **Account Is Disabled** Selecting this check box disables the user account, preventing anyone from using it to log on.

8. Click Create. The new account is added to the user list and the console clears the dialog box, leaving it ready for the creation of another user account.

9. Click Close.

10. Close the Computer Management console.

Creating a local group

To create a local group with the Local Users And Groups snap-in, use the following procedure.

1. In Server Manager, on the Tools menu, select Computer Management to open the Computer Management console.

2. Expand the Local Users and Groups node and click Groups to display a list of local groups.

3. Right-click the Groups folder and then, from the shortcut menu, select New Group. The New Group dialog box opens.

4. In the Group Name text box, type the name you want to assign to the group. This is the only required field in the dialog box. If desired, specify a Description for the group.

5. Click Add. The Select Users dialog box opens.

6. In the text box, type the names of the users whom you want to add to the group, separated by semicolons and then click OK. The users are added to the Members list. You can also type part of a user name and click Check Names to complete the name or click Advanced to search for users.

7. Click Create to create the group and populate it with the user(s) you specified. The console then clears the dialog box, leaving it ready for the creation of another group.

8. Click Close.

9. Close the Computer Management console.

Local groups have no user-configurable attributes other than a description and a members list, so the only modifications you can make when you open an existing group are supplying a description and adding and removing members. As noted earlier in this lesson, local groups cannot have other local groups as members, but if the computer is a member of a Windows domain, a local group can have domain users and domain groups as members.

Understanding User Account Control (UAC)

One of the most common Windows security problems arises from the fact that many users perform their everyday computing tasks with more system access than they actually need. Logging on as an Administrator or as a user who is a member of the Administrators group grants the user full access to all areas of the operating system. This degree of system access is not necessary to run many of the applications and perform many of the tasks users require every day; it is needed only for certain administrative functions, such as installing system-wide software and configuring system parameters.

For most users, logging on with administrative privileges all the time is just a matter of convenience. Microsoft recommends logging on as a standard user and using administrative privileges only when you need them. However, many technical specialists who do this frequently find themselves encountering situations in which they need administrative access. There is a surprisingly large number of common, and even mundane, Windows tasks that require administrative access, and the inability to perform those tasks can negatively affect a user's productivity.

Microsoft decided to address this problem by keeping all Windows Server 2012 R2 users from accessing the system using administrative privileges unless those privileges are required to perform the task at hand. The mechanism that does this is called *User Account Control (UAC)*.

Performing administrative tasks

When a user logs on to Windows Server 2012 R2, the system issues a token, which indicates the user's access level. Whenever the system authorizes the user to perform a particular activity, it consults the token to see if the user has the required privileges.

In versions of Windows prior to Windows Server 2008 and Windows Vista, standard users received standard user tokens and members of the Administrators group received administrative tokens. Every activity performed by an administrative user was therefore authorized using the administrative token, resulting in the problems described earlier.

On a computer running Windows Server 2012 R2 with UAC, a standard user still receives a standard user token, but an administrative user receives two tokens: one for standard user access and one for administrative user access. By default, the standard and administrative users both run using the standard user token most of the time.

When a standard user attempts to perform a task that requires administrative privileges, the system displays a credential prompt, as shown in Figure 6-12, requesting that the user supplies the name and password for an account with administrative privileges.

FIGURE 6-12 A UAC credential prompt

When an administrator attempts to perform a task that requires administrative access, the system switches the account from the standard user token to the administrative token. This is known as Admin Approval Mode.

Before the system permits the user to employ the administrative token, it might require the user to confirm that he or she is actually trying to perform an administrative task. To do this, the system generates an elevation prompt, as shown in Figure 6-13. This confirmation prevents unauthorized processes, such as those initiated by malware, from accessing the system using administrative privileges.

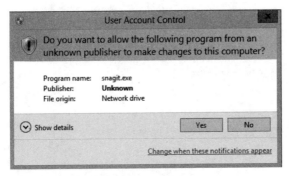

FIGURE 6-13 A UAC elevation prompt

Using secure desktop

By default, whenever Windows Server 2012 R2 displays an elevation prompt or a credential prompt, it does so by using the secure desktop.

The secure desktop is an alternative to the interactive user desktop that Windows normally displays. When Windows Server 2012 R2 generates an elevation or credential prompt, it switches to the secure desktop, suppressing the operation of all other desktop controls and permitting only Windows processes to interact with the prompt. The object of this is to prevent malware from automating a response to the elevation or credential prompt and bypassing the human reply.

Configuring UAC

Windows Server 2012 R2 enables UAC by default, but it is possible to configure its properties and even to disable it completely. In Windows Server 2012 R2, there are four UAC settings available through the Action Center in Control Panel, as shown in Figure 6-14. The four settings are as follows:

- Always Notify Me
- Notify Me Only When Apps Try To Make Changes To My Computer
- Notify Me Only When Apps Try To Make Changes To My Computer (Do Not Dim My Desktop)
- Never Notify Me

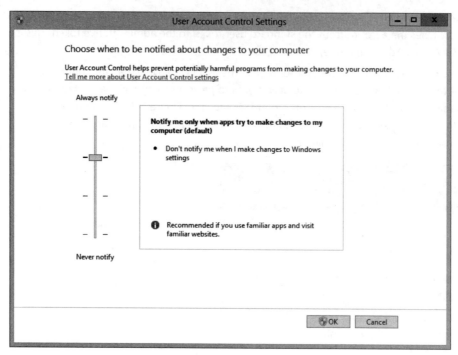

FIGURE 6-14 The User Account Control Settings dialog box

Although the Control Panel provides some control over UAC, the most granular control over UAC properties is through the Security Options node in Group Policy and Local Security Policy.

Thought experiment

Deploying security templates

In the following thought experiment, apply what you've learned about this objective to predict what steps you need to take. You can find answers to these questions in the "Answers" section at the end of this chapter.

You are a network administrator planning a security template deployment on a network that consists of 100 workstations. The workstations are all running various versions of Microsoft Windows, broken down as follows:

- Windows 7: 30 workstations
- Windows XP Professional: 40 workstations
- Windows XP Home Edition: 20 workstations
- Windows 2000 Professional: 10 workstations

In the past, some computers on the network have been compromised because end users modified their workstation security configurations. Your task is to deploy your security templates on the workstations in such a way that end users cannot modify them. To accomplish this goal, you decide to use Group Policy to deploy the templates to an AD DS OU object that contains all of the workstations.

Based on the information provided, answer the following questions.

1. How many of the workstations cannot receive their security template settings from a GPO linked to an AD DS container?

2. Which of the following methods can you use to deploy your security templates on the workstations that do not support Group Policy, while still accomplishing your assigned goals?

    A. Upgrade all the computers that do not support Group Policy to Windows 7.

    B. Run the Security Templates snap-in on each computer and load the appropriate security template.

    C. Create a logon script that uses Secedit.exe to import the security template on each computer.

    D. Run the Security Configuration and Analysis snap-in on each computer and use it to import the appropriate security template.

Objective summary

- Most security-related settings are found within the Windows Settings node of the Computer Configuration node of a GPO.

- Local policy settings govern the actions users can perform on a specific computer and determine if the actions are recorded in an event log.

- Auditing can be configured to audit successes, failures, or both.

- Administrators can use security templates to configure local policies, group memberships, event log settings, and other policies.

- When a standard user attempts to perform a task that requires administrative privileges, the system displays a credential prompt, requesting that the user supply the name and password for an account with administrative privileges.

- User Account Control is enabled by default in all Windows Server 2012 R2 installations, but it is possible to configure its properties and even to disable it completely.

Objective review

Answer the following questions to test your knowledge of the information in this objective. You can find the answers to these questions and explanations of why each answer choice is correct or incorrect in the "Answers" section at the end of this chapter.

1. Which of the following tools are used to deploy the settings in a security template to all the computers in an AD DS domain?

   A. Active Directory Users and Computers

   B. Security Templates snap-in

   C. Group Policy Object Editor

   D. Group Policy Management console

2. Which of the following are local groups to which you can add users with the Windows Control Panel? (Choose all that apply.)

   A. Users

   B. Power Users

   C. Administrators

   D. Non-Administrators

3. Which of the following tools are used to modify the settings in a security template?

   A. Active Directory Users and Computers

   B. Security Templates snap-in

   C. Group Policy Object Editor

   D. Group Policy Management console

4. The built-in local groups on a server running Windows Server 2012 R2 receive their special capabilities through which of the following mechanisms?

    A. Security options

    B. Windows Firewall rules

    C. NTFS permissions

    D. User rights

5. After configuring and deploying the Audit Directory Service Access policy, what must you do before a computer running Windows Server 2012 R2 begins logging Active Directory access attempts?

    A. You must select the Active Directory objects you want to audit by using the Active Directory Users and Computer console.

    B. You must wait for the audit policy settings to propagate to all the domain controllers on the network.

    C. You must open the Audit Directory Service Access Properties sheet and select all the Active Directory objects you want to audit.

    D. You must add an underscore character to the name of every Active Directory object you want to audit.

Objective 6.3: Configure application restriction policies

The options in the Software Restriction Policies node provide organizations greater control in preventing potentially dangerous applications from running. Software restriction policies are designed to identify software and control its execution. In addition, administrators can control who will be affected by the policies.

This objective covers how to:

- Configure rule enforcement
- Configure AppLocker rules
- Configure Software Restriction Policies

Using software restriction policies

The Software Restriction Policies node is found in the Windows Settings\Security Settings node of the User Configuration or the Computer Configuration node of a GPO. By default, the Software Restriction Policies folder is empty. When you create a new policy, two subfolders appear: Security Levels and Additional Rules. The Security Levels folder enables you to define the default behavior from which all rules will be created. The criteria for each executable program are defined in the Additional Rules folder.

In the following sections, you learn how to set the security level for a software restriction policy and how to define rules that will govern the execution of program files.

Enforcing restrictions

Prior to creating any rules that govern the restriction or allowance of executable files, it is important to understand how the rules work by default. If a policy does not enforce restrictions, executable files run based on the permissions that users or groups have in the NTFS file system.

When considering the use of software restriction policies, you must determine your approach to enforcing restrictions. There are three basic strategies for enforcing restrictions, as follows:

- **Unrestricted**   This approach enables all applications to run except those that are specifically excluded.
- **Disallowed**   This approach prevents all applications from running except those that are specifically allowed.
- **Basic User**   This approach prevents any applications from running that require administrative rights, but enables programs to run that only require resources that are accessible by normal users.

The approach you take depends on the needs of your particular organization. By default, the Software Restriction Policies area has an Unrestricted value in the Default Security Level setting.

For example, you might want to enable only specified applications to run in a high-security environment. In this case, you would set the Default Security Level to Disallowed. By contrast, in a less secure network, you might want to allow all executables to run unless you have specified otherwise. This would require you to leave the Default Security Level set as Unrestricted. In this case, you would have to create a rule to identify an application before you could disable it. You can modify the Default Security Level to reflect the Disallowed setting.

Because the Disallowed setting assumes that all programs will be denied unless a specific rule permits them to run, this setting can cause administrative headaches if not thoroughly tested. You should test all applications you wish to run to ensure that they will function properly.

To modify the Default Security Level setting to Disallowed, use the following procedure.

1. In Server Manager, on the Tools menu, select Group Policy Management to open the Group Policy Management console.

2. Expand the forest container and browse to your domain. Then expand the domain container and select the Group Policy Objects folder. The GPOs that currently exist in the domain appear on the Contents tab.

3. Right-click a GPO and select Edit. A Group Policy Management Editor window opens.

4. Browse to the Software Restriction Policies node under either Computer Configuration or User Configuration.

5. Right-click Software Restriction Policies and select New Software Restriction Policies. The folders containing the new policies appear.

6. In the details pane, double-click Security Levels. Note the check mark on the Unrestricted icon, which is the default setting.

7. Right-click the Disallowed security level and, from the shortcut menu, select Set As Default. A Software Restriction Policies message box appears, warning you of your action.

8. Click Yes, and then close the Group Policy Management Editor and Group Policy Management consoles.

You have now modified the Default Security Level for a software restriction policy.

Configuring software restriction rules

The functionality of software restriction policies depends first on the rules that identify software and then by the rules that govern its usage. When you create a new software restriction policy, the Additional Rules subfolder appears. This folder enables you to create rules that specify the conditions under which programs can be executed or denied. These rules can override the Default Security Level setting when necessary.

You create new rules of your own in the Additional Rules folder using a dialog box like the one shown in Figure 6-15.

FIGURE 6-15 The New Path Rule dialog box

There are four types of software restriction rules that you can use to specify which programs can or cannot run on your network:

- Hash rules
- Certificate rules
- Path rules
- Network zone rules

There is also a fifth type of rule—the default rule—that applies when an application does not match any of the other rules you have created. To configure the default rule, select one of the policies in the Security Levels folder and, on its Properties sheet, click Set As Default.

The functions of the four rule types are explained in the following sections.

HASH RULES

A hash is a series of bytes with a fixed length that uniquely identifies a program or file. A hash value is generated by an algorithm that essentially creates a fingerprint of the file, making it nearly impossible for another program to have the same hash. If you create a hash rule and a user attempts to run a program affected by the rule, the system checks the hash value of the executable file and compares it with the hash value stored in the software restriction policy. If the two match, the policy settings will apply. Therefore, creating a hash rule for an application executable prevents the application from running if the hash value is not correct. Because the hash value is based on the file itself, the file will continue to function if you move it from one location to another. If the executable file is altered in any way, for example, if it is modified or replaced by a worm or virus, the hash rule in the software restriction policy prevents the file from running.

CERTIFICATE RULES

A certificate rule uses the digital certificate associated with an application to confirm its legitimacy. You can use certificate rules to enable software from a trusted source to run or to prevent software that does not come from a trusted source from running. You can also use certificate rules to run programs in disallowed areas of the operating system.

PATH RULES

A path rule identifies software by specifying the directory path where the application is stored in the file system. You can use path rules to create exceptions that allow an application to execute when the Default Security Level for software restriction policies is set to Disallowed, or you can use them to prevent an application from executing when the Default Security Level for software restriction policies is set to Unrestricted.

Path rules can specify either a location in the file system where application files are located or a registry path setting. Registry path rules provide assurance that the application executables will be found. For example, if an administrator uses a path rule to define a file system location for an application, and the application is moved to a new location, such as during a network restructuring, the original path in the path rule would no longer be valid. If the rule specifies that the application should not function unless it is located in a particular path, the program would not be able to run from its new location. This could cause a significant security breach opportunity if the program references confidential information.

In contrast, if you create a path rule using a registry key location, any change to the location of the application files will not affect the outcome of the rule. This is because when you relocate an application, the registry key that points to the application's files is updated automatically.

NETWORK ZONE RULES

Network zone rules apply only to Windows Installer packages that attempt to install from a specified zone, such as a local computer, a local intranet, trusted sites, restricted sites, or the Internet. You can configure this type of rule to enable Windows Installer packages to be installed only if they come from a trusted area of the network. For example, an Internet zone rule could restrict Windows Installer packages from being downloaded and installed from the Internet or other network locations.

Using multiple rules

You can define a software restriction policy by using multiple rule types to allow and disallow program execution. By using multiple rule types, it is possible to have a variety of security levels. For example, you might want to specify a path rule that prevents programs from running from the \\Server1\Accounting shared folder and a path rule that enables programs to run from the \\Server1\Application shared folder. You can also choose to incorporate certificate rules and hash rules into your policy. When implementing multiple rule types, systems apply the rules in the following order of precedence:

1. Hash rules

2. Certificate rules

3. Network zone rules

4. Path rules

When a conflict occurs between rule types, such as between a hash rule and a path rule, the hash rule prevails because it is higher in the order of preference. If a conflict occurs between two rules of the same type with the same identification settings, such as two path rules that identify software from the same directory, the more restrictive setting will apply. In this case, if one of the path rules were set to Unrestricted and the other to Disallowed, the policy would enforce the Disallowed setting.

Configuring software restriction properties

Within the Software Restriction Policies folder, you can configure three specific properties to provide additional settings that apply to all policies when implemented: Enforcement, Designated File Types, and Trusted Publishers.

ENFORCEMENT PROPERTIES

As shown in Figure 6-16, the Enforcement properties enable you to determine whether the policies apply to all files or whether library files, such as dynamic link library (DLL) files, are excluded. Excluding DLLs is the default. This is the most practical method of enforcement. For example, if the Default Security Level for the policy is set to Disallowed and the Enforcement properties are set to All Software Files, you would have to create a rule that checked every DLL before the program could be allowed or denied. By contrast, excluding DLL files by using the default Enforcement property does not require an administrator to define individual rules for each DLL file.

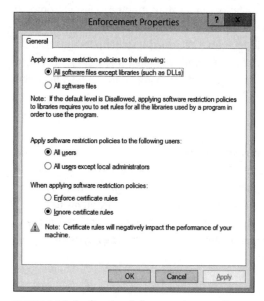

FIGURE 6-16 Configuring Enforcement properties

DESIGNATED FILE TYPES PROPERTIES

The Designated File Types properties within the Software Restriction Policies folder, as shown in Figure 6-17, specify file types that are considered executable. File types that are designated as executable or program files are shared by all rules, although you can specify a list for a computer policy that is different from one that is specified for a user policy.

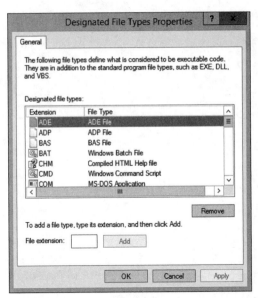

FIGURE 6-17 Configuring Designated File Types properties

TRUSTED PUBLISHERS PROPERTIES

Finally, the Trusted Publishers properties enable an administrator to control how systems handle certificate rules. In the Properties dialog box for Trusted Publishers, shown in Figure 6-18, the first setting enables you to specify which users are permitted to manage trusted certificate sources. By default, local computer administrators have the right to specify trusted publishers on the local computer and enterprise administrators have the right to specify trusted publishers in an OU. From a security standpoint, in a high-security network, users should not be allowed to determine the sources from which certificates can be obtained.

The Trusted Publisher Properties sheet also lets you decide if you wish to verify that a certificate has not been revoked. If a certificate has been revoked, the user should not be permitted access to network resources. You have the option of checking either the publisher or the time stamp of the certificate to determine if it has been revoked.

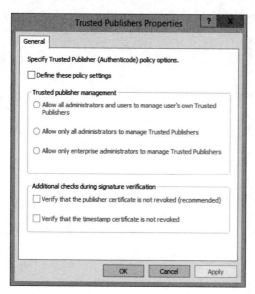

FIGURE 6-18 Configuring Trusted Publishers properties

Using AppLocker

Software restriction policies can be a powerful tool, but they can also require a great deal of administrative overhead. If you elect to disallow all applications except those matching the rules you create, there are many programs in Windows Server 2012 R2 itself that need rules, in addition to the applications you want to install. Administrators must create the rules manually, which can be an onerous chore.

AppLocker, also known as *application control policies*, is a Windows feature that is essentially an updated version of the concept implemented in software restriction policies. AppLocker also uses rules, which administrators must manage, but the process of creating the rules is much easier, thanks to a wizard-based interface.

AppLocker is also more flexible than software restriction policies. You can apply AppLocker rules to specific users and groups and also create rules that support all future versions of an application. The primary disadvantage of AppLocker is that you can apply the policies only to computers running Windows 7 and Windows Server 2008 R2 or later.

Understanding rule types

The AppLocker settings are located in GPOs in the Computer Configuration\Windows Settings\Security Settings\Application Control Policies\AppLocker container, as shown in Figure 6-19.

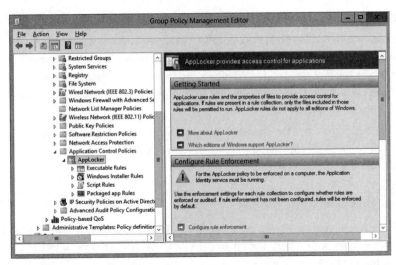

FIGURE 6-19 The AppLocker container in a GPO

In the AppLocker container, there are four nodes that contain the basic rule types:

- **Executable Rules** Contains rules that apply to files with .exe and .com extensions
- **Windows Installer Rules** Contains rules that apply to Windows Installer packages with .msi and .msp extensions
- **Script Rules** Contains rules that apply to script files with .ps1, .bat, .cmd, .vbs, and .js extensions
- **Packaged App Rules** Contains rules that apply to applications purchased through the Windows Store

Each of the rules you create in each of these containers can allow or block access to specific resources, based on one of the following criteria:

- **Publisher** Identifies code-signed applications by means of a digital signature extracted from an application file. You can also create publisher rules that apply to all future versions of an application.
- **Path** Identifies applications by specifying a file or folder name. The potential vulnerability of this type of rule is that any file can match the rule, as long as it is the correct name or location.
- **File Hash** Identifies applications based on a digital fingerprint that remains valid even when the name or location of the executable file changes. This type of rule functions much like its equivalent in software restriction policies; in AppLocker, however, the process of creating the rules and generating file hashes is much easier.

Creating default rules

When enabled, AppLocker blocks all executables, installer packages, and scripts (except for those specified in Allow rules) by default. Therefore, to use AppLocker you must create rules that enable users to access the files needed for Windows and the system's installed applications to run. The simplest way to do this is to right-click each of the four rules containers and select Create Default Rules from the shortcut menu.

The default rules for each container are standard rules that you can replicate, modify, or delete as necessary. You can also create your own rules, as long as you are careful to provide access to all the resources the computer needs to run Windows.

> **IMPORTANT APPLYING APPLOCKER POLICIES**
>
> To use AppLocker, the Application Identity service must be running. By default, this service uses the manual startup type, so you must start it yourself in the Services console before Windows can apply the AppLocker policies.

Creating rules automatically

The greatest advantage of AppLocker over software restriction policies is the ability to create rules automatically. When you right-click one of the rules containers and select Automatically Generate Rules from the shortcut menu, the Automatically Generate Rules Wizard starts.

After specifying the folder to be analyzed and the users or groups to which the rules should apply, you will see a Rule Preferences page, enabling you to specify the types of rules you want to create. The wizard then displays a summary of its results on the Review Rules page and adds the rules to the container.

Creating rules manually

In addition to creating rules automatically, you can do it manually by using a wizard-based interface you activate by selecting Create New Rule from the shortcut menu for one of the rule containers.

The wizard prompts you for the following information:

- **Action** Specifies whether you want to allow or deny the user or group access to the resource. In AppLocker, explicit deny rules always override allow rules.

- **User Or Group** Specifies the name of the user or group to which the policy should apply.

- **Conditions** Specifies whether you want to create a publisher, path, or file hash rule. The wizard generates an additional page for whichever option you select, enabling you to configure its parameters.

- **Exceptions** Enables you to specify exceptions to the rule you are creating by using any of the three conditions: publisher, path, or file hash.

Thought experiment

Using AppLocker

In the following thought experiment, apply what you've learned about this objective to predict what steps you need to take. You can find answers to these questions in the "Answers" section at the end of this chapter.

Sophie is planning on using AppLocker to control access to applications on a new network she has constructed for the Research and Development department at a major aerospace firm. The software developers in the department have recently deployed a new application called Virtual Wind Tunnel, which is based on government project research and is therefore classified. All of the full-time personnel have sufficient clearance to use the application, but the interns in the department do not. Sophie has placed the user accounts for everyone in the department into a security group called ResDev. The interns are also members of a group called RDint.

How can Sophie use AppLocker to provide everyone in the department with access to the Virtual Wind Tunnel application without changing the group memberships and without having to apply policies to individual users?

Objective summary

- Software restriction policies enable the software's executable code to be identified and either allowed or disallowed on the network.

- The three Default Security Levels within software restriction policies are Unrestricted, which means all applications function based on user permissions; Disallowed, which means all applications are denied execution regardless of the user permissions; and Basic User, which enables only executables to be run that can be run by normal users.

- Four rule types can be defined within a software restriction policy. They include, in order of precedence, hash, certificate, network zone, and path rules. The security level set on a specific rule supersedes the Default Security Level of the policy.

- Software restriction policies are Group Policy settings that enable administrators to specify the programs that are allowed to run on workstations by creating rules of various types.

- AppLocker enables administrators to create application restriction rules much more easily than was previously possible.

Objective review

Answer the following questions to test your knowledge of the information in this objective. You can find the answers to these questions and explanations of why each answer choice is correct or incorrect in the "Answers" section at the end of this chapter.

1. Which of the following is *not* one of the software restriction rule types supported by Windows Server 2012 R2?

   A. Hash rules

   B. Certificate rules

   C. Path rules

   D. Firewall rules

2. Which of the following strategies for enforcing software restrictions will prevent any executable from running except for those that have been specifically allowed by an administrator?

   A. Basic user

   B. Disallowed

   C. Power user

   D. Unrestricted

3. Under which of the following conditions will a hash rule in a software restriction policy cease to function? (Choose all that apply.)

   A. When you move the file on which the hash is based to a different folder

   B. When you update the file on which the hash is based to a new version

   C. When the file on which the hash is based is modified by a virus

   D. When you change the permissions for the file on which the hash is based

4. Which of the following rule types applies to files with an .msi extension?

   A. Executable rules

   B. Windows Installer rules

   C. Script rules

   D. Packaged app rules

5. Which of the following services must you manually start before Windows can apply AppLocker policies?

   A. Application Identity

   B. Application Management

   C. Credential Manager

   D. Network Connectivity Assistant

Objective 6.4: Configure Windows Firewall

You might have locked the door to the computer center in which the servers are located, but the computers remain connected to the network. A network is another type of door, or rather a series of doors, that can allow data in or out. To provide services to your users, some of those doors must be open at least some of the time, but server administrators must make sure that only the right doors are left open.

A firewall is a software program that protects a computer or a network by allowing certain types of network traffic in and out of the system while blocking others. A firewall is essentially a series of filters that examine the contents of packets and the traffic patterns to and from the network to determine which packets they should allow to pass through.

The object of a firewall is to permit all of the traffic that legitimate users need to perform their assigned tasks yet block everything else. Note that when you are working with firewalls, you are not concerned with subjects like authentication and authorization. Those are mechanisms that control who is able to get through the server's open doors. The firewall determines which doors are left open and which are shut tight.

> **This objective covers how to:**
> - Configure rules for multiple profiles using Group Policy
> - Configure connection security rules
> - Configure Windows Firewall to allow or deny applications, scopes, ports, and users
> - Configure authenticated firewall exceptions
> - Import and export settings

Understanding Windows Firewall settings

Windows Server 2012 R2 includes a firewall program called Windows Firewall, which is activated by default on all systems. In its default configuration, Windows Firewall blocks most network traffic from entering the computer. Firewalls work by examining the contents of each packet entering and leaving the computer and comparing the information they find to a series of rules, which specify which packets are allowed to pass through the firewall and which are blocked.

The Transmission Control Protocol/Internet Protocol (TCP/IP) is used by Windows systems to communicate functions by packaging application data using a series of layered protocols that define where the data comes from and where it is going. The three most important criteria that firewalls can use in their rules are as follows:

- **IP addresses**   *IP addresses* identify specific hosts on the network. You can use IP addresses to configure a firewall to only allow traffic from specific computers or networks in and out.

- **Protocol numbers**   *Protocol numbers* specify whether the packet contains TCP or User Datagram Protocol (UDP) traffic. You can filter protocol numbers to block packets containing certain types of traffic. Windows computers typically use UDP for brief message exchanges, such as Domain Name System (DNS) and Dynamic Host Configuration Protocol (DHCP) transactions. TCP packets usually carry larger amounts of data, such as the files exchanged by web, file, and print servers.

- **Port numbers**   *Port numbers* identify specific applications running on the computer. The most common firewall rules use port numbers to specify the types of application traffic the computer is allowed to send and receive. For example, a web server usually receives its incoming packets to port number 80. Unless the firewall has a rule opening port 80 to incoming traffic, the web server cannot function in its default configuration.

Firewall rules can function in two ways, as follows:

- Admit all traffic, except that which conforms to the applied rules
- Block all traffic, except that which conforms to the applied rules

Generally, blocking all traffic by default is the more secure arrangement. From the server administrator's standpoint, you start with a completely blocked system, and then begin testing your applications. When an application fails to function properly because network access is blocked, you create a rule that opens up the ports the application needs to communicate.

This is the method that Windows Firewall uses by default for incoming network traffic. There are default rules preconfigured into the firewall that are designed to admit the traffic used by standard Windows networking functions, such as file and printer sharing. For outgoing network traffic, Windows Firewall uses the other method, allowing all traffic to pass the firewall except that which conforms to a rule.

Working with Windows Firewall

Windows Firewall is a single program with one set of rules, but there are two distinct interfaces you can use to manage and monitor it. The Windows Firewall control panel applet provides a simplified interface that enables administrators to avoid the details of rules and port numbers. If you just want to turn the firewall on or off (typically for testing or troubleshooting purposes) or work with the firewall settings for a specific Windows role or feature, you can do so by using just the control panel. For full access to firewall rules and more sophisticated functions, you must use the Windows Firewall With Advanced Security console, as discussed later in this objective.

In many cases, administrators never have to work directly with Windows Firewall. Many of the roles and features included in Windows Server 2012 R2 automatically open the appropriate firewall ports when you install them. In other situations, the system warns you of firewall issues.

For example, the first time you open File Explorer and try to access the network, a warning appears, informing you that Network Discovery and File Sharing are turned off, preventing you from browsing the network.

Network Discovery is just a set of firewall rules that regulate the ports Windows uses for network browsing, specifically ports 137, 138, 1900, 2869, 3702, 5355, 5357, and 5358. By default, Windows Server 2012 R2 disables the inbound rules associated with these ports, so the ports are closed, blocking all traffic through them. When you click the warning banner and choose Turn On Network Discovery And File Sharing from the shortcut menu, you are in effect activating these firewall rules, thereby opening the ports associated with them.

In addition to the menu commands accessible through the warning banner, you can control the Network Discovery and File Sharing rules in other ways. The Network and Sharing Center control panel, through its Advanced Sharing Settings page, provides options that you can use to turn Network Discovery, File Sharing, and other basic networking functions on and off.

The Windows Firewall control panel has an Allow An App Or Feature Through Windows Firewall link, which opens the Allowed Apps dialog box. The Network Discovery check box in this dialog box enables you to control the same set of rules as the Network Discovery control panel in the Network And Sharing Center.

Finally, you can access the individual Network Discovery rules directly by using the Windows Firewall With Advanced Security console. When you select the Inbound Rules node and scroll down in the list, you can see nine Network Discovery rules.

As you can see by examining the rules in the console, Network Discovery is a complex Windows function that would be difficult to control if you had to determine by trial and error which ports it uses. This is why Windows Firewall includes a large collection of rules that regulate the ports that the applications and services included with the operating system need to operate.

Using the Windows Firewall control panel applet

The Windows Firewall control panel applet provides the easiest and safest access to the firewall controls. These controls are usually sufficient for most server administrators, unless the system has special requirements or you are working with custom server applications.

When you open the Windows Firewall window from the control panel, as shown in Figure 6-20, you see the following information:

- Whether the computer is connected to a domain, private, or public network
- Whether the Windows Firewall service is turned on or off
- Whether inbound and outbound connections are blocked
- The name of the currently active network
- Whether users are notified when a program is blocked

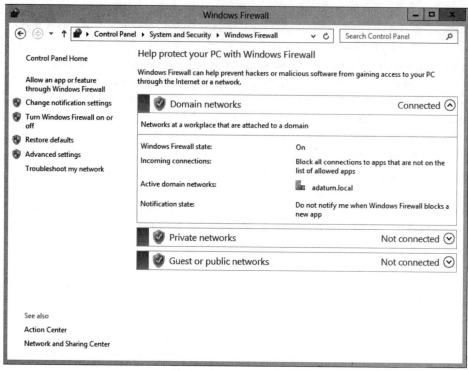

FIGURE 6-20 The Windows Firewall control panel

On the left side of the window is a series of links, which provide the following functions:

- **Allow An App Or Feature Through Windows Firewall**   Opens the Allowed Apps dialog box, in which you can select the applications that can send traffic through the firewall

- **Change Notification Settings**   Opens the Customize Settings dialog box, in which you can adjust the notification settings for each of the three profiles

- **Turn Windows Firewall On Or Off**   Opens the Customize Settings dialog box, in which you can toggle the state of the firewall in each of the three profiles

- **Restore Defaults**   Returns all firewall settings to their installation defaults

- **Advanced Settings**   Launches the Windows Firewall With Advanced Security console

- **Troubleshoot My Network**   Launches the Network and Internet troubleshooter

Customizing settings

Several of the links in the Windows Firewall window point to the same place: a Customize Settings dialog box that contains controls for some of the most basic firewall functions.

The Customize Settings dialog box, shown in Figure 6-21, is organized according to three areas, corresponding to the three profiles on a Windows computer. Windows Firewall uses these profiles to represent the type of network to which the server is connected. The profiles are as follows:

- **Public** The public (or guest) profile is intended for servers that are accessible to unauthenticated or temporary users, such as computers in an open lab or kiosk.

- **Private** The private profile is intended for servers on an internal network that are not accessible by unauthorized users.

- **Domain** The domain profile is applied to servers that are members of an AD DS domain in which all users are identified and authenticated.

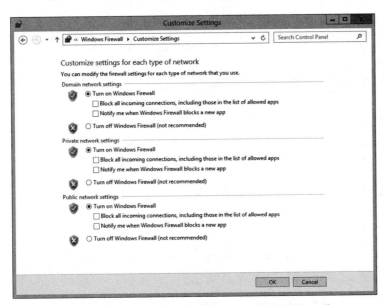

FIGURE 6-21 The Customize Settings dialog box for Windows Firewall

In Windows Firewall, the three profiles are essentially separate sets of rules that apply only to computers connected to the designated network type. Administrators can control the environment for each type of network by configuring separate rules and settings for each profile.

The Customize Settings dialog box has the following controls for each of the three network profiles:

- **Turn On/Off Windows Firewall** Toggles the Windows Firewall on and off for the selected profile

- **Block All Incoming Connections, Including Those In The List Of Allowed Apps** Enables you to increase the security of your system by blocking all unsolicited attempts to connect to your computer

- **Notify Me When Windows Firewall Blocks A New App** Causes the system to notify the user when an application's attempt to send traffic through the firewall fails

Allowing applications

There are times when administrators might be required to modify the firewall settings in other ways, typically because a specific application requires access to a port not anticipated by the firewall's default rules.

To do this, you can use the Allowed Apps dialog box in the Windows Firewall control panel, as shown in Figure 6-22.

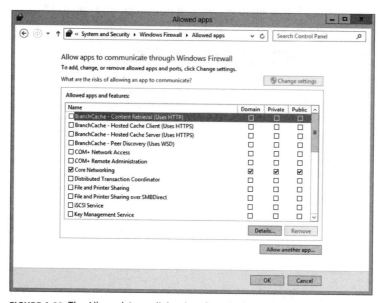

FIGURE 6-22 The Allowed Apps dialog box for Windows Firewall

Opening up a port in a server's firewall is an inherently dangerous activity. The more open doors you put in a wall, the greater the likelihood that intruders will get in. Windows Firewall provides two basic methods for opening a hole in your firewall: opening a port and allowing an application. Both are risky, but the latter is less so. This is because when you open a port by creating a rule in the Windows Firewall With Advanced Security console, the port stays open permanently. When you allow an application through the firewall by using the control panel, the specified port is open only while the program is running. When you terminate the program, the firewall closes the port.

EXAM TIP

Previous versions of Windows refer to allowed applications as exceptions, meaning that they are exceptions to the general firewall rules closing off all the computer's ports against intrusion. Exam candidates should be prepared to see questions containing either term.

The applications listed in the Allowed Apps dialog box are based on the roles and features installed on the server. Each listed application corresponds to one or more firewall rules, which the control panel activates and deactivates as needed.

Unlike earlier versions, the Windows Server 2012 R2 version of the Windows Firewall control panel does not provide direct access to port numbers. For more precise control over the firewall, you must use the Windows Firewall With Advanced Security console, which you can access by clicking Advanced Settings in the Windows Firewall control panel or by selecting it from the Tools menu in Server Manager.

Using the Windows Firewall With Advanced Security console

The Windows Firewall control panel is designed to enable administrators and advanced users to manage basic firewall settings. For full access to the Windows Firewall configuration settings, you must use the Windows Firewall With Advanced Security snap-in for the MMC.

To open the console, open Server Manager and, from the Tools menu, select Windows Firewall With Advanced Security. The Windows Firewall With Advanced Security console opens, as shown in Figure 6-23.

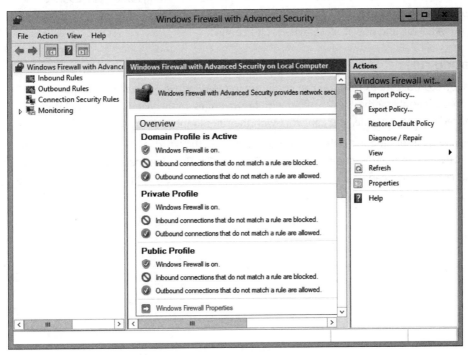

FIGURE 6-23 The Windows Firewall With Advanced Security console

Configuring profile settings

At the top of the Windows Firewall With Advanced Security console's middle pane, in the Overview section, there are status displays for the computer's three network location profiles. If you connect the computer to a different network (which is admittedly not likely with a server), Windows Firewall can load a different profile and a different set of rules.

The default Windows Firewall configuration calls for the same basic settings for all three profiles, as follows:

- The firewall is turned on.
- Incoming traffic is blocked unless it matches a rule.
- Outgoing traffic is allowed unless it matches a rule.

You can change this default behavior by clicking the Windows Firewall Properties link, which displays the Windows Firewall With Advanced Security On Local Computer dialog box.

In this dialog box, each of the three network location profiles has a tab with identical controls which enable you to modify the default profile settings. You can, for example, configure the firewall to shut down completely when it is connected to a domain network and you can configure the firewall to turn on with its most protective settings when you connect the computer to a public network. You can also configure the firewall's notification options, its logging behavior, and how it reacts when rules conflict.

Creating rules

The allowed applications that you can configure in the Windows Firewall control panel are a relatively friendly method for working with firewall rules. In the Windows Firewall With Advanced Security console, you can work with the rules in their raw form.

Selecting either Inbound Rules or Outbound Rules in the left pane displays a list of all the rules operating in that direction, as shown in Figure 6-24. The rules that are currently operational have a check mark in a green circle next to them; the rules not in force are unavailable.

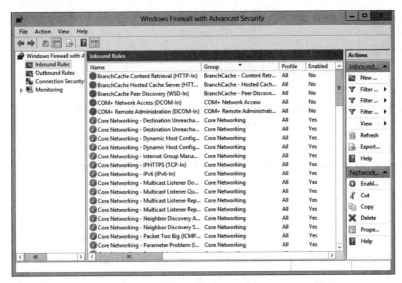

FIGURE 6-24 The Inbound Rules list in the Windows Firewall With Advanced Security console

Creating new rules by using this interface provides much more flexibility than the Windows Firewall control panel. When you right-click the Inbound Rules (or Outbound Rules) node and select New Rule from the shortcut menu, the New Inbound (or Outbound) Rule Wizard takes you through the process of configuring the following sets of parameters:

- **Rule Type**   Specifies whether you want to create a program rule, a port rule, a variant on one of the predefined rules, or a custom rule. This selection determines which of the following pages the wizard displays.

- **Program**   Specifies whether the rule applies to all programs, to one specific program, or to a specific service. This is the equivalent of defining an allowed application in the Windows Firewall control panel, except that you must specify the exact path to the application.

- **Protocol And Ports** Specifies the network or transport layer protocol or the local and remote ports to which the rule applies. This enables you to specify the exact types of traffic that the rule should block or allow. To create rules in this way, you must be familiar with the protocols and ports that an application uses to communicate at both ends of the connection.

- **Predefined Rules** Specifies which predefined rules defining specific network connectivity requirements the wizard should create.

- **Scope** Specifies the IP addresses of the local and remote systems to which the rule applies. This enables you to block or allow traffic between specific computers.

- **Action** Specifies the action the firewall should take when a packet matches the rule. You configure the rule to allow traffic if it is blocked by default or block traffic if it is allowed by default. You can also configure the rule to allow traffic only when the connection between the communicating computers is secured using IPsec.

- **Profile** Specifies the profile(s) to which the rule should apply: domain, private, or public.

- **Name** Specifies a name and (optionally) a description for the rule.

The rules you can create by using the wizards range from simple program rules, like those you can create in the Windows Firewall control panel, to highly complex and specific rules that block or allow only specific types of traffic between specific computers. The more complicated the rules become, however, the more you have to know about TCP/IP communications in general and the specific behavior of your applications. Modifying the default firewall settings to accommodate some special applications is relatively simple, but creating an entirely new firewall configuration is a formidable task.

Importing and exporting rules

The process of creating and modifying rules in the Windows Firewall With Advanced Security console can be time-consuming, and repeating the process on multiple computers even more so. Therefore, the console makes it possible for you to save the rules and settings you have created by exporting them to a policy file.

A policy file is a file with a .wfw extension that contains all the property settings in a Windows Firewall installation and all its rules, including the preconfigured rules and those you have created or modified. To create a policy file, select Export Policy from the Action menu in the Windows Firewall With Advanced Security console, and then specify a name and location for the file.

You can then duplicate the rules and settings on another computer by copying the file and using the Import Policy function to read in the contents.

> **NOTE** **IMPORTING POLICIES**
>
> When you import policies from a file, the console warns you that all existing rules and settings will be overwritten. You must therefore be careful not to create custom rules on a computer and then expect to import other rules by using a policy file.

Creating rules by using Group Policy

The Windows Firewall With Advanced Security console makes it possible to create complex firewall configurations, but Windows Firewall is still an application designed to protect a single computer from intrusion. If you have a large number of servers running Windows Server 2012 R2, manually creating a complex firewall configuration on each one can be a lengthy process. Therefore, as with most Windows configuration tasks, administrators can distribute firewall settings to computers throughout the network by using Group Policy.

When you edit a GPO and browse to the Computer Configuration\Policies\Windows Settings\Security Settings\Windows Firewall With Advanced Security node, you see an interface that is nearly identical to the Windows Firewall With Advanced Security console.

You can configure Windows Firewall properties and create inbound, outbound, and connection security rules, just as you would in the console. The difference is that you can then deploy those settings to computers anywhere on the network by linking the GPO to an AD DS domain, site, or OU object.

When you open a new GPO, the Windows Firewall With Advanced Security node contains no rules. The preconfigured rules that you find on every computer running Windows Server 2012 R2 are not there. You can create new rules from scratch to deploy to the network, or you can import settings from a policy file, just as you can in the Windows Firewall With Advanced Security console.

Group Policy does not overwrite the entire Windows Firewall configuration like importing a policy file does. When you deploy firewall rules and settings by using Group Policy, the rules in the GPO are combined with the existing rules on the target computers. The only exception is when you deploy rules with the identical names as existing rules. In that case, the GPO settings overwrite those found on the target computers.

Creating connection security rules

Windows Server 2012 R2 also includes a feature that incorporates IPsec data protection into the Windows Firewall. The IP Security (IPsec) standards are a collection of documents that define a method for securing data while it is in transit over a TCP/IP network. IPsec includes a connection establishment routine, during which computers authenticate each other before transmitting data, and a technique called *tunneling*, in which data packets are encapsulated within other packets for their protection.

In addition to inbound and outbound rules, the Windows Firewall With Advanced Security console enables you to create connection security rules by using the New Connection Security Rule Wizard. Connection security rules define the type of protection you want to apply to the communications that conform to Windows Firewall rules.

When you right-click the Connection Security Rules node and select New Rule from the shortcut menu, the New Connection Security Rule Wizard takes you through the process of configuring the following sets of parameters, as follows:

- **Rule Type**   Specifies the basic function of the rule, such as to isolate computers based on authentication criteria, to exempt certain computers (such as infrastructure servers) from authentication, to authenticate two specific computers or groups of computers, or to tunnel communications between two computers. You can also create custom rules combining these functions.

- **Endpoints**   Specifies the IP addresses of the computers that will establish a secured connection before transmitting any data.

- **Requirements**   Specifies whether authentication between two computers should be requested or required in each direction.

- **Authentication Method**   Specifies the type of authentication the computers should use when establishing a connection.

- **Profile**   Specifies the profile(s) to which the rule should apply: domain, private, public, or a combination thereof.

- **Name**   Specifies a name and (optionally) a description for the rule.

Thought experiment
Configuring Windows Firewall

In the following thought experiment, apply what you've learned about this objective to predict what steps you need to take. You can find answers to these questions in the "Answers" section at the end of this chapter.

Ralph is a junior network administrator at Wingtip Toys. He has been left in change of the IT department while everyone else is out of town at a conference. Ralph receives a call from the company's best customer, reporting that the customer is unable to place orders through the company's website. Ralph examines the logs for the Windows web server and notices a huge amount of incoming traffic that began that morning.

Ralph suspects that the server is the target of a denial of service (DoS) attack, but he doesn't have access to the network firewall and does not know anything about the firewall configuration his company uses. Ralph does have access to the Windows Firewall running on the web server, however. What temporary modifications can he make to that firewall to block the attack and allow the customer to submit orders as usual?

Objective summary

- A firewall is a software program that protects a computer by allowing certain types of network traffic in and out of the system while blocking others.

- A firewall is essentially a series of filters that examine the contents of packets and the traffic patterns to and from the network to determine which packets they should allow to pass through.

- The default rules preconfigured into the firewall are designed to admit the traffic used by standard Windows networking functions, such as file and printer sharing. For outgoing network traffic, Windows Firewall allows all traffic to pass the firewall except that which conforms to a rule.

- The Windows Firewall control panel is designed to enable administrators to perform basic firewall configuration tasks as needed.

- For full access to the Windows Firewall configuration settings, you must use the Windows Firewall With Advanced Security snap-in for the MMC.

Objective review

Answer the following questions to test your knowledge of the information in this objective. You can find the answers to these questions and explanations of why each answer choice is correct or incorrect in the "Answers" section at the end of this chapter.

1. Which of the following mechanisms is used most often in firewall rules to allow traffic onto the network?

   A. Hardware addresses

   B. IP addresses

   C. Protocol numbers

   D. Port numbers

2. Connection security rules require that network traffic allowed through the firewall use which of the following security mechanisms?

   A. EFS

   B. IPsec

   C. UAC

   D. Kerberos

3. Which of the following actions *cannot* be performed from the Windows Firewall control panel?

   A. Allowing an application through the firewall in all three profiles

   B. Blocking all incoming connections for any of the three profiles

   C. Creating firewall exceptions based on port numbers for all three profiles

   D. Turning Windows Firewall off for all three profiles

4. Which of the following tools *cannot* enable and disable the Network Discovery firewall rules?

   A. File Explorer

   B. B. Network and Sharing Center

   C. Action Center

   D. Allowed Apps dialog box

5. Which of the following statements about Windows Firewall are true? (Choose all that apply.)

   A. Applying firewall rules by using Group Policy overwrites all the firewall rules on the target computer.

   B. Applying firewall rules by using Group Policy combines the newly deployed rules with the ones already there.

   C. Importing firewall rules saved from another computer overwrites all the rules on the target system.

   D. Importing firewall rules saved from another computer combines both sets of settings.

Answers

This section contains the solutions to the thought experiments and answers to the objective review questions in this chapter.

Objective 6.1: Thought experiment

Alice must create another GPO containing the following setting, link it to the domain, and modify its Security Filtering by adding the Executives group and removing the Authenticated Users group. This GPO must take precedence over the Device Restrictions GPO.

- Prevent installation of devices not described by other policy settings - Disabled

Objective 6.1: Review

1. **Correct answer:** B

   A. **Incorrect:** Group Policy tools that use the older style administrative template (ADM) files do not look for them in the Central Store.

   B. **Correct:** Group Policy tools look for XML-based administrative template (ADMX) files in the Central Store by default.

   C. **Incorrect:** GPOs are stored in the Active Directory database, not the Central Store.

   D. **Incorrect:** Security templates are not found in the Central Store.

2. **Correct answer:** D

   A. **Incorrect:** Local GPOs are applied first, before the administrators, non-administrators, and user-specific local GPOs.

   B. **Incorrect:** Administrators local GPOs are applied after local GPOs and before user-specific local GPOs.

   C. **Incorrect:** Nonadministrators local GPOs are applied after local GPOs and before user-specific local GPOs.

   D. **Correct:** Of the local GPO types, user-specific local GPOs are applied last.

3. **Correct answer:** C

   A. **Incorrect:** GPO linking applies Group Policy settings to the entire contents of an AD DS container.

   B. **Incorrect:** Administrative templates are the files defining the registry-based settings that appear in GPOs.

   C. **Correct:** Security filtering is a Group Policy feature that enables you to restrict the dissemination of Group Policy settings to specific users and groups within an AD DS container.

   D. **Incorrect:** Starter GPOs are templates used to create new GPOs.

4. **Correct answer:** A

   A. **Correct:** Starter GPOs are templates that you can use to create multiple GPOs with the same set of baseline Administrative Templates settings.

   B. **Incorrect:** Starter GPOs are not applied by clients.

   C. **Incorrect:** Starter GPOs use the same interface as standard GPOs.

   D. **Incorrect:** Starter GPOs do not contain all the settings found in the default Domain Policy GPO.

5. **Correct answer:** A

   A. **Correct:** A Not Configured policy setting has no effect on the existing setting of that policy.

   B. **Incorrect:** A Disabled setting remains disabled if you apply a GPO with a Not Configured value for the same setting.

   C. **Incorrect:** A Not Configured setting will not change a Disabled setting to Enabled.

   D. **Incorrect:** Policy setting conflicts result in overwritten settings but not errors.

Objective 6.2: Thought experiment

1. 20. Of the workstation operating systems listed, only Windows 7, Windows XP Professional, and Windows 2000 Professional are able to use Group Policy.

2. A. The only way to ensure that end users do not change the security settings on their computers is to deploy them by using Group Policy, which would require you to upgrade the operating system. Answers c and d would enable you to successfully deploy security templates on the computers, but the users would be able to modify the settings afterward.

Objective 6.2: Review

1. **Correct answer:** C, D

   A. **Incorrect:** You cannot use Active Directory Users and Computers to apply a security template to a domain.

   B. **Incorrect:** You cannot use the Security Templates snap-in to apply a security template to a domain.

   C. **Correct:** You must use the Group Policy Object Editor to import a template into a GPO before you apply it to a domain.

   D. **Correct.** After importing the security template into a GPO, you can link it to a domain object and deploy the template settings.

2. **Correct answers:** A, C

   A. **Correct:** By creating a standard user in Windows Control Panel, you are adding the account to the local Users group.

   B. **Incorrect:** You cannot add users to the Power Users group by using the Windows Control Panel.

   C. **Correct:** Granting a user administrative privileges in the Windows Control Panel adds the account to the local Administrators group.

   D. **Incorrect:** There is no Non-Administrators local group in Windows.

3. **Correct answer:** B

   A. **Incorrect:** You cannot use Active Directory Users and Computers to modify the settings in a security template.

   B. **Correct:** You use the Security Templates snap-in to modify the settings in a security template.

   C. **Incorrect:** You cannot use the Group Policy Object Editor to modify the settings in a security template.

   D. **Incorrect:** You cannot use the Group Policy Management console to modify the settings in a security template.

4. **Correct answer:** D

   A. **Incorrect:** Security options cannot provide the capabilities granted to the built-in local groups.

   B. **Incorrect:** Windows Firewall rules cannot provide the capabilities granted to the built-in local groups.

   C. **Incorrect:** NTFS permissions cannot provide the capabilities granted to the built-in local groups.

   D. **Correct:** Built-in local groups on a server running Windows Server 2012 R2 receive their special capabilities through user rights.

5. **Correct answer:** A

   A. **Correct:** The Audit Directory Service Access policy audits only the objects you select in the Active Directory Users and Computers console.

   B. **Incorrect:** There is no need to wait for the policy settings to propagate to all the domain controllers.

   C. **Incorrect:** You configure the objects to be audited in the Active Directory Users and Computers console, not in the policy itself.

   D. **Incorrect:** Modifying the object names will have no effect.

Objective 6.3: Thought experiment

Sophie has to create two rules: an allow rule that grants the ResDev group access to the application and a deny rule that applies only to the RDint group. Because deny rules take precedence over allow rules in AppLocker, the interns will not be able to access the application.

Objective 6.3: Review

1. **Correct answer:** D

   A. **Incorrect:** Hash rules is one of the software restriction rule types.

   B. **Incorrect:** Certificate rules is one of the software restriction rule types.

   C. **Incorrect:** Path rules is one of the software restriction rule types.

   D. **Correct:** Firewall rules is not one of the software restriction rule types.

2. **Correct answer:** B

   A. **Incorrect:** The Basic User strategy prevents any application from running that requires administrative rights, but enables programs to run that only require resources that are accessible by normal users.

   B. **Correct:** The Disallowed strategy prevents all applications from running except those that are specifically allowed.

   C. **Incorrect:** There is no Power User strategy for enforcing software restrictions.

   D. **Incorrect:** The Unrestricted strategy enables all applications to run except those that are specifically excluded.

3. **Correct answers:** B, C

   A. **Incorrect:** The hash is based on the file, not on its location, so moving it does not affect its functionality.

   B. **Correct:** Substituting a different version of the file renders the hash unusable.

   C. **Correct:** Modifying the file in any way renders the hash unusable.

   D. **Incorrect:** Changing the file's permissions does not modify the file itself, so the hash remains functional.

4. **Correct answer:** B

   A. **Incorrect:** Executable rules apply to files with .exe and .com extensions.

   B. **Correct:** Windows Installer rules apply to Windows Installer packages with .msi and .msp extensions.

   C. **Incorrect:** Script rules apply to script files with .ps1, .bat, .cmd, .vbs, and .js extensions.

   D. **Incorrect:** Packaged app rules apply to applications purchased through the Windows Store.

5. **Correct answer:** A

   A. **Correct:** To use AppLocker, Windows Server 2012 R2 requires the Application Identity service to be running.

   B. **Incorrect:** The Application Management service is not necessary for Windows to apply AppLocker policies.

   C. **Incorrect:** The Credential Manager service is not necessary for Windows to apply AppLocker policies.

   D. **Incorrect:** The Network Connectivity Assistant service is not necessary for Windows to apply AppLocker policies.

Objective 6.4: Thought experiment

As a temporary measure, the administrator could create an IP address–based Windows Firewall rule that admits the traffic from the customer's computer and blocks all other traffic. This would prevent the system from processing the DoS files.

Objective 6.4: Review

1. **Correct answer:** D

   A. **Incorrect:** Firewalls can conceivably use hardware addresses to filter network traffic, but this is rarely a practical solution.

   B. **Incorrect:** Firewalls typically filter specific types of network traffic, not entire IP addresses.

   C. **Incorrect:** Filtering by protocol number typically does not provide the granularity needed to create an efficient firewall configuration.

   D. **Correct:** Firewalls typically use port numbers to allow traffic onto the network.

2. **Correct answer:** B

   A. **Incorrect:** Encrypting File System only provides security for the storage medium, not for network traffic.

   B. **Correct:** Connection security rules require that network traffic allowed through the firewall use IPsec for security.

   C. **Incorrect:** User Account Control cannot restrict network traffic.

   D. **Incorrect:** Kerberos is an authentication protocol. It cannot restrict network traffic.

3. **Correct answer:** C

   A. **Incorrect:** You can allow an application through the firewall for all three profiles by using the Windows Firewall control panel.

   B. **Incorrect:** You can use the Windows Firewall control panel to block all incoming connections for all three profiles.

   C. **Correct:** You cannot block traffic based on port numbers for all three profiles by using the Windows Firewall control panel.

   D. **Incorrect:** You can use the Windows Firewall control panel to turn the firewall on and off for any of the three profiles.

4. **Correct answer:** C

   A. **Incorrect:** File Explorer displays a link that enables the Network Discovery rules.

   B. **Incorrect:** The Network and Sharing Center control panel contains a link that provides access to controls for the Network Discovery tools.

   C. **Correct:** The Action Center control panel does not contain Network Discovery controls.

   D. **Incorrect:** The Allowed Apps dialog box contains controls for the Network Discovery rules.

5. **Correct answers:** B, C

   A. **Incorrect:** Firewall rules applied with Group Policy combine with the existing rules.

   B. **Correct:** Firewall rules applied with Group Policy combine with the existing rules.

   C. **Correct:** Importing Windows Firewall rules from another system overwrites all the existing rules.

   D. **Incorrect:** Importing rules overwrites the existing rules; it does not combine them.

Index

Symbols

6to4 mechanism, IP transitioning, 213

A

AAAA (Address) resource records, 245
A (Address) resource records, 245
ABE (access-based enumeration), 76
access-based enumeration (ABE), 76
access control entries (ACEs), 77
access control list (ACL), 77
accessing
    files, configuring share access, 71–89
        folder shares, 72–77
        NTFS quotas, 87–88
        permissions, 77–86
        Volume Shadow Copies, 86–87
        Work Folders, 89
access tokens, 300
Account Operators group, 292
ACEs (access control entries), 77
ACL (access control list), 77
Action parameter (New Inbound Rule Wizard), 366
Activate instance ntds command, 268
Activate Scope page (New Scope Wizard), 224
active/active configuration (Switch Independent
        Mode), 22
Active Directory Administrative Center console, 277
    creating computer objects, 288
    creating single AD DS users, 278–282
Active Directory Domain Services. *See* AD DS
Active Directory-integrated zones, 243–244
Active Directory objects, management, 288–293
Active Directory Object Type page (Delegation of
        Control Wizard), 299

Active Directory Sites And Services console, 273
Active Directory tab
    adding servers in Server Manager, 114
Active Directory Users and Computers console, 277
    Copy Object-User Wizard, 282
    creating computer objects, 287
    creating user templates, 282–283
    New Object - User Wizard, 279
Active Directory Zone Replication Scope page (New
        Zone Wizard), 244
active/standby configuration (Switch Independent
        Mode), 22
adapters, virtual networks, 181–185
    advanced network adapter features, 185
    emulated adapters, 183–184
    hardware acceleration settings, 184–185
    synthetic adapters, 183–184
Add action, LDIFDE.exe utility, 284
Add-DnsServerPrimaryZone cmdlet, 245
Add Exclusions And Delay page (New Scope
        Wizard), 223
Add Features That Are Required dialog box, 32
Add Features That Are Required For Active Directory
        Domain Services dialog box, 258
Add Features That Are Required For Hyper-V dialog
        box, 137
adding
    print servers, 107, 107–108
    servers, Server Manager, 113–114
Additional Drivers dialog box, 100
Additional Options page (AD DS Configuration
        Wizard), 264
Additional Rules folder (Software Restriction Policies
        node), 346
Additive permission management task, 79
-addmbr <members> command-line parameter, 307
Add Or Remove Snap-Ins dialog box, 325

H

N

Q

R

X

Z

About the Author

CRAIG ZACKER is the author or co-author of dozens of books, articles, and websites on operating systems, networking topics, and PC hardware, including Microsoft Learning's *Windows Small Business Server 2011 Administrator's Pocket Consultant* and *MCITP Self-Paced Training Kit for Exam 70-686: Windows 7 Desktop Administrator.* He has also been an English professor, a network administrator, a webmaster, a corporate trainer, a photographic technician, a library clerk, a student, and a newspaper delivery boy. He lives in a little house with his beautiful wife and a neurotic cat.

Now that you've read the book...

Tell us what you think!

Was it useful?
Did it teach you what you wanted to learn?
Was there room for improvement?

Let us know at http://aka.ms/tellpress

Your feedback goes directly to the staff at Microsoft Press, and we read every one of your responses. Thanks in advance!